COLONIAL EDUCATORS

COLONIAL EDUCATORS

The British Indian and Colonial Education Service
1858-1983

Clive Whitehead

I.B. TAURIS
LONDON · NEW YORK

Published in 2003 by I.B.Tauris & Co Ltd
6 Salem Road, London W2 4BU
175 Fifth Avenue, New York NY 10010
www.ibtauris.com

In the United States of America and in Canada distributed by Palgrave
Macmillan, a division of St Martins Press, 175 Fifth Avenue, New York NY
10010

ISBN 1 86064 864 9

A full CIP record for this book is available from the British Library
A full CIP record for this book is available from the Library of Congress

Library of Congress catalog card: available

Printed and bound in Great Britain by MPG Books Ltd, Bodmin
from camera-ready copy supplied by the authors

In memory of my father and C.E.B.,
with heartfelt thanks.

Contents

Tables

Abbreviations

CES   Colonial Education Service
CO   Colonial Office
DE   Director of Education
DPI   Director of Public Instruction
ICS   Indian Civil Service
IES   Indian Education Service
ODA   Overseas Development Administration
ODM   Overseas Development Ministry

Foreword by
Anthony Kirk-Greene

Underlying much of the recent research into Britain's modern imperial century — say the period from 1858, when the Crown assumed the administration of India, to 1966, when the Colonial Office was disbanded — has been a shift away from the classic focus on why imperial rule came about and what it accomplished towards a new-found avenue of enquiry; who the colonial executives on the ground were in socio-educational, and hence attitudinal, terms and how they achieved their tasks. In short, the argument has been repositioned onto the primary thesis that one cannot expect to grasp what imperialism was until one first understands who the imperialists were. Such an approach calls for the study of the personnel *in situ* as a defining element in the study of policy *in vacuo*. The socio-educational who's who of those who implement can be as rewarding and revealing as the minds and motives of those who plan. It is in this ongoing context of the new historiography of imperial research that Clive Whitehead's study stands out as an important contribution to evaluating the dynamics of colonial rule.

At the same time his book is not only a reinforcement of such research but also an extension to the field. For whereas up to now the bulk of the interest in who the imperial agents were, in terms of such influential attributes as family provenance, social millieu, educational (including athletic) accomplishments and pre-career determinants, has been directed at Britain's 'Sanders of the River' administrators — the Indian Civil Service, the Sudan Political Service and the Colonial Administrative Service, — Whitehead's anatomy of the hands-on executives of colonial government relates to the cadres of professional educators: the men and women who established western education in the Indian and later the Colonial Empire.

Coincidentally but conveniently, this two chosen foci dovetail in their chronology. The Indian Education Service, which was not a large department and never exceeded 300 members, was set up in 1896. Recruitment stopped in 1924. That was also the year of the inaugural meeting of the Colonial Secretary's newly appointed Advisory committee on Education in British Tropical Africa. Its milestone 1925 report and subsequent reconstitution as a standing Committee on Education in the Colonies were to dominate the formulation of colonial educational policy for the next 35 years. Despite the fact that for a long time education in the colonies meant missionary initiatives rather than government involvement, and although the Colonial Education Service was not formalized until 1938, the Colonial Office had already recruited some 600 education officers before the second world war, a figure which doubled in the immediate post-war years alone. By then, too, Women Education Officers had become a prominent feature of the colonial educational scene.

It is these cadres of professional educators, in India and in the colonies, British graduates and qualified teachers, women as well as men, whom Whitehead introduces in his widely-researched study. Following an outline of the founding and nature of the two Services, the core of his presentation, combining immense personal and career detail with sustained readability, lies in a series of narrative mini-biographies of a generous spread of the Directors of Public Instruction in India and many of those who played a key role in government education in the colonies. A well-thumbed index of personal names can be anticipated! In many ways Whitehead's chosen method of presentation might be described as a joined-up personal file or narrative *Who's Who* entry, the minutiae enriched by additional personal data, incidents drawn from official files, and interpretative comment. In this respect, one cannot help noticing how accessible the India Office personal files are, when set beside the restrictions placed on access to the Colonial Office files. Such a range of biographical detail means, in Whitehead's skilled and knowledgeable hands, that these colonial educators are meaningfully brought to life in the discussion of their professional achievements as well as of their occasional career failings.

In the case of the Colonial Education Service, which accounts for two-thirds of Whitehead's study, the mini-biography approach is supplemented by substantial biographical essays on half a dozen top level colonial educators whose careers Whitehead considers to have been exemplary. One — the most substantial — of these portraits, on the elusive yet distinguished Hanns Vischer, is written by an invited scholar, Sonia Parkinson. Two of them are devoted to famous female educators, Margaret Read and Freda Gwilliam. One relates to a major colonial educator still alive, William Dodd. It is — once again — a neat coincidence and continuum that Arthur Mayhew, who appears on the opening page of the book making his way in 1903 by train to Marseilles en route to India to take up his appointment as an inspector of schools in Madras, should feature, forty years on, in the final chapter, now as the joint secretary with Vischer of the Advisory Committee on Education the Colonies. Such is the wealth of biographical information and career elaboration provided for these colonial educators, whether in the mini-biographies or in the fuller biographical essays, that many readers will come away from this absorbing study of who Britain's colonial educators were feeling that they, as Whitehead himself did, could well have known some of them.

When it comes to an evaluation of the colonial record and legacy, the one-time Indian Education Service and the Colonial Education Service will have good reason to be grateful to Clive Whitehead for having put the nature of their work and the calibre of their professionalism into perspective and given them their proper recognition. In the critical terms of their family background, intellectual formation and career development, Clive Whitehead has provided scholars with a substantial and significant study of the colonial educator in India and Africa. No longer can 'Sanders of the River' leave 'Carruthers of the Classroom' in underserved obscurity.

Anthony Kirk-Greene
St. Antony's College, Oxford
December, 2002

Preface

The renewal of interest by the British in recent years in the history of their former empire vindicates the late Dame Margery Perham, that *doyenne* of academics interested in colonial matters, who claimed, now more than a quarter of a century ago, that a time would come in the not too distant future when the British would be increasingly interested to review their imperial record more dispassionately.[1] For more than thirty years there has been a steady stream of books and articles mostly condemning the British as cultural and economic imperialists who needlessly exploited the colonies for their own aggrandisement. More than three decades on, the tumult and the shouting have largely subsided, and Kipling's captains and kings have long since departed. In the interval a new generation has also grown to maturity for whom the former empire is not even a distant memory. It is, therefore, perhaps timely to revisit the past again and especially to become better acquainted with the men and women who established western education in India and the Colonial Empire 'lest we forget' their contribution to Britain's imperial legacy.

The need is especially true of those who were responsible for spreading western education throughout India and the colonial empire, for their influence may well prove to be the most enduring and far-reaching of all aspects of Britain's imperial rule. Paradoxically, while they outnumbered many other types of colonial officers, they seem to have been largely forgotten. Traditionally, it has been the former governors and their administrative retinues that have occupied centre stage. Philip Mason immortalised the Indian Civil Service in his study of *The Men Who Ruled India*,[2] and Anthony Kirk-Greene has recently given a strong civil service or administrative flavour to his *On Crown Service*.[3] The need to broaden the focus in the study of British overseas administration to include those who worked in areas such as education, health, agriculture and forestry, was duly recognised at a conference on 'Administering Empire' held at the University of London under the auspices of the Institute for Commonwealth Studies in May 1999.[4] This study is partly a response to that need.

This volume is not a study of British education policy in India and the Colonial Empire but rather of the men and women who were central to its implementation. For more than a century — from 1860 to the late 1960s — many hundreds of British university graduates served in India, Africa, the West Indies, Southeast Asia and the Pacific, establishing and maintaining education systems based on the western model. Their backgrounds, their strengths and weaknesses, and their careers, are in every sense as much a part of Britain's imperial history as are those of governors and senior administrators. Indeed, a greater knowledge of those who served in aspects of colonial administration beyond the confines of government house may well shed new light on the true nature of colonial rule. Countless men and women devoted the greater part of their working lives, often in remote parts of the world, to developing agriculture, forestry and education, building and maintaining a variety of public works, providing medical, dental and veterinary services, and maintaining law and order. A comprehensive account of their contribution to colonial rule is yet to be written and may force many critics of empire to reassess their judgements.

Writing a book of this nature always runs the risk of becoming a study in hagiography. By emphasising the faults of some as well as the virtues of the many men and women included in this volume I hope to have gone some way to offsetting this charge. During many years of studying British colonial rule at the grass roots level I have never been convinced that the imperial record was as black as some writers would have us believe.[5] I am constantly reminded of a point made by the late Dr C. E. Beeby, a former Director of Education in New Zealand [1940–60], a former Deputy Director-General of Unesco, a very close friend and confidant of Sir Christopher Cox, and within the Colonial Office, perhaps the most widely respected authority on education within the British Commonwealth. When discussing education policy whether in Fiji, Trinidad, Uganda or Bengal, he always sought to know what the viable alternatives were *at the time*. As he was wont to say, it is easy to be an armchair critic and claim, with the clarity of hindsight or the insight of some new all encompassing social or economic theory, that this or that should or should not have been done, but officials on-the-spot who had to make decisions at the time did not have that luxury.

No one seriously denies that there were major problems associated with the way the British developed western education in India or that the pace of educational progress in the colonies prior to the outbreak of war in 1939 was slow, but more often than not there were compelling reasons to account for the shortcomings. This is not to attempt to exonerate the British from all blame for the many problems encountered in promoting education in India and elsewhere. There are good grounds for arguing that education was never a top government funding priority in India or the colonial empire generally when compared with the need to maintain Britain's place in the balance of world power or the health of the domestic economy. As J. R. Bunting, a former Chief Federal Adviser on Education in Nigeria, claimed, a succession of British governments felt neither the necessity nor the compulsion to tackle the educational needs of the colonial territories properly. To have done so would have needed far more personnel and money than contemporary political priorities dictated.[6] There is, however, much evidence to suggest that those personally responsible for promoting education in the dependencies were motivated by a genuine concern for the welfare of indigenous peoples but they could only work within the confines of what was feasible at the time.

It would have been difficult not to be impressed by the dignity and wisdom of a deeply religious man like Frank Ward, and little wonder that he was greatly respected for his forthright honesty as a British delegate at Unesco meetings. He, and others like him, cared deeply about the welfare of Africans and other indigenous peoples but there was only so much they could do. To suggest that men like Ward, and Arthur Mayhew, two of the most knowledgeable men of their generation about the problems of extending western education to Africa and India respectively, were cultural imperialists in any pejorative sense as many anti imperial critics would have us believe, is surely to stretch credibility to breaking point unless, of course, one believes that members of the Indian and Colonial Education Services were all living under a great illusion which has only been revealed with the benefit of hindsight!

This volume arises from study extending over many years into British education policy in India and the Colonial Empire in which I was privileged to meet the likes of Sir Christopher Cox, the former Educational Adviser to the Colonial Office, Freda Gwilliam, Adviser to the Colonial Office on Female Education in the Colonies, and Frank Ward, Cox's Deputy. In the late 1980s I catalogued the voluminous collection of government and semi-government papers that Cox amassed during the thirty years that he worked in Whitehall. This incredibly rich archive of primary source material now resides in the Public Record Office at Kew [Ref. No. CO 1045]. I was also privileged to enjoy a regular correspondence with Ward for over a decade before his death in 1997. As a frequent visiting research scholar at the London Institute of Education over the past twenty years it has also been my good fortune to know William 'Bill' Dodd and his long-time mentor and friend John Cameron, who served in Tanganyika for many years before taking up an academic appointment at the London Institute of Education. On numerous occasions I have enjoyed their convivial company and the scholarly insights of their accumulated wisdom on British colonial rule.

I am much indebted to several living relatives of people whose lives feature in this volume. They include Arthur Mayhew's daughter, Ms Felicity Harlow, and his granddaughter, Ms Felicity Groom; Freda Gwilliam's niece Ms Philippa Gwilliam; Eric Hussey's son Lord Hussey, a former Chairman of the BBC, and Dr Joan Read and Mr John Read, niece and nephew respectively of the late Professor Margaret Read. All gave me access to family records and some made me very welcome in their homes. I also wish to thank Dr Sonia Parkinson for contributing the comprehensive essay on Sir Hanns Vischer to this volume; Mr Anthony Kirk-Greene, Emeritus Fellow at St Antony's College, Oxford, for his interest in my colonial research over the years; Dr Paul Sharp, the Editor of the *Journal of Educational Administration and History* for permission to include the essays on Cox, Ward, Mayhew and Gwilliam, which first appeared in print in that journal; and also Dr Lester Crook of I. B. Tauris

& Co Ltd for supporting the publication of this volume. I am also deeply indebted to Mrs Zan Blair, the Education Faculty Administrative Officer at the University of Western Australia, for preparing a camera-ready copy of the typescript. Finally, I acknowledge my debt to the University of Western Australia for generous provision of overseas study leave without which my long-term research into British colonial education would not have been possible. Only my immediate family can comment on the many occasions that they spent together coping with everyday life while I was absent.

NOTES

1. Foreward to Sir James Robertson, *Transition in Africa: from direct rule to independence: a memoir*, London, C. Hurst, 1974
2. Philip Woodruff [Philip Mason], *The Men Who Ruled India*, London, Jonathon Cape, 1953–54
3. Anthony Kirk-Greene, *On Crown Service A History of HM Colonial and Overseas Civil Services, 1837–1997*, London, I. B. Tauris, 1999
4. John Smith [ed.], *Administering Empire The British Colonial Service in Retrospect*, University of London Press, 1999
5. For an extended discussion of this theme in relation to education see the author's essay 'British colonial education policy: a synonym for cultural imperialism?' in J. A. Mangan [ed], *Benefits Bestowed? Education and British Imperialism*, Manchester University Press, 1988, pp 211–230
6. J. R. Bunting [Aide Memoire] Mss Afrs 1755(41) Box XI, Rhodes House Library, Oxford

PART ONE

THE INDIAN EDUCATION SERVICE

1. The Origins and Nature of the Indian Education Service

It would be difficult to overestimate the importance of the functions which are fulfilled by the European officers of the [Indian Education Service]. Their number is insignificant compared with the great body of teachers and inspectors included in the system of State Education and it devolves on this handful of men and women to set a model for the whole educational system of the country and to guide its course.[1]

Arthur Mayhew[2] was fast approaching 25 years of age as he made his way by train from Victoria station in London to the southern French port of Marseilles to connect with the Peninsula & Oriental Steam Ship Company's vessel *S. S. Peninsula* sailing for Bombay on 10 July 1903.[3] From there he probably made his way by train across southern India to his final destination, the city of Madras. Several weeks earlier he had been appointed to the Indian Education Service [IES] as an inspector of schools in Madras. The third son of The Rev. Anthony Mayhew, Chaplain of Wadham College, Oxford, Arthur Mayhew was educated at Winchester, and later New College, Oxford. He graduated with what was widely considered the epitome of academic excellence in late Victorian England — a first class honours degree in classics or *Literae Humaniores*. He then studied pedagogy, or the science of teaching, at the universities of Berlin and Jena before taking a post as lecturer in English history and literature at Culham Teachers' Training College in Oxfordshire. A year later he set sail for India.

The sea voyage to India at the turn of the century was a virtual P & O monopoly and the company ran a regular weekly train to Marseilles for passengers bound for India who sought either to cut the journey time by several days or to avoid the bad weather traditionally associated with sailing through the Bay of Biscay *en* route to Gibraltar. The India Office in London provided Mayhew with a first class ticket — then worth upwards of £45 — which he was expected to repay if he resigned within the first two years of his contract. His journey took him through the Mediterranean Sea to Port Said; then through the Suez Canal into the Red

Sea where there was a brief coaling stop at Steamer Point in Aden, and then across the Arabian Sea to Bombay, traditionally the gateway to British India.

The trip from London to Bombay usually took about 17 days so Mayhew would have had ample time to enjoy the pleasures of shipboard life. One wonders whether, like seasoned travellers, he was fortunate to share a cabin on the port or left side of the ship which faced north and so avoided the hot sun experienced east of Suez.[4] At the turn of the century there was a steady movement of people to and from India and passengers tended to belong to one of several well defined groups. Mayhew probably mixed with 'government people' rather than the military types, the tea planters, the commercial or 'box-wallah' set, the missionaries, or the numerous mothers and children going out to rejoin husbands and fathers. Sailing in July meant that he missed the 'fishing fleet' of young spinsters who traditionally went out to India in the cold weather season from November to February, looking for husbands, but late July was not the best time to arrive in India because it was one of the hottest months of the year and the monsoon rains had often arrived by then. Nevertheless, for most young men of Mayhew's age and background the voyage would have been the experience of a lifetime.

Sir Henry Sharp, one of the most illustrious members of the former IES, recounted his experience of sailing to India in the period before the First World War.[5] For him the voyage heightened the contrast between the luxurious, pleasure-seeking late Victorian/ Edwardian years in which Britain reached the zenith of its material prosperity, and the simple and seemingly timeless Orient, dominated by immemorial custom and the all-pervasive caste system. In India he found none of the frantic hurry of modern life in Europe. Instead, the Orient reminded him of a more primitive past. At Bombay passengers disembarked by crowded tenders and then engaged in a mad scramble on the quayside for ramshackle horse-drawn cabs to take them to fragile-looking hotels, consisting mainly of verandas perched perilously above the crowded streets. Again one wonders whether Mayhew had similar thoughts when he experienced India for the first time — the constant noise and bustle of the narrow streets, people in colourful and exotic dress, blue-clad police, yellow-clad porters, Arabs, pedlars, hawkers, soothsayers, astrologers, snake-charmers — in short, the strange medley of the East. And beyond the hustle and bustle of downtown Bombay lay the *mofussil* — the vast hinterland of mountains, mighty rivers, deserts, fortresses, giant temples, the magnificence of Delhi. As Sharp concluded after a lifetime spent in India, 'No lapse of years can stale India's infinite variety, nor can length of time fathom her absorbing riddles'.[6]

On closer acquaintance Mayhew would soon have experienced the multitude of servants and customs which dictated the course of daily life and the importance, for most Europeans, of club life with its polo, tennis, cards, billiards, endless short drinks and gossip. Accommodation was often very basic, especially for young bachelors, and in rural districts one had to contend with the constant presence of numerous wild animals. Mayhew would also have soon been aware of the widespread poverty and disease found throughout India and the ubiquitous social divide between the British ruling class and their Indian subjects. Despite the many practical drawbacks to a career based in India, Mayhew prospered. As will be outlined in greater detail in a subsequent chapter, by the time he left India in 1922, he was married with three children and had risen to be the Director of Public Instruction [DPI] in the Central Provinces. In the 1920s he was destined to establish himself as a leading scholarly authority on British education in India

The Origins of the Indian Education Service

In examining the origins of the IES it is important to clarify its precise meaning because there is a tendency to use the term to refer to all Europeans and even Indians who taught in Indian schools and universities and administered education generally during the time of the *Raj*. Strictly speaking, the IES was established in 1896 and overseas recruitment formally ceased in 1924. Prior to 1896 Europeans were recruited for educational work in India on an *ad hoc* basis by the various provincial governments as and when required. Those recruited belonged to the various provincial education services. Only in 1896 did the India Office create an all-India service with common salary scales and working conditions.

The foundations of British education in India were established in the first half of the nineteenth century and are forever linked to Lord Macualay's Minute of 1836 which sanctioned the policy of introducing western education through government schools and colleges via the medium of the English language. But an even more significant milestone was Sir Charles Wood's Education Despatch of 1854 which set out a blueprint for the future development of western education throughout British India. It included provision for the establishment of provincial education departments, government and voluntary schools, and universities based on the London model of affiliated colleges in Calcutta, Madras and Bombay. The Indian Mutiny followed soon after the 1854 Despatch but Wood's education policy was reaffirmed by Lord Stanley's Despatch of 1859 after control of India had passed from the East India Company to the Crown. Thereafter, education policy was the primary concern of the Secretary of State for India and the Viceroy in Calcutta. The administration of policy was delegated to provincial governments.[7]

The 1854 despatch foreshadowed the need to establish a bureaucratic structure to administer and impart western education but it was never the intention of the British to establish a popular state system of schooling across India. Instead, in keeping with English educational tradition, it was intended that Indians should be encouraged to establish and maintain their own schools assisted financially by government grants-in-aid. At the same time, the government acknowledged the need to establish some schools and colleges as 'models' for the Indians to emulate. These were to set academic standards, generate healthy competition, and enhance the quality of non-government schools. Similarly at the university level, the government saw fit to establish some government affiliated colleges. The Presidency Colleges at Calcutta and Madras and Elphinstone College in Bombay were destined to become the premier university colleges in India. Their primary role was to set academic standards and to train a modern professional elite. The Christian missions were also encouraged to provide schools and colleges but the Indian government's strict policy of religious neutrality often strained relations between missionaries and government officials. The development of western education in nineteenth century India was also far from uniform. Bengal had an over-whelming proportion of privately run and predominantly Hindu schools, whereas Madras had a far greater missionary presence. Bombay, by contrast, had a far greater number of government schools.

As with all aspects of colonial government, the British chose to import professional talent from home to fill the highest administrative and technical positions, and education was no exception. The Indian Civil Service [ICS] was the epitome of this policy but India also boasted its own legal, public works, police, medical, forestry and agricultural services, all of which were run at the highest levels by British officials recruited in Britain. The IES was a comparative latecomer in this regard. The educational positions traditionally reserved for Europeans comprised those which carried administrative and policy responsibilities. These included the DPIs in the various provinces, school inspectors, headmasters and principals in selected high schools and training colleges, and professors in the English language colleges affiliated to the universities and Oriental institutes. The traditional *ad hoc* method of recruitment resulted in wide discrepancies in salaries and conditions of service from one province to another. Moreover, any increase in salary could only be achieved by applying for a more senior position. This meant that promotion was dependent more often than not on someone in a more senior post retiring or dying. As education expanded the demand for more honours graduates from British universities increased but they were unlikely to be attracted to administrative and teaching posts in India unless there were financial and career incentives.

William Atkinson, the DPI in Bengal in 1864, was especially outspoken in his criticism of how educational staff were recruited and the comparatively low salaries they were paid. To attract and retain more highly qualified staff he recommended an increase in salaries and the introduction of a graded system of appointments with automatic salary increases spread over five years within each grade. Promotion from one grade to another was to be at the discretion of the provincial government but in practice it was to be based mainly on seniority. Atkinson's scheme was introduced into Bengal in 1865 and was applied progressively to other Indian provinces in 1869 and thereafter. It cost more than the previous system but was successful in attracting a higher calibre of applicant.[8]

Senior education staff, recruited in Britain, were commonly referred to as the 'superior' service. Those occupying lesser posts, comprising both Europeans and Indians recruited in India, were termed the 'inferior' service. The superior service was always small in number. In 1879, for example, it comprised no more than 102 positions, the distribution of which from province to province is illustrated in Table 1.

Table 1
Distribution of superior personnel in Indian Education 1879

Province	D.P.I.	Grade 1	Grade 11	Grade 111	Grade 1V	Total
Bengal	1	2	5	12	18*	38
Bombay	1	2	4	5	6	18
Madras	1	1	2	6	5*	15
N-W Provinces	1	1*	4	3	6	15
Punjab	1	-	2	3	3	9
Central Provinces	1**	-	-	2	1	4
British Burma	-	-	1***	1	-	2
Assam	-	-	1***	-	-	1
Total	6	6	19	32	39	102

Source: Government of India, *Proceedings, Home Dept., Education, June 1879.*
*   Vacant positions included
**   Official title, inspector-general of education
***   Served as director of public instruction but recruited from the Bengal Education Service.

Some 20 years later, when Lord Curzon compiled his opening speech for the education conference that he convened at Simla in 1901, he noted that the superior service, or what was by then officially termed the IES, comprised a mere 92 members. He found it 'quite staggering' that they, together with a further 213 inferior or provincial service personnel, were responsible for an enterprise which controlled some 4.5 million pupils with an annual budget the equivalent of £2.3 million.[9]

The introduction of a graded service and enhanced salaries raised the quality of personnel recruited from Britain but it also led to the rapid bureaucratisation of provincial education departments. Moreover, as the provincial departments grew in size the number of appointments in the lower grades rose much faster than those in the upper grades. As a consequence many staff were compelled to spend long periods in the lower grades and promotion became an increasingly difficult hurdle.

This was heightened by the twin functions of administration and teaching performed by superior staff. The primary function of provincial education departments was administration but the majority of superior staff held teaching appointments. Consequently, when the most senior positions were filled the tendency was to opt for men who had been inspectors of schools rather than principals of colleges. Inspectors travelled widely and knew at first hand the manifold problems which confronted provincial governments, many of which were not necessarily purely educational. Principals of colleges were frequently outstanding teachers and administrators within their respective institutions but they often lacked a full appreciation of the political, social and economic aspects of educational administration at the provincial level.

The selection of DPIs long remained a contentious issue within the ranks of the IES because the Indian government consistently upheld the right of provincial governments to choose men from non-educational backgrounds when deemed necessary.[10] This was justified on the grounds that the pool of potential applicants from within a province was often very small and it was quite likely that none of them had the necessary qualities to deal with educational matters that were often of great public interest because they involved delicate social and political issues concerning race, caste and religion. Nor did they always have the qualities to deal with a wide variety of people and organisations. Even appointments to the post of DPI from within the ranks of the IES or the earlier graded service could generate strong feelings of resentment if unsuccessful candidates thought that their claims had been unfairly overlooked or rejected.

The appointment of Archdale [later Sir Archdale] Earle as successor to Alfred Croft as DPI in Bengal in 1906, was a classic example.[11] Earle was a senior member of the ICS and Secretary to Bengal's General and Revenue Departments when he reluctantly accepted the post. At the time he thought the move was a retrograde step in his career but he was later rewarded for his apparent sacrifice by being appointed Secretary of the Home Department of the Indian government and later still Chief Commissioner in Assam. The appointment of William Hornell as DPI in Bengal in 1913, in succession to George Kuchler, also generated heated controversy.[12] Hornell had been an inspector of schools in Bengal but resigned his post in 1908 in order to return to Britain to take up a senior position with the Board of Education in Whitehall. His reappointment to India generated strong opposition especially from H. R. James, the principal of Presidency College, and other IES staff in Bengal who thought that James had been unfairly overlooked.

The case of John Nesfield was another prime example of an educator being overlooked in the appointment of a DPI in favour of a member of the ICS.[13] Nesfield, the son of a Wiltshire cleric and a BA graduate of Merton College, Oxford (1860), was a professor at Presidency and Krishnagarh colleges in Bengal before becoming DPI and inspector of schools in Lower Burma in 1872. From there he went to be director in the then autonomous state of Oudh. When Oudh was amalgamated for administrative purposes with the Northwest Provinces, he became principal of Benares College for a year before joining the inspectorate in Oudh in 1879. In 1885 he applied unsuccessfully for the post of DPI in the Northwest Provinces and Oudh. Instead, the post went to Edmund White, a member of the ICS, who had held a variety of administrative and legal positions in both Bengal and the Northwest Provinces. Nesfield felt sufficiently aggrieved that he sent a strongly worded memorial to Viscount Cross, the Secretary of State. He referred to previous government statements on the policy of appointing DPIs; to his own varied and successful career up to that point in time; and to what he thought was the very unfair appointment of someone over him who had had no previous educational experience. The Indian government transmitted his memorial to London without comment, which was tantamount to saying that it saw no grounds for supporting Nesfield's case. As might be expected, the Secretary of State rejected his appeal. Nesfield then wrote two further letters of protest to the Lieutenant-Governor of the Northwest Provinces but was again rebuffed. He then made a personal appeal to the Viceroy but again his case was rejected. Finally, he asked unsuccessfully, to see the evidence on which the decision was determined. He did derive some small recompense, however, when he was appointed as DPI for the last two years of his service in India after White retired in 1892. It is significant that during White's term as DPI, he carried the major responsibility for preparing the case, and a draft bill, for the new university at Allahabad. That is probably the primary reason why the government chose him ahead of James.

The formal establishment of the IES in 1896, as opposed to the broad generic use of the term as explained earlier, arose out of the *Report of the Public Service Commission* of 1886–87, presided over by Sir Charles Aitchison, then Lieutenant-Governor of the Punjab.[14] The Commission was established in response to the growing resentment of Indians at their exclusion from the higher levels of the Civil Service. It was the Commission's task to examine the employment of Indians across all branches of civil administration with a view to enhancing their rate of participation. The Commission made five principal recommendations regarding education.

The first and most far-reaching was the abolition of the graded service: 'The result of the system and of the modes of recruitment adopted has been to secure a body of officers who, with brilliant exceptions, are not superior to the average graduates of British universities, and are in no sense specialists in the subjects they are required to teach'.[15] The Commission was also highly critical of the interchange of professors and inspectors and called for a clear distinction to be drawn between teaching or professional staff and the inspectorate. There was support for each province having at least one college with a professional staff capable of teaching to the highest European standards but in general, the Commission favoured gradually reducing the number of government colleges and schools in line with the recommendation of the Education Commission of 1883. The Commission also argued that professional staff should be recruited from England for a stipulated number of years. Finally, the Commission believed that the inspection of schools should be done by a separate agency recruited from a different source. To this end it recommended a reduction in the number of inspectors recruited from England and the recruitment of the majority of inspectoral staff from within India on terms common to the rest of the inferior or provincial services.

Elsewhere in the report, the Commission stated that the claims of Indians for access to more high level appointments in the Civil Service could best be provided for by reducing the existing covenanted civil service to a small *corps d'elite* and opening up all other appointments to local provincial services. In the case of education the Commission sought to go even further by largely eliminating the idea of any elite graded service altogether. In general terms the Commission sought to reduce the number of officers recruited in Britain in all areas of civil administration but to raise the quality of those who remained. As the Chief Secretary in the Bombay provincial government remarked, 'imported Europeans should be as good as possible, as few as possible, and as highly paid as possible'.[16] It was argued that the cost savings generated by recruiting fewer personnel from England could be used to raise salaries to attract the highest quality honours graduates. Numerous interviews conducted by the Commission highlighted the fact that promotion in the graded system was uncertain and almost entirely dependent on death or retirement rather than healthy competition. When A. M. Nash, an inspector of schools in Bengal, was asked if he thought competition produced the best men for the public service, he replied, 'I do not think that it always gives you the best men, but it secures you against getting the worst'.[17] The Commission's outspoken criticisms and radical recommendations met with a mixed reaction from provincial governments and the Viceroy's executive council in Calcutta.

It took what seemed like an inordinate amount of time to circulate the Commission's report and get back the responses of provincial governments but eventually the Indian government despatched its comments to the Secretary of State in London in March 1891. It strongly opposed the abolition of the graded system mainly because it was far from clear what would take its place, and feared that fixed-term appointments without any leave or pension entitlements would not attract professors of high enough standard from Britain. It was also felt that academics appointed to senior teaching positions in India needed prior Indian experience. The Indian government also strongly rejected the notion of recruiting most of its school inspectors from within India and entrusting the inspection of schools primarily to native born Indians. It was claimed that the inspection process would not be thorough enough, especially as the government progressively withdrew from direct control of most of its educational institutions. It was feared that some Indian school inspectors might be compromised by bribes and obligations generated by religion, caste and social relationships. It was thought imperative, therefore, to retain the European element in the inspectorate to provide a corrective. This should be supplied by recruits from Britain, the precise number to be determined by local circumstances. Alfred Croft, the DPI in Bengal, also emphasized the need for the inspectorate to provide intellectual and social leadership as it did in the United Kingdom:

> Successful school-masters in England, are made Assistant Inspectors; Inspectors are almost invariably recruited from the Universities. The reason is clear. It is found desirable to entrust the control and direction of education as distinguished from the regulation of its details, *to a class of men of superior culture*, and a wide range of knowledge and ideas. In India, too, if education is to be progressive, if educational systems are to be tempered with fresh ideas, some at least of the Inspectors should be men of the highest Western education.[18]

Finally, the Indian government claimed that the Commission had not resolved the problem of what constituted adequate salaries to attract the best graduates.

Some 10 months later [January 1892] the Secretary of State agreed to the retention of the graded system but emphasized the need to improve promotion prospects, for example, by allowing all professors to rise within 10 years service to a salary of R 1000 per mensem. Emphasis was also placed on the utmost importance of providing from England 'a teaching agency of the highest quality and character'. There was general agreement with all other points in the Viceroy's despatch. Then followed another protracted process whereby the Indian government approached each of the provincial governments to determine which posts should be included in a revised graded service and what salaries should be paid at each level. This exercise generated much discussion about the nature and functions of the superior and inferior services and the cost implications for each province. The use of the term superior service was also questioned. Madras suggested calling it the 'Imperial' education service but the Indian government preferred the term 'European'. The Secretary of State rejected the term 'European' on the grounds that it suggested a distinction based on race and was inadequate to describe a service performed in India. Instead, it was decided to adopt the term 'Indian' Education Service.[19] The inferior branch of the service was henceforth to be called the Provincial Education Service of Bengal, Madras etc. In the final analysis the newly established IES was to consist initially of 92 positions. It was not envisaged at the time that provincial staff would be eligible for promotion to the IES but this ruling was to change after the First World War.

The Nature of the Recruits

There was a steady stream of young IES recruits like Mayhew who made their way to India in the years leading up to the outbreak of war in August 1914 and the India Office files contain details of their social backgrounds, education and training, and teaching experience up to the time of their appointments. These records provide a valuable social history of IES recruitment and an equally interesting insight into the education of the middle classes in late Victorian/Edwardian Britain.

Not surprisingly, many recruits came from families that already had strong ties with India. John Watson,[20] who had a first class honours degree in history and a second class honours degree in classics, both from Edinburgh University, was appointed as the vice-principal of the teachers' college at Allahabad in 1909. At the time both his father and brother-in-law were chaplains in the Indian ecclesiastical establishment. Harry Wetherill,[21] appointed to the IES in 1913, as headmaster of the government high school in Allahabad, had been born in Calcutta in 1876 and lived in India between the ages of 10 and 15. He also had a brother, by then deceased, who had been a member of the elite 'heaven-born' Indian Civil Service and he still had family members and many friends in India. Guy Hunter,[22] an Oxford first class honours graduate in modern history, joined the IES as a professor[23] of history at Jubblepore College in 1912. His father had been a member of the Indian Police Service and both his grandfathers had served in India, one in the police and the other in the army. Raymond Goffin,[24] appointed as a professor of English at Cotton College, in Assam, in 1914, had been born in Madras, the son of a retired missionary. At the time of his Indian appointment he also had a cousin who was a professor of mathematics in Calcutta. Gerald Small,[25] an honours graduate in classics and history from Trinity College, Dublin, joined the IES as an inspector of schools in Eastern Bengal and Assam in 1911. His father was a retired colonel in the Indian army and he also had two brothers both holding commissions in the Indian army. Moreover, one of his referees was Colonel Riach of the Cameroon Highlanders. Amongst his accomplishments Small mentioned that he had a riding certificate from the Riding Master of the 5th Dragoon Guards!

One of the most interesting of all the IES recruits to have a strong family link with India was Lady Alice Henrietta Lawrence,[26] the only member of the British aristocracy known to have joined the IES. Her father, Sir Henry Hayes Lawrence, who died when she was only three years old, was the grandson of Sir Henry Montgomery Lawrence, who was killed defending the Residency at Lucknow during the Indian Mutiny. Her father, educated at Eton and Trinity College, Cambridge, was the second Baronet Lawrence of Lucknow, a Justice of the Peace and High Sheriff in the County of Dublin. Alice, the second of his three daughters, deliberately took up teaching as a career in order to go to India. She attended Cheltenham Ladies' College and then Lady Margaret Hall, Oxford, graduating in 1918 with second class honours in modern history. She then enrolled at the Bedford College for women and gained a London University diploma in pedagogy in 1920. When she sailed for India in November 1921, she was one of the last women to be recruited in England for the IES. She went out as an 'Inspectress' of teacher training institutions for women in the United Province of Agra and Oudh, and was based in Allahabad. It was hardly surprising that such an eligible young spinster of 26 years of age should be married within the year to Sir Hopetoun Stokes, a leading government official in Madras. As a consequence her IES career ended somewhat abruptly although she and her husband lived on in Madras until he retired in the late 1930s. During that time, Lady Alice was deeply involved in welfare work and was awarded the prestigious *Kaiser-I-Hind* [Empress of India] Gold Medal in 1935 in recognition of her social services to India. Her husband died in London in November 1951 but she lived on until January 1975. By then she was a qualified surgeon and a leading advocate of homoeopathy. In her will she left various personal family papers to the South Asian Archive at the University of Cambridge. Her life story, like those of so many IES officers mentioned in this chapter, deserves to be studied in greater detail. Hers, in particular, would provide the basis for an excellent novel.

The motives which prompted young men and women to go out to India were diverse. Mayhew readily admitted that serving the Empire was a very popular fashion at Oxford at the turn of the century. For many it was a family tradition, for others it was a source of adventure, an opportunity to do something different. In most cases India provided an income and a style of life hard to emulate at home. Inevitably there were some recruits who went to India to escape from life's misfortunes but most, being single and in their mid twenties, were imbibed with a strong sense of adventure and a genuine willingness to serve their country in far off lands. Even so, they often paid a high price for their patriotism. Separation from family and friends, the oppressive climate — 'the heat of summer had to be endured much like toothache'[27] — strange languages and social customs, the acute lack of female or male company, the strong sense of isolation from the mainstream life of Europe, long intervals between leave or 'furlough', and frequent separation from wives and children, all took their toll. Many loved the life, some endured it, while a few voted with their feet.

Arthur Jones[28] was one of the latter. A brilliant young student from Manchester, he started life as a pupil teacher in his home city but later won a succession of scholarships which enabled him to go to university and get first class honours in both history [1905] and Celtic studies [1907], the latter being the first such award at Manchester University. He then lectured at the universities of Manchester and Oxford before joining the IES in 1910 as the principal of Jubblepore College. His professor at Manchester judged his honours degree in history to have been the equal of any comparable Oxbridge degree, and even the Vice-Chancellor saw fit to provide him with a glowing reference. When interviewed for the IES he stated that he hoped to publish a book on his Celtic studies in the near future and was attracted to India by the opportunity to further his historical research by being close to public records etc. Perhaps he was too scholarly for the relatively mundane job of a college principal because he resigned from his post after five months and returned to England.

Douglas Schulze[29] lasted an even shorter time. The son of a naturalised German father who was a grain merchant, and a Scottish mother, he was educated at the Glasgow Academy and Fettes College before going to Merton College, Oxford, where he graduated with second class honours in classics in 1904. Thereafter, he completed a teacher's diploma at Manchester University before teaching at Dulwich College, St Pauls and the Royal Naval College at Dartmouth. He excelled at rugby football and represented Scotland at national level between 1905 and 1908. He joined the IES as an inspector of schools in Burma, arriving in Rangoon on 7 June 1908. One can only imagine what went through his mind when he landed but within a week he was most anxious to leave. Even a personal interview with the Lieutenant-Governor failed to change his mind and he formally resigned on the 25 June. Within a week he left for England, more than happy to refund the passage money of £47 6s.

Another Burma recruit who didn't stay long was Gordon Luce,[30] a brilliant classics scholar from Emmanuel College, Cambridge. The son of an Anglican cleric, he was appointed as a professor of English at the government college in Rangoon. When he went to Burma in 1912 he was a raw 23 year old graduate with no prior teaching experience whatsoever. The Board of Education selection committee described him as being somewhat eccentric because of his unconventional manner and lack of taste for anything like methodical or business habits. He also had no love of sport, not because he was incompetent but because he had other interests. Nevertheless, one of his tutors at Cambridge had no hesitation in claiming him as the most gifted man Emmanuel College had had for many years. At the time of his appointment to the IES he was clearly a young man still revelling in student life and hardly ready for the relatively mundane life of teaching Indian undergraduates. It comes as no surprise to learn that he resigned his post before his two year probationary period was completed.

Fortunately for the India Office, for every IES recruit that failed to adjust to life in India there were many more who did, and who went on to enjoy highly successful careers. Some, like John Bottomley,[31] lived on in India after retirement and eventually died there. Bottomley joined the IES in 1911 as a professor of mathematics at the government college in Dacca. He was born in Napier, New Zealand, but reared in Ormskirk in Lancashire, where his father ran a drapery business. He won scholarships to the Merchant Taylor's School in Liverpool and to Christchurch, Oxford, where he graduated with second class honours in mathematics. His college tutors all agreed that he was a first rate mathematician. H. T. Gerrans, a tutor at Worcester College, described him as 'just one of our best type: straightforward, stimulating, free from "side", [and] well supplied with initiative. It is not often I exhibit enthusiasm on paper with regard to any man'. His former headmaster at Merchant Taylor's remarked that he had come from a small Lancashire town and was by birth not of much social standing but he was nonetheless instinctively a gentleman. The Dean of Christchurch suggested that Bottomley's failure to gain first class honours may have been partly attributable to his having found the body of his fellow lodger who died suddenly owing to a fit during 'finals'. Bottomley was destined to occupy a variety of teaching and inspectoral appointments in India, including principal of Presidency College in Calcutta, before he was eventually appointed DPI in Bengal in 1933. In 1917, he married the daughter of a lieutenant-colonel in the Indian Army. He retired in 1943 but lived on in Burma until his death in 1960.

In some cases IES recruits subsequently enjoyed illustrious careers in other countries or outside the sphere of education. Duncan Sloss,[32] who was appointed to the IES in 1920 and became Principal of the University College, Rangoon, later went on to be Vice-Chancellor of the University of Hong Kong [1937–49] and played a leading role in the decision to rebuild the university after the Second World War.

David [later Sir David] Meek,[33] joined the IES in 1911 as a professor of physics at the government college in Dacca. Reared and educated in Glasgow, he proved to be an outstanding student and graduated from the university with a first class MA degree in mathematics and natural philosophy and later a DSc. His career changed direction as a result of the First World War. In 1918 he was appointed Assistant Controller of Munitions in India. Later appointments included Director of Industries in Bengal and Director-General of Commercial Intelligence and Statistics before he became Indian Trade Commissioner in London in 1935. He was knighted in 1937. In 1944 he became Deputy High Commissioner for India in London.

Robert Gilchrist[34] was also born in Scotland. The son of a retired farmer, he was educated in Aberdeen at both the grammar school and the university. In 1909 he graduated MA with triple honours in economic science, history and mental philosophy. At university he was on the student council, president of the debating society, and editor for two years of *Alma Mater*, the Aberdeen University magazine. He took up his IES appointment as a professor of English and philosophy in Bengal in 1911. During the war he was principal of Krishnagar College. Afterwards he worked for the Indian government in a variety of labour and commercial appointments before becoming Labour Commissioner in Bengal. He later served as a Principal in the India Office in London (1940–48) before retiring to Aberdeen, where he sat on the Board of Management of Aberdeen General Hospitals (1951–57).

The Selection of Indian Education Service Officers

Traditionally recruits to the graded service were appointed by the Secretary of State, aided by an *ad hoc* committee consisting mainly of members of the India Office. After the Board of Education was created in England in 1899, the selection committee was chaired by the Board's director of special enquiries and reports. Others on the committee included permanent representatives from the India Office, the Scottish Education Department and invited others. An officer from the Board acted as secretary and maintained a list of applicants for employment. Various teaching institutions in Britain, including the universities, were kept informed of employment opportunities and sometimes posts were advertised if applicants could not be obtained by informal means. The same system continued after the creation of the IES in 1896.

The selection criteria were similar to those applied at a later date by Sir Ralph Furse[35] when recruiting for the Colonial Education Service although less emphasis appears to have been given to sporting prowess. As with Furse, a major emphasis was placed on character. In testimonials on behalf of applicants, referees repeatedly emphasized the hallmarks of honesty, trust and loyalty. Playing the game and not letting the side down were aspects of character synonymous with the public school tradition which most applicants had experienced in their youth. Oxbridge tutors, in particular, frequently spoke of their former students as in every respect scholars and gentlemen. Lawrence Watkins, appointed to the IES in 1913 as headmaster of the government high school in Peshawar, was a typical example.[36]

The son of a former Archdeacon of Lucknow, he was educated at the King's School, Canterbury, and Corpus Christi College, Cambridge, where he graduated with third class honours in classics. Thereafter, he taught at the Bradford Grammar School and King William College on the Isle of Man before his Indian appointment. Despite his third class degree his tutor at Cambridge described him as 'in every respect a gentleman'. The Dean of Corpus Christi described Watkins as probably the most popular and influential man in the college in his last year, largely because he was captain of the university boat club. He was, the Dean concluded, 'a gentleman who can be thoroughly trusted to do what he has to do with capacity and loyalty'.

Like Watkins, Charles Ransford,[37] son of Colonel Ransford, of the Indian army retired, was also handicapped by a poor academic record — in his case a fourth class in *Literae Humaniores* from Worcester College, Oxford. After teaching in Argentina and South Africa, he joined the IES as headmaster of a school at Mercara in Coorg. His former Oxford tutor wrote of him: 'He is a gentleman and has the ways and feeling of a gentleman, with good manners, good appearance and a pleasant address'. Another Oxford tutor wrote: 'He is in the fullest sense of the word a gentleman, high principled, courteous in manner and certain to exercise a good influence over his pupils'.

By contrast, Francis Storrs[38] had an upper second class honours degree in classics from Jesus College, Cambridge, when he applied to join the IES in 1910 as a professor of English at the government college in Rangoon. His classics tutor described him as 'an English gentleman in the best sense of the word' while the Master of his College added that he was 'an absolutely trustworthy and thoroughly well-educated gentleman'.

His father was the Dean of Rochester. He also had an elder brother Sir Ronald Storrs who had an illustrious career in the Egyptian and later Colonial Service as Governor of Jerusalem [1917–20], Cyprus [1926–32] and Northern Rhodesia [1932–34]. Thereafter, he served on the London County Council [1937–45].

Occasionally the IES attracted a candidate from one of the dominions like Robert George[39] who hailed from New Zealand. He was educated in Auckland before going up to St John's College, Oxford, where he graduated with second class honours in English in 1913. When he applied to join the IES as a professor of English at the government college in Lahore, the Dean of Christ Church and the Vice-Chancellor of Oxford both referred to him as a 'Colonial' but hastened to add that he was 'a thoroughly well-educated gentleman'. Lord Plunket, a former Governor-General of New Zealand said that he knew his family, that he came from 'good stock', and was a scholar and a gentleman. The selection committee considered it relevant to comment that he had 'little or no trace of a Colonial accent!'

The graded service and later the IES comprised two branches — teaching and administration — and candidates opted for one or the other, although it was made clear to them at the time of recruitment that they could be transferred if necessary. In practice, most of those who joined as professors but who later held high administrative positions transferred at an earlier date to inspectoral duties. All applicants had to be male, except for a very small number of posts open to women as 'inspectresses' of girls' schools or principals of female training colleges; aged between 23 and 30, although some exceptions were made at the upper limit; and British subjects. They also had to produce evidence of a 'liberal education' which meant in most instances a public school education or its equivalent and a good university honours degree i.e. first or second class honours, preferably from Oxford or Cambridge. After 1900 fewer Oxbridge graduates were recruited but there was a substantial increase in graduates from Scottish universities. Candidates underwent a searching interview in London but unlike candidates for the ICS, there was no additional qualifying examination. In theory, the selection criteria were weighted in favour of a 'good honours' degree, teaching experience, and qualifications in special areas depending on the nature of the vacancy, in that order. In appointing school inspectors special emphasis was placed on linguistic talent, capacity for organisation, and practical and theoretical knowledge of educational methods. In practice, it would seem that any Oxbridge candidate with a first or second class honours degree, especially in classics or modern history, had a headstart over all other applicants. All candidates underwent a searching medical examination but even so, the rigours of the Indian climate frequently took their toll either in premature death or enforced early retirement.

H. C. Norman,[40] a graduate of Edinburgh and Oxford, who was appointed as a professor of English literature at Queen's College in Benares in 1905, was a case in point. He died in April 1913, aged 32 years.

His mother was granted a gratuity payment of £400 by the Indian government as her son had been her sole means of support. A. C. Bray,[41] appointed as a professor of English at Morris College in Nagpur in 1907, resigned within six months of taking up his post. He cited family reasons but the civil surgeon in Nagpur reported that Bray was unsuited to the Indian climate because of a delicate constitution and a nervous temperament. The fact that he had done good work since his arrival meant that the Secretary of State did not seek a refund of the cost of his passage to Bombay. Dr A. D. Imms,[42] professor of biology at the Muir Central College, resigned on health grounds in October 1910, some three years after taking up his post. He claimed that he was constitutionally unfit to live in India's hot rainy season. Soon after arriving in India he contracted malaria and then jaundice. He took six months' sick leave but after resuming work he was again afflicted with malaria. George Stuart,[43] an outstanding mathematics graduate from Emmanuel College, Cambridge, who was also a member of the English Bar, joined the IES in 1882 but died in Madras in 1903 at the age of 51. His son George Stuart, likewise a graduate of Emmanuel College, joined the ICS in 1901 but died at Madras in 1921 aged only 41 years. Yet another Emmanuel graduate, Kenneth Ward,[44] described as 'socially and intellectually ... quite the right type for the IES', went to Burma as a professor of physics in 1911, and died in 1927, aged 40. His father was James Ward, the first Professor of Mental Philosophy and Logic at Cambridge [1897–1925]. Kenneth Ward also had two uncles teaching in India — Arthur Ward, Professor of Physics at Canning College in Lucknow, and Professor Ernest Tipple, Professor of Mathematics and Physical Science at Thomason College, Roorkee.

Conditions of Service

Candidates accepted into the graded service and later the IES, signed on for an initial probationary period of five years, later reduced to two, during which they had to pass an indigenous language test. The same requirement later applied to those appointed to the Colonial Education Service. Failure to pass the test, in some cases after several attempts, resulted in termination of their contract, although there was at least one celebrated case where this rule was not followed. H. B. Matthews,[45] the Professor of Electrical Engineering in the College of Engineering at Madras in 1916, was exempted after appealing against the requirement, mainly one suspects because of the near impossibility of replacing him at the time. Matthews, then aged 39 years, claimed that he had never had occasion to use a vernacular language, and that, having had no previous practice at learning a language, he found it very difficult at his time of life. The need to speak a vernacular language clearly carried less weight at the college level where teaching was mainly in English but for inspectors who travelled around the country visiting vernacular schools it was essential that they spoke the local language.

Writers like J. A. Mangan[46] have made much of the importance attached to athletic prowess in the selection of personnel to rule the empire. Athletic ability and experience in the organizing of sport in schools were certainly important qualities looked for in applicants for teaching posts in the IES but they were frequently overlooked if candidates had outstanding academic records. Occasionally one comes across a candidate with outstanding athletic qualities but in most cases sporting activity was confined to school or college teams. Mention has already been made of Schulze who played rugby football for Scotland at the turn of the century. L. G. Owen,[47] a first class honours graduate in mathematics from Jesus College, Oxford, who became a professor of mathematics at the government college in Rangoon in 1915, likewise played soccer, or association football as it was more commonly called then, for Wales. Dr Kenneth Caldwell,[48] who had a doctorate from the University of Leipzig and who was appointed as a professor of chemistry at Patna College in 1909, had once been chosen as twelfth man for Wales against Scotland at hockey. Several others had played rugby and cricket at provincial or near county level; others had won 'Blues' at their respective universities. Leslie Taylor[49] had represented Oxbridge in athletics against Harvard and Yale — his Cambridge tutor referred to him as the one 'who runs about'. John Bulkerley[50] was the French record-holder for the long jump; while George Stewart[51] had been the 1899 Scottish inter-universities 100 yards sprint champion. At least two IES recruits — Philip Robertson,[52] a New Zealander, and John MacLean,[53] a Canadian — were Rhodes Scholars, and one of the key selection criteria for the award was outstanding athletic ability. Robertson played hockey while MacLean rowed for Worcester College. By contrast, other equally successful IES recruits claimed little or no sporting prowess. Several even listed golf and walking! One can only conclude that sporting achievement was a bonus but by no means the decisive factor in any IES appointment.

Either party could withdraw from the initial contract within the probationary period without penalty provided three months notice was given but rates of pay, recreation and sick leave, and retirement and pension provisions were all designed, at least in theory, to make India an attractive career option. Under the old graded system new appointees started on R 500 per mensem or the equivalent of about £400 per year, rising in five annual steps to R 750 per mensem or £600 per year. Higher grades, also arranged in five incremental steps, went to £800, £1000 and £1200 per year respectively. The creation of the IES was accompanied by a new salary structure. Henceforth, all new appointees started as before on R 500 per mensem but then rose in 10 annual steps of R 50 to R 1000 per mensem or about £800 per year. Thereafter, annual R 50 junior and senior allowances were payable, again over a five year period. Junior allowances ranged from R 1000 to R 1250 per mensem, the equivalent of £1000 per year, and senior allowances from R 1250 to R 1500 per mensem or £1200 per year. The new scales were an improvement on the old but they were not comparable with the salaries and allowances paid to the ICS.[54] They were, however, sufficient to attract good quality staff until the years leading up to the First World War. By then mounting political tensions associated with the Indian independence movement had made India a less attractive career option while educational expansion in the United Kingdom was providing improved employment opportunities for British university graduates at home. Rapid inflation of the Indian rupee both during and after the First World War also intensified recruitment problems for the IES.

NOTES ON CHAPTER

1. *Proceedings of the Government of India* [P] 9193 Education [ED] January 1913. Govt. of India to Sec. of State 21 May 1910
2. For details of Mayhew's life and work see chap. 8 in Part Two of this study.
3. P 6661 ED June 1903. For details of the P & O services at the turn of the century see *The Times*. For life aboard ship see Boyd Cable, *A Hundred Year History of the P & O 1837–1937*, Ivor Nicholson and Watson, London, 1937. There is a full-page colour plate of the *S. S. Peninsula*, the ship on which Mayhew sailed to India, facing p 144. For more on the P & O and the India run see Peter Padfield, *Beneath the House Flag of the P & O*, Hutchison, London, 1981; and David Howarth and Stephen Howarth, *The Story of the P & O*, Weidenfeld and Nicolson, London, 1986.
4. Charles Allen (ed), *Plain Tales From The Raj*, Futura Pubs. Ltd., London, 1975, esp. chap. 3
5. Sir Henry Sharp, *Good-Bye India*, OUP, London, 1946
6. *Ibid.*, p 16
7. For a comprehensive coverage of these events see S. Nurallah and J. P. Naik, *A History of Education in India*, Macmillan & Co., (2nd ed) 1951
8. For details of the origins of the graded system and the influence of Atkinson see the Introduction in J. P. Naik and Surresh Chandra Ghosh (eds), *Selections from Educational Records* (New Series) Vol. 1, Pt. 1, Zakir Husain Centre for Educational Studies, Jawaharlal Nehru University, New Delhi, 1976. See also Irene A. Gilbert, 'The Organization of the Academic Profession in India: The Indian Educational Services, 1864–1924', in S. H. Rudolph & L. I. Rudolph (eds), *Education and Politics in India. Studies in Organization, Society and Policy*, Harvard University Press, Cambridge, Mass. 1972
9. Curzon Papers, British Library, India Office Records, Mss European F. 111/ 248c. Handwritten notes on education in India for speech at education conference, Simla, 1901
10. Govt. of India, *Selections from the Records of the government of India*, Home Dept., No. 24. Papers relating to the Re-organization of the Educational Service in India 1891–1897 (Calcutta). Govt. of India to S of S, Despatch No.8 of 1886 (Home Dept.) Education, 28 Sep 1886
11. P 7314 ED May 1906
12. P 9195 ED Sep 1913
13. For details of Nesfield's career see *India Office List 1911*, p 606. For details of his appeal see *Selections from the Records of the government of India* …. Papers relating to the Re-organization of the Educational Service…, pp 275–287. Controversy was to surround Nesfield right up to the point of his retirement and beyond over a matter concerning textbooks used in schools in the Northwest Provinces. A question was addressed in the House of Commons to the Secretary of State for India as to whether a large number of the textbooks, both English and vernacular, prescribed for use in the

schools in the Northwest Provinces had been compiled as a private enterprise by Mr Nesfield, the DPI, and whether such an arrangement operated to create a monopoly and exclude other text-books from the schools. When the Indian government finally responded, in October 1894, Nesfield had retired. It transpired that he had compiled the books when he was an inspector *at the request* of the then Director, Edmund White. The books were published at Nesfield's own risk, with government approval, but they were not meant to establish a monopoly. Indeed, quite the reverse. The books were written to fill a desperate need for suitable texts. On his retirement, Nesfield disposed of the copyright to a London publishing house. On receipt of this advice, the Indian government advised London that it considered the matter was now closed. During his time in India Nesfield published several studies of the tribespeople of Oudh and northwest India but he is perhaps best remembered for his *Manual of English Grammar and Composition*, first published in 1898. It was twice revised and went through endless reprints, and was still available from booksellers as late as 1954. See India Office Records, L/P & J/3/159 – pp 571–574

14. C.5327 (1887) India Office Records V/26/210/1
15. *Report of the Commission ...*, para. 99
16. *Proceedings of the sub-committee of the Public Service Commission.* Education Dept., Simla 1887, p 87. India Office Records V/26/210/11
17. *Ibid.*, p 23
18. P 3881 ED Oct 1891 Croft to the Govt. of Bengal, 1 Aug 1891. Author's emphasis
19. *Selections from the Records of the government of India ....* Papers relating to the Re-organization of the Education Service .... S of S to Govt. of India 12 Mar 1896, Despatch No. 22, (Public) Education
20. P 8155 ED Nov 1909
21. P 9196 ED Nov 1913
22. P 9193 ED Feb 1913
23. In India the term professor was used to designate all college/university teaching staff regardless of seniority. In the case of someone like Hunter, he was going out in modern parlance to the equivalent of a junior lecturing position. The use of this nomenclature was questioned by Henry Sharp [p 13] and William Hornell [p 115] in the *Appendix to the Report of the Commissioners* [Royal Commission on the Public Services in India 1915], Vol.XX Minutes of Evidence relating to the Education Department [Cd.7908].
24. P 9445 ED Aug 1914
25. P 8698 ED Apr 1911
26. P 11209 ED Jan 1922 See also *Burke's Peerage*, 102nd ed MCMLIX (1959) and *Who's Who*
27. Charles Allen (ed), *Plain Tales from the Raj,* Futura Publications, London, 1976, p 144
28. P 8434 ED Sep 1910
29. P 7876 ED May 1908
30. P 8943 ED Dec 1912
31. P 8698 ED Jan 1911
32. P 10828 ED Sep 1920
33. P 8698 ED Jan 1911
34. P 8698 ED Feb 1911
35. Major Sir Ralph Furse, *Aucuparius Recollections of a Recruiting Officer*, London, OUP, 1962, esp. chap.x
36. P 9195 ED Oct 1913
37. P 8432 ED Feb 1910
38. P 8698 ED Jan 1911
39. P 9708 ED Feb 1915

22 COLONIAL EDUCATORS

40. *P* 7050 ED Sep 1905
41. *P* 7877 ED Jun 1908
42. *P* 8432 ED Apr 1910
43. *Alumni Cantabrigiensis*, Part 11, Vol. VI, p 72
44. *P* 8698 ED Mar 1911
45. *P* 9942 ED Jan 1916
46. J. A. Mangan, *The Games ethic and imperialism: aspects of the diffusion of an ideal*, Harmondsworth, Middlesex, Viking, 1986
47. *P* 9708 ED Mar 1915
48. *P* 8432 ED Feb 1910
49. *P* 9708 ED May 1915 Taylor was educated at Oundle and Clare College, Cambridge, and joined the IES in 1915 as a school principal in Burma.
50. *P* 7591 ED Dec 1906 Bulkerley was educated at King William College, Isle of Man, and Keble College, Oxford. He joined the IES in 1906 as Principal of the Rangoon Collegiate School.
51. *P* 8698 ED Jan 1911 Stewart had first class honours in history from Glasgow University and joined the IES in 1911 as a professor of history at Muir Central College, Allahabad.
52. *P* 8155 ED Oct 1909 Robertson was a graduate of Trinity College, Oxford and joined the IES as a lecturer in science at Rangoon College.
53. *P* 7877 ED Aug 1908 MacLean had a second class honours degree in classics from Oxford and joined the IES in 1908 as a school inspector in Bengal.
54. The disparity in pay between the two services was maintained until recruitment to the IES ceased in 1924. By then an ICS officer with 15 years service was on R 1950 per month whereas his IES counterpart was on R 1250. The gap widened still further after 23 years service to R 2500 and R 1600 per month respectively.

2.   The Intellectual Calibre of the Indian Education Service

Much has justifiably been written about the intellectual calibre of members of the ICS but so far little recognition has been accorded to the equally talented group of British administrators and scholars who laid the foundations of modern education in India.[1] Prior to the First World War, despite the earlier somewhat derogatory remarks of the Public Service Commission in its report of 1887, most high-ranking education officials had good honours degrees, including many Firsts, especially from Oxford but also from Cambridge, while many other equally talented staff were graduates of London, Trinity College, Dublin, and the Scottish universities. Some of the most outstanding officials were also knighted for their services to education in India. Men like Alfred Croft, Alexander Pedler, Henry Sharp, Alfred Bourne, Hugh Orange, Joseph Stone, Thomas Arnold and George Anderson spring readily to mind but it is a measure of the comparative lack of interest in the history of education in British India by contemporary educational historians that so few of them would readily recognise these names from the past or know of their achievements. To paraphrase Kipling, the *Raj* and its educational officials have long since departed from India. If we wish to know more about them we must search amongst the records and listen to their silent voices. In more prosaic terms we need to search diligently through the main biographical sources and India Office records if we are to appreciate more fully who they were and their place in British imperial history.

Of those who served education in British India none was more highly revered in his day than Alfred Woodley Croft, who occupied the important post of DPI in Bengal for 20 years from 1877 until his retirement in 1897. He was born in Plymouth in 1841 and educated at the Mannamead School and Exeter College, Oxford, from whence he graduated BA in philosophy in 1863 and MA in 1871. He lectured at Exeter College for a short while after graduation before going out to Calcutta to join the Bengal Education Service in 1866 as a professor of philosophy at Presidency College.

He must have greatly impressed his superiors because after 10 years as a professor, school inspector, and acting principal of Presidency College, he was appointed DPI at the relatively young age of 35 years. As Charles Buckland, a former member of the Bengal Civil Service, said of him in a *Times* obituary, he spent many of his early years as a school inspector in the *mofussil* or Indian hinterland and developed a deep knowledge of the needs and possibilities of the rural population as opposed to those in the large cities. In a career spanning almost 31 years he oversaw major advances in education in Bengal, including a rapid expansion of schools and university colleges.

Croft also served on the Indian Education Commission of 1882–3 and wrote much of the voluminous report which exceeded 600 pages. The report and its 13 volumes of appendices constitute one of the most valuable sources of information on British education policy and practice in nineteenth century India. In the light of his contribution to the report, Croft was commissioned to write the first [1886–87] of an ongoing series of quinquennial reports on the progress of education in India. The Secretary of State for India saw fit to thank him personally for the quality of his report. He was also closely linked to the development of the University of Calcutta as a Fellow, Registrar and later as Vice-Chancellor [1893–96]. In recognition of his services to the University he was awarded an honorary degree of Doctor of Law on the occasion of his retirement in 1897. In 1884 he was made a Companion of the Order of the Indian Empire [CIE] for his services to education and knighted three years later. Between 1887 and 1892 he was also an influential member of the Bengal Legislative Council. When he retired the Indian government gave him a special supplement of R 1000 per year to add to his pension in recognition of his outstanding service to education in Bengal.

Some indication of the high esteem felt for Croft in government circles in Bengal was provided by the Lieutenant-Governor, Sir Charles Elliot, in his comments on the 1893/94 Report on Education compiled by Croft: It was impossible, he wrote, to rise from a perusal of the Report without feeling impressed by its remarkable merits, not only on the score of literary skill and grasp of the subject, but also for the marks it bore of wise reflection, large experience, and administrative ability. There was literally no branch of the subject, however small, which Sir Alfred Croft had not illuminated by his penetrating and instructive remarks. Charles Buckland also wrote of Croft's studious mind and of his combination of culture and administrative ability. He was the first DPI to be a member of the Bengal government, he was highly trusted in official circles, and always a power behind the throne. As a DPI he won universal esteem from Europeans and Indians alike for his fairness, unfailing courtesy and administrative ability. He never married and lived out his retirement in south Devon amongst his books and flowers. In his latter years he was almost blind. He died aged 84 on 29 October 1925.

The longest serving DPI in British India was K. M. Chatfield. Appointed when he was only 31 years of age, he occupied the post in Bombay for 23 years from 1874 through to his retirement in 1897. Born in 1841, the son of an Anglican cleric, he won a scholarship to Corpus Christi College, Oxford, in 1860 and graduated BA in 1864. Two years later he went out to Bombay as principal and professor of logic and moral philosophy at Elphinstone College and remained there until his appointment as Director. After retirement he disappeared from all known sources of biographical data on IES personnel. A more detailed study of his life is clearly needed.

Another able and long serving DPI in Bengal was William, later Sir William W. Hornell. A product of Radley and later Trinity College, Oxford, Hornell joined the IES in 1901 as a professor at Presidency College in Calcutta. He then spent three years as an inspector of schools and two years as assistant DPI before going back to England to be a junior examiner at the Board of Education. In 1910 he was made Assistant Director of special inquiries and reports which involved him actively in the selection of IES candidates. A year later he acted as secretary to the Imperial Education Conference held in London. Then, in 1913, he went back to Calcutta as DPI in Bengal. His appointment was highly controversial because he was no longer a member of the IES and many people thought that the post should have gone to Henry James, the Principal of Presidency College, but Hornell's selection proved to be a wise choice despite the fact that much of the progress hoped for in Bengal education when he became director was subsequently hindered by political unrest and the onset of war.

In later years (1917–19) he served with great distinction on the Calcutta University Commission. He received the CIE in recognition of his work for education in 1918. He left Bengal in 1924, after 11 years as director, to become Vice-Chancellor of the University of Hong Kong. While there he oversaw a major reorganisation of the institution and was knighted in 1931. He was also awarded an honorary LL when he retired in 1937. Thereafter, he lived in London acting as honorary Resident Adviser to the College of the Sea, which aimed at encouraging study and culture among seamen. This link with seafarers was probably related to the fact that he had a much decorated elder brother, Vice-Admiral Sir Robert Hornell, who died in 1949. Hitherto single, in 1946 Sir William finally married a widowed friend he had known since his youth. He died in Nottingham in 1950. It was probably his niece, Dorothy Hornell, who married William, later Sir William Armstrong, who joined the IES in 1917 and eventually became DPI in the Punjab from 1936 to 1947.

Another long term DPI was Sir Alfred Gibbs Bourne, a distinguished scientist, who held the senior post in Madras from 1903 through to his retirement in 1914. He was born in Lowestoft in 1859, the son of Alfred Bourne, Secretary to the British and Foreign Schools Society, and educated in London at the University College School, the Royal School of Mines, and University College, where he completed a DSc in zoology. As a Fellow of University College he was engaged in scientific research at the Zoological station in Naples for six years before taking up an appointment as a professor of biology at Presidency College in Madras in 1885. From 1891 to 1899 he was Registrar of the University of Madras and also government botanist in Madras [1897–98]. In 1902 Lord Curzon invited him to sit on the Indian Universities Commission, set up to reform the administrative structure of the universities. A year later Bourne assumed administrative control of education throughout Madras. For much of his 11 years as director he was also a member of the Legislative Council. After retirement he spent a further six years as director of the recently established Indian Institute of Science in Bangalore. He eventually settled in Dartmouth when he retired and served a term as local mayor [1922–23]. He died in July 1940, aged 81 years. In 1908 he was made a Companion of the Order of India and knighted shortly before he retired as DPI. His scientific work was recognised by his election to membership of the Royal Society.

Sir Alexander Pedler was another leading figure in the IES. Born in Dulwich, then a leafy suburb of south London, in 1849, he was educated at the City of London School and the Royal College of Science. Like Croft, he also joined the Bengal Education Service, in his case as a professor of chemistry at Presidency College in 1873. He served the College with distinction for 24 years, including the last four as principal, before succeeding Croft as DPI in 1897. His time in the top post coincided with Lord Curzon's concerted attempts to reshape and reform education in India. At Presidency College Pedler was a pioneer of modern scientific research and largely responsible for the pre-eminence of its science department. As DPI Pedler served on the Legislative Council of Bengal. Like Bourne, he was also a member of the Indian Universities Commission of 1902. In the last two years of his career in India he was also Vice-Chancellor of the University of Calcutta. A member of the Royal Society, he was knighted in 1906, and also awarded a R 1000 increase in his retirement pension in recognition of his outstanding service to India. Thereafter, he lived in London until his death in May 1918.

Sir Henry Sharp was a eminent member of the IES better known to later generations because of his published work which included two quinquennial reviews of education in India [1907–12, 1912–17], a volume of selected early educational records of the government of India, a study of the city of Delhi and its buildings, a book of Indian reminiscences entitled *Good-Bye India*, a translation of the Indian classic the *Agamemnon*, and three novels written in later life. On the occasion of his death in late January 1954, *The Times* saw fit to publish an informative obituary. Born in Colwyn Bay in June 1869, his educational pedigree speaks for itself — Rugby and New College, Oxford, and a First in *Literae Humaniores*. He went to India in 1894 as principal of the government college at Jubblepore in the Central Provinces but four years later he became an inspector of schools. In 1906 Sir Joseph Fuller, the High Commissioner in Assam finally succeeded in getting Sharp appointed as DPI in East Bengal and Assam.

Prior to Sharp's appointment, Fuller had been responsible for replacing William Booth as director on the grounds of administrative incompetence.[2] Booth, a graduate of mathematics from Trinity College, Dublin, had served for 28 years in India, including five years as director in Assam but Fuller reluctantly concluded that he was so deficient in administrative capacity that it was no longer possible to trust him even in matters of petty detail. Fuller claimed that Booth's control of his subordinates was very lax and capricious, and owing to an eccentric manner, which might have been excusable in a professor, his inspections of schools were alarming and confusing rather than instructive. Fuller claimed that he had been obliged to run education himself in Assam for the past two years. The Indian government sympathised with Fuller and Booth was sent back to Bengal as a school inspector. He retired a year later. In defence of Booth it should be said that he held office in Assam at a time of rapid educational expansion and because of overwork his health broke down while he was on tour in 1903. As a consequence he was bed-ridden for seven weeks suffering from phlebitis, pleurisy and pneumonia. Fuller wanted quick results in his programme of educational expansion but the administrative burden proved too much for Booth. Fuller requested Sharp as Booth's successor but the job went to N. L. Hallwood from the Bengal Education Department on a two-year trial basis. He and Fuller subsequently fell out and Hallwood was not confirmed as director. Hallwood then resigned and returned to Bengal. At that point Fuller finally got his way and Sharp, then aged 37, the man Fuller had wanted from the start, was appointed as director in Hallwood's place. Sharp's move created a vacancy in the inspectorate in the Central Provinces and Arthur Mayhew's name was mentioned, together with six others, as a possible replacement but nothing came of the idea.

Four years later, in 1910, when the Indian government finally created its own separate Department of Education, Sharp was appointed Joint Secretary. The following year he was made an additional member of the Governor-General's Executive Council. In 1915 he became the first Educational Commissioner to the Indian government and in 1918 the first Educational Secretary. It was during that time that he wrote the two quinquennial reviews and edited the volume of educational records mentioned earlier. He was knighted in 1922 but also retired in the same year at the comparatively young age of 52. He returned to England but led no life of ease. Between 1923 and 1926 he was secretary of the Statutory Commission on Oxford University and then secretary of a similar commission on the University of London [1927–28] before becoming secretary to the Cathedral Commissioners for England for 11 years [1931–1942]. He married late in life and lived in Pall Mall nearby his beloved *Athenaeum*. He was also a devout member of the congregation of St James' church in Piccadilly where he served on the parochial church council. Like Sir Alfred Croft, Sharp too, went almost blind in his latter years. Lord Hailey, a former governor of the Punjab, wrote of Sharp's exacting sense of duty, his love of sport, his equal devotion to the classics, his legendary feats of memory and the immense courtesy and consideration that he always showed for the feelings of others.

Sir Hugh Orange spent only a relatively short part of his educational career in India but few members of the 'heaven born' ICS could better his credentials. Born in April 1866, the son of Dr William Orange, he won a scholarship to Winchester. From there he went to New

College, Oxford, and graduated in 1889 with a First in classics. He started life as a journalist before becoming a junior examiner at the Board of Education in London. Later he became private secretary to Sir George Kekewich, the Permanent Secretary at the Board of Education, at a time of hectic activity leading up to the 1902 Education Act. It was during this period that he came to the notice of Lord Curzon, then Viceroy of India, who selected him to be the first Director-General of Education in India.

The appointment arose out of an educational conference convened by Curzon at Simla in 1901. Curzon was impressed by the sheer size of the educational enterprise in India and the relatively small number of European officers who administered it. But he was equally concerned that it was run on a purely provincial basis and that the government of India was not as fully in touch with all that went on as he thought it should be. Accordingly, he sought to appoint an expert to keep him fully informed and to advise him on educational matters. As he told the DPIs assembled at Simla, he did not want an imperial education department packed with pedagogues and crested with officialism, nor did he advocate a minister or a member of the executive council for education but he did want someone located in Calcutta who could prevent the government 'drifting about like a deserted hulk on chopping seas' over educational matters.[3] Orange was chosen largely on the recommendation of Michael (later Sir Michael) E. Sadler,[4] who was then Professor of the History and Administration of Education at the Victoria University in Manchester, but the appointment was never a great success, not because Orange was incompetent but because his role was never clear, especially after Curzon left India. For eight years Orange ran what amounted to a bureau of education, which generated a variety of publications on education in India and elsewhere, and a clearing house for information but it came as no surprise when Orange returned to England in 1910 to become the Chief Inspector of Elementary Schools in England and Wales. Two years later he was appointed Accountant-General to the Board of Education, a post he held with distinction until his retirement in 1928. He was made a Companion of the Order of India in 1906 and later, in England, he received a CB in 1914, and a knighthood in 1919. When he retired he was made a Knight Commander of the British Empire. He lived in rural Sussex in his latter years and eventually died in 1956 at the age of 90.

Three further men to receive knighthoods for their services to Indian education were Joseph Stone, Claude De la Fosse and Alexander Campbell. Stone, born in Coventry in 1858 and educated at Floundes College, Ackworth, and King's College, Cambridge, went to Madras in 1886 as professor of history at Presidency College. In 1895 he became principal of Kumbakonam College and later an inspector of European schools and training colleges before returning to Presidency College in 1907 as both principal and professor of English literature. In 1912 he became deputy DPI, and two years later director. He retired in 1919, the same year in which he was knighted. He then returned to England and took a major interest in his father's box making business in Banbury, duly becoming chairman of Henry Stone and Company in 1925. He died in 1941, aged 83.

By contrast, De la Fosse pursued his career in the United Provinces of northern India. Ten years younger than Stone, he was the son of a major-general in the Indian army. Educated at Bath College and Trinity College, Oxford, he started his career in India as principal of Victoria College in Kuch Behar, in 1893. Later he was a professor of English literature and logic at Queen's College in Benares, and inspector of schools, before being appointed assistant DPI in 1901. Seven years later he became director. He remained stationed in Allahabad for the next 15 years before retiring in 1923. For much of that time he was also a member of the legislative council of the United Provinces. In 1919–20 he was stationed in Delhi on special duties with the Indian government and sat on the Indian legislative council. He then returned to Allahabad for a brief spell as Vice-Chancellor of the university before retirement. In 1922 he was knighted and also awarded an honorary DLitt. He retired to Guildford in Surrey, where he later served as a borough councillor and vice-chairman of the RSPCA. He was the author of a much used school textbook *A History of India for High Schools*. He died in 1950, aged 81.

Alexander Campbell[5] was one of a generation of men old enough to participate in the First World War and still young enough to fight in the Second. Born in Perth in 1892, the son of a police inspector — on his application form to join the IES it was stated that his father's whereabouts were unknown but that his mother held a *Decree Nisi* — he was educated at the Perth Academy and Edinburgh University, where he obtained an MA degree with first class honours in English. At the same time he attended the Edinburgh Provincial Training College and acquired a general teaching certificate. He was also a first class rugby player. When he was appointed as a professor of English at the government college in Rangoon in 1915, he was 23 years old, and had been teaching at a public school for one year. Within 12 months he was serving in the army in East Africa where he won the Military Cross. In 1921 he became Registrar of Rangoon University. Twelve years later he joined the school inspectorate and soon became Assistant DPI [1935] and subsequently DPI [1939]. War again interrupted his career and he saw active service in South-East Asia and Burma as a lieutenant-colonel in the Burma Auxiliary Force. He was knighted in 1944 and also awarded the Efficiency Decoration. In 1945 he was Officer-in-Command of the Advance Party of the British Military government which reoccupied Burma. Prior to retirement in 1946, he helped to re-establish Rangoon University and the education system. In the period 1947–52, he was Registrar of the University College of South West England, later called Exeter University. He died in July 1963, aged 71.

Whereas the aforementioned all ultimately pursued administrative careers in education, Sir Thomas Arnold was one of the most renowned Oriental scholars of his generation and the subject of a lengthy entry in the *Dictionary of National Biography*. He was born in 1864 and educated first at Plymouth High School and latterly at the City of London School from where he won a scholarship to Magdalene College, Cambridge. He graduated in 1886 and shortly afterwards went out to India to a special appointment as professor of philosophy at the Anglo-Oriental College, later renamed and reconstituted as the Moslem University, located at Aligarh. During this time he became totally absorbed in the study of Moslem culture and even dressed like a Moslem. After 10 years at Aligarh he moved to a Chair in philosophy at the government college in Lahore, later becoming dean of the Oriental faculty at the Punjab University. He left India in 1904 to become assistant librarian at the India Office in London, where he did invaluable work collecting and classifying Indian manuscripts. In 1921, the same year in which he was knighted, he took up the Chair of Arabic and Islamic studies at the University of London. During his time at the India Office he also acted as an educational adviser to the India Office (1917–20) and to numerous Indian students studying in Britain. He died suddenly in June 1930, aged 66, while still a professor at London University. As the author of many significant publications on Islamic culture he won wide acclaim, including an honorary doctorate from the *Deutsche Universitat* in Prague. He clearly rates as one of the most illustrious members of the IES. Like so many former Indian administrators and literary men he was also a member of the renowned *Athenaeum* club in Pall Mall.

Ralph L. Turner[6] was another equally outstanding Oriental scholar who spent several years in the IES before taking up a Chair in Sanscrit at the School of Oriental and African Studies [SOAS] in London. Later still he became Director of the School and was knighted in 1950. The son of a former schoolteacher and lawyer, he was born in Charlton, a suburb of southeast London, and educated at Bedford and later Perse grammar schools. From there he progressed to Christ's College, Cambridge where he graduated with first class honours in classics and Oriental languages and was duly elected a Fellow of his College in 1912. He joined the IES two years later, initially as a professor of English literature at Queen's College in Benares, but he soon started lecturing in Sanscrit. His appointment was clearly considered as something of a coup by the India Office as the post he took up was never advertised and he started on a salary of R 750 rather than the normal R 500 per month. In 1914 he also lectured in philology at Bombay University. Between 1915 and 1919 he saw war service with the Gurkha Rifles and won the Military Cross. After the war he became Professor of Linguistics at the Hindu University in Benares, formerly known as Queen's College, but left in 1923 to take up the Chair of Sanscrit at SOAS. In 1937 he became Director of SOAS and retained the position for the next 20 years before retiring in 1957. He died in April 1983, in his 95th year.

Amongst the many esteemed teachers in the IES none ranked more highly than Henry Rosher James, the long-standing principal of Presidency College, Calcutta, although his career was to end on a somewhat sour note. James was born in Penzance in 1862 but a Queen's scholarship took him to Westminster School where he was Captain of School in 1880–81 and a prominent fencer and boxer. From there he went to Christ Church, Oxford, where he graduated with a First in *Literae Humaniores* in 1885. After a year as an assistant tutor at Christ Church, he joined the IES as a professor of moral philosophy at Patna College and became principal in 1905. Two years later he was appointed to the top position at Presidency College. By then he had already acquired an envious reputation as a classical and literary scholar having translated Boethius' *De Philosophise Consolatione* and published Macaulay's essays on Milton, together with an introduction and explanatory notes. In 1911 he published a series of articles in the Calcutta *Statesman* which traced the origins and development of British education in India. These were later published as a book — *Education and Statesmanship in India 1797–1910*. His primary aim was to explore the link commonly made between education and political unrest in India. He blamed the press not education for student unrest and claimed that the great majority of students were neither revolutionaries nor conspirators, and that colleges were not 'hotbeds of sedition'. He was a long-standing Fellow of Calcutta University and frequently clashed in the Senate, as did Sir Henry Sharp, with Sir Ashutosh Mukarji, the outspoken critic of Curzon's university reform policy in India at the turn of the century. James also served on a variety of government committees and in 1909, acted as DPI while Croft was on furlough.

The first of two major controversies in his career occurred in 1913 when he was passed over for the post of DPI in favour of William Hornell.[7] At the heart of the controversy lay the issue of whether or not the post of director should be confined to members of the IES. When Hornell's appointment was announced there was outrage in Calcutta and the daily English newspaper devoted many columns to condemning the decision. James' claims to the appointment were also pressed in Parliament by Lord Ampthill, Bonar Law and Sir Henry Craik, and in *The Times* by no lesser person than Sir Alfred Croft. James also sent a personal petition to the Secretary of State requesting a public inquiry but unbeknown to him the government of India gave no support whatsoever to his request and it was rejected.

The reason for overlooking James was never stated publicly but in official correspondence from the provincial government in Bengal to the government of India it was stated that James was passed over because he did not have the necessary qualities to head up a major drive to expand education, especially at the primary level. The government in Bengal sought a man of 'general experience and wide outlook' with sound administrative and practical experience. Unfortunately for James, he had spent most of his career as a professor and principal of a college. It was also pointed out that the Bengal inspectorate was very weak at that time and that the new director would need to spend much of his time instructing and supervising his inspectors in carrying out new government initiatives in both primary and secondary education. James was certainly the obvious choice from within the department but the governor vetoed his appointment on the grounds that he did not possess the particular qualifications needed for the post at that particular time. It was true that James had spent a year as acting director in 1909 but, as the governor claimed, without any 'marked success' i.e. without evidence of any great constructive ability or driving power. Even more doubtful was his ability to inspire, instruct and guide the body of inspectors. Consequently, the Bengal government looked further afield. The governor was fully aware that his decision would cause pain for James and be resented by other members of the IES in Bengal but he felt that the public interest had to take precedence. The Indian government had made it clear enough in several previous statements that it reserved the right for provincial governments to select DPIs from outside the IES. In hindsight, the governor's decision proved to be a wise one as James subsequently got embroiled in a conflict with the Bengal government which did nothing to enhance his reputation while Hornell proved to be an outstanding director.

James' long career at Presidency College ended in further controversy when he was suspended over his actions resulting from a student attack on one of his staff in February 1916.[8] The origins of the dispute lay in growing student indiscipline in schools fanned by the Indian independence movement. As a subsequent committee report on the whole sorry story commented, the trouble started with certain students termed 'revolutionary propagandists' who sought to exploit problems and generate trouble. Such students, it was claimed, were full of their so-called rights but made no mention of their responsibilities. The attack on Professor Oaten, a member of the college staff, was in response to his objection to the noise the students were making in a corridor next to the room where he was working. The incident might have been minimised had Oaten not been assaulted, whereupon the government closed the college and appointed an investigative committee. Up to this point James' actions in the matter had been conciliatory and correct. The investigative committee was chaired by James' old advisary Sir Ashutosh Mukharji, and included both Hornell and James. The appointment of Mukharji and Hornell appears to have been the underlying reason for what followed.

James still deeply resentful at having been supplanted by Hornell as DPI, went in a highly agitated state to P. C. Lyon, the Vice-President of the Governor's executive council and the Member responsible for education, to protest against the inclusion of Mukharji and Hornell on the investigative committee. He claimed that they would both be prejudiced against him and his work at the College. James refused to sit on the committee while the other two were included and said he intended to resign as principal and from the IES. According to Lyon's account of the meeting, James lost control of himself during the interview and his manner and language were grossly insulting. Mr Peake, a senior professor at Presidency College, was then appointed to replace James on the committee.

The day after the committee first met, the government received a letter from James stating his objection to Mukharji and Hornell on grounds of bias. James said he was prepared to provide evidence either in writing or confidentially to the governor. He also sent a copy of the letter to the secretary of the investigative committee, an act which constituted a gross breach of public service rules. Mukharji, as president of the committee, said he could no longer preside over the matter so the committee's deliberations were adjourned *sine die*. The governor then removed James from his post as principal and suspended him pending disciplinary proceedings. A more contrite James then wrote to the government expressing regret for any offence that he may have given Mr Lyon. He also claimed that in sending a copy of his letter to the committee he had not intentionally meant to break public service rules. The governor was not satisfied that this was an adequate apology or that James realised the gravity of what he had done but he gave him another opportunity to apologise. James did so, and at this point the governor appeared satisfied and cancelled the suspension order. At the same time James was granted overseas leave until November 1917.

The committee's subsequent report, which was endorsed by the Bengal government, made it clear that the students had deliberately misrepresented what had happened in the attack on Professor Oaten and James was completely vindicated in his handling of the matter. On the strength of this finding James then sent a memorial to the Viceroy seeking reinstatement and financial compensation for his removal from office as principal but he was unsuccessful. The Viceroy ruled that James had been removed from office because he had shown himself unfit for the responsibility of the post. Despite James' long and meritorious service the Viceroy still considered him unfit to return and he was forced to retire. It was a sad end to an illustrious career. He went to Tangier where he wrote two volumes of *Our Hellenic Heritage*, which were highly praised in scholarly circles, and an entry on Indian education in the 1931 edition of the *Encyclopaedia Brittanica*. He returned to London, already seriously ill, some two weeks before he died in June 1931. As stated in his *Times* obituary, he was one of the most gifted members of the IES and made valuable contributions to education and classical studies.

Dr G. W. Leitner[9] was undoubtedly one of the most colourful and unusual educators to serve in British India. Born in Pest, Hungary, in 1840, and educated at the Protestant college in Malta, he was appointed at the tender age of 15 years as chief interpreter to the British Commissariat in the Crimean war with the rank of colonel! From there he went to the Muslim theological college in Constantinople. Thereafter, he attended King's College, London, and in 1859 became a lecturer there in Arabic, Turkish and modern Greek. His early education in mosque schools had also made him fluent in Turkish and Arabic and other Levant languages. In 1861 he was appointed Professor of Arabic and Moslem Law and effectively founded the Oriental section of King's College. He then obtained MA and PhD degrees from the university at Frieberg before

becoming principal of the government college in Lahore in 1864. Later he
was the first Registrar of the Punjab University of which he was the
principal originator and founder. He was also one of the first educators to
convey western knowledge in indigenous languages:

> The Oriental University of the Punjab was the first serious
> attempt in northern India to infuse life into the dry bones of the
> educational system of the government; to interest princes and
> people in educational work by conveying the knowledge and
> science of the West through the medium of the vernacular
> languages of India; and to engage the religious teachers of the
> people, pandits and mullahs, on the side of scientific education,
> instead of leaving them, as the government department had
> done, altogether aloof or hostile.[10]

For many years Leitner was a major educational figure in the Northwest
Provinces of India and provided valuable evidence on the nature and
condition of Moslem education to the Indian Education Commission in
1882. Shortly afterwards he wrote a *History of indigenous education in the
Punjab since annexation and in 1882*, which was reprinted in 1971.
He succeeded in gaining support and raising funds for education from
local rulers and also published various journals in Urdu, Arabic and
English. One of the latter, *Indian Public Opinion*, once employed Rudyard
Kipling as its assistant editor and published many of his earliest verses and
stories. Leitner retired to England to live in 1887, and opened an Oriental
Institute at Woking for the training of young Indians of good family.
He also edited the *Asiatic Quarterly Review* and continued to publish widely
in academic journals. As a linguist he probably had no living rival. It was
claimed that he had a more than passing acquaintance with some
50 languages, many of which he spoke fluently. In 1869 he married a
daughter of the German and American Consul in Brusa, Turkey. He died
in Bonn in 1899.

Occasionally the IES made 'special appointments' related
to Islamic studies. Alexander Harley[11] was a case in point. Born in 1882,
in Hamilton, he was educated at The Academy, and Glasgow, Edinburgh
and Berlin Universities. A brilliant student of languages, he won major
prizes in Hebrew and Arabic at Edinburgh University, and had a working
knowledge of German, French, Italian, Spanish, Arabic, Hebrew, Syriac,
Coptic and Persian. He joined the IES in 1911 as Principal of the Madrasa
[Moslem College] in Calcutta. The Calcutta Madrasa, founded by Warren
Hastings in 1782, was the first college established by the English in India.
The position to which Harley was appointed called for a good knowledge
of Arabic and Persian and he was expected to promote Moslem studies in
Bengal. Initially, Harley had planned to train for the Scottish
Congregational Ministry, hence his study of Hebrew when he was at
university, but he subsequently grew to dislike the dogmas of Christianity
and finally took a job in 1905 as an assistant lecturer in Hebrew and

Arabic at Edinburgh University. In 1910 he worked briefly for the British Museum as a cataloguer of Arabic and Coptic printed books and manuscripts. While in London he also worked with Professor T. W. Arnold on his Encyclopaedia of Islam and Arnold may have been instrumental in Harley's decision to go to India. He remained Principal of the Madrasa until 1926. Then he became Principal of Islamia College in Calcutta until he returned to London in 1937 to be a Reader at SOAS. He died in January 1951 aged 69.

It was no less a figure than Alfred Croft who described Charles H. Tawney 'as one of the most distinguished men that ever came to India in the service of government in any capacity'.[12] Born in 1838, the son of The Rev. Richard Tawney, he was educated at Rugby, where he was Head of School, and at Trinity College, Oxford, where he was Senior Classic in 1860. He was elected a Fellow in the same year. In December 1864 he went to Bengal as a specialist in English literature and spent most of the next 28 years as Professor and Principal of Presidency College. During that time he also served as Registrar of the University of Calcutta and acting DPI on no less than five occasions. He also acquired a reputation as a notable Sanscrit scholar. When he retired in 1892, Croft successfully supported his application for a special R 1000 grant to supplement his pension. No one, Croft claimed, had done more to advance higher education in Bengal or to uphold academic standards. After leaving India Tawney spent the next 10 years as Assistant Librarian at the India Office in London. He died in 1922.

Mention has already been made of how service in India had long been a tradition amongst many British families but few could boast of three brothers all serving together like the Covernton family. Two of them joined the IES while a third joined the ICS. The eldest, James, was born in 1868 in north London and educated at Merchant Taylor's School and St John's College, Oxford, where he graduated with a First in *Literae Humaniores*. His younger brother Alfred, born four years later, had an identical educational background even down to the First in classics from St John's. Each, in turn, joined the IES. James was first appointed as a professor of English literature at Elphinstone College in 1894. Four years later he became a school inspector in Sind. In 1906 he transferred to Burma where he was DPI for the next 11 years. In 1917 he returned to a similar position in Bombay which he occupied until his retirement in 1923. Alfred Covernton followed in his brother's footsteps, spending three years as an assistant-master at Merchant Taylor's before also going out to India to be a professor of English and history at Elphinstone College. Like his brother he too joined the inspectorate [1905–8] but then their career paths diverged. While James went to Burma, Alfred went back to Elphinstone College as Principal and Professor of English literature. From 1913 to 1915 he acted as deputy DPI in Bombay before returning once more to Elphinstone College. He retired in 1927. Alfred died in 1939 and his younger brother in 1957. The youngest of the three brothers,

Stephen, also went to Merchant Taylor's and St John's College and served in the ICS in Bengal until he retired in 1936.

Edward Giles was another member of the IES with strong Elphinstone connections. Born in 1849, the fourth son of Archdeacon Giles, Canon and Presenter at Lincoln Cathedral, he was educated at Westminster and Christ Church, Oxford, from whence he graduated with a First in history. He also rowed for Oxford in the annual boat race against Cambridge in 1871. Two years later he went to India as a professor of history at Elphinstone College. Thereafter, he followed the familiar pattern of joining the inspectorate before eventually becoming DPI in Bombay in 1897. In his final year before retirement in 1908, he served as Acting Director-General of Education in India while Orange was in Britain assessing Scottish and Irish universities as potential recruiting grounds for IES candidates.

Another example of a family tradition of service in India was provided by H. J. Allen whose father had served in the Bengal Civil Service. Educated at St Columba's College and Trinity College, Dublin, and King's College, Cambridge, he was admitted to Lincoln's Inn in 1893 but seven years later he took up a teaching position as a professor of history and economics at Presidency College in Madras, and later served as Principal from 1915 to 1921.

David Duncan, MA, DSc and LLD, had a rather different background before joining the IES. Born in 1839, he was educated at the Grammar School in Aberdeen and the universities of Aberdeen, Edinburgh and Berlin. He started out in adult life as private secretary to Herbert Spencer, the eminent sociologist [1867–70] before going to Madras as a professor of logic and moral philosophy at Presidency College. In 1884 he became Principal of the College and in 1892 DPI. He retired in 1899, having spent his final year in India as Vice-Chancellor of Madras University. He later wrote *The Life and Letters of Herbert Spencer*. A member of the *Athenaeum* in his latter years, he died in 1923.

John van Someren Pope was another notable member of the IES. He was born into a distinguished family, his father being The Rev. George Pope, D.D., reader in Tamil and Telugu and Chaplain of Balliol College, Oxford, and his uncle The Rev. William Pope, for many years Tutor of Systematic Theology at Didsbury College, and in 1877, President of the Wesleyan Conference. John Pope was born in 1850, in Plymouth, where his grandfather was a shipowner and a prominent figure in local municipal affairs. He was taken to India in infancy and educated for a time at Snowden College in Ootacamund, in southern India, before returning to Plymouth to attend the Mannamead School. From there he went to Trinity Hall, Cambridge, and graduated BA in 1871. After several years of private tutorial work he moved to Bengal where he held various positions at Patna, Dacca and Presidency Colleges before going to Rangoon in 1889 as the first DPI in Burma. In adult life he acquired a passion for Oriental languages and passed numerous proficiency tests in Urdu, Hindi, Bengali, Sanscrit and Canarese. After retiring from the IES in 1906, he held various appointments including Reader in Bengali at Cambridge University; instructor in Hindustani and Persian at the Army Staff College, and instructor in Hindustani at the Royal Military Academy at Woolwich. In 1909, he returned to Cochin State in southern India to act as adviser on education for two years. During the First World War he worked as a censor for Indian languages at the War Office in Whitehall. He then acted as an examiner for the ICS before becoming Professor of Oriental languages at Trinity College, Dublin. He died in 1932, aged 82. He had a son Major-General Sydney B. Pope who served in the Indian Army and a daughter who married Colonel H. S. Bush, also of the Indian Army.

Not all members of the IES were destined to be DPIs but men like Richard Prior still left their mark. Born in 1858, Prior was educated at Bedford Grammar School before going up to Queen's College, Cambridge. In 1881 he graduated BA and also rowed for the 'light blues' in the annual boat race. His whereabouts during the next few years are uncertain but in 1889 he was appointed Headmaster of Poona High School in the Bombay Presidency. Four years later he became Principal of Elphinstone College. A further four years on, in 1897, he became a school inspector and remained so until he retired in 1913. The quiet semi-rural life that he retired to in England was rudely shattered a year later by the outbreak of war and like many other retirees of his generation, he re-entered the teaching profession for the duration of the war as an assistant master at Shrewsbury public school. When he died in January 1928, *The Times* saw fit to publish a tribute to his lifelong service to education. The writer commented that office routine irked him and that his heart was always with the simple Maratha village schoolmasters among whom, as an inspector, he had done his best work.

> His stern commanding figure and his wise and humorous criticisms (for he could jest in fluent Maratha) will long be remembered and pass into legend …. Into legend too, will pass the story of his having cured the habit of unpunctuality at Poona High School by the simple process of standing in the porch one morning and caning all the latecomers there and then. There were 200 boys in the school and they were all late — and the temperature was over 90 in the shade.

The writer claimed that readers would find Prior appreciatively portrayed in Percival Wren's first published novel *Dew and Mildew A loose tale of Hindustan.*

Of those who served in the IES with distinction in the latter years of the *Raj,* perhaps the most memorable were Richard Littlehailes, J. R. Cunningham, James Richey and Sir George Anderson. Littlehailes was born in 1878 and educated at the Bede School in Sunderland, Balliol College, Oxford, and Kiel University. After spending a year as a demonstrator and lecturer at the Clarendon laboratory in Oxford, he joined the IES in 1903, the same year as Arthur Mayhew. He eventually became DPI in Madras in 1919, and in 1927, Educational Commissioner to the government of India. In 1933 he spent a year as Educational Adviser to the state of Baroda and a further three years prior to retirement [1934–37] as Vice-Chancellor of Madras University. The author of the ninth quinquennial report *Progress of Education in India* 1922–27, he died at his home in Fleet, Hampshire, in December 1950.

John Cunninham was of Scottish descent. Born in 1876, he was educated at the Grammar School in Campbeltown, and at St Andrew's and Edinburgh Universities where he acquired MA and LLB degrees. He joined the IES in 1907 as a professor of English literature and language at Pachiappa's College in Madras. Later, he held a similar position at Presidency College, Calcutta, before becoming DPI in Assam in 1912. He served there for the next 19 years until his retirement in 1931. In 1935–36 he came out of retirement to participate in the Assam University Enquiry. He died in Campbeltown in May 1942, aged 66.

Few men were held in higher regard for their services to Indian education under British rule than James Alexander Richey. Not only did he merit a *Times* obituary but no lesser figures than Sir Philip Hartog and Sir Henry Sharp also wrote glowing tributes. Richey, the son of Sir James Richey, who served in the ICS, was born in 1874 and educated at Rugby and Balliol College, Oxford, where he graduated with honours in classics. His father died when he was only 16 and this may have influenced his later, somewhat unusual decision to go to South Africa where, for a short time, he lectured at the Diocesan College at Rondebosch in the Cape Colony. Richey's grandfather had been a Rector in Devon and the grandson may have briefly contemplated following in his footsteps. Instead, in 1902, after the Boer War, he moved north to the Transvaal, and worked for the next six years for the newly established Transvaal Education Department. In 1908 he joined the IES as Assistant DPI in East Bengal and Assam. Three years later he became DPI in the Northwest Provinces and later still DPI in the Punjab [1917–20]. In 1920 he succeeded Sir Henry Sharp as Educational Commissioner to the Indian government, a post he retained until he retired in 1928. He is perhaps best remembered as the author of the eighth quinquennial report *Progress of Education in India* [1917–22] and the second volume of *Selections from Educational Records* of India. He was also the author of a most informative but less publicised report entitled *Grants-in-aid to schools in British India* published in 1923 by the Bureau of Education.

Throughout his time in India he was widely regarded for his tireless efforts to generate mutual sympathy and understanding between the different races. Hartog, who knew him well throughout the 1920s, wrote of his keen intellect and valiant efforts to introduce a more agriculturally biased curriculum into vernacular middle schools in the Punjab. His elevation to Educational Commissioner coincided with the devolution of control over education to the provinces, nevertheless, he worked hard to generate a greater interest across India in common educational problems by encouraging conferences of DPIs from the various provinces. He was also responsible for the first Indian inter-university congress held at Simla in 1924. Hartog also referred to ill health which dogged Ritchey throughout his life but which had not adversely affected his humour and commonsense, his unruffled sanity, and his eternal optimism. In a concluding comment Hartog was critical of what he considered inadequate official recognition of Richey's work. He clearly thought Richey should have been knighted but 'his modesty exceeded his merit'.

Sir Henry Sharp endorsed all Hartog had said. He also wrote of Richey's earlier pioneering work in East Bengal and Assam where the quality of education was poor, and institutions were squalid, ill-distributed and inadequately financed:

> The difficulties inherent in organising a department which dealt with a number of schools far in excess of that contained in England and Wales, with an inadequate staff and in the teeth of considerable opposition and prejudice, was enormously increased by a violent agitation against the formation of the new province and the fact that the agitators used schools (and occasionally teachers) as their agents. In these circumstances a mass of irritating labour requiring for its proper discharge diligence, tact, and scrupulous care, fell to Richey's lot.

In conclusion, like Hartog, Sharp also referred to the ill-health that increasingly afflicted Richey in the 1920s but which never dampened his zeal or the freshness of his mind. He died at sea in 1931, aged 57. He had been seriously ill for some months in Switzerland and had intended to spend the winter in South Africa.

No survey of leading figures in the IES, however cursory, would be complete without reference to Sir George Anderson. He was born in 1876 and educated at Winchester and University College, Oxford. An honours graduate in history, he started out in life, much like Richey, teaching briefly in Eastbourne before going out to work for the Transvaal Education Department [1902–10]. From there he moved to India as a professor of history at Elphinstone College. Later he became Assistant Secretary to the Education Department of the Indian government in Delhi. During that time he served as secretary of the important Calcutta University Commission [1918–19]. In 1920 he was appointed DPI in the Punjab and knighted four years later. In 1927 he sat on the committee of enquiry into Aligarh University. A year later he was a member of the Auxiliary Committee of the Indian Statutory Commission (popularly known as the Hartog Committee) which reported on the quality and progress of Indian education since 1921, the year in which it became a provincial responsibility. In 1933 Anderson became the Educational Commissioner to the Indian government and wrote the tenth quinquennial report on the *Progress of Education in India 1927–1932*. He retired in 1936 but was soon active in London as a highly respected member of the Colonial Office Advisory Committee on Education in the Colonies. The author of several books on India, he died in May 1943, on his 67th birthday.

In *The Times*, Sir Philip Hartog claimed that Anderson would long be remembered for his work in the Punjab. Hartog had specifically in mind the development of vernacular rather than English medium schools for the rural population, designed to make secondary schooling relate more closely to daily life through the use of agriculture as a means of mental discipline and training. This was a policy initiated by his distinguished predecessor James Richey. Hartog also thought that Anderson would be remembered for his determined efforts to promote increased educational opportunities for girls. Anderson's outstanding administrative ability was also matched by political astuteness. As Lord Hailey, who was Governor of the Punjab during five years of Anderson's directorship, told Hartog, Anderson was popular in the Legislative Council with Moslems and Hindus alike and steered several issues through which in less skillful hands might have faltered.

Traditionally, the senior ranks of the graded education service were reserved for Europeans recruited in the United Kingdom but there was one notable exception, Jagadis, later Sir Jagadis Chandra Bose. Born near Dacca in 1858, the son of a deputy magistrate, Bose was destined to become the first Indian scientist of world renown. He was educated at St Xavier's College in Calcutta and subsequently at University College, London, and Christ's College, Cambridge, where he graduated with honours in natural sciences in 1883. Later, he obtained a PhD from the University of London. When he returned to India in 1883 Lord Ripon's Indian government appointed him to a Chair in Physical Sciences at Presidency College, Calcutta. At first the appointment was on a temporary basis and made amid protests from both the Principal of the College and the DPI but Bose quickly showed his outstanding ability as a scientist. His research into chemistry and electricity, and especially his work on Hertzian waves which led to wireless telegraphy, generated world-wide interest and the Indian government made repeated financial grants to Bose to further his research. He was made a Companion of the Order of the Indian Empire in 1903, a Companion of the Order of the Star of India in 1911, and finally knighted in 1917. During his academic career he was also awarded honorary degrees from the universities of Aberdeen, Calcutta, Lahore, Allahabad, and Benares. He officially retired in 1915 but he was so highly regarded that for some years he retained his Chair as Emeritus Professor on full pay. He died in 1937, aged 78.

This brief catalogue of some of the more illustrious British teachers and administrators who served in the IES in the second half of the nineteenth and early decades of the twentieth centuries is by no means comprehensive. But it does suggest that contrary to the comments of the Public Services Commission in its report of 1887, teaching and educational administration did attract many of the best honours graduates from Oxford and Cambridge. However, the files of the Indian government also reveal that by no means all IES staff were successful in pursuing a career in India.

NOTES ON CHAPTER

1. Biographical details of leading figures in the IES have been gleaned from a variety of sources including *Alumni Oxonienses* and *Alumni Cantabrigienses*, *Who Was Who*, *Who's Who*, *India Office List*, *Dictionary of National Biography*, *The Times* obituaries and tributes, C. E. Buckland, *Dictionary of Indian Biography*, and India Office Records.
2. *P* 7049 ED Feb 1905 and *P* 7050 ED Oct 1905
3. *P* 6111 ED Oct 1901
4. *Curzon Papers* India Office Records Mss European F 111/ 161 Sir Arthur Godley (U/Sec of State for India) to Curzon, 13 Jan 1902
5. *P* 9708 ED Apr 1915
6. *P* 9443 ED Jan 1914
7. *P* 9195 ED Sep 1913
8. *P*/CONF/17 ED Jun 1916 and *P* 9443 ED Nov 1916
9. In addition to the biographical sources already cited, there is an informative obituary of Leitner in *The Bombay Educational Record and Literary Journal*, Vol.XXXII, July 1899, No. 1, pp 12–13 (See Sydney University library)
10. *Ibid.*, p 12
11. *P* 8698 ED Jan 1911. See also *Who Was Who*, Vol. 5 [1951–60]
12. *P* 3881 ED Oct 1891

3. The Trials and Tribulations of the Indian Education Service

Resignations and Contracts Terminated

There were various reasons why men resigned or had their contracts terminated. Some were predictable, others were sad, even tragic. One of the saddest concerned W. Knox Johnson,[1] the Principal at Jubblepore College, in the Central Provinces, who committed suicide by shooting himself in June 1906. He had been suffering from acute depression — not uncommon in India among men often situated in remote areas cut off from European contact for many months at a time — and had recently received news that his father was very ill with cancer. Johnson was also suffering from a delusion that a group of Indian students were trying to blacken his character by abusing him outside his home. In a meeting with the DPI he dwelt on his solitary life in Jubblepore and said that he wanted to retire and leave India. His colleagues confirmed that he was living the life of a recluse but was well liked at the college. He was examined by the civil surgeon who could only report that he was suffering from delusions. At that meeting Johnson told the surgeon that he wanted to arrange for some financial settlement regarding his wife *who had not been in India for many years*.[2] One wonders how many men spent large periods of their service lives in India separated from immediate family and what psychological as well as physical impact it had on them. Soon after the medical examination Johnson shot himself with a revolver. He left a note addressed to the DPI in which he asked that a stone ['expense of my people'] be put over his grave with the following inscription:

> Ask not my name, O friend,
> He only who hath known each man
> From the beginning can
> Remember each unto the end.

The official enquiry into his death found that he committed suicide 'while temporarily insane'.

There were numerous instances of staff taking extended sick leave in Europe or resigning on health grounds, some after many years of service, others after no more than a few months. The medical report on Arthur Jones,[3] Principal of the government college in Jubblepore, who served for only five months, stated that he suffered from chronic dyspepsia and nervous depression — 'almost a complete breakdown'. It was further observed that he had only one stump of a tooth in his head! He was adjudged to be permanently incapacitated for further service of any kind in India. In 1911 the Indian government expressed its concern at the number of IES appointees who had resigned for health reasons. It cited no less than 10 cases in recent years, including that of G. R. Watt, a professor of English at Presidency College, Calcutta, whose 'lamentable death took place almost immediately on his arrival in India'. A renewed emphasis was placed on the importance of recruiting fit young men. It was impossible, the government claimed, to exaggerate the importance of physical fitness to withstand the Indian climate.[4]

There is little doubt that life in India under the *Raj* was synonymous for many Europeans with the regular consumption of substantial quantities of alcohol which frequently led to health and social problems. William Bell,[5] the DPI in the Punjab in the early 1900s, fell victim to the ravages of alcoholism with predictable results. Early in 1906 it became clear that Bell had 'contracted habits of intemperance and that the fact had become a matter of public notoriety'. Further enquiries established beyond doubt that Bell had for some years been 'an habitual drunkard and that the matter had become both socially and departmentally a public and notorious scandal of the most serious character'. It was clear that this behaviour could not continue. Bell was 48 at the time. In 1885 he had been specially selected to be the Principal of the new central teachers' training college in Lahore. Two years later he was promoted to the graded education service and became a professor and later Principal of the government college in Lahore. Later still, he became an inspector of schools. Throughout that time he did 'admirable work'. He had been director in the Punjab since May 1901 and was specially selected from among other directors to be the inspector of chiefs' colleges in India. But for his recent lapse of grace his service record was 'exceptionally meritorious'.

In handling the matter, the Lieutenant-Governor decided to get rid of Bell as quietly as possible to avoid further scandal. He gave Bell two options: a year's furlough and then retirement or a public inquiry and the possibility of dismissal and loss of his pension. Bell chose a year's leave — 'he had', he claimed 'no option'. He duly went on leave in October 1907 and retired a year later. In view of his outstanding service in former years, the Lieutenant-Governor sought a compassionate allowance for him of R 200 per year. The Indian government endorsed the move and in a rare case of generosity even suggested R 300 per year, on the grounds that until recently he had been considered one of the most efficient members of the IES. His was considered 'a particularly sad case'. The Secretary of State was not quite so forgiving and agreed to an extra sum of R 200.

Another equally sad case of dismissal, which also provides an interesting insight to the social mores of the late Victorian period, involved W. Young,[6] the Principal of Jubblepore College and Superintendent of the Rajkumar school in the Central Provinces. His 20-year-old daughter had an affair — 'an improper intimacy' — with a young 20-year-old Indian student at the Rajkumar school. Evidently rumours of the affair had been rife for some time in Jubblepore and had seriously compromised Young's position as superintendent as it became progressively more difficult for him to retain the respect of his pupils. Young reacted to the crisis by seeking urgent compassionate leave on the grounds that his wife and daughter were seriously ill and had been ordered to take a sea voyage. In truth Young closed the school and fled to Colombo where he and his family took ship to Australia to prevent the marriage of his daughter. Prior to these events there had been complaints about Young's administration at both Jubblepore College — where it was alleged that discipline had become lax — and at the Rajkumar school. The High Commissioner recommended that Young be given a transfer elsewhere but there were no other positions available and he was forced to retire in 1892 on a measly pension of R 197 per month. He did, however, subsequently obtain other employment, presumably in Australia. While waiting for a ship in Colombo he wrote to a friend to explain his flight, saying that a fearful calamity had happened, the exact nature of which he could not possibly talk about. At a subsequent enquiry it was recommended that the Indian youth be expelled from the school but there is no record of his ultimate fate.

Occasionally, new staff like Francis Buckler[7] failed to make the grade and were dismissed before their probationary period was completed. Buckler was a 23-year-old Cambridge graduate when he set sail for Bombay in September 1914. He had been appointed as a history professor at the Muir Central College in Allahabad after having already spent a year teaching at the Madras Christian College. A product of Trinity Hall, where he obtained second class honours in history, he was described by the selection committee as a pleasant looking person with agreeable manners who was very anxious to return to India. From the outset his appointment turned to disaster. E. G. Hill, the Principal of Muir College, described him as full of energy and keenness but added that he displayed a large degree of youthful irresponsibility. Hill claimed that no member of the staff had much confidence in Buckler's ability as a teacher. His delivery was described as 'extraordinarily bad' and Hill had to stop his first public lectures because they were so appalling. He had also proved of little use in extra-curricular activities being an athlete of 'mean prowess'. De la Fosse, the DPI, claimed that Buckler would never make a first rate professor of history because he lacked adequate ability and powers of expression, dignity and a sense of responsibility: 'Mr Buckler's work is … poor, his interest in his pupils indifferent and he commands no respect'. Fosse was also very critical of Buckler's failure — for the third time — to pass the vernacular language test. This was a sign of inefficiency and a lack of application and it was clearly not in the best interests of Muir College to retain him.

H. Y. Langhorne[8] was another unsatisfactory appointment. He had gone to India in 1906 to be Headmaster of the Central Model School in the Punjab. In the first two years he failed to pass the vernacular language test and was given an extension of time. He was also transferred to a teaching post at Daly College, Indore, but he resigned from there within a month. The principal of the college thought he was unsatisfactory because he disregarded instructions and showed no interest in the work. He was then given a temporary job at the government college in Lahore but he lasted only a few weeks there before his employment in the IES was terminated.

Some staff resigned for personal reasons. Ada Browning,[9] head assistant mistress at the Dow Hill girls' boarding school at Kurseong, in Bengal, returned to Britain without formal permission after she found life in the school untenable because of her 'relations' with the principal, Elinor Greene. The file on Miss Browning contains several long letters which highlight how petty the matters of dispute really were between the two women but maybe the case reflected an aspect of life in India which was especially applicable to women who were both unmarried and socially isolated. In such circumstances all events could readily take on an exaggerated countenance. Miss Browning, emphasized the fact that she was 'a London Board trained teacher' and claimed that she had not been treated with due respect by Miss Greene. Having reviewed the matter, the Indian government recommended waving the cost of Miss Browning's outward passage which she was liable to refund because she had returned to Britain within her probationary period without permission.

There were also instances, like that of Richard Varley,[10] where staff recently appointed to the IES simply disappeared from the annual *India Office List* for no apparent reason. Varley, who was appointed in 1906 as Superintendent of English training colleges in Bengal and Principal of the teachers' college at Hooghly, had been Captain of School in his last two years at St Paul's, and then won an Exhibition scholarship to Balliol College, Oxford, where he was also a Craven university scholar. His tutor at Oxford made reference to work interruptions due to ill-health to account for his eventual second class honours degree but hastened to add that he thought him 'an excellent Latin and Greek Scholar'. At his selection interview Varley had said that he hoped to attend a course of training at the London Day Training Centre and also to study German teaching methods with a view ultimately of becoming a school inspector. In 1908 he disappears without trace from the India Office records. Perhaps he resigned for health reasons or was offered a better post back in England.

The case of Ernest Kilroe

In one instance a member of the IES was effectively 'blackballed' by all the provincial governments from re-employment in India after the First World War and the Secretary of State had to intervene and override them.

The case concerned Ernest Kilroe[11] who joined the IES in 1909 as an inspector of schools in the Central Provinces. He had been Captain of School at the South Eastern College in Ramsgate before going up to St John's College, Oxford, where he obtained a second class honours degree in classics in 1904. He was also a good all-round sportsman and boxed for Oxford against Cambridge. He then taught for two years in Ramsgate before becoming a private secretary in a law firm and studying for the Bar. He must have decided that he preferred a career in teaching because he left the law firm in 1908 and completed a short teacher training course at Oxford before applying to join the IES. Thereafter, he performed creditably 'except for a tendency to be impatient of detail and slapdash in his methods' until some of his private correspondence came to light in the course of normal war censorship in 1917, which caused some major misgivings in official circles.[12] Two letters in particular, copies of which are no longer in existence, were purported to have contained expressions which indicated 'abnormal tendencies' which made him 'unfit from a moral point of view to be in control of the education of the young'. In the letters he also expressed sympathy with student strikes in government schools against the orders of his superiors and allowed himself to be a means of communication between Sinn Fein in Ireland and the Indian National Congress.

After going to India, Kilroe had developed a strong sympathy for Annie Besant's political views, which were decidedly hostile to the British administration in India, and to Theosophy, a semi mystical cult that Besant adopted in 1889.[13] By 1907 she was President and spiritual leader of the Theosophical Society in both Europe and India, and deeply involved in the Indian independence movement. She accused the British of ruling India autocratically and selfishly without due respect for Indian culture, and she dismissed talk of Britain ruling India as a trustee as nothing but cant. Even during the First World War she campaigned for Indian self-government, which made her highly unpopular in the United Kingdom, and she was eventually interned in 1917. She also expressed strong sympathies for Irish Home Rule and the Easter rising, women's suffrage and republicanism. It is hardly surprising, therefore, that senior Indian government officials viewed with deep suspicion Kilroe's sympathies for Besant's political agenda. But it was his link with Theosophy that really set the alarm bells ringing, and especially a reference in one letter to 'C.W.L.' and the possibility that they would go on a visit together.

The initials stood for Charles Webster Leadbeater, a highly controversial figure and Besant's partner in the Theosophical movement.[14] It had been widely rumoured for years that Leadbeater liked pubescent boys, a belief that was strengthened by a celebrated court case in 1906, in which two 14-year-old boys claimed that Leadbeater made them sleep with him and taught them how to masterbate. Leadbeater had spent time in India in the 1880s before he teamed up with Besant, and the hype surrounding him was well-known to British officials in India.

Sir Reginald Craddock, the Lieutenant-Governor of Burma, who knew Kilroe because the latter had served under him in the Central Provinces, was especially outspoken in his condemnation of him. Craddock already knew of Kilroe's interest in Theosophy but until he read the revelations contained in the letters he had no idea of its extent. Craddock was adamant that no department of education could employ a man capable of 'writing such letters'. Disloyalty, insubordination and 'that sexual perversion which Theosophy seems to have encouraged' were, said Craddock, 'disclosed to such an extent and in a manner which would make Kilroe's appointment to any post connected with schoolboys and students, too serious a risk to take'. Craddock claimed to have come across other cases in the IES in which brilliant capacity was found conjointly with erotic and wholly undisciplined tendencies. Given the potential danger to Indian students from contact with such characters, he considered Kilroe totally unfit for further service in the IES. Craddock added that he was most anxious to keep 'this particular kind of poison out of Burma' which had so far escaped the taint. Other provincial governors felt likewise. One thought it advisable that Kilroe should 'worship' Besant 'at a distance' while another suggested that the 'gravely objectionable tendencies' disclosed in Kilroe's letters would not diminish with the passage of time. Given the overwhelmingly negative response from the provinces, the Indian government asked the Secretary of State to prevent Kilroe from returning to India after the war. In the meantime, to escape the furore, Kilroe went to England to seek enlistment in the Royal Air Force.

He was subsequently called to the India Office in London to give his side of the story and, much to the indignation of government officials in the Central Provinces, the Secretary of State decided that there was insufficient concrete evidence to support the allegations. Kilroe was permitted to join the Air Force until the war ended and then authorised to resume his former position as an inspector of schools in the Central Provinces. He duly returned to India after the war, one imagines much to the chagrin of local officialdom, and eventually retired seemingly unscathed in 1932. Kilroe's case is interesting not only as a revelation of social attitudes towards homosexuality at the time but also because of the way in which the India Office seemingly maintained an impartial, detached attitude towards the issue in the face of overwhelming passion and prejudice amongst officials in India.

Government Parsimony

In retrospect, the early 1900s appear to have been the high noon of the IES. Thereafter, as the expansion of Indian education gathered momentum it became increasingly difficult to recruit high quality Oxbridge graduates and recourse was made increasingly to graduates from elsewhere, especially the Scottish universities, London, and Trinity College, Dublin. The prospects of a life-long career in India were also diminished as Indian political activity intensified and grew more violent. The falling value of the rupee also remained a major cause for concern both for existing and potential members of the IES. The value of retirement pensions was being steadily eroded and for those contemplating joining the IES there were equally if not potentially more attractive career openings in the United Kingdom where there was a comparable expansion of education at secondary and university levels after 1900. In the early years of the new century there was also a growing feeling of discontent in the ranks of the IES as salaries and working conditions steadily deteriorated. This was not helped by the highly bureaucratic outlook of both the Indian and provincial governments and the constant cry of poverty when officials were challenged to increase educational expenditure. At the personal level the bowels of compassion of officialdom appear to have been rarely stirred.

When Arthur Barrett,[15] formerly a professor of English literature at the Deccan College in Poona, applied for a small top up to bring his annual retirement pension to R 5000 [then about £340], the Bombay government supported him. He had performed creditably as Principal of Elphinstone High School, Professor of English literature at Elphinstone and Deccan Colleges, and as DPI in the Hyderabad Assigned Districts, but the Indian government, while aware of his dedicated service, regretted that it could not consider his services so exceptional as to warrant making a recommendation in his favour to the Secretary of State. T. C. Lewis,[16] the Principal of the government college in Lahore, likewise, was disappointed when he applied unsuccessfully for promotion to the first grade of the old graded service in 1891. An outstanding mathematician — he was sixth wrangler at Cambridge in 1875 and two years later elected to a Fellowship at Trinity College — he was told that he had received more rapid promotion in Lahore than he would have got in Bengal. He was also fobbed off with the claim that as a result of the report of the Public Service Commission of 1887, it was likely that the graded service would be phased out in the near future.

When Edward Giles[17] became DPI in Bombay he was 49 years old. He requested that he be paid the maximum salary of R 2500 per month as he would otherwise never achieve that salary based on 10 incremental steps before he reached the retirement age of 55. He expressed the hope that the Indian government would not condemn him to spend the rest of his service in pursuit of a salary which, 'like the phantom mirage of the desert, was before his eyes but beyond his reach'. After consultation with the government in Bengal, which also stood to be affected by the ruling, it was agreed to reduce the number of incremental steps to five but, Giles did not get his R 2500 as requested.

The parsimonious nature of Indian government officials also extended to W. J. Goodrich,[18] a professor of history at the Muir Central College in Allahabad, when he sought payment of his return passage to England. He had suffered a physical and mental breakdown in his health and took leave on half pay for six months but did not, as directed, seek medical treatment. After a further deterioration in his health a medical board declared him unfit to resume teaching. At this point the Lieutenant-Governor had no option but to terminate his appointment whereupon Goodrich had gone back to England of his own accord without seeking his passage money. Both the Northwest provincial and Indian governments rejected his subsequent appeal. Given that he got six months on half pay and did nothing to restore his health, the Indian government did not think that 'a further indulgence should be accorded him at the public expense'.

John van Someren Pope,[19] likewise, was refused a rise in salary as DPI in Burma when he argued for one on the grounds of a rapid growth in schools. Pope compared his work with that of the DPI in the Punjab who was paid more. In rejecting his request Indian government officials highlighted the fact that the Punjab had a university which entailed much extra work for the director. Not to be deterred, Pope reapplied. He stressed that his job entailed much travel over rugged mountain terrain, high living expenses, and a depressing climate. He also stressed the fact that he spoke Bengali, Hindi, Urgu, Tamil, Canarese and Santhali. While in Burma he had also learnt Pali, Burmese and Karen. He also outlined in some detail his work with the seven Christian missions that operated schools in Burma and the fact that in 21 years of service he had taken only one year, five months and 13 days leave. In Burma, he claimed to be cut off from any further hope of promotion. He argued that it would be difficult to imagine getting anyone to replace him on his salary of R 1250 rising to R 1500 per month. The Lieutenant-Governor strongly supported Pope's case and suggested increasing his salary to R 1500 rising to R 2000 per month. If that was accepted, he thought that Pope should start at R 1800 as he had already completed eight years of service in Burma and had only six more years to serve before retirement. The Indian government still did not think that the Burma 'Appointment' merited a rise in pay but it did acknowledge the good work that Pope had done in Burma. Eventually it was agreed that he should be paid a special personal allowance of R 250 per month. Still not satisfied, Pope later applied, again unsuccessfully, to have the grant increased by five increments of R 50 to R 500 per month.

Occasionally the Indian government did show a compassionate side to its operations. When Dr A. F. R. Hoernle,[20] the Principal of the Calcutta Madrussa, retired in 1899 on a meagre pension of R 324 per month, the Bengal government asked that it be increased in the light of his outstanding work in archaeology and eastern scholarship. The Indian government agreed that his pension was too low and granted him an additional R 1000 per year. It was also not uncommon for men who had served with distinction as DPIs to be granted the additional R 1000 bonus when they retired. David Duncan,[21] who was Director in Madras for eight years, James Willson,[22] who was Director in Assam, and George Thompson,[23] acting Inspector-General in the Central Provinces, who had to retire for health reasons, were all recipients of the Indian government's *largesse*. Not so lucky was T. B. Kirkham,[24] an inspector in Bombay, who had completed more than 30 years of service in India. When his application for the R 1000 bonus to his pension was refused in 1899, he was told that his service was 'not of a nature not ordinarily falling within the duty that may be expected of his office'.

Traditional government parsimony in financial matters was clearly uppermost when Archdale Earle, who succeeded Pedler as Director of Public Instruction in Bengal, sought permission in 1907 to buy a car to expedite his frequent tours of inspection.[25] This was the first request of its kind made by a DPI and indicative of the onset of a new age of technology. Earle sought to purchase a Darracq 10 h.p. car for R 5825 or the equivalent of about £388. This sum comprised the cost of the car R 5300 [£353], plus a Stepney wheel and tyre complete R 175 [£11.10s], an Acetylene headlamp R 100 [£6.10s], and a Cape Cart Hood with side curtains and glass hood R 250 [£16.10s]. Running expenses were calculated at up to R 50 per month plus the hire of a driver for R 60 per month. Earle claimed that the car would save him valuable time. He also pointed out that on occasions he already hired a car to get around Calcutta. The Bengal government supported his request but as might have been predicted the Indian government initially turned down the request. It was claimed that Calcutta streets were narrow and overcrowded and that a motorcar would be no advantage over a horse-drawn vehicle. Beyond Calcutta it was argued that most places the director was likely to visit were well serviced by railways, hence a car was not a necessity. The government had no objection, however, should the director chose to provide himself with a car from his own funds. Suffice to say that this decision was later reversed after further consultation with Bengal officials.

There is a sequel to this story.[26] In August 1914, it was stated that the same car, purchased in 1908, was no longer fit for use. Indeed, it had been out of commission since 1912, and Hornell, then the Director, sought a replacement. His offer to contribute towards the cost of the car was agreed to by the Indian government but then a dispute arose over the running costs which had increased substantially since 1908. There is little point in continuing the saga. Suffice to say that nothing changes with the passage of time when it comes to bureaucrats parting with government funds.

Broadening the Recruitment Base

To overcome the decline in the number of high quality Oxbridge graduates applying to join the IES, a revised set of terms and conditions of appointment were drawn up in 1904.[27] The main change was the reduction in the length of the probationary term after recruitment from five years to two. While it was still thought highly desirable that recruits should undergo a basic course in teacher training before going out to India, it was clearly not practical to enforce any prescribed period of training because men were often needed to fill vacancies immediately or at short notice and also throughout the year. It was also agreed that, contrary to popular opinion, the pool of potential candidates for the IES was not large and there was no point to be gained by making the selection criteria too onerous. Furthermore, some of the best candidates were already in employment. The need to widen the scope of recruitment to include universities other than Oxford and Cambridge was also acknowledged, albeit reluctantly in some quarters.

Broadening the scope of recruitment to the IES was a matter pursued in detail by both Henry James and Sir Hugh Orange, in his capacity as director-general of education. James spent time in Britain in 1908 specifically gathering information on the training of secondary teachers which was subsequently published as a study by the bureau of education.[28] The report contains a wealth of valuable historical information not readily available elsewhere. At the outset James highlighted the contrasting attitudes in the United Kingdom towards teacher training. Many headmasters of leading secondary schools rejected or simply ignored it on principle but it was widely agreed that primary school teachers should be trained. The latter generally did not have university degrees and they 'instructed' rather than educated the lower classes. Most university graduates were educated middle class gentlemen who taught boys from middle and upper middle class backgrounds. Their degrees were thought to ensure that they were competent to teach!

Training for secondary school teaching — the IES was not directly involved in primary teaching — was of recent origin and offered in 13 universities and colleges in England and Wales, including Oxford, Cambridge and London. The earliest certificate course was started at Cambridge in 1880, followed by London in 1883, and Oxford in 1896, although the College of Preceptors had conducted teaching examinations since 1847. A further nine colleges or training departments attached to colleges for women only, provided secondary training towards the Cambridge certificate or the London diploma. Only Cherwell Hall provided a course for the Oxford diploma. In Scotland there were combined training courses for both primary and secondary teachers at the universities of Edinburgh, Aberdeen and Glasgow. Edinburgh also had a separate women's college. Edinburgh and St Andrews were the first British universities to establish Chairs in Education in 1876. Teaching diplomas were also granted by Trinity College, Dublin, and the Royal University of Ireland, but the main emphasis in Ireland was on training primary teachers. When James conducted his survey, the numbers attending many courses, especially at civic universities, were often very low, even single figures. In contrast to present practice, every course included a study of the history of education. At London, one of the most influential training centres, the three principal components of the course, besides practical teaching experience, comprised the historical evolution of educational ideals; the works and writings of great teachers; and studies of school systems at home and abroad.

Orange also visited the United Kingdom, specifically to check on the nature and quality of the degree courses offered at the four Scottish universities and Trinity College, Dublin.[29] He concluded that while the structure of Scottish degrees was markedly different from those at Oxford and Cambridge, for practical purposes the best Scottish and Irish degrees had to be treated as the equal of the best Oxbridge degrees. Moreover, many staff at Scottish and Irish universities were Oxbridge graduates. Much the same conclusion was reached about the Universities of London and Durham, and the civic universities which had been established in Manchester, Liverpool, Leeds, Birmingham and Sheffield, and the University of Wales. Orange made two statements in his report which emphasized the essential social class structure of English education and the IES. In the first he stressed the importance of 'personal qualifications' in the candidates recruited into the IES. It was clearly desirable, he said, that all candidates should have a good academic degree and practical teaching experience, they should also have 'the bearing and behaviour of gentlemen, in the wide sense in which that term is applied to members of the *superior official class*'.[30] It is little wonder that referees, and especially headmasters and university dons, regularly claimed that those they spoke on behalf of, were true gentlemen in every sense of the term. In another comment, Orange also said that 'the men whom we require are those who have received a liberal school and university education, and have been trained as secondary teachers, not those who have been educated as pupil teachers and qualified as elementary teachers'. One wonders what Orange would have thought of the appointment of Arthur Baldwin as Principal of the Collegiate School in Rangoon in 1911.

Baldwin,[31] who came from a working class background, was originally a pupil teacher at the Rothschild school in Brentford, from whence he won a King's scholarship to Cheltenham Teachers' College. He graduated from there with a Board of Education teaching certificate in 1903. In the Michaelmas Term of 1908, while still teaching at a school in Cowley, he enrolled at St John's College, Oxford, as a commoner. Three years later he graduated BA with upper second class honours in English literature, in a year in which there was only one First awarded in that school. By all accounts he was an outstanding IES candidate. His tutor at Magdalen College, thought he was suitable in every respect for the Rangoon appointment:

> I have had only one pupil who knew more about English literature than Mr Baldwin, and I have had none who was his superior in lucidity and force. In my weekly classes .... I have usually relied upon him to lead discussion. He just missed a First ... the reason, I imagine, was that *for the first half of the course he was teaching half the day.* He is a man of exceptionally robust physique, good at most games, and a colossal worker.

Sir W. M. Raleigh, Professor of English Literature, likewise sang his praise: 'He is a first rate solid man, a slogger at work, and a good fellow …. I think he would be splendid for the Rangoon post. He has the White Man's *morale*, I think, at all points. I don't see how you could get a better man'. The Board of Education selection committee comments on him said it all:

> Mr Baldwin's social origin is not that of the usual IES candidate. He appears, however, to have held his own in the social life of Oxford, as in addition to athletic success [he had played cricket and soccer for Brentford, rowed at St John's, and also boxed and played tennis, rugby and hockey] he was a member of the Prince of Orange club at St John's College and of the scribblers' club, a University literary society of which he became president. This evidence goes to show that he might be expected to win the respect of the natives of Burma and *to pass muster in European society in Rangoon* …. His whole career may be said to give evidence of strength of purpose and tenacity of character'.

His subsequent career proved that the selection committee's judgement was not misplaced. After four years of military service he became a school inspector in 1919. Five years later he was appointed Assistant DPI in Burma, a position he retained until he retired in 1936.

In the years immediately prior to the outbreak of war in 1914 and thereafter, there were others who also joined the IES who had started out in life with Board of Education certificates and later completed degrees. James Holme,[32] appointed as a professor of English at Presidency College, Calcutta, in 1910, had obtained a first class certificate in primary teaching from the Board of Education before going on to graduate with first class honours in English literature at the University of Liverpool in 1907. When interviewed he stated that he had entered into an agreement with the Board of Education to repay fees and grants made to him while he had been a training college student but it was not clear whether he had earlier been a pupil teacher or not. John Murray,[33] appointed Principal of the government and normal schools, Moulmein, in 1913, had been a pupil teacher at Torphichen Street public school in Edinburgh before training to be a teacher at Moray House Training College. Thereafter, he obtained an MA degree from the University of Edinburgh. The selection committee said of him: 'a big man and very pleasant manner. He may be regarded with confidence as a very good candidate for the IES'. Unfortunately, he resigned his post in July 1914, after less than 12 months in the job. He had been a keen member of the officer training corps before going out to India so he may have gone home to enlist. Francis Blair[34] was another IES recruit from Scottish working class origins — his father was a butcher. He was a pupil teacher at the West Kilbride school and then trained as an elementary school teacher. He studied part-time at Edinburgh University and eventually obtained an MA degree with second

class honours in English literature. One referee suggested that he missed
out on a First because he was a part-time student. He went on to have
a successful career in east Bengal as an inspector, principal, deputy
director, and eventually DPI in Bihar before he retired in 1938.

Alfred Dix,[35] who went out to the Central Provinces as a
headmaster in 1914, had obtained an elementary teacher's certificate from
Cheltenham Training College before attending the North London
polytechnic institute and obtaining a BSc with second class honours in
chemistry from the University of London. He gained his early teaching
experience in the east end of London in the districts of Islington and
St Pancras before spending a year teaching science in a government
secondary school in Cairo. He held various appointments in the Central
Provinces including tutor to the Maharaja of Nabha before he retired
in 1937.

John Armour[36] also started life as a pupil teacher at the turn of the
century in his native Glasgow, and then went on to complete his teacher's
certificate at the Church of England training college. Between 1904 and
1911 he completed a part-time MA degree at Glasgow University with
first class honours in English. He then won a scholarship to Balliol
College, Oxford, where he studied modern history. Regrettably, he only
gained third class honours. His tutor at Balliol said that he was
handicapped by having to take 'compulsory Greek' — but for that he
might have gained a First. His tutor also commented that he was 'Scotch,
but not too Scotch', in temperament and manner, a man of strict
principles and sound standards, and would make a very good public
servant. Another referee said of him: 'He is not a man from whom one
would expect bursts of brilliance but his work [will] never fall below
a high level of efficiency'. He was above all 'a safe appointment'. The
selection committee thought he was exceedingly able and had made a
mistake at Oxford in reading modern history rather than English. He had
also been unlucky at Glasgow in not obtaining a university lectureship
in English. He went to India in 1914 as a professor of English at Patna
College in Bankipur. In 1935 he became Principal of the college and
retired in 1941.

The onset of war in 1914 saw the age of IES candidates rise.
Harold Tinker[37] was 36 and had already applied without success for
teaching positions in South Africa, Canada, Cairo and Lahore, before
being appointed as a professor at the training college in Allahabad in the
United Provinces. Moreover, unlike most applicants he was married with
two children but said that he did not propose to take them to India in the
first instance. Born in Manchester, he began his education as a pupil
teacher in Derbyshire. He then attended the St Paul's training college
in Cheltenham. While teaching, he studied science part-time at the
technical school in Stockport. Eventually he gained entry to the University
of London and over the period 1903–8, attended classes at Birkbeck
College, East London University College, and the South West Polytechnic
before eventually obtaining a first class honours degree in geology. Still

not satisfied, in 1911 he studied for and gained the Cambridge teacher's training certificate. He held a variety of teaching positions in his early career but at the time of his IES appointment he had been the master of teaching method and lecturer in education for three years at the same St Paul's training college where he had formerly trained to be a teacher. The selection committee thought he was a nice looking, attractive person with open and frank manners who looked younger than his age. They were also impressed by his teaching record. In 1920 he became the Principal of the training college in Agra. He later joined the inspectorate before becoming acting Principal of the Teachers' College in Allahabad, in 1930. He retired four years later.

Growing Indian resentment at being excluded from the IES prompted Sir Charles Lyall, a Secretary in the India Office, to produce a paper in January 1908, outlining the origins of the so-called 'superior' and 'inferior' education services.[38] He was at pains to emphasize that nominally there was no difference in the status of the IES and the provincial education services. He claimed that the difference in pay scales in favour of the IES was designed to attract Europeans to India and not to attract Indians! Moreover, to saddle India with a scale of salaries designed to attract Europeans but applied to Indians serving in their own country would be an unjustifiable extravagance. The higher salaries paid to Europeans were justified on the grounds that their living costs, like house rents and food, were higher; they had to pay for their children to be educated in Britain, and most Europeans were married. Lyell also maintained that to 'promote' Indians from the provincial education services to the IES was to suggest that one service was superior to the other which was not the original intent. Unfortunately, for Lyall, this was not how it was generally perceived, and his rationalisation of the differences in salaries found little or no support amongst Indians. Even he had to agree, when challenged, that there was merit in the argument for higher salaries in some senior posts in the provincial education services.

NOTES ON CHAPTER

1. P 7315 ED Aug 1906
2. Author's emphasis
3. P 8942 ED Feb 1912
4. P 8699 ED Jul 1911
5. P 7876 ED Feb 1908
6. P 4343 ED Jun 1893
7. P 9445 ED Nov 1914
8. P 8432 ED Apr 1910
9. P 6111 ED Aug 1901
10. P 7315 ED Oct 1906
11. P 8154 ED Jan 1909
12. P 10585 ED Jul 1919
13. The definitive biography on Mrs Annie Besant (1847–1933) is the two volume work by Arthur H. Nethercot, *The First Five Lives of Annie Besant*,

1961, and *The Last Four Lives of Annie Besant*, 1963, both published by
Rupert Hart-Davies, London. A shorter and more recent study is that by
Rosemary Dinnage, *Annie Besant*, Penguin Books, London, 1986.

14. For more on Leadbeater see Gregory Tillett, *The Elder Brother: A Biography of Charles Webster Leadbeater*, Routledge & Kegan Paul, London, 1982
15. P 4960 ED Jul 1896
16. P 3881 ED Jan 1891
17. P 5415 ED Mar 1898
18. P 4960 ED Jul 1896 and P 4749 ED May 1895
19. P 5182 ED 1897 and P 5415 ED Feb 1898
20. P 5641 ED Aug 1899
21. P 5875 ED Mar 1900
22. P 5875 ED Jun 1900
23. *Ibid.*
24. P 5641 ED Mar 1899
25. P 7592 ED Aug 1907
26. P 9445 ED Aug 1914
27. P 6344 ED Oct 1902 and P 6807 ED Mar 1904
28. H. R. James, *The Training of Secondary Teachers in the United Kingdom*, Occasional Reports No. 5. Bureau of Education, New Delhi 1909
29. P 8154 ED May 1909
30. Author's emphasis
31. P 8942 ED Jan 1912
32. P 8698 ED Jan 1911
33. P 9196 ED Nov 1913
34. P 9443 ED Jan 1914
35. P 9445 ED Nov 1914
36. P 9445 ED Sep 1914
37. P 9709 ED Sep 1915
38. P 7876 ED Jan 1908

4. The Female Members of the Indian Education Service

The provision of western education for women and girls had long been a contentious subject in India. The Education Commission of 1882 had drawn attention to the manifold problems facing those who sought to promote it but solutions were almost impossible to find. As one deputy inspector in the Central Provinces said shortly after the First World War, female education was carried on in response to a demand that did not exist.[1] In October 1915 a deputation, headed by Mrs Philippa Fawcett, presented a memorial to the Secretary of State [Austen Chamberlain], calling for more to be done to expand education for females in India.[2] Amongst over 400 signatures to the memorial were those of Ramsey Macdonald, the Aga Khan, Mrs Sydney Webb, Mrs Sophie Bryant, The Rev. William Miller, and the writer H. G. Wells. The deputation wanted Chamberlain to establish a committee to look into the matter but he did not think the time was opportune in the middle of a world war. He did, however, agree to pass on the memorial to the Indian government in Delhi for its consideration. He expressed support for their concern but felt that the demand for female education had to come from Indians in India, not from Europeans in London.

The Indian government subsequently invited provincial governments to obtain the views of local people and interested groups and to forward their findings plus their own observations. In due course the Indian government amassed an enormous amount of material comprising more than 1000 foolscap pages on the subject.[3] It was difficult to generalise for the whole of India because conditions were not uniform but there was general agreement on the paucity of provision everywhere. Overall, approximately one per cent of the female population was receiving some form of instruction. Of that one per cent some nine tenths were enrolled at the primary level. Only two per cent of girls undergoing instruction were enrolled at the secondary level, and most of those were in schools run by voluntary agencies. It was estimated that just over 900 females were enrolled in collegiate or university courses.

The Indian government claimed that the absence of female education had its roots in the very fabric of society and only a radical nationwide change in life, customs and ideals would generate a solution. There was widespread public apathy towards the issue because there were no obvious material advantages to be gained from investing in the education of females. In Moslem communities there was widespread parental unwillingness to send girls to school or to allow them to remain beyond marriageable age. Communal or sectarian feeling might stimulate girls' schooling in large centres of population for specific communities but most communities, whether Hindu, Moslem or Sikh etc, would not send their daughters to a common school. There were also more specific practical problems including a supply of competent teachers. Men were not welcome and there were really only three possible sources — widows, teachers' wives, and Indian Christians. It was also well-nigh impossible to get Indian women to serve as school inspectors. The job involved endless travelling and staying overnight in a variety of types of accommodation which was quite unacceptable to Moslems and Hindus alike. Despite the time and effort spent on responding to the London memorial, the Indian government saw little hope of any real progress until Indian women themselves started to demand change.[4]

In the circumstances the number of women required for the IES was small. Their main tasks were to inspect girls' schools in receipt of government grants-in-aid and to act as principals in the few government schools and teacher training colleges for young women. In 1913, there were 17 female IES officers, comprising 12 inspectresses, as they were then called, and five superintendents.[5] A perusal of the backgrounds of some of the European women who served in India provides a rare insight into the education of middle class women in the late nineteenth and early twentieth centuries.

Indian government records provide details of most women appointed to the IES between 1905 and 1922 when recruitment ended. Over that time the average age of the 17 appointed was close to 30 years. Male appointments, by comparison, averaged closer to 26 years of age. The academic credentials of women varied; some had good quality honours degrees, others did not, but all had teacher training qualifications of one sort or another. When appointed, all were single, but many did not stay in the IES for very long. Little is known of what happened to them after they resigned but it is likely that many got married while others, finding Indian pay and conditions not to their liking, sought and found positions elsewhere. Previous or existing family links with India were also much in evidence amongst female IES recruits.

Gladys Heuer[6] was 26 when appointed as a mistress of method at the Dow Hill Training College in Kurseong in 1906. Born in Liverpool, she had been a pupil teacher before winning a Queen's Scholarship to the Edge Hill Training College. She completed her Board of Education teaching certificate in 1902 and then spent a further year in France at a Normal School in Limoges, where she passed the *Brevet Elementaire de l'Academie de Poitiers*. At the time of her appointment to the IES she was teaching at the Ethelburga Street council school in Battersea. The chairman of the selection committee described her as a fresh-looking, healthy girl, who was very calm and self-possessed, with a touch of superiority in her manner. She was clearly a cut above the average elementary teacher in qualifications and probably in ability and the chairman said that her year's training in France had impressed the committee. She had no academic degree, and no male would have been appointed to the IES without one, but that was not considered essential as her work in India was to focus mainly on the training of infant teachers.

By contrast, Mary Honeyburne[7] was 32 years old and a first class honours graduate in classics from Victoria University, Liverpool, when she was appointed as a junior inspectress in Bengal in 1907. She also had a teaching certificate from the Cambridge Training College for Women. The daughter of an Anglican cleric, she was born and reared in Liverpool. She attended the prestigious Liverpool High School for girls before winning a scholarship to Victoria University. When she applied to join the IES she already had six years teaching experience, including two years spent in government schools in Cairo and another 21 months in India at the All Saints Diocesan High School in Naini Tal. She also had a knowledge of French, German, Latin and Greek, and Egyptian Arabic!

Ethel West[8] was born in Calcutta — her father was a botanist and seed merchant — and educated at the esteemed La Martiniere College for girls. Her mother ran a training school and orphanage for Eurasian children and Miss West did honorary work there when she left school. As a result she became a fluent speaker of Urdu. Later she taught at La Martiniere College before going to England in 1902 to study at Girton College, Cambridge. In 1905 she achieved third class honours in the Mathematics Tripos but it was not until 1947 that Cambridge awarded degrees to women. Instead, she took advantage of a temporary *ad eundem* arrangement and took out a BA degree from Trinity College, Dublin.[9] At the time people like her were called 'mailboat graduates' because they crossed to Dublin, often for the first time in their lives, by the mailboat to pay their fee and receive their degree. She then completed a teacher's diploma at St Mary's College, Paddington, and taught for two years at the girls' high school in Dover. By then she was 30 years old and anxious to return to India. The comments of the selection committee chairman were more revealing of contemporary social attitudes to race than they were of Miss West's qualities as a teacher. It was stated that she probably had

> *a slight trace of Indian blood.* In connection with this suspicion, together with her Indian upbringing, special enquiries were made as to a *possible deficiency in energy and initiative* but the result confirmed the impression she conveyed when she was interviewed, that she was lacking in neither of the necessary qualities mentioned.[10]

Tragically, within a few months of her return to India she died, and the IES lost one of its most promising female recruits.

Miss West's replacement was Helen Stuart,[11] a 30-year-old Englishwoman, who had been educated at Cheltenham Ladies College, during the headship of the famous Miss Beale, St Hilda's College, Oxford, and the Maria Grey Training College in London. Like Miss West, she too was a 'mailboat graduate' having taken out a BA degree in classics, from Trinity College, Dublin, under the *ad eundem* provision. A speaker of French, Latin and Greek, she had taught for five years, including nine months in Canada, before applying to join the IES. Her subsequent career is unknown.

Mary Garrett,[12] appointed in 1908 as an inspectress of schools in Eastern Bengal and Assam, was born in Ceylon where her missionary father administered some 50 mission schools and 5000 pupils. She was educated privately until the age of 16. Then she went to England and completed a first class teaching certificate at the ladies' training college in Cheltenham. The selection committee thought she was 'pleasant looking and [had] an interesting and intelligent face'! She spent the next 10 years touring Assam each year as a school inspector before resigning in 1920.

Jessie Parsons[13] was 37 years old, with 17 years teaching experience to her credit, when she was appointed Principal of the training college for Indian girls at Bankipore in 1909. She too, had been born in India, in Madras, where her late father had been an officer in the government secretariat. She attended the Doveton Girls' School and later the Doveton College in Madras before entering Presidency College in 1889. She graduated with a BA degree in history in 1891, and was one of the first women to do so. She then obtained a licentiate in teaching from the government training college at Saidapet in Madras. Thereafter, she held various teaching posts in India and also ran a boarding school for European children in Penang from 1896 to 1904. She had two brothers; one, Dr L. D. Parsons, was the Colonial Post Officer in Gibraltar, while the other was a barrister in London. In 1908 she spent a year at the London Day Training College catching up on the latest ideas and techniques in the training of teachers. The selection committee thought she was eminently sensible, though not a brilliant person. In appearance she was described as plain but her voice was pleasant and despite being born in India she was of pure English descent! Her widespread knowledge of India was thought to make her far less of a risk than some younger girl who knew nothing of India. She was also thought to possess 'that solidarity of purpose and equability of temperament which in pioneer work is invaluable'.

Mary Somerville[14] was another former pupil teacher who subsequently obtained a university degree after combining a course at teachers' college with part time university study. When she sailed for Calcutta in January 1911 to take up a post as an inspectress of schools in East Bengal and Assam, she was 25 years old. She hailed from Edinburgh where her father worked in the Inland Revenue department. She was educated initially at the Edinburgh Ladies' College before becoming a pupil teacher at the North Merchiston public school for four years. She then completed a certificate of teaching specialising in secondary and higher education at the Established Church of Scotland

Training College. While training as a teacher she also attended the University of Edinburgh and graduated MA with second class honours in English in 1908. Thereafter she taught at the Leith Academy and at the Edinburgh Ladies' College. She was also assistant secretary of the historical society of the University of Edinburgh. Some two years before she applied to join the IES she had been engaged to be married to a young ICS man in Bengal but he was accidentally drowned. Thereafter she was determined to go to India. In 1908 she had unsuccessfully applied for the principalship of the training college at Patna. Her referees all spoke very highly of her teaching ability and the selection committee was clearly impressed by her determination to acquire a degree under difficult conditions. She was described as a 'nice-looking Scotch girl .... In manner she is very quiet and though she seems to be of a distinctly gentle disposition, she impresses one as having plenty of "grit" and determination. She speaks well'. She resigned in October 1914 and was replaced by Miss Garrett.

The file on Miss Somerville's appointment also contains a poignant letter from F. R. Jamieson, of the Scottish Education Department, to the India Office on the subject of Indian and Colonial appointments.[15] He claimed to know of a lady with a far better claim to the post that Miss Somerville was after — someone educated at Wycombe Abbey, Girton College, and both the Manchester and the Oxford training centres for teachers, 'but she would not look at it .... She was quite contemptuous of the place' [India]. He mentioned this in order to warn the India Office that it would probably not be overrun with candidates of the first order: 'Generally, I find that to be the trouble with the Indian and Colonial places; they are not good enough for the best kind of people; and second-best people don't seem to be likely to hold up their end creditably — in India at least'.

One wonders whether Jamieson would have approved of Gladys Broughton,[16] appointed as an inspectress in the Central Provinces in 1912. She was born in India and lived there until she was 11 years old. Her family had very strong links with India. Her late father had been a captain in the British army. Her maternal grandfather, Sir Michael Filose, had been a lieutenant-colonel in the Indian army and Chief Secretary to the Maharaja of Gwalior. Lieutenant-Colonel Clement Filose, then Military Secretary in Gwalior, was her cousin. She also had two brothers serving in the Indian army and another seeking entry. After the death of her father, her mother went to London, trained as a nurse, and then served in the Indian Medical Service until her second marriage.

Miss Broughton was educated at Bedford High School and won a scholarship to University College, London, where she obtained a BA degree in 1907 with second class honours in philosophy. In 1912 she obtained a University of London teaching diploma as a student in the training department at Bedford College. She had no teaching experience when she sailed for India from Marseilles in December 1912 but she was described as a bright and extremely capable young woman — she was 29 at the time — and 'intensely in sympathy with India'. She was later approached to accept the position of principal at Bethune College, the foremost women's university college in Bengal, but she refused on the grounds that the pay was insufficient. Soon afterwards, in 1915, while on leave in the United Kingdom, she resigned from the IES but later rescinded her decision.

Ethel Chamier[17] was another member of the IES who was born and spent her childhood in India. However, unlike many female appointees she remained in her post as a school inspectress in the Central Provinces until she retired in 1940, aged 55. The year before she retired she was awarded the OBE for her services to female education in India. She hailed originally from Madras where her father was a prison governor. She was educated at Bishop Cotton's School in Bangalore and was a fluent speaker of Hindustani before she went to England in 1903. There she attended Princess Helena College in London before going up to St Hilda's Hall, Oxford, to study science. She majored in chemistry and gained her diploma with fourth class honours which the Principal of her College attributed, in part, to nervousness under examination pressure and a period of poor health. From there she returned to India where she worked as an educational inspector in the Bengal provincial education service. She clearly impressed the selection committee with her glowing references, her extensive knowledge of India, academic qualifications, previous teaching experience, and enthusiasm for science. Two of her most supportive referees were Misses Garrett and Somerville. Their faith in her ability was amply justified in her subsequent career.

One of the best qualified female candidates to join the IES was Elsa Spencer,[18] whose father was an HMI. Born in Cambridge, she attended the St Felix School in Southwold before winning a scholarship in 1907 to Royal Holloway College 'probably the best women's college connected with the University of London'. There she completed a London degree with upper second class honours in classics. One of her referees claimed that she would have got a First but for illness at a critical time. From Holloway she went to the Clapham High School secondary training department to train as a teacher for two years. This was followed by a winter spent in further study at Gottingen University. Her teaching experience included a year at the *Lycee de jeunes filles* in Rheims, as well as posts as a language teacher first at the prestigious Croydon High School for girls, and later at the equally famed North London Collegiate School for girls. She was described as dark, serious looking, pleasant and of good appearance, self-possessed, and intelligent. She was also keen to go to India. The selection committee was especially impressed by her knowledge of Latin and Greek and her capacity to speak French and German fluently. Unfortunately, her subsequent career in India is not recorded.

Helen Brander[19] was an equally promising IES candidate but she lasted only a year before being forced to resign for health reasons. She suffered from appendicitis in the summer of 1916 and went to Darjeeling for an operation but suffered post-operative complications for some time afterwards. In her letter of resignation in March 1917, she said she felt unequal to the strain of school work and the climate. She was also annoyed at the lack of free living quarters as originally promised. She had gone to India as Principal of the government girls' high school in Bankipore, Bihar. The daughter of a Scottish bank manager, she was born in San Francisco and lived in California for five years before the family returned to Edinburgh. There she was educated at George Watson's Ladies College, where she won a succession of scholarships, before enrolling at Edinburgh University. She graduated MA in 1908, having majored in Latin, French and German. She then spent a year in France at the University of Clermont — Ferrand where she completed a *Dip d'etudes francaises*. Then followed teaching posts at Blackburn High School for girls, Camborne County School for girls, and Bournmouth Collegiate School for girls before spending the 1914–1915 academic year at Bedford College acquiring a London University teacher's diploma. Described as a pleasant, sensible Scotch girl who was likely to do well in India, her career in India appeared doomed from the start but she subsequently recovered her health and eventually, at the age of 32, was reappointed to her original post which had remained unfilled on a permanent basis since her resignation. Prior to her reappointment she taught at the Loretto Convent School in Darjeeling and was briefly Headmistress of the Dow Hill School and Training College in Kurseong, Bengal.

The war years made it virtually impossible to recruit female staff from Britain because of a wartime ban on women travelling by sea through 'the dangerous zone' for fear of submarine attack. The same rule also prevented Miss M. V. Irons,[20] an inspectress of schools in Bengal, from returning to England after her resignation from the IES. In the immediate post war years many more appointments were made from candidates already domiciled in India. In some cases, as with Eunice Dawson, the normal age limit was also waived.

Miss Dawson[21] was 37 when she was appointed as an inspectress of schools in Bihar and Orissa in 1919. She was born in Burnley, Lancashire, but lived much of her childhood in the Punjab as her father was an Anglican missionary there before later returning to be a parish priest in Rugby. Miss Dawson was educated at the Clergy Daughters' School in Bristol and later at Durham University, where she graduated BA in classics in 1903. The following year she gained a Durham diploma in the theory and practice of teaching. She then held several teaching appointments at girls' grammar schools before going out to India in 1913 to be first assistant mistress and subsequently Headmistress of the European High School for girls and the Lawrence School in the Punjab. In 1918 she was offered but declined the post of educational secretary to the YMCA, preferring instead, to take a temporary position in the IES as a school inspectress. This position was made permanent in 1919. She presumably resigned in 1921 as her name disappeared from the *India Office List* thereafter.

Una Tilley[22] was an example of someone already serving in India who was appointed to the IES after the First World War. Initially, she joined the Burma provincial education service as Headmistress of the government normal school in Rangoon at the start of 1918. Three years later she obtained an IES post as assistant lecturer in education at the University of Rangoon. Born in London in December 1890, she was educated at Blackheath High School for girls (1900–1910). From there she won a scholarship to Somerville College, Oxford, where she gained a second class honours diploma in history in 1914. This was followed by a further year at the Clapham High School training department and the award of a Cambridge certificate of secondary teaching. Miss Tilley then taught at schools in Kennington and Bromley for two years, and spent another two years as a secretary in the War Trade Intelligence Department before eventually fulfilling a long cherished wish to go out to India. The selection committee thought her rather young for a senior Indian appointment but she impressed them with her marked capacity and strength of character. It was noted, for example, that while at Oxford she had played hockey for her College XI and also been president of the boating club! Her only drawback was her weak eyesight. It was considered acceptable for the initial two-year probationary term but would need to be tested again if her appointment was to be made permanent. Some three years later her eyesight must have been considered acceptable for her to be appointed to the IES as a university lecturer.

There appear to have been three female IES appointments in 1922 but thereafter recruitment ceased. Mention has already been made in some detail of Alice Lawrence. Others who joined included Miss I. H. Lowe and Gladys Harrison. Miss Lowe[23] was London born and the daughter of a senior examiner in the Patent Office. After private schooling she attended Westfield College where she obtained a University of London BSc degree in 1913 with honours in geology. In the period 1914–20, she was a demonstrator in geology at Bedford College. In 1920 she was awarded an MSc degree in geology and also began reading for a diploma in geography from the University of Oxford. When she applied in 1920 to join the IES as an inspectress of schools in Madras she was told that her appointment would be conditional on her first obtaining a teaching diploma. She met this requirement the following year at Bedford College by obtaining a Cambridge certificate of teaching and sailed for India, aged 32, in February 1922. The Principal of Bedford College referred to her as a woman of character and ability who had won the esteem of her teaching colleagues. She was trustworthy and in her last year at Westfield College she had been elected as senior student. The selection committee noted that she came from a cultured family and was a person of refinement and high character. Perhaps this was the female equivalent of being in all respects a true gentleman!

Gladys Harrison[24] was probably the last female appointed to the IES. Born in Buckingham in 1888, she attended Oxford High School and Royal Holloway College, graduating BA in 1909, with second class honours in French and English. The next year she studied for the London teachers' diploma in pedagogy at St Mary's College, Paddington. From there she went out to Calcutta to teach at the Pratt Memorial High School for two years before returning to England to teach at St Mary's Abbots School in Bromley. From 1917 to 1919, like Miss Tilley, she too worked for the War Trade Intelligence Department. In 1920 she returned to India as Vice-Principal of Queen Mary's College in the Punjab. It was from there that she was appointed to the IES as Principal of a new intermediate college for girls in Lahore.

There are grounds for believing that the Indian government was never anxious to increase the number of women employed in the IES beyond the bare minimum. Many recruits did not stay in India for very long because they got married or found better teaching posts elsewhere. Some also found the job too demanding. The harsh Indian climate and the hazards of travel, especially in rural India, deterred many women from making a lifelong career in the IES. Traditionally, they were also paid less than men on the grounds that they did not have families to support. The response of the Indian government towards Lilian Brock's request for an increase in salary seemed indicative of its attitude in general towards females in the IES.[25] Miss Brock, an inspectress of schools in Bengal, applied for an increase in salary in 1905, a year after arriving in India. She claimed that her salary, which was pegged at R 600 per month, was inadequate 'to meet the expenses of an English lady living in Calcutta'. Unless her salary was increased she said that she would terminate her contract. The provincial government of Bengal strongly supported her claim. She had a first class honours degree in English from the University of London, a diploma in teaching from Cambridge University, and was very highly thought of in her work. The Indian government, mindful of the fact that it had not experienced any difficulty of late in procuring good female candidates for similar positions on existing pay, expressed sorrow at her probable departure but declined to support her claim. Not deterred, she made a second attempt but that too was unsuccessful. Then, early in 1906, the female missionaries in Bengal petitioned Pedler, the DPI, to prevent her from resigning. At this point the Secretary of State got to hear about the matter and eventually terms were agreed and she stayed.

The difficulties faced by many female members of the IES were highlighted in the evidence they gave to the Public Services Commission in 1913. Miss H. G. Stuart,[26] Chief Inspectress of schools in the United Provinces, criticized the poor salaries and especially the harsh pension conditions. She argued that few, if any, women could complete 25 years service. The work was very exacting, especially for inspectresses, who spent much of their time travelling and staying overnight in *dak* [post] bungalows, and most would be well over 50 before they qualified for a full pension if they stayed that long. In her opinion 20 years was an ample requirement for the pension. The problems associated with constant travelling had surfaced some years earlier when the Indian government had agreed to pay special local travel allowances to inspectresses in the Central Provinces.[27] At the time the point was made that men often travelled alone and covered many miles on horseback but this was not always possible for women. Moreover, as Miss Stuart remarked, 'A lady is seldom physically strong enough to do her work and inspections after long and fatiguing rides for any length of time together, and there is no [male] inspector in [the Central Provinces] who is called upon to cover so large an area as the inspectress'. When Miss Garrett resigned in 1920, after spending 10 years as an inspectress of schools in Assam, she commented, 'I feel that 10 years as a touring officer in this climate is as much as can be fairly expected of any woman …'.[28] Miss Stuart also pointed out how difficult it was to recruit Indian women as assistant inspectresses because of social custom. In the Central Provinces, for example, the isolation of women from the mainstream of life, a custom called *purdah*, was still rigidly enforced. Miss Stuart was also critical of the way in which women were recruited into the IES. She said that she got her job in India via someone on the Board of Education in London mentioning the post to a friend in the training department at Bedford College. The friend, in turn, mentioned Miss Stuart as a possible candidate. Miss Stuart claimed initially that she had known nothing of the post nor had she ever considered working in India. She was convinced that most female teachers were not aware of career opportunities in the IES and that more advertising and information were needed. She also spoke of the long period that elapsed before leave was due and the undermining effects of the climate on personal health and vitality.

These views were endorsed by those of Miss J. Patterson[29] from Madras. When asked to comment on female education in India arising from a memorial presented to the Secretary of State by Philippa Fawcett *et al*, she suggested that the paucity of female school inspectresses was a major reason for heavy workloads and frequent health breakdowns:

> the life of an officer is a very hard one. She is cut off almost entirely from home life and society. She experiences all kinds of discomforts, is obliged to put up in travellers' bungalows, chatrams, chavadis, school rooms; and even in the open air under the shade of some friendly tree. She encounters innumerable hindrances and irritations small and big. Sometimes the latter are so constant that the strain results in a nervous breakdown. It is a life of pure self-sacrifice and only those who are really interested in their work continue in it and contrive ways and means of meeting expenses, overcoming difficulties and enduring with patience the trials of life.

At the same time she readily admitted that the work was fascinating, and that there was no officer who could not relate a score of interesting anecdotes to show why they bore the burden bravely and unflinchingly.

Miss C. M. Lynch,[30] another inspectress in Madras, made some interesting comparisons when she referred to the low salaries paid to women in the IES. She claimed that female inspectors in England were paid from £200 to £400 per year. A teacher at a top school like Cheltenham College could earn up to £1000 per year. A teacher at the North London Collegiate School earned up to £500 per year, while other teachers could earn £300 per year or £200 in small schools. By comparison, women in the IES started on the equivalent of about £320 per year rising in most instances to no more than about £600 at the very most.

NOTES ON CHAPTER

1. *Report on the state and progress of Education in the Central Provinces and Berar for the year 1919–20*, p 12
2. P 9942 ED Mar 1916
3. P 10167 ED Oct 1917
4. P 10585 ED Oct 1919
5. *Appendix to the Report of the Commissioners* Vol.XX Evidence given by Henry Sharp, p 7
6. P 7314 ED Feb 1906
7. P 7592 ED Oct 1907
8. P 7591 ED Apr 1907
9. For more on the *ad eundem* provision see J. V. Luce, *Trinity College Dublin The First 400 Years*, Trinity College Dublin Press, 1972, pp 120–21, and R. B. McDowell and D. A. Webb, *Trinity College Dublin 1592–1952. An Academic History*, CUP, London, 1982, p 352
10. Author's emphasis
11. P 7877 ED Jun 1908
12. P 7877 ED Nov 1908
13. P 8154 ED Feb 1909
14. P 8698 ED Mar 1911 and P 9445 ED Dec 1914
15. P 8698 ED Mar 1911
16. P 9193 ED Feb 1913
17. P 9445 ED Oct 1914
18. P 9709 ED Oct 1915
19. P 9942 ED Apr 1916 and P 10828 ED Feb 1920
20. P 10369 ED Feb 1918
21. P 10585 ED Jul 1919
22. P 10360 ED Feb 1918 and P 11041 ED Mar 1921
23. P 11209 ED Apr 1922
24. P 11209 ED Jun 1922
25. P 7049 ED May 1905
26. *Appendix to the Report of the Commissioners* Vol. XX, pp 36–38
27. P 7877 ED Jul 1908
28. P 10584 ED Jan 1919
29. P 10167 ED Oct 1917
30. *Appendix to the Report of the Commissioners Vol. XX*, p 198

5.   The Demise of the Indian Education Service

The Royal Commission on the Public Services in India 1915

Mention has already been made of the rapid growth of education throughout India in the decade prior to the outbreak of war in 1914 and of the equally rapid development over the same period of Indian demands for greater participation in the government of the country. Both trends generated even greater pressure than before for enhanced participation and equal status of Indians in the various branches of the Civil Service, including education. To meet this demand the Indian government finally established a Royal Commission in December 1912, under the chairman-ship of Sir John Islington, to examine ways of enhancing Indian participation, especially at the senior levels of administration. The Commission took some two and a half years to complete its task, partly due to the outbreak of war in August 1914. The report was finally presented to the Indian government in August 1915 but it was not printed until January 1917.[1] The main educational recommendation — to abolish the distinction between the Indian and provincial education services — was rejected but the subsequent Government of India Act of 1919, which introduced the concept of dyarchy, paved the way for popularly elected Indian provincial governments to take over much of the day-to-day running of the country, including education. As a consequence unified provincial education services replaced the long-standing distinction between 'Indian' and 'provincial' education officials after 1922, and recruitment for the IES formally ceased in 1924.

The majority of witnesses interviewed by the Commission all favoured removing the distinction between the Indian and provincial education services. In their place the Commission recommended a threefold breakdown of staff based not on salary but on the nature of the position and the work done. The three proposed categories were *Administration* which included headmasters, training college principals, and inspectors of schools; *College professors*; and *Special appointments*. Each category would then have been sub-divided into class 1 and class 2 appointments and there would have been no interchange between categories except in exceptional cases. There was strong support for the idea from the Indian National Congress, which passed a resolution in favour of the complete nationalisation of Indian education in 1917, but the reactions of the provincial governments were mixed. Bengal, for example, favoured a single education service but was undecided on the need for, and extent of European influence. Arthur Mayhew,[2] by then DPI in the Central Provinces, adopted a characteristically cautious approach in his response to the Commission's report.

In a specially prepared paper, he claimed that there was almost universal agreement to 'obliterate' all racial distinctions between the Indian and provincial education services in order to make education a more attractive career for Indians and to expand the field of recruitment but the Commission recommended a gradual phasing in of Indians to senior posts. Hence the question really at stake was not any longer whether Indians should be accepted into the IES but how rapidly the senior ranks of educational administration should be Indianised. That was an issue which generated much passionate debate with many people being fearful of rapid and radical change. Mayhew supported the Commission's main recommendation but he also wanted a greater European presence *at all educational levels*[3] to improve the quality of what was offered. He believed that Indian parents still greatly valued European teachers and institutions and he feared for the consequences if they were rapidly displaced. He favoured a single education service in each province and a single pay scale with the most responsible posts going to those qualified by age, experience and ability as in the ICS or the Indian army. Moreover, pay should be incremental and not tied to a particular post, and there should be an efficiency bar. In essence he advocated a common career structure for Europeans and Indians alike, based on open and fair competition. That would help to remove the racial distinctions embedded in the existing educational service structure that gave so much offence to Indians, and also remove a similar offence whereby young and inexperienced European graduates were placed over mature Indians because they belonged to another service. At the same time though, he still supported differential pay for Indians and Europeans because the latter had higher living costs, a fact that was duly recognised by the Public Services Commission. If India was to succeed in recruiting high quality British graduates, recruitment policy would need to be geared to market forces. Mayhew was convinced that Europeans would not serve in India if they were going to be out-of-pocket.

After much deliberation the Indian government retained the two existing educational services but sanctioned a major increase in the number of Indians recruited into the IES. This policy was partly dictated by the exigencies of war. In August 1915 IES recruitment of men was suspended in Britain except for cases of extreme urgency for which it was impossible to make temporary arrangements.[4] Many European education officers serving in India also joined the armed forces. This left the door open for the appointment of many Indians to temporary IES posts, many of which were confirmed after the peace. The immediate postwar years saw even greater numbers of Indians join the IES as education expanded and many former provincial posts were upgraded to IES status. At the same time it also became increasingly difficult to recruit suitable graduates from Britain because of the equally rapid expansion there of schools and universities. The high inflation of the Indian rupee after the war also continued to make serious inroads into the value of IES salaries even after they were increased. In February 1919, 73 people, all recruited in India, were either appointed to, or confirmed in IES positions.[5] The majority were Indians with British degrees. Almost half had Oxbridge degrees and most of the others had British degrees of one sort or another. Several appointees had degrees from Columbia, Harvard, California, Paris and Berlin. Some idea of the rapid growth of the IES can be gauged from the following figures. In 1907 there were 148 IES staff. This number rose to 202 in 1913. By 1920 the number had reached 277 and provincial governments were recommending that a further 112 positions should be transferred to the IES. By then Indians filled almost half the IES appointments.[6]

The rapid rise in IES numbers resulted in a decline in their quality much to the consternation of some government officials. The appointment of Francis R. Tomkinson[7] to the IES as a headmaster in the Punjab was a case in point. Tomkinson was 32 when appointed. He had been educated at Repton and Clare College, Cambridge, but had graduated with only third class honours in history. Thereafter, he taught at several preparatory schools before going to Egypt as secretary, librarian, and house master at the Engineering College in Gizeh. At the time of his IES appointment he was teaching at a school in Cairo. The selection committee admitted that he was by no means brilliant but he impressed them as being in every way a perfect gentleman and an essentially 'safe man'. As one of his referees in Cairo remarked: 'He is not a great scholar but … would be a capable Head Master on whom his employers might always count for honest work'. Unfortunately, the government of the Punjab thought otherwise and suggested that he be placed elsewhere in India. It was claimed that he did not fit the criteria stipulated: he had a third class degree, his teaching experience was gained in Egypt, he had no formal qualification in teaching method or experience from a training college, and he was initially pronounced medically unfit because he had myopia, or short-sightedness. It was also noted that he had no aptitude for games. In reply, the Indian government rejected any bid to transfer him elsewhere 'where his alleged defects might be equally embarrassing'. If he proved unsuitable it was assumed that the Punjab authorities would terminate his contract at the end of the two-year probationary period. The attitude of the Punjab officials was not very charitable but perhaps they felt they were getting the short straw! In the event, Tomlinson went on to serve competently in a variety of posts until his untimely death in 1925, aged 48.

The apparent decline in the academic quality of IES recruits was one of Henry Sharp's primary concerns when he gave evidence to the Public Services Commission in 1914.[8] He gave a detailed breakdown of the academic qualifications held by IES staff in 1907 and 1913 respectively, which showed that the number of Firsts had dropped appreciatively. He also emphasized the fact that the IES was increasingly composed of younger men because many of the older and experienced staff had retired of late because of poor pay and conditions and the inflation of the rupee. Sharp strongly supported the exclusive nature of the IES because he believed that it represented 'the irreducible minimum of the Western element needed to maintain a European education system'. His response to Indian demands for promotion was to suggest reshaping the provincial education services to that end. He also agreed that a bifurcation of administrative and professional roles was urgently needed. Administration had become increasingly complex in recent years and professors were not able to keep up-to-date on all the changes. Likewise, it was no longer possible for an inspector to step into a professional teaching role.

The lowered status of the IES in the years prior to the outbreak of war was also emphasised by De la Fosse when he met the Commission.[9] He claimed that the failure to attract men of high calibre from the United Kingdom was due to reasons beyond the control of the IES. These included the poor rates of pay and inadequate pensions, the nature of the work, and the subordinate position of education in the Indian administrative structure. He also singled out the vernacular language requirement, claiming that many scientists, in particular, were not prepared to spend their valuable time acquiring a capacity to speak a vernacular language for which they had no aptitude or probable use. Given the rapid expansion of schooling in India, he argued forcefully for a large increase in the inspectorate if the quality of education was not to be further eroded. Finally, he forecast a raid increase in female education in future years which would necessitate the recruitment of more European women as principals and inspectresses.

The quality of William Hornell's evidence to the Commission provided ample evidence of why he was appointed DPI in Bengal ahead of Henry James.[10] At the outset he concentrated on the selection process for IES candidates. For three years he had acted as the chairman of the selection committee in London. Contrary to what some critics might say, he contended that the India Office did all it could to ensure that vacant posts were widely circulated. He was especially keen to promote the professional training of IES personnel but was confronted with similar problems to those experienced by the Colonial Office in the 1920s when it, too, attempted to provide training for Colonial Education Service recruits. The number of recruits was never large, men were often needed at short notice, and recruitment was occasional rather than on a regular annual basis. Hornell thought it was high time that the recruitment and preparation of educational staff for India was more clearly thought out and systematised. He suggested that IES candidates might undertake a special preparatory course on Indian languages, history and culture at the proposed Oriental school, later known as the School of Oriental and African Studies, established as part of the University of London after the First World War. He also suggested that the Board of Education might arrange a course on the nature and structure of the various Indian provincial education systems. He even envisaged the Oriental school becoming a centre for the study of educational problems in India.

Hornell also confirmed the widespread feeling of discontent amongst IES officials in Bengal and elsewhere at their deteriorating pay and conditions. He gave a colourful account of life for a young professor or inspector in India. The young professor often taught young students and was part of a giant examining system and a rigidly defined curriculum. The inspector was caught up in a maze of petty administration, and both might still be doing the same job years later because opportunities for promotion were severely limited. Pension provisions were a major reason for low morale in the IES. Like salaries, they compared most unfavourably with those in the ICS. Education staff had to complete 30 years service to receive a full pension whereas the qualifying period in the ICS was 20 years. As A. L. Covernton remarked to the Commission: 'As long as the [IE] Service is felt to mean banishment from Europe for a lifetime, the scholar and research-worker will not be willing to enter it'.[11] Hornell agreed that it must be galling to Indians to be prevented from joining the IES, and he certainly thought that the restriction should be removed from university apppointments, but he observed that most government services in India were divided into imperial and provincial branches, and he saw no sign that this would change in the near future. He was, however, adamant in his belief that the IES was no closed caste open only to Englishmen of social class.

The main problem that he encountered while on the selection committee was the fact that there were *never* enough good people — British or Indian — to satisfy the demand. Moreover, with many new opportunities opening up in Britain for university graduates, there was no longer any need for them to seek an uncertain career in India. He acknowledged that some bright young men went to mission schools and colleges in India but they were fired with idealism and had no wish to work in government institutions. Indeed, many of them shared the view that a government servant was a 'carefully sterilized machine'. Hornell also voiced the view of several other witnesses to the Commission when he said that the word 'professor' had come to be used in a very 'promiscuous' way in India, which had led to confused ideas in Britain about teaching posts in the IES. People immediately conjured up thoughts of eminent academics like Huxley whereas most professors in Indian colleges were akin to tutors or lecturers in British universities.

The Commission's interview with H. F. Heath,[12] the chairman of the IES selection board, which had been created as a standing committee of the Board of Education in 1910, confirmed the declining popularity of the IES. He claimed that contact was regularly made with between 70 and 90 different people, including university staff, school inspectors and leading headmasters, who might know of likely candidates. If this failed then positions were advertised. In recent years it was clear, said Heath, that the IES was no longer a popular career choice. It was rare to attract first class Oxbridge men and even the Scottish and Irish candidates were a mixed bunch. Amidst the many different problems experienced in attracting men to India Heath emphasised that there was always the climate! He told the Commission that many good candidates failed to be selected for medical reasons related to the climate, and that no less than eight well-qualified men had been lost for this reason within the last 15 months. Heath's observations were confirmed by M. C. Seton from the India Office.[13] He claimed that most recruits to the IES appeared to have a genuine interest in Indian education and its progress but recruitment was severely hindered because it was sporadic, whereas it was widely known that the ICS recruited annually.

J. G. Covernton[14] said that he had found that most under-graduates at Oxford and Cambridge had never heard of the IES and those that had rarely knew anything about it. In what some critics might argue was one of the most insightful comments made to the Commission, Covernton claimed that the IES would never be a popular service in India or Burma because the average Englishman had no enthusiasm for education. It was not yet a science, and as an art he found it extremely dull. It dealt mainly with children rather than adults, it did not involve questions of life or death, or justice, and it didn't raise much obvious revenue. There was also the widespread fear amongst Europeans that higher education might well generate political trouble.

Amongst the British governing elite in India there was still a strong belief in the need for an essentially European *corps d'elite* like the IES to oversee the development of education on Western lines and in accordance with Western standards. As Sir James Meston, the Lieutenant-Governor of the United Provinces, argued, a certain number of educational posts should be reserved to constitute 'the indispensable European minimum'.[15] Sir Archdale Earle, by then Lieutenant-Governor in Assam, told the Commission that he favoured allowing Indians into the IES but only if they were of exceptional ability and on the same terms as Europeans.[16]

The Rev. C. F. Andrews, the Cambridge educated but outspoken critic of British rule in India, who was then Principal of St Andrew's College in Delhi and a Fellow of the Punjab University, told the Commission that there was an increasing need to separate the university world from that of the school inspector.[17] University development had now passed the crude initial stage and separate teaching universities were being established together with post-graduate research: 'The whole situation is altered from the earlier days when a teacher's work could be interchanged with inspection work and *vice versa*'. He supported the elimination of the IES, but even more so, the 'Service' concept within the university sphere. University work, he claimed, should constitute a career in itself and no longer be a stepping stone to becoming a DPI. He concluded his interview with the Commission by saying that while in England the previous year he found the IES looked down upon at

Cambridge. He also knew of one possible recruit to the IES who was strongly advised not to join by a very high ranking officer in the Punjab.

One of the most memorable interviews with the Commission was that in which Aftab Ahmad Khan, a Trustee of the Aligarh College in Delhi, challenged the logic underlying the claim made by the Secretary of State that the IES and the provincial education services were equal in status even though pay and conditions differed.[18] Surely, Khan contended, those on higher pay and better conditions must be superior to those on lower pay etc: 'It is nothing but a fiction to hold that men employed on different terms can ever hold the same status, or form one service on sound lines'. If high pay etc were needed to attract good Europeans to the education service surely the same argument applied to attracting the best Indians?

The End of a Proud Tradition

The groundswell of rising discontent amongst both men and women in the IES over their pay and career prospects in the years immediately prior to the First World War was widely acknowledged by provincial governments[19] but this still did not stop petitions being sent to the Indian government in 1913 from IES staff in both Bihar and Orissa and the United Provinces, seeking a basic salary level of up to R 1000 per month.[20] The government stalled claiming that it was waiting for the recommendations of the Public Services Commission but IES staff argued that they had been waiting for several years already for improved service conditions.

In November 1913, in response to the mounting difficulty of recruiting suitable staff, the Bombay provincial government proposed that the vernacular language requirement be left to the discretion of provincial governments to apply.[21] Several cases were cited of professors in the engineering college at Poona who had experienced great difficulties in passing. They saw the requirement as a waste of their time. All their lectures were delivered in English, the students expected the professors to converse in English, and the latter never had any chance to develop their vernacular skills. Moreover, the students at the college spoke a variety of vernacular languages. The Bombay government even suggested waiving the requirement altogether for special posts of a technical nature related to collegiate education although officers engaged in general educational work would still be required to pass the test.

The Indian government rejected the suggestion outright. The view was strongly reiterated that all career officers in India should learn at least one vernacular: 'By no other means will he be able to obtain a knowledge of the ways and thoughts of the people, which, even if his activities are confined to special college classes, it is eminently desirable that he should obtain'. Extensions of time to pass the test would still be allowed but the rule was to remain.

Government officials in   Delhi, were not unsympathetic to   IES demands for higher pay etc, and it was not their fault that the Public Services Commission took so long to deliver its report. Nor could they be blamed entirely for the slow response to a report with far-reaching implications presented in the midst of a major war. Nevertheless, future career prospects for Europeans looked increasingly insecure after 1918.

The Express, an Indian English language newspaper came out strongly in favour of a complete nationalisation of all educational services in India in November 1917: 'There is a strong demand throughout the country for the complete nationalisation of Indian education and a resolution emphatically embodying this view was adopted at the last session of the Indian National Congress'.[22] This was not a view endorsed by the Public Services Commission but a Bengal provincial government committee, set up to review the Commission's report, favoured a single education service and claimed that in the near future the normal staff requirements of the education department could be safely recruited solely in India. The wide variety of views expressed by provincial governments on the future of the educational services in India, and especially the need for, and extent of European influence soon became a highly controversial issue.

Meanwhile, unrest continued to simmer within the ranks of the IES with further memorials being sent to the Secretary of State. The women, in particular, objected to their inferior rates of pay. In August 1920, Miss Dawson and Miss Brander claimed equal pay for equal qualifications with men but their claim was not supported by the provincial government of Bihar and Orissa, which reasserted the Secretary of State's earlier statement about men having higher living costs because they supported families.[23] Miss Chamier and Miss Mahony also sent a memorial of protest along similar lines to London which received some support from the government of the Central Provinces.[24] They argued that most women in the IES were as academically well qualified as the men, and better qualified professionally. They emphasized the point that few women would have been appointed without pedagogical diplomas or prior teaching experience whereas the same rule did not apply to many male appointments. They also pointed out that women were generally older when appointed and maximum salary was only achieved after 20 years service which few, if any, women achieved. Travel and work conditions were claimed to be more arduous for women, they had less support staff, and they experienced constant financial and health worries. The base salary of R 400 per month was said to be totally inadequate for a European women to live on in Calcutta, Jubblepore or Bombay. Indeed, it was inadequate before the war and by 1920 living expenses had increased 100 per cent and were still rising. Pension rules were also a bone of contention; males could retire on half pensions after 20 years service whereas women could retire on only one-third pensions after the same period of service.

Two similar memorials were also sent to London by Lilian Brock and Miss Irons with the support of the Bengal government.[25] They too, criticized the low rates of pay and increments, overseas allowances, the low percentage of senior posts open to women, and the unfavourable pension rates, but the Indian government remained unmoved, claiming that no further revision of salaries was called for as it was finding no difficulty in getting the few female staff needed. Finally, Maud Ebbutt sent a similar memorial to London on behalf of female IES staff in Madras.[26] She placed particular emphasis on the recent increase in living costs, estimated at 64 per cent since 1914 by the Salaries Board in India but more like 150 per cent according to the Board of Trade in the United Kingdom. What many IES staff found especially galling was the fact that the private sector had received salary increases of between 50 and 75 per cent over the same period.

The IES underwent major changes in December 1919, including the creation of a separate Women's Service. Salaries were increased, pay scales were reorganized, the period of service required for full pension rights was reduced from 30 to 25 years, and the Service was divided into three distinct branches comprising administration, collegiate and special. Henceforth, Indians were to occupy approximately 50 per cent of positions and recruitment was no longer to be confined to Britain. All appointments were also to be vetted by provincial governments although the final decision to appoint was still to rest with the Secretary of State.[27] Political events ensured that these changes were relatively short-lived.

The India Act of 1919 was meant to dampen down political unrest but it had the reverse effect. Indian nationalists continued to agitate for still more Indianization of the All-India Civil Services, including the IES, and the Indian government eventually responded with yet another Commission in 1924.[28] Despite the transfer of education to provincial control in 1921, existing IES staff were still answerable to the Indian government which was clearly an anomaly. To correct it, the Commission recommended that recruitment to the IES should cease and that all educational staff should henceforth be recruited by provincial governments. The rights of existing IES staff were to be protected but as they retired or left they were not to be replaced. As a consequence, after 1924 the IES literally faded gradually into history as its numbers were progressively depleted and not replaced.

In retrospect, regardless of the recommendations of the Civil Services Commission, it was the First World War that brought about the ultimate demise of the IES. For all practical purposes the supply of suitable recruits from the United Kingdom simply dried up and thereafter Indians increasingly took their place. The war also served to intensify political changes in India which resulted in the control of education being transferred to popularly elected provincial governments in 1921. A year later the Legislative Council of the Central Provinces passed a motion seeking to abolish the distinction between the IES and the provincial education services but the government of India did not consider it was feasible at the time.[29]

It was Sir Reginald Craddock, a former Lieutenant-Governor in Burma, who expressed the thoughts of many in the IES when he claimed that: 'The Indian Educational Service [had] produced many distinguished men, and [had] played a very valuable part in the educational development of India'[30] but for many European officers the transfer of education to the care of popularly elected provincial governments and the rapid post-war Indianisation of the IES indicated that it was time to depart. One of those who did so, in 1922, was Arthur Mayhew, albeit a lot older and wiser than when he had first set sail for India from Marseilles as a raw recruit back in July 1903. When he left India he was fast approaching his 44th birthday and still had many years of professional life ahead of him. For the next six years he taught classics at Eton before being appointed in 1929 as Joint-Secretary of a revamped and expanded Advisory Committee on Education in the Colonies. Throughout the 1930s his Indian experience contributed to the influential role that he played in developing the Colonial Education Service in Africa, the Caribbean, South-East Asia, and the Pacific. No other British colonial educator bridged the gap between the worlds of Rudyard Kipling and Somerset Maughan quite like Mayhew.

NOTES ON CHAPTER

1. Cd. 8382 *Report of the Commissioners* Vol.1
2. P 10585 ED Aug 1919 pp 1726–1743
3. Author's emphasis
4. P/CONF/5 ED Aug 1915 and P 9709 ED Jun 1915
5. P 10584 ED Feb 1919
6. P 11041 ED Jun 1921
7. P 8434 CO Sep 1910 and 8598 ED Jan 1911
8. Cd. 7908 *Appendix to the Report of the Commissioners Vol. XX Minutes of Evidence relating to the Education Dept.*, pp 5–15
9. *Ibid.*, pp 38–43
10. *Ibid.*, pp 106–116
11. *Ibid.*, p 218
12. *Ibid.*, p 246
13. *Ibid.*, pp 243–245
14. *Ibid.*, pp 215–221
15. *Ibid.*, p 252
16. *Ibid.*, p 262
17. *Ibid.*, pp 46–50
18. *Ibid.*, pp 50–55
19. P 9193 ED Jan 1913
20. P 9196 ED Oct 1913
21. P 9193 ED Feb 1913
22. P 10585 ED Aug 1919
23. P 11041 ED Nov 1920
24. *Ibid.*
25. *Ibid.*
26. *Ibid.*

27.   A useful summary of these changes is included in chap. 2 of the *Eighth
      Quinquennial Review Progress of Education in India 1917–1922*, edited by J. A.
      Richey
28.   Cmd. 2128 *Royal Commission on the Superior Civil Services in India* (1924)
29.   P 11209 ED 1922 Despatch No. 5 Govt. of India to S of S, 29 Jun 1922
30.   *Report of the Royal Commission on Superior Civil Services* [1924] p 133

PART TWO

THE COLONIAL EDUCATION SERVICE

6. The Origins and Nature of the Colonial Education Service

... if there is any class of men and women who have really and without equivocation served disinterestedly the peoples whose affairs we have temporarily administered it is those who have gone out to teach and extend education. They are men and women who have not sought praise. But it is only just that something more should be known of their work and their spirit, by their countrymen and by the new generation in the countries and territories they served.[1]

Recruitment for the IES officially ended in 1924, the same year as the Colonial Office Advisory Committee on Education in British Tropical Africa began its deliberations. This committee, enlarged and renamed in 1929 as the Advisory Committee on Education in the Colonies, ushered in a new dimension to British colonial policy. During the Committee's 37-year history [1924–61] it oversaw the growth and development of education in the Colonial Empire and, like the India Office before it, called on further generations of British university graduates to achieve its task.[2]

Initially, as its name suggests, the Committee was responsible for promoting education in the African colonies, but the Colonial Office conference of 1927 agreed to enlarge the committee's responsibility to include all colonies that sought its help from the start of 1929. This decision gave rise to the need for an increase in the Committee's administrative staff. Initially, there was one secretary, Hanns [later Sir Hanns] Vischer, a former DE in Northern Nigeria. In January 1929, he was reappointed, and joined by Arthur Mayhew, fresh from his experience of teaching classics at Eton. Henceforth, they were referred to as joint secretaries. Vischer assumed responsibility for African matters while Mayhew dealt with the concerns of the non African colonies.

The colonial empire was understood to mean that myriad of crown colonies, protectorates and trusteeship territories that fell within the orbit of the Secretary of State for the Colonies. Most were located in tropical Africa but there were also many others in the West Indies, including British Guiana and British Honduras, South-East Asia, and the Pacific. There was also a multitude of minor territories scattered as far afield as the Mediterranean [Gibraltar, Malta, Cyprus], the Middle East [Palestine, Aden, Somaliland], the Indian Ocean [Mauritius, the Seychelles, the Maldives] the Atlantic Ocean [St Helena, the Falklands], and the China Sea [Hong Kong]. Southern Rhodesia and Ceylon did not fall within the responsibility of the advisory committee. They did not have dominion status like Australia, Canada, New Zealand and South Africa, but they were largely responsible for their own internal affairs, including education.

The 1920s ushered in a new era in the development of Britain's colonial empire. The initial phase of establishing sovereignty and a semblance of law and order belonged for the most part to the late Victorian and Edwardian years but the First World War also resulted in the acquisition of several former German colonies. As a consequence, in the 1920s Britain became responsible for the welfare of some 450 million people embracing almost every race and creed, spread across some fourteen million square miles of territory. It was the largest empire the world had ever known. In hindsight, it appears to have been a relatively straightforward matter acquiring such an empire compared to the far more difficult problem of knowing what to do with it thereafter, and especially how to promote the welfare of its many millions of subject peoples.

Until after the First World War education was almost exclusively a mission preserve. In some instances the Christian missionaries had established themselves and started schools long before they were followed by the British flag and the formal proclamation of British sovereignty. The missions were, however, acutely aware that after 1918, their educational position would be progressively challenged by colonial governments as the popular demand for education grew and civil authority was regularized and progressively extended. The establishment of the Advisory Committee in 1924 was part of a mission strategy to establish a partnership arrangement whereby the missions would be both formally recognised as partners with colonial governments in the promotion of education and also receive financial assistance in the form of grants-in-aid towards both the capital and recurrent costs of running schools.[3] The success of this strategy was evident in the first major statement — *Education Policy in British Tropical Africa* — issued by the Advisory Committee and published as a government White Paper in March 1925.[4] This document incorporated the long-standing English practice of 'voluntaryism', whereby non-governmental bodies were encouraged to establish and operate schools with government financial assistance, as an integral feature of British colonial education policy for the next 40 years.

In the 1920s it was confidently predicted that there would be a rising demand for education throughout the colonies and that this would necessarily become a growing concern for all colonial administrations. As in India in the last century, specialist staff would need to be recruited from Britain to administer and supervise the growth of education, and to teach in key institutions. Hitherto, colonial administrations had employed very few, if any, educational experts. The administration of schooling had been minimal and left largely to civil service personnel. The 1920s marked the beginning of a new phase of government involvement in education in many colonies, in which departments of education were established for the first time. It would be their primary task to supervise the growth of schools run by voluntary agencies and where deemed appropriate, to establish and maintain separate government institutions.

The inter-war years were akin to a pioneering phase and progress was slow — far too slow in the view of many critics of empire, especially in the mid to late 1930s[5] — but funds were severely limited and trained personnel were thin on the ground. The period was also marked by a prolonged economic depression which effectively halted almost all social and economic development in the early to mid 1930s. The Second World War ushered in a new age as the balance of world power changed. In hindsight the inter-war years now seem like the classic age of colonialism in which few people seriously doubted that the British Empire would extend long beyond their lifetimes. After 1945, colonial rule became increasingly difficult to justify and was rapidly superceded by the era of decolonization.[6] What seemed like the often leisurely pace of educational development of the inter-war years was soon replaced by a race against time to provide the necessary skilled manpower to sustain colonies after independence. Increased financial aid was made available from Britain through the Colonial Development and Welfare Acts of 1940 and 1945 respectively, but above all, there was a rapid increase in the recruitment of British university-trained staff — the Colonial Education Service [CES] — to help develop colonial education, especially at the secondary and tertiary levels.

For many years the CES, like its Indian counterpart, was a term used loosely to describe all those who worked in education in a colonial setting. Until 1938 there was no CES as such, and even thereafter, men and women continued to join the education departments of specific colonies rather than some unified global service. After 1938, however, recruitment, and various aspects of the terms and conditions of service were standardized and officers could be transferred or request a transfer from one colony to another. Even so, salaries, pensions and leave entitlements still varied from one territory to another. Broadly speaking, however, the process of recruitment and the conditions of service were similar to those of the former IES.[7]

Prospective education officers had to be of European descent and British subjects. They were also required to have a university honours degree from a British university and a recognized teaching diploma or certificate. The latter could be obtained after selection by attendance at a training course extending over one academic year, held annually at the London Institute of Education from 1927 onwards, for which a monthly allowance of £20 was paid. Candidates had to be between 22 and 35 years of age although a strong preference was given to those under 30. Initially, most recruits were expected to work as teachers in secondary schools or higher grade colleges and teacher training institutions. In contrast to the IES, new appointees were called education officers or superintendents rather than professors. In time, some education officers were promoted to inspectoral duties. The senior ranks of the service were filled by promotion from below. Again, in contrast to the IES, the most senior official was called the DE rather than the Director of Public Instruction, a title which had decidedly Victorian overtones. The DE was generally assisted by a deputy or assistant DE.

All newly appointed education officers underwent a two or three year probationary period during which they had to pass an elementary local language test. Subsequent promotion was also dependent on passing a more advanced language test. All candidates had to pass a medical examination and, as in India, new appointees were not encouraged to marry prior to their first posting. This was partly on account of the relatively low starting salaries paid to junior appointments and the difficulties often experienced initially in finding suitable accommodation for a married man. The need to travel frequently in underdeveloped areas in some territories was another disincentive. Once established in a post, officers were given every encouragement to have their wives and children join them although in most colonies they still required official permission. As in India, the retirement age was set at 55.

Those who sought to make the CES their life career were supplemented by others who went to the colonies on fixed term contracts. One of the earliest and most important achievements of the Advisory Committee in London was to pave the way for short-term contract staff to preserve their superannuation rights in Britain by payments from their colonial salaries. In the inter-war years the CES also included a small number of female appointments. Many of these were filled locally but others were recruited through the Board of Education in London. The number of female appointees grew rapidly after 1945 as the education of girls gathered increasing momentum but getting the right people always proved difficult. As Freda Gwilliam commented, most female teachers preferred to stay and teach in the United Kingdom where standards of work were higher, chances of promotion were clearer, environmental conditions were more congenial, and positions were mostly non-residential.[8]

The CES was never envisaged as an elite service like the IES although its members were expected to perform similar teaching and administrative roles. Nor was there any presumption that the service should be dominated by Oxbridge graduates. They still constituted the single largest group but over a 40 year period [1921–61] there were many recruits who had London, 'red-brick', Scottish and Irish degrees.

In most colonies there were few officials with specific educational expertise immediately prior to and after the First World War. In many instances officers from the civil administration were responsible for inspecting schools and administering grants-in-aid to voluntary agencies. This slowly changed as the Colonial Office and colonial governments adopted a more systematic approach to the development of education. By 1935 education was fast becoming an established aspect of colonial administration although not every governor and/or his colonial secretary necessarily welcomed it because schooling consumed scarce financial and human resources in an age which had yet to appreciate the idea that investment in 'human capital' was a necessary element in economic growth and social change. In many colonies education was still viewed as a 'spending' or 'Cinderella' department and ranked low in the administrative pecking order.[9]

A perusal of the *Colonial Office List* for 1935[10] provides a useful snapshot of the extent to which education departments had been established and the nature of the officials who controlled them. Some 45 territories were listed. Of these only 23 — the Bahamas, Bermuda, British Guiana, Ceylon, Cyprus, Fiji, Gibraltar, the Gold Coast, Hong Kong, Jamaica, Kenya, the Straits Settlements, the Federated Malay States, Malta, Nigeria, Northern Rhodesia, Nyasaland, Palestine, the Seychelles, Tanganyika, Trinidad and Tobago, Uganda and Zanzibar — had formally constituted education departments, and many of these were still very small and rudimentary. Only Ceylon, Fiji, the Gold Coast, Hong Kong, Kenya, the Straits Settlements, the Federated Malay States, Malta, Nigeria, Palestine, Tanganyika and Uganda could be said to have passed the initial stages of development. Some colonies employed a director of education while others relied on an inspector of schools to administer education. Territories where educational administration was absent or still very rudimentary, included the High Commission territories in South Africa, British Guiana, British Honduras, the Falklands, the Windward and Leeward Islands of the West Indies, Mauritius, Northern Rhodesia, Nyasaland, St Helena, the Seychelles, Somaliland, the island territories of the Western Pacific, Zanzibar, North Borneo and Sarawak. By 1935, the majority of directors of education were university graduates but none had undergone any systematic training in education.

Of 17 directors holding university qualifications, 12 had Oxbridge [9 Oxford and 3 Cambridge], and 4 Scottish degrees. Other universities represented included London, Leeds and Cape Town [in two instances directors had degrees from two universities]. The graduate of Cape Town University was John B. Clark, a Rhodes Scholar, who also completed a BA honours degree in classics at Balliol College, Oxford. In 1927 he was appointed Director of European Education in Northern Rhodesia. Major William Gray, the DE in British Guiana was better qualified academically than most. He had a first class honours MA degree and a PhD from Edinburgh University and a BLitt from New College, Oxford. At one time he had also been a Carnegie Research Fellow. He joined the army in 1912 after lecturing at the Technical College in Brighton, and eventually, after holding a variety of senior military appointments, became a major in the Army Educational Corps in 1920. From there he went to British Guiana in 1924 and became DE in 1927. On various occasions he also acted as deputy for both the colonial secretary and the governor. James Cullen

[Cyprus], Gerald Power [Gold Coast], Edward Morris [Kenya], Frederick Morten [Straits Settlements], Eric Hussey [Nigeria], Humphrey Bowman [Palestine], and Albert Isherwood [Tanganyika], were all Oxford graduates, while Cambridge was represented by Alfred Lacey [Nyasaland], Wilfred Farrell [Palestine], and Lachlan Macrae [Ceylon]. Hussey is the subject of an extended biographical essay later in this volume.

Another of the early directors worthy of note was Humphrey Bowman, 'a very pleasant boy-scout kind of man who was an old Etonian and proud of it'.[11] Born in 1879, he also attended New College Oxford, and graduated with second class honours in modern history. He entered the service of the Egyptian Ministry of Education in 1903 but was seconded to the Sudan for two years in 1911. In 1913–14 he was adviser to Egyptian students in the United Kingdom before enlisting in the army at the outbreak of war. He saw service with the British Expeditionary Force in France in 1915–16, and then worked as a staff captain at the headquarters of the Northern Command for two years [1916–18]. He was seconded for a further two years as DE in Mesopotamia [1918–20] before retiring with the rank of major. In 1920 he was again seconded, this time as DE to the government in the newly created British colony of Palestine and remained there until his retirement in 1937. Bowman's successor and long time understudy in Palestine was Wilfred J. Farrell, 'a remarkable man' with an Irish Catholic background, who was a graduate and Fellow of Jesus College, Cambridge.[12] He taught at both Rugby and Haileybury public schools, interspersed with war service, before becoming civilian education officer and later acting DE in Iraq. He went to Palestine as a senior education officer in 1923, became deputy DE in 1929, and succeeded Bowman as Director in 1937.

By way of contrast Joseph Cutteridge MBE had started out in life [1906–8] as a student teacher at the Borough Road Training College in London. He acquired a teacher's certificate with four distinctions and later an advanced teaching certificate from the Board of Education before the war intervened. After military service he was briefly a mathematics and drawing master in Liverpool before becoming Principal of the government teachers' college in Trinidad. Thereafter he served in various administrative positions including senior inspector of schools, before becoming DE in 1934. Frederick Reid [Basutoland], Henry Dumbrell [Bechuanaland and Swaziland], Wilton Albury MBE [Bahamas], Albert Dillon [Trinidad], and Charles Follows [Gibraltar], were all further examples of non-graduates occupying leading educational positions.

Some indication of the academic calibre of the CES in the late 1930s can be gleaned from data on the Malayan Educational Service as supplied in the *Malayan Civil List* of 1939.[13] The Service comprised 102 people, of whom 14 were females. Only six officers were under 30 years of age, a reflection no doubt of the virtual cessation of recruitment in the 1930s. A further 49 officers were aged between 30 and 40 years, while the remaining 47 officers were all aged over 40. There were no women employed under 30 years of age; eight were aged between 30 and 40 years; and the remaining six were over 40.

The school backgrounds of education officers were varied and included English public schools, reputable English grammar schools, and a variety of Scottish academies. The public schools included Shrewsbury, Christ's Hospital, Charterhouse, King Edward V1 [Birmingham], Uppingham, Lancing, Rossall, Fettes, Sedbergh, Whitgift, and Stoneyhurst. There were also graduates from no less than 17 universities, including two from New Zealand and one from Australia. The universities included Oxford [21], Cambridge [12], London [9], Trinity College, Dublin [5], the National University of Ireland [4], Edinburgh [3], St Andrews [3], Wales [3], Bristol [2], Manchester [2], Birmingham [2], Durham [2], Aberdeen [2], Glasgow [1], Adelaide [1], Otago [1] and Auckland [1]. The Oxbridge graduates were drawn from no less than 20 different colleges. Only Queen's College, Cambridge, with four graduates, had more than the standard one or two per college. The teaching qualifications were from equally diverse origins including the London Day Training College, later renamed the London Institute of Education; Moray House Training College, Edinburgh; Homerton College, Cambridge; the Froebel Training College at Bedford; Culham Training College, [Oxford Diocesan]; the Sheffield City Training College; the Episcopal Training College in Edinburgh; Aberdeen Training College; Southlands College, London; St Mark's College, Chelsea; and St John's College, Battersea. As in the IES, many women did not have degrees but most had recognised teaching qualifications of one sort or another.

Recruitment trends in the CES over a 40 year period are illustrated in Table 2. There was steady although fluctuating recruitment into the CES throughout the 1920s but this came to a virtual standstill at the height of the great economic depression of the early 1930s and had only very slowly recovered before the outbreak of war in 1939. The early years of the Second World War again saw recruitment reduced to a trickle but by 1944 the tide of war had turned in favour of the Allies. Thereafter, CES recruitment began to escalate rapidly as educational expansion took on an hitherto unprecedented socio-political importance. In all the colonies, however small or remote, education departments experienced a rapid increase in popular demand for primary schooling. By then also, there was widespread acceptance of the need to promote secondary and tertiary education to provide the skilled manpower needed for political, social and economic development. In the corridors of Whitehall there was also a growing recognition that the continuation of imperial rule was no longer politically acceptable and that independence for the colonies was rapidly becoming only a matter of time. The figures also show that while men still comprised the majority of recruits, there was also a rapid and significant expansion of female appointments after 1945. By the early 1960s the era of decolonization was almost over and the demand for recruits began to wane rapidly. Moreover, in 1961, the work of the

Advisory Committee on Education in the Colonies came to an end when the Colonial Office transferred its responsibility for education to the newly formed Department of Technical Co-operation.

Table 2

Colonial Education Service recruitment 1921 – 1961

Year	Total	Women	Year	Total	Women
1921	43	-	1942	10	5
1922	39	-	1943	19	13
1923	30	-	1944	62	54
1924	43	-	1945	110	52
1925	46	-	1946	197	49
1926	76	-	1947	172	58
1927	64	-	1948	190	69
1928	74	-	1949	236	91
1929	62	-	1950	233	109
1930	65	-	1951	222	99
1931	18	-	1952	258	118
1932	4	-	1953	*	*
1933	1	-	1954	*	*
1934	5	-	1955	*	*
1935	9	-	1956	*	*
1936	9	-	1957	329	119
1937	14	-	1958	300	119
1938	14	-	1959	250	92
1939	22	-	1960	168	72
1940	8	-	1961	168	61
1941	2	-			

* Figures not available.

Compiled from tables included in Anthony Kirk-Greene, *On Crown Service A History of HM Colonial and Overseas Civil Services 1837–1997*, London, I. B. Tauris, 1999, pp 22, 24, 26 & 37.

If the 1890s and early 1900s were the high point in the IES, the period from 1945 through to the early 1960s was a period of similar significance for the CES. By the mid 1950s there were education departments in more than 40 colonial territories and the CES was numbered in the hundreds. There was still a preponderance of Oxbridge graduates in the most senior positions but other English, Scottish and Irish universities were also well represented. A survey of 30 of the most senior colonial education officials serving in 1956,[14] shows that 10 were Oxford, and eight Cambridge graduates. For no apparent reason Oxford graduates were in charge of predominantly African education departments. These included Nigeria [Lagos], Western Nigeria, Tanganyika, Uganda, Zanzibar, Kenya and Nyasaland, together with Malta, Bermuda, and Sarawak. Cambridge graduates ran education departments in more diverse and far-flung locations including Eastern Nigeria, Somaliland, St Vincent, Jamaica, Aden, Singapore, Malaya and Fiji. Officials in charge of other colonial education departments were graduates of Exeter [2], Southampton, Bristol, Nottingham, Edinburgh, Glasgow, St Andrews, Queen's Belfast, University College Bangor, Victoria University Wellington, and Rhodes and Natal universities in South Africa.

Secondary school backgrounds were also diverse in origin but several leading English schools were represented, including Dulwich [2], Bede, King Edward VII, Rugby, Westminster, Haileybury and Manchester Grammar School. By the late 1930s, many senior officers had also undergone some form of professional training, mainly at the London Institute of Education, where the Colonial Department had its origins in the training course established by Sir Percy Nunn for prospective colonial educators in 1927.[15] After 1945 the Colonial Department, later renamed the Department of Education in Developing Countries, grew rapidly and attracted possibly the richest cultural mix of students to be found in any university department in Britain. Moreover, its graduates were to be found in senior educational posts throughout the Colonial Empire and later the Commonwealth of Nations.

Subsequent chapters in this study deal at length with a selection of men and women who exercised key roles in the work of the CES, but in a service which included several hundred members at any given point in time, it is inevitable that the contributions of most will receive either scant mention or go unrecorded. Like their predecessors in India, they have been relatively neglected until now by historians of education. Some 30 years ago, I was privileged to meet and to be greatly assisted in my doctoral study of government education policy in Fiji by Gordon Rodger, the long-serving DE in that remote outpost of empire. A product of Repton and Pembroke College, Cambridge, and a former education officer in the Gold Coast before his move to Fiji in 1955, he played a central role in developing education in Fiji, including the University of the South Pacific, in the 1960s and beyond, before eventually retiring in New Zealand. A highly intelligent man and a model of tact and diplomacy, he firmly believed in the virtues of the traditional English policy of encouraging the creation of voluntary schools assisted by government grants-in-aid, and maintaining amicable relationships with the missions. As a result he was much respected by both Fijians and Indians alike, and by both Australian and New Zealand officials with whom he worked closely.[16] Had he been a member of the IES in India at the turn of the century he would doubtless have been described in the language of that period as in all respects a scholar and a gentleman.

Unfortunately, the same could not be said of Howard Hayden,[17] another DE in Fiji in the years immediately after the Second World War. Hayden, was a graduate of Cambridge who started life as a Shakespearean actor. In 1937 he became a school inspector with the London County Council. In 1943 he was appointed as the first DE in Barbados. In the relatively short time that he spent there he made a major impression, establishing a department of education and introducing new teaching methods and revised school curricula, but in 1945 his wife had a brief affair with a local doctor and the Acting Governor told the Colonial Office that it would be in Hayden's best interests to have him transferred. To be fair to Hayden, the Acting Governor made it clear that the reasons for seeking his transfer were in no way a reflection on his ability as a DE. He was undoubtedly an officer of outstanding mental calibre with exceptional energy and drive but he did rather tend to suffer fools gladly.

Hayden applied for a vacancy in Trinidad but the Governor thought it would be better if he went further afield and he was eventually posted to Fiji. The move was not a promotion and he was never happy there — he really wanted a civil administrative post — and his letters to Colonial Office staff in London were invariably flippant and condescending about the people he worked with. Unbeknown to him, within the Colonial Office he was described privately as 'an able fellow but something of a social snob'. His main failing in Fiji was his inability to get on with the many New Zealand teachers and administrators who had worked there since 1926 as part of a scheme of educational co-operation between the New Zealand and Fiji governments. In private correspondence with Christopher Cox, the Chief Educational Adviser at the Colonial Office, Hayden described the often young and inexperienced teachers as 'raw pups' and added, 'They can all milk cows and it is reported that some of them can read'.

Hayden made few friends while he was in Fiji. The most damning indictment of him came from Freda Gwilliam, the highly esteemed Colonial Office adviser on female education in the colonies. While on tour in the South Pacific, Cox asked her for a candid assessment of Hayden as he was being considered for the director's job in Hong Kong. She described him as intelligent with wide cultural interests and the best bridge player in Fiji, much to the Governor's delight, but she thought he lacked the qualities of humanity, personal selflessness, and deep concern for the indigenous people that were the hallmarks of 'our' best colonial educationalists. She also thought that he was more interested in 'H. H.' and the advancement of his career than in the welfare of Fiji's people. On his attitude towards the New Zealanders, she was especially outspoken: 'He *has* to work with New Zealanders — a nice, bluff, limited but honest bunch. Instead of cherishing them, encouraging them, making allowances for them, he makes them *feel* they are not first class. He thinks of everything in terms of H. H. — his reputation — his comfort — his convenience. Every minute I spent with him and his wife became a greater strain ...'. It should be noted that a third party also informed Cox that

Hayden disliked Freda Gwilliam, so the hostility was mutual. She was also scathing about his plans for promoting education in the Solomon Islands which were linked administratively to Fiji at the time. Hayden had seemingly managed to get offside with both the missions and the colonial administration. As an afterthought, written on the side of an aerogram to Cox, Freda wrote; 'H. H. has ambitions to be Resident Commissioner in the Solomons: that would complete their ruin!' Needless to say, Hayden did not get the posting to Hong Kong.

In private correspondence with Hayden, Cox expressed sympathy for his wish to leave Fiji and hastened to reassure him that although he had recently missed out on a job in Trinidad [1950], there was not the slightest danger of his being forgotten in considering future appointments. Behind this facade of pleasantry, however, there was a genuine concern in London at the way he was running education in Fiji. Several European teaching staff recruited from Britain proved most unsatisfactory and a subsequent inquiry did little to enhance Hayden's reputation. Cox minuted that for all Hayden's brilliance, he and his wife seemed to lack human interest and sympathy so far as the European staff in the Education Department were concerned. Cox also noted that Hayden had little time for New Zealanders and they knew it. Both Dr C. E. Beeby, the DE in New Zealand, and F. R. J. Davies, the Officer for Islands Education and a former Deputy DE in Fiji, told Cox personally that Hayden was not liked by his New Zealand staff, yet as Cox noted, 'we are dependent on New Zealanders who have for so long been the not very supple backbone of our educational staffing there; if it were not for the scheme of co-operation with Fiji we should educationally be in the soup'. In response to a third party comment that Gwilliam's dislike of Hayden was mutual, Cox claimed that wherever Gwilliam went she left encouragement and inspiration behind her: "The same was not unfortunately true of the Haydens'.

After missing out on a job at the new University College of the West Indies in 1950, Hayden eventually got a posting back to the Caribbean in June 1953, as DE in Trinidad but after a year he left to take up an appointment with the United Nations in Korea. Soon after Hayden's departure from Fiji, Max Bay, a New Zealander and a highly respected education officer in Fiji, wrote to Cox and commented on the pleasant atmosphere that now existed among departmental officers: 'We now receive courtesy, and are no longer treated like overgrown schoolchildren'. It was, to say the least, ironic, that after all he had said about New Zealanders, Hayden chose to live in Auckland in retirement in the 1970s.

Another DE who caused major problems for the Colonial Office was Harold Jowitt, who *did the unthinkable*.[18] Not only did he convert to Roman Catholicism in 1942, at a time when relationships between Protestant and Catholic missions were strained throughout the African colonies, but he did so when in charge of education in Uganda, a colony in which education had long been divided into distinct Catholic and non-

Catholic religious fiefdoms. Jowitt's origins are unknown but he was born in 1893, probably in South Africa. He was a graduate of the University College of Southampton, but completed an educational diploma in South Africa. He started his educational career in Natal, first as Headmaster of the Edendale Training College and later [1918] as senior inspector of schools. In December 1924 he moved to Southern Rhodesia as Director of Native Education. He became DE in Uganda in 1934. By then he had established himself as an expert on native teaching methods and school organisation.[19] In the late 1930s he fell foul of Sir Philip Mitchell, the Governor of Uganda, because of disputes over the funding of the missions and especially the payment of grants to the Roman Catholic Church for the payment of teachers' salaries when the teachers, who were predominantly 'religious', performed their duties without payment. The late 1930s was also a period when the colonial government in Uganda began to challenge the mission monopoly of education much to the alarm of Catholics and Protestants alike. Jowitt had a Roman Catholic wife, and it had been known for some time that he had leanings towards the Catholic faith but it was not until Palm Sunday 1942, that he publicly went to mass. His conversion to Catholicism confirmed the worst fears of the leaders of the Protestant missions who called him 'The Dictator of Education' because of widespread allegations that he used the Code of Education Regulations to further Catholic interests. By 1942 his position as DE was fast becoming untenable and he requested a transfer but it was not easy to relocate him during the war and he had to stay on in Uganda until April 1945 when he moved to be DE in Bechuanaland. Later still, he worked at the University College in Roma, Basutoland. Within the Colonial Office there was some sympathy for him in the belief that Mitchell was equally to blame for their falling out in the late 1930s, but his conversion to Catholicism complicated what was at best a very trying time for the Ugandan administration as it sought to change the balance of power in Ugandan schooling.

Occasionally, as with D. S. Tomblings,[20] an illustrious career in the CES came to a sad end. For many years [1926–39] he was Principal of Makerere College in Uganda and a close friend of Christopher Cox. After retirement he was asked to go to Fiji to rejuvinate the Queen Victoria School, established in 1906 to educate the sons of Fijian nobility. The full story behind Tombling's downfall may never be known but in November 1947, he performed an 'African dance' on the beach in the moonlight. One version of the incident suggests that he was ringed by young boys and that he and the boys were all near naked. There is also some suggestion that Tomblings had been drinking. The incident was seemingly watched by a number of male and female pupils, and by the assistant headmaster who got wind that something untoward was happening. Apparently he witnessed the dance from the seclusion of some nearby sandhills and duly reported the incident to F. R. J. Davies, the Acting DE in Suva. When called to account for his actions, Tomblings immediately resigned and within days was on a plane back to his retirement cottage in Uganda.

In a letter which must have been very difficult for him to write, he tried to explain to Cox why he had left Fiji at such short notice. He did not attempt to deny the facts but hastened to assure Cox that his 'lunatic lapse' had not harmed the school in any way and that his resignation was in the School's best interest. He went on to say that after a good deal of 'pressure' [from whom was not stated] he agreed to do an African dance on the beach in the moonlight. He hastened to add that he in no way defended his action: 'It was damn foolish but it was private and personal'. He admitted that he had behaved very badly due, he felt, to 'repression for many years' but he assured Cox that it was now quite definitely past and done with. There was nothing in his actions, he claimed, beyond exhibitionism: 'It had nothing to do with the School ... or boys, and during my whole time in Fiji I never had anything to do with the girls, nor did I on this occasion so much as shake hands with them'. Evidently, the Acting Governor, J. F. Nicoll, was understanding and wrote him a consoling letter, but the incident, which Tomblings tried to dismiss as at most 'a passing impulse', was a terrible blow for a man who had been awarded the CMG for his services to education in Uganda, and a sorry way to end 35 years in the Colonial Service.

Amongst colonial officials in general who served for long periods overseas it was widely recognized that a few of their colleagues sometimes went 'tropo', i.e. they displayed bizarre behaviour, and this is probably the explanation for Tomblings' moonlight dance and the acting governor's sympathetic response. Going 'tropo' often took the form of an alcoholic binge lasting for several days or in more severe cases prolonged symptoms of mental depression. It was often induced by prolonged exposure to a humid tropical climate; geographical isolation and a heightened sense of loneliness brought about by long separations from wife and family; sexual frustration; prolonged personal animosities between European staff who were forced to live in close proximity to each other for long periods; and the constant need to act in public in ways that preserved distinctions based on hierarchy and race. Correspondence between Cox and his senior administrators in the colonies frequently highlighted the great personal strain imposed on education officers by broken marriages, the cost of children's education and their separation from the family for long periods due to the practice of sending them back home to attend British boarding schools, personal animosities amongst European staff, failed promotion applications, and the financial implications of poor pension provisions and compulsory retirement at 55 years of age.

In one celebrated instance a DE was sacked by a colonial governor for his alleged lack of 'drive, confidence and vision'. The case concerned James Cullen,[21] then DE in Uganda. Cullen was a classics graduate of Balliol College, who went to Uganda as DE in 1945 after a spell of no less than 15 years in charge of education in Cyprus. Before that he had taught at Winchester. In the immediate post-war years, in line with the rest of the colonies, major efforts were made to promote the rapid growth of education in Uganda, but Andrew Cohen, the Assistant Under-Secretary of State for the Africa division at the Colonial Office, was highly critical of the slow progress achieved under Cullen's direction. When Cohen was appointed Governor of Uganda in 1952, one of his first acts was to send Cullen into premature retirement.

Cullen's demise appears to have originated when Uganda was visited by the East and Central African Study Group in late 1951, as a prelude to the Cambridge Education Conference of 1952.[22] Freda Gwilliam, a member of the group, was especially critical of Cullen's lack of leadership and told Cox in no uncertain terms: 'I think we [the three person study group] shall all burst soon! The rich material here in Africans and the grim reality of delay, procrastination, negation, lack of drive, lack of plan, lack of initiative and general futility, has worn our courtesy so thin and our discretion so holey, that it is just as well we are leaving Uganda soon .... A clean sweep appears to us to be what the country needs. There is no confidence either in the [Education] Department or in James [Cullen].' She went on say that education policy was preventing African development. Evidently, Cullen was opposed to more English education for Africans on the grounds that it would encourage a move to the townships from the rural areas and the possibility of political unrest: 'that piece of ignorant escapism nearly produced apoplectic fits from [Professor] Fletcher and me'.

Gwilliam was not alone in her criticisms of Cullen. Christopher Bell, subsequently Deputy DE in Uganda, later told Cohen that under Cullen there was no direction or policy in the Department and implied that the internal organisation was completely chaotic. When Frank Ward, Cox's deputy in Whitehall, visited east Africa in October 1951, he was approached by various people in Uganda asking that something be done about Cullen. To be fair to Cullen, Gwilliam did point out that he lived under the verdict of the late governor that education was an 'unproductive service', and a financial secretary, who was similarly critical of education. The latter, clearly the power behind the throne, used the financial committee to discuss all *details*[23] of policy. As a result Cullen was frequently over-ruled. The knowledge that 'Entebbe [could] always queer the pitch' meant that there was little or no confidence in Cullen or his department. Cullen's demise was a difficult matter for Cox to handle because they had known each other since their student days at Oxford and Cox was the godfather of one of Cullen's children. After returning to Britain Cullen taught briefly at Epsom College before becoming senior classics master at Oundle.

Cullen was replaced by Douglas [later Sir Douglas] Miller,[24] a product of Westminster and Merton College, Oxford. After graduating with second class honours, he joined the CES in 1930 as a superintendent of native education in Northern Rhodesia. Over six feet tall and well built, he was said to have cut an imposing figure as he strode through the African bush with his bearers strung out behind him carrying tents, fresh water, and piles of textbooks. He was born in Ontario but his father, an English-born schoolmaster, saw to it that he was educated in England. Miller spent 15 years in Northern Rhodesia before moving to Basutoland in 1945 as one of the youngest DEs in the CES at the time. He was there during the visit of the Education Commission, chaired by Sir Fred Clarke, and played the leading role in reshaping education policy in the light of the Commission's recommendations. In 1948 he moved to Nyasaland as DE, and it was from there that he replaced Cullen in Uganda in 1952. By all accounts he was the man of the moment. In close collaboration with Andrew Cohen, he oversaw a major expansion and improvement in the quality of education, especially at the secondary level, and a significant increase in the colony's teacher-training capacity. He was fortunate in having Cohen's backing and also access to substantial government financial reserves which had been accumulated to offset any major collapse in cotton or coffee prices, the main sources of Uganda's income.

Miller spent six successful years in Uganda before moving to Kenya as DE in the lead up to independence. He was persuaded to move by the Governor of Kenya, Sir Evelyn Baring, who had known him when they both served in Basutoland after the war. In 1959, Miller became Permanent Secretary in the newly created Ministry of Education, and a year later acted as temporary Minister for Education before retiring in 1961. Thereafter he became secretary of the King George Jubilee Trust [1961–71] and also industrial adviser to the Duke of Edinburgh's Award Scheme. He was awarded the OBE in 1948, the CBE in 1956, and knighted [KCVO] in 1972. He had a reputation for being slightly aloof and a stubborn taskmaster but he also had acute political judgement and an irreverent sense of humour. He died in 1996, aged 89.

Some indication of the importance attached to the Ugandan situation in Whitehall can be gauged from the fact that Miller was also given a new assistant DE to help him in his task. That role went to Christopher Bell, who had been the DE in Somaliland since 1943. Born in Brighton, the son of an Anglican cleric, he was educated at Winchester and Brasenose College, Oxford, where he studied history. He also completed a post graduate teachers' certificate course at the London Institute before joining the CES in 1935 and serving in Kenya until the outbreak of war. In conversation with the author[25] he recalled being interviewed for the CES by Major Furse — one of about 100 applicants for the post. Furse was impressed by the fact that Bell was a cricket player of well above average ability and a good all-rounder. He spent much of his military service in Dar-es-Salaam putting his knowledge of Italian to good use in censorship work before he became DE in Somaliland under the British Military Administration after the Italians were driven out in 1943, and later civilian director in 1946. To quote him, he 'effectively restarted education in the war torn territory'. Shortly before Uganda became independent in 1962, Bell returned to England where he became involved in local politics and textbook publishing.

Dr H. W. Howes[26] was perhaps the least conventional of all the directors that Cox recommended for appointment. He started out in life as a teacher with the London County Council and then studied for his doctorate in anthropology under Professor Malinowski at the London School of Economics in the 1930s, before becoming the principal of a technical school and a college of art. In 1944, at the age of 47, Howes was appointed as DE in Gibraltar, although Cox claimed that he was 'not the type of man nor the age that we had in mind'. It was wartime and there was an acute shortage of suitable applicants and Howes made a short list of four. The best applicant then withdrew, another 'proved impossible', while the other was a woman who would have been totally unacceptable in Gibraltar. Cox described Howes as a rather 'Pickwickian looking man with horn-rimmed spectacles, certainly to look at neither an inspiring leader nor a man of the world'. Nevertheless, he appeared to be 'a quietly cheerful and confident, alert, friendly person, with whom you would have no danger of friction or rows'. He was also a Roman Catholic 'but not a fanatical one'! What Cox didn't say was that Howes was scruffy in appearance, loquacious, spoke Spanish and was well acquainted with Spain, which was just as well as he faced a tough assignment in Gibraltar.[27]

Traditionally, the Roman Catholic Church had run schools for the almost exclusively Catholic population in the colony but the quality of schooling was poor and most of the teaching force were Irish priests and nuns whose loyalty to the British Crown was suspect during the Second World War. In 1940 the worsening war situation in Europe forced the government to evacuate all the children from Gibraltar. In their absence the government was anxious to wrest control of education from the exclusive control of the Roman Catholic Church without precipitating a major political crisis. The success of the ensuing negotiations owed much to Howes' handling of a very delicate and potentially explosive situation. Cox described him as 'a funny little man' but he was impressed with Howes' knowledge of his job, his enthusiasm and energy, and thought he had done well in the circumstances. He was, however, quite unlike any other director that Cox dealt with during his 30 years as Educational Adviser.

During his time in Gibraltar and also on a later assignment as DE in British Honduras [Belize], Howes regularly bombarded Cox with long letters describing in intimate detail what he was doing and how successful he thought he was. Such behaviour was unusual and not always appreciated by Colonial Office staff. In 1959, Howes went to British Honduras to sort out denominational rivalry or, as Harold Houghton, Cox Deputy, somewhat facetiously termed it, 'to tackle the affairs of British Honduras'. Again Howes was successful in getting Catholics and non-Catholics to co-operate in the provision of schooling. In one of many letters to Cox he spoke of the 'religious peace which now reigns in the educational field, and of the new spirit of co-operation between the denominations'. It had, he claimed, been 'a slow, planned and carefully developed task, as I realised that one false step and the whole apple-cart would be upset'. He was now working, he said, to get the denominations separately and collectively to become real partners with the government in education — 'The secret is that I enabled them to claim full credit for the [my] bright idea'.

Howes' lack of modesty in a service where understatement was an integral part of the administrative culture made some senior officials in Whitehall want 'to throw up'. In 1960 he wrote an article in *The Catholic Herald* extolling both the virtues of British policy in steering colonies to independence and the work of the Catholic missions in colonial education. Cox sent a copy of the article to Sir Hilton Poynton, the Permanent Under-Secretary of State, with the added comment — 'The irrepressible Dr Howes has asked me to let you see the enclosed which need only detain you for a moment'. Poynton scribbled a cryptic reply — 'Yes I remember him well'. When Howes left Gibraltar in 1949 to become the first permanent DE in Ceylon after independence, Cox and his colleagues in Whitehall were quite taken aback. Clearly, they knew nothing of his application and were amazed that he got the job. Later still, he served as Unesco Adviser on Education to the Caribbean Commission.

At the risk of being accused of hagiography, there is widespread evidence in Colonial Office records to suggest that most of those who achieved the highest positions in the CES were men of considerable ability. There was no better example of this than the small group of men who worked with Cox in Whitehall as assistant educational advisers in the late 1940s and early 1950s, when virtually all the colonies were drawing up and implementing development plans for education. The group included T. R. Rowell, a former Principal of Northcote Teachers College in Hong Kong, who joined Cox in 1941; L. McD. Robison, a former DE in Ceylon, who returned to London in 1943; R. A. McL. Davidson, who later became DE in Nigeria; T. H. Baldwin, a former deputy DE in Nigeria, who read original Greek texts for relaxation; R. S. Foster, formerly DE in Kenya; R. J. Harvey, a former DE in Zanzibar, and Harold Houghton, who served as DE in Jamaica before returning to London to work as Cox's deputy after Frank Ward retired in 1956. J. R. Bunting, a former Chief Federal Adviser on Education in Nigeria, described Houghton as 'the most professional of the Advisers, sound, shrewd, approachable and intolerant of humbug'.[28]

Sir Herbert S. Scott,[29] another former DE, who became a most valued member of Cox's wartime staff, also deserves special mention. He was born in London in 1873 and educated at St Paul's School, Eton, where he was a King's Scholar for five years, and Hertford College, Oxford, from where he graduated with honours in classics in 1984. He and Humphrey Bowman [DE Palestine] are the only two old Etonions known to have served in the CES. After graduation Scott chose to pursue a career in teaching.

In 1990 he was appointed to the staff of the Borough Road Training College but two years later he left to join the Transvaal

Education Department as acting principal of the newly created Normal School. Before leaving England he completed a teaching certificate course at the London Day Training Centre. In the Transvaal he became a district headmaster and inspector. Spending much time up-country he taught himself Africaans and gained much practical knowledge of the territory. In 1913 he was made Secretary for Education, a post which made him virtually second in command.

During the First World War he volunteered for active service but was employed in munitions in the United Kingdom and eventually held a senior post in the financial department at the Board of Trade. After the war he returned to the Transvaal and spent much time and effort laying down lines of procedure, revising regulations, and consolidating and rewriting subject syllabuses. Almost single-handedly he also compiled a digest of various education laws. In 1924 he overcame strong opposition from Dutch nationalists to succeed Dr Adamson as DE. At the time his name was mentioned by J. H. Oldham as a possible candidate for the post of secretary to the proposed Colonial Office Advisory Committee on Education in British Tropical Africa.[30] In 1928, after 26 years of service, he reached pensionable age. He was then appointed DE in Kenya, a post he occupied until his return to England in 1935. In Kenya he sponsored a new education act and was awarded the CMG for his work when he retired.

He settled in Woking, near London, and joined the Advisory Committee on Education in the Colonies. In the late 1930s he soon acquired a reputation as an academic expert on British education policy in the colonies and wrote the chapter on education in Lord Hailey's *African Survey*.[31] He also made important contributions to *The Year Book of Education* published annually by the London Institute of Education in partnership with Evans Bros. His article in the 1937 edition called 'Educational Policy in the British Colonial Empire' was the first of its kind. This was followed in 1938 by an article on the education of the African in relation to western contact. A year later Scott prepared a section in the Year Book on language problems in colonial education, including an article by himself on the general study of the problem. Finally, in the 1940 edition, he was responsible for a section on educational policy and problems in the African colonies. During the war years he edited the *Colonial Review*, a digest of articles on colonial matters produced by the Colonial Department of the London Institute of Education, and also worked for the Ministry of Information. He was knighted in 1948 and died four years later.

Christopher Cox wrote an appreciation of his work for *The Times*[32] in which he emphasized the varied ways in which Scott had contributed, especially behind-the-scenes, to the advance of colonial education since his return from Kenya. Cox thought his work on committees and his private counsel were of especial significance: 'Acute, clear-headed, wise, liberal, thorough, he drew on a lifetime of experience with a racy relevance and a total absence of egotism, and many times it was he, though he would not dream of admitting it, who piloted the ship to port'.

Sir Richard [Olaf] Winstedt,[33] was yet another illustrious member of the CES who spent much of his career in Malaya, where he became a leading scholar of the Malayan language. Born in 1878 and educated at Magdalen College School and New College, Oxford, he joined the Malayan Civil Service as a cadet in 1902. Thereafter he held a variety of offices in the civil administration before being appointed DE in the Straits Settlements and the Federated Malay States [1924–31]. He also served as President of Raffles College [1921–31]. In 1935 he was knighted and retired to England where he became a member of the Advisory Committee on Education in the Colonies [1936–39] and Reader in Malay at the University of London [1937–47]. He also became a member of the Governing Council and a Fellow of SOAS, and wrote extensively on the Malay language and Malay history before his death in 1966.

The education of women and girls had made minimal progress when war broke out in 1939, consequently there were no women in what might be termed senior administrative or teaching positions in the CES. The education of females, especially in Africa, was addressed in detail by a sub-committee of the Education Advisory Committee in the early 1940s.[34] As a result several female education officers were appointed in 1943–44 in Tanganyika, Nigeria, Zanzibar, Uganda and Trinidad respectively, with the prospect of more to follow, but recruitment of well qualified ex-patriate women proved to be a perennial problem for a variety of reasons not the least of which was the ever present 'Damocletian sword of marriage'.[35] There is also evidence to suggest that some male members of the CES found female ex-patriate staff a mixed blessing.

Muriel Pelham-Johnson, a leading female figure in the CES in the immediate postwar years, was a case in point. Born in 1903 and educated at the Royal School for Officers' Daughters in Bath, she qualified with a first class teaching diploma in domestic subjects and became a superintendent of female education in Tanganyika in 1939. Ten years later she was appointed Assistant DE [girls and women], a position she retained until her retirement in 1958. During her time in Tanganyika she acquired a redoubtable reputation as a staunch advocate of female education but the constant struggle to recruit suitable ex-patriate staff was at times a demoralising experience as she confessed to Freda Gwilliam in a letter written in the mid 1950s.[36] She admitted to being 'utterly depressed' by the whole business of female education and feared that all she had fought for during the past 17 years was disintegrating. She sighted the attitude of the DE [Randall Ellison] as a major contributing factor. She described his attitude to women as 'courteous and sympathetic but hardly inspiring. He makes no bones of the fact that he considers women totally unfit to be Provincial Education Officers – though they can be useful as assistants!' She also claimed that Ellison did not consider her 'capable' of discussing policy. Gwilliam sympathized with her, saying that it was the same story in every territory. In her efforts to recruit female staff Gwilliam claimed that most women preferred to stay and teach in the United Kingdom where standards of work were higher, chances of promotion were clearer, environmental conditions were more congenial, and most teaching appointments were non-residential. It was, she claimed, the ordinary group of form mistresses that it was so difficult to get and hold. Moreover, once attracted to join the CES, 'each one has to be of such proven calibre before being accepted as the equivalent of an *ordinary* man in positions of responsibility'.[37]

Ellison was not the only DE, however, to have mixed feelings about Miss Pelham-Johnson. Shortly before she retired she was considered for an advisory mission to the Solomon Islands but W. W. Lewis-Jones, formerly the DE in Fiji, who had recently replaced Ellison as DE in Tanganyika, advised strongly against her appointment. In a private letter to Cox, he readily admitted that she had done good work in her early days in the territory but it seemed to him that she had been allowed to 'build an empire' in girls' education. He expressed grave concern at the poor quality of female education in Tanganyika despite the 'very considerable' sums of money being spent on it. He went on to say that on the surface she seemed very popular but many female staff had become tired of her set up and approach. He also claimed that her administrative ability was very poor – 'In view of her many years of service I have tried to let her serve this last year without making major changes and without hurting her but it has not been easy ...'[38] Cox thanked him for his frankness. Needless to say Miss Pelham-Johnson was not asked to undertake the advisory mission. She was, however, still destined to go to the Solomon Islands on a two year appointment in charge of women's education.

There were undoubtedly many very able women who served in the CES, especially after 1945, but they often served on short term contracts or left when they married and there is often little biographical information about them in official records readily available to researchers. Theirs is clearly a story yet to be written. Miriam Janisch, Assistant DE in Kenya in the early 1950s, is typical of such women. Another was Mrs L. M. Moody, who was prominent in Jamaican education in the early 1940s. Not only was she a member of the Schools Commission which controlled education in the territory but she also served on the committee, chaired by Professor L. L. Kandel, which reported on the future of secondary education in 1943.

The career of Lady [Dr] Constance Alexander, although perhaps not typical of most female CES officers, nevertheless provides evidence of what might prove a rich vein of historical research. She was the Chief Woman Education Officer in Northern Nigeria in the period 1948–1952. She had an MSc degree from the University of New Zealand and originally trained as a teacher at the London Day Training College in 1927–1928. Thereafter, she taught in India eventually becoming Principal of the Lahore College for Women. She returned to the United Kingdom in 1948, the year in which she completed her PhD at Cambridge, and then went to Northern Nigeria. From 1952 to 1957 she was Assistant Director of Women's Education, later becoming Reader and Professor of Education at the University College of Ibadan.[39] In 1959 she married Norman Alexander, the Professor of Physics at University College, Ibadan, who later became Vice-Chancellor of Ahmadu Bello University. He was knighted in 1966.

Another woman of note in the CES was Mrs E. D. Mather who spent 20 years in mission and government education service in Nigeria. Educated at the Birkenhead secondary girls' school and Liverpool University, she went to Nigeria as an assistant mistress in 1937. Later she became, in turn, the Principal of the Government Women's Training College, Enugu, and Queen's College, Enugu. In both instances she literally created both institutions and set both the tone and standards they subsequently displayed.[40] She retired in 1957.

Gladys Plummer BA, DipEd, had the distinction of being the first woman in the CES to act as the head of an education department when the DE in Nigeria was absent from the territory for several months in 1947.[41] Born in 1891, Miss Plummer was educated at the County Secondary School in Streatham, University College, London, and the London Day Training College. She went to Nigeria as an education officer in 1931. In 1945 she was appointed as the first Assistant DE [Women and Girls] 'an outward and visible sign of the Education Department's concern with women's education'.[42] She was later awarded the OBE for her services to female education.

Dr Anne McMath, was another to receive the same decoration for her services to female education in Africa. Born in Scotland in 1900 and educated at the Morgan Academy in Dundee and St. Andrew's University, she went out to teach in Sierra Leone in 1937 later moving to Nigeria in 1945 to become a senior Women's Education Officer.[43] Ema Clarke was another female member of the CES to serve in west Africa. She qualified as a domestic science teacher in the 1920s and subsequently took up a position as a lecturer in the government teachers' training college in Trinidad. In 1939 she became the organising instructress for domestic science in Uganda. After the war she became a senior education officer and Assistant DE in the Gold Coast.[44]

This brief mention of female members of the CES would not be complete without reference to Helen M. Neatby, who was Assistant DE in Uganda in the 1940s. She was educated at the King Edward VI High School in Birmingham, and Girton College, Cambridge, where she graduated with second class honours in history and a Cambridge Teacher's Certificate. Later in life she was a member of the Association of Headmistresses and completed a Diploma in Theology at the University of London. Details of her early teaching career are unknown but she seemingly went direct from the United Kingdom to take up a newly created position as an Assistant DE in Uganda in 1944.[45] She contributed 10 years' 'energetic' service before her retirement in 1954.[46] Finally, another female officer of the CES to serve in Uganda was Agnes

B. Robertson MA. Born in 1901, she was a graduate of Edinburgh University and also held a general teaching certificate issued by the Scottish Education department. In 1934 she became an inspector of schools in Uganda. Ten years later she was an education officer in Zanzibar but moved back to Uganda after two years and was appointed as a Provincial Education Officer in 1948. She was the author of a variety of arithmetic books designed for use in primary schools in Uganda.[47]

The 1960s marked the beginning of the end for the CES as colonial rule rapidly became a fast-fading memory. When Rodger was asked why he had stayed so long as DE in Fiji, he replied that by the late 1960s there were few places left where one could go. Most CES officers eventually returned to Britain to retire or to take up further employment in education in the United Kingdom. They left behind perhaps the most enduring legacy of colonial rule. Western education led to the social, economic and political transformation of what was commonly referred to as the developing countries in the post independence era, and continues to shape their hopes and aspirations in the so-called global village of the 21st century.

This introduction to the CES, with its emphasis on the varied assortment of men and women who served in it, provides the context for the eight detailed biographical essays which follow. The first two focus on the two joint-secretaries of the Advisory Committee on Education in the Colonies: Sir Hanns Vischer, the first DE in Northern Nigeria, and Arthur Mayhew, who has already featured in this study. The third essay relates the life and work of Eric Hussey, the archetypal DE of the pioneering period between the two world wars. After serving initially in the Sudan, he went on to establish an education department in Uganda and was the first overall DE in Nigeria.

Christopher Cox, the subject of the fourth essay, was the Education Adviser to the Colonial Office and its successors for 30 years [1940–70]. He was undoubtedly one of the most influential civil servants of his generation although he preferred to work behind-the-scenes and rarely spoke in public. During his long tenure in Whitehall he was at the centre of most colonial education intitiatives and played an especially critical role in the development of colonial universities.[48] He also exercised a key influence on the career paths of numerous CES personnel, and senior appointments. He travelled around the colonies constantly acquiring a vast fund of on-the-spot information and corresponded regularly with all his senior officers regardless of where they were serving. In Britain, he knew everyone that mattered, especially in university circles, and was much respected by his senior colleagues in other government departments in Whitehall.

Cox's deputy was Frank Ward, the subject of the fifth essay. One of the original staff to accompany The Rev. A. G. Fraser to West Africa to establish Achimota College in the Gold Coast in the mid 1920s, he went on to become a leading historian of Africa and the first DE in Mauritius before taking up his Whitehall appointment in 1945. Thereafter, he played a leading role in recruiting for the CES, representing British interests at various United Nations conferences, editing *Oversea Education*, the journal initially established by Mayhew in 1929, and being a trusted adviser on policy matters and administration in colonial education in general. Freda Gwilliam, the 'Woman Education Adviser', appointed in 1947, was Cox's indomitable offsider and the subject of the sixth essay. Like Cox, she repeatedly travelled the empire in the cause of female education, while in Britain she worked tirelessly to recruit women education officers for the colonies. Perhaps more so than any other woman of her generation she epitomized the struggle to overcome the deep-seated prejudice against the education of women and girls which characterized the cultures of so many colonies. She was never a member of the CES — her early career was spent as a teacher and later as the principal of a training college in Brighton — but few civil servants exerted more influence on the careers of so many CES female officers.

Professor Margaret Read, another woman who also never served as a member of the CES, is the subject of the seventh essay. A social anthropologist who conducted fieldwork in both India and East Africa in the inter-war years, she was destined to become head of the Colonial Department at the London Institute of Education during and after the Second World War. A close confidant of Cox, she played a significant role in reshaping British colonial education policy in the mid 1940s, especially in the areas of mass education or what was later called community development. As head of the Colonial Department she exerted a decisive influence in shaping the nature and content of the professional training received by CES officers in the post-war years.

The career of William Dodd, the subject of the eighth and final essay, straddled the colonial era of the 1950s and early 60s and the post independence era. After war service in India and a brief period teaching in Ipswich, he joined the CES and went out to Tanganyika in 1952. At the time of independence he was a senior official there in the Ministry of Education. He returned to Britain in 1965, and after lecturing for several years at the London Institute of Education, joined the Ministry of Overseas Development, later renamed the Overseas Development Administration, as an Educational Adviser. By then Britain had few colonies left but the distribution of educational aid to developing countries in the form of finance for capital projects or the provision of human expertise on a short term contractual basis for activities like teacher training, curriculum reform and educational planning, had become a major governmental concern. In the late 1970s Dodd became Chief Educational Adviser and subsequently Under Secretary at the ODA before retiring in 1983. He is the only one of the eight people chosen for detailed study who is still alive today. Despite the passing of the years he still leads a very active life in his home town of Sevenoaks and continues to be an active member of the MCC and an avid follower of the fortunes of Kent and English cricket.

NOTES ON CHAPTER

1. H. L. Elvin, Foreword to W. E. F. Ward, *Educating Young Nations,* London, Allen & Unwin, 1959
2. For a brief history of the Advisory Committee see the author's article 'The Advisory Committee on Education in the [British] Colonies 1924–1961', *Paedagogica Historica* [New Series]. XXVII/3 (1991) pp 385–421
3. For the background to the establishment of the Advisory Committee see the author's article 'Education Policy in British Tropical Africa: the 1925 White Paper in Retrospect', *History of Education,* X/3 (1981) pp 195–203
4. *Education Policy in British Tropical Africa,* Cmd.2374 (London, 1925)
5. For a study on the critics of empire in the inter-war years see Penelope Hethrington, *British Paternalism and Africa 1920–40,* London, Frank Cass, 1978
6. For a comprehensive study of decolonisation see John Darwin, *Britain and Decolonisation The Retreat from Empire in the Post-War World,* London, Macmillan, 1988
7. *His Majesty's Colonial Service Information Regarding The Colonial Education Service,* Colonial Service Recruitment No.5, Colonial Office, Jun 1939
8. Freda Gwilliam to Miss Pelham-Johnson, 30 Oct 1955, Sir Christopher Cox Papers, CO 1045/356, PRO Kew
9. Informal discussions with W. E. F. Ward, 1987
10. *Dominions Office and Colonial Office List,* 1935
11. Interview with S. J. Hogben (Deputy DE, Palestine, 1936–1946), Eastbourne 1971. Mss Brit. Emp. S. 389, Rhodes House Library, Oxford
12. *Ibid.*
13. *The Malayan Civil List 1939,* Singapore, Government Printing Office, 1939
14. See biographical information contained in *The Colonial Office List 1957,* HMSO, 1957
15. For details of the origins of the training course see the author's paper 'Not Wanted on the Voyage' A study of the Colonial Department, ULIE 1927–1956, DICE Occasional Papers No. 11, March 1988, Department of International and Comparative Education, Institute of Education, University of London
16. For a detailed account of Rodger's work in Fiji see the author's *Education in Fiji Policy, Problems and Progress in Primary and Secondary Education, 1939–1973,* Canberra, The Australian National University, 1981
17. Material relating to Hayden quoted here is derived from various files of correspondence in the Sir Christopher Cox Papers located at the PRO Kew
18. Author's emphasis. Material on Jowitt is derived mainly from the Ugandan correspondence files in the archives of the Conference of British Missionary Societies 1912–1970, and Colonial Office files [CO 536] on Uganda located in the PRO at Kew
19. See H. Jowitt, *The Principles of Education for African Teachers in Training* (1932) and *Suggested Methods for the African School* (1934), both published in London by Longmans Green and Co
20. Information derived from correspondence in the Sir Christopher Cox Papers and an interview with F. R. J. Davies in Auckland, 1973
21. Material derived from correspondence in the Sir Christopher Cox Papers
22. See *Report of the East and Central Africa Study group in African Education A study of educational policy and practice in British Tropical Africa,* Oxford, The Nuffield Foundation and the Colonial Office, 1953
23. Gwilliam's emphasis
24. See *The Times* obituary and photograph 19 Jul 1996
25. Nov 1997

26. Material on Howes derived from correspondence in the Christopher Cox Papers

27. For greater detail on the reorganisation of education in Gibraltar during the Second World War see the author's article 'Education in Far Away Places: Evidence from the Periphery of Empire of the Problems of Developing Schooling in British Colonies', *Education Research and Perspectives*, Special edition on Comparative Education, 16/1 (1989) esp. pp 61–67

28. J. R. Bunting (Aide Memoire) Mss Afrs. 1755(41) Box XI, Rhodes House Library, Oxford

29. Material derived from various sources including A. K. Bot, *The Development of Education in the Transvaal 1836–1951*, Pretoria, Govt. Printer, 1951, pp 97–99, and Colin Hickey, 'Fine Clean Healthy Looking Lads!' Elementary Education and Imperialism: the diffusion of athleticism into training colleges in empire. A paper presented at the combined History of Education Society/Australia New Zealand History of Education Society conference, Swansea, Dec 2002, pp 30–31.

30. See Chap. 7 [Vischer] p 16

31. I am indebted to Professor John W. Cell for this information

32. 21 Mar 1952

33. Who Was Who, VI p 1219

34. *Report of a Sub-Committee on the Education and Welfare of Women and Girls in Africa*, Colonial Office, Feb 1943. Colonial No, 1169

35. The phrase was used in a Statement on Recruitment to the CES compiled by E. R. Edmunds and presented to the ACEC at its meeting in Mar 1951.

36. Miss Pelham-Johnson to Freda Gwilliam 7 Oct 1955. Cox Papers, PRO. CO 1045/356

37. Freda Gwilliam to Miss Pelham-Johnson 30 Oct 1955. Cox Papers, PRO. CO 1045/356

38. Lewis-Jones to Cox 18 Sep 1958. Cox Papers, PRO CO 1045/1493

39. Mss African 1755(33) box viii, Rhodes House Library, Library.

40. Education Department, Eastern Region, Nigeria, *Annual Report 1957*, p 3

41. Nigerian Education Department, *Annual Report 1944/45*, p 1

42. *Ibid.*

43. *The Colonial Office List 1950*, p 550

44. *Ibid.* p 467

45. *Ibid.* p 563

46. Uganda Protectorate, *Annual Report of the Education Department 1953*, p 29

47. *The Colonial Office List 1950*, p 583

48. It is perhaps a measure of Cox's ability to influence events from behind the scenes that he was hardly mentioned in a recent study of the founding of the first universities in West and East Africa. See Apollas O. Nwauwa, *Imperialism, Academe and Nationalism*, Frank Cass, 1997.

7.   Sir Hanns Vischer

Champion of African Cultures: a portrait of an adviser on colonial education[1]

Sonia F. G. Parkinson

Hanns was unique. So was his contribution to the modern colonial story.'[2] Sir Ralph Furse wrote this in 1961, 16 years after Sir Hanns Vischer's death, and it is a judgement that should be considered seriously, coming as it did from the man who was responsible for the development of the whole pattern of recruitment to the British Colonial Service between 1918 and 1948, during which time he must have interviewed and assessed a generation of applicants. Furse met Vischer, then DE for Northern Nigeria, when he came to Furse in London in 1912 to arrange for the recruitment of his first batch of Education Officers. Furse liked Vischer's clarity, he knew the task he had set himself and the sort of men he wanted as assistants to give effect to his educational plans. Furse sympathised with the priority Vischer gave to character ahead of academic qualifications. He also discerned 'a deep but reserved and discriminating love for the African'[3] in his new acquaintance. Their friendship developed in London after Vischer's appointment in 1923 as member and Secretary of the newly-created Advisory Committee on Native Education in British Tropical Africa, a post he held until 1929. Then, when the Committee's brief was widened to Education in the Colonies, Vischer remained as a Joint-Secretary with the newly-appointed Arthur Mayhew until they both retired in December 1939.

Hanns Vischer was never a permanent Colonial Office official but during 15 years as Secretary of the Advisory Committee he was uniquely placed to influence educational matters. He brought to the Colonial Office an extraordinary background being Swiss by birth, European in outlook, and British by naturalisation. Add that he had been a lay missionary with the Church Missionary Society from 1900 to 1902 serving in Northern Nigeria before becoming a Political Officer there and subsequently DE, and clearly in 1923 Vischer could bring several perspectives to his work on the Advisory Committee. That alone would

have made him unique, but Furse was referring to his personality as much
as to his career.

Hanns Vischer was a complex man, well-read, multi-lingual,
cosmopolitan, naturally urbane and convivial, but only those as perceptive
as Furse realised that there was a private core which no one except
Vischer's wife, Isabelle, was privileged to know. 'You might think yourself
verging on intimacy and then, with perfect courtesy, he would swiftly
withdraw into some private *seigneurie* of his own where you could not
follow.'[4] With this reticence went a modesty which made him generous in
giving credit to others, a trait which Lord Lugard termed his self-negation.
Typical of that modesty is that one looks in vain for a picture of the
author among the forty-odd illustrations in the book[5] Vischer published
in 1910 about his dangerous journey across the Sahara from Tripoli to
Bornu, despite the fact that the *Illustrated London News* published his
portrait that year as one of 'The Great Explorers of the Moment'
alongside others such as Shackleton and Amundsen.[6]

Besides the courage of the explorer, Vischer possessed both
a strong aesthetic streak and a deep historical sense. These qualities
surface in his private papers rather than in official reports, however much
they influenced the latter, and there is a good example in his private
account of his journey to Vienna, Warsaw, Prague and Budapest in the
spring of 1919 as a Major in British Intelligence on a military mission.
New countries were emerging from the wreck of the Austro-Hungarian
Empire, and the invitation he had received on this occasion was from the
wife of a Minister in Vienna representing one of these.

> We are received by a flunkey who has seen better days and
> shown into a magnificent chamber. There are old Flemish
> pictures on the walls and some furniture — Louis XVI — about
> and a lovely Louis XVI stove. There is also a Maple pink plush
> settee and three armchairs. Behind the settee there are some
> cheap photographs of scenes from Schiller's 'Glocke' and on the
> settee sits a jolly fair Viennese lady, the Minister's wife. The
> queer furniture is the lady's home within a home. There is also a
> Paraguayan Consul here who has long lived in Vienna and
> represents the proper Diplomatic background or entourage.
> A white-whiskered Englishman with a red face, the Reuter
> correspondent of before the war, is also here. After half an hour
> of banal conversation, during which you could hear the tears of
> the glorious old room drip on the unpolished floor, the Minister
> rushes in ....[7]

Vischer could not only evoke an atmosphere with words, he was a good
amateur water colourist and a competent draughtsman whose sketches
illustrated not only his travel book but also the Hausa textbooks produced
in Northern Nigeria before 1914 and the English reader for the Sudan
published much later in 1932.[8] He was, moreover, an inveterate doodler

during committee meetings, sometimes in the margin of official papers now in the Public Record Office which offer unexpected light relief to the researcher. At committee meetings Furse 'always tried to sit next to him to get a sight of the lightning sketches and caricatures he made of our colleagues'.[9]

However, this acute and perceptive observer possessed *gravitas*, for he was a man indelibly stamped with the beliefs and standards he had absorbed from childhood in Basle. Hanns grew up in an evangelical household, among a family in which religious, commercial and academic interests mingled. The Vischers trace their ancestry to the Hans Vischer who was born in Bavaria at Lechausen in 1486 and died at Augsburg in 1546, where the family's name appears in the records of the local guilds. His son moved to Colmar where the family established itself as merchants and landholders and were granted their coat of arms in 1593 by the Emperor Charles V. However, the religious wars of the seventeenth century forced the Protestant Vischers to move to 'the relatively stable Protestant town of Basle'.[10] Here Matheus Vischer III worked hard to re-establish the family's fortunes, and from the time that he was elected Warden of his Guild and also asked to assist in making the inventory of the collection of books which had once belonged to Erasmus, he set the pattern of that mixture of religion, commerce and civic duty which thereafter linked the family's history with that of Basle.

In the nineteenth century, academic interests and connections with England were added to Hanns' heritage. His paternal grandfather, Wilhelm Vischer, was Professor of Classical Greek at Basle University to which he supported the appointment of Nietzsche. The latter became particularly friendly with Wilhelm's second son, Adolf, later to become Hanns' father. Wilhelm also founded an Antiquarian Society in Basle which he organised for some 30 years, but he combined academic interests with civic duties by becoming a member of the Basle Parliament.

Hanns (1876–1945) was the fifth of the eight children born to Adolf Eberhard Vischer and Rosalie Sarasin. Three of the children died young, but the other five (three boys and two girls) remained close all their lives, despite Hanns and Marcus both opting to become British citizens. Their father, Adolf, was a highly successful silk merchant specialising in silk ribbons. Between 1860 and 1864 he was in China studying the silk trade and establishing business connections, which was as enterprising an episode as it was dangerous. There he encountered 'Chinese' Gordon, later to go down in history as 'Gordon of Khartoum', and developed an admiration for Gordon with whose evangelical Christianity he was in accord. Adolf had links with evangelicals in England. He was something of an Anglophile, admiring the English public school system, and Hanns was to spend a year at St Lawrence's College, Ramsgate, improving his English, before entering Emmanuel College, Cambridge, in 1896 to read Modern Languages. One of his younger brothers, Marcus, followed him to Emmanuel in 1897 to read theology. In about 1890, the strengths of his religious beliefs led Adolf

Vischer to give up business and devote himself and the family's fortune to charitable work. This plan entailed considerable financial sacrifices (including the sale of the splendid family house designed by his architect brother, Edouard, that Adolf had had built on the Gartenstrasse in Basle), but was supported by all the family.[11] Brought up in such an environment, it is hardly surprising that his three surviving sons became respectively, a missionary, a clergyman, and a doctor, and their sisters both married clergymen.

Through his mother, Rosalie Sarasin, Hanns was linked to another family prominent in Basle. The Sarasins' history in part parallels that of the Vischers. The family is descended from Jacques, Comte Sarasin, who was living in Pont-à-Morisson in Lorraine in 1477. His Protestant descendants arrived in Basle by way of Colmar in 1628. Hanns' maternal grandfather, Felix Sarasin (1797–1862), built one of the first cotton mills in Switzerland after studying the industry in England. A man of enterprise, he became Burgomaster of Basle. Rosalie's brothers, Fritz and Paul were naturalists. They worked as far afield as Ceylon, the Celebes and New Caledonia, and their friend, Professor Leopold Rutimeyer, encouraged the young Hanns to take an interest in ethnology. These influences helped to turn the boy's eyes to horizons beyond Europe, but Hanns' father had written *A Child's History of Basle,* and Hanns had a profound historical sense, knowledge of his family's past, and a feeling for 'roots' which undoubtedly pre-disposed him to support the theory of adaptation in colonial education. For him, to have become *dépaysé* would have blighted his existence, for although he became a British national in 1903 and served Britain whole-heartedly in peace and war, his British nationality only came about because by 1903 he thought he could better serve Africa in the British Colonial Service than as a member of the Church Missionary Society. Until his death in 1945 he remained throughout 'a true and eminent son of his native land'.[12]

This position was reinforced by his marriage in 1911 to Isabelle de Tscharner, daughter of a distinguished Bernese house. Their four sons were always to be aware of their Swiss blood and dual heritage, reinforced by many contacts with their relatives. Years later, the two younger sons met fleetingly in an orchard near Caen. It was June 1944: both were participating in the Normandy invasion, one serving in the Parachute Regiment and the other with the Royal Artillery, and they greeted each other in Schwytzerdeutsch. That must have appealed to both their father's sense of humour and his traditionalism, for he had taken the motto of the Swiss mercenaries, *Honneur et Fidélité*, for himself and his sons, feeling it peculiarly appropriate to one in his position.[13]

Africa began to assert its attraction on the young Swiss quite early. His sons believe the attraction pre-dated his coming to England in 1895. He went to Tripoli in his last long vacation from Emmanuel College, Cambridge, in order to study Hausa, and from then on Africa exerted a major influence on his life. After graduation, he continued his studies at Ridley Hall. He did not present a conventional picture of a Church

Missionary Society candidate. He had arrived at Cambridge 'shy and lonely, with not too good a command of English', but on the river met a second-year student, Evelyn Howell, who already had his First Boat Colours and had been in the crew which won the Thames Cup at Henley that year. Hanns had been only 13 years old when granted a licence to row a Weidlig[14] on the Rhine at Basle, and Howell saw his potential and took him into his crew for the College Senior Trials. Vischer subsequently rowed in the 2nd May Boat. Through the Boat Club he found his niche at Emmanuel, as Howell remembered years later:

> With a little encouragement he rapidly expanded and became one of the most popular men in the College .... In 1900 we sent a crew to Henley. I was First Boat Captain and being in my 5th year was not eligible to row for the Ladies Plate. So I stood down and Swissy to his great delight took my place and got his First Boat Colours. I forget what the crew did at Henley, but I shall always remember 'Swissy' without any clothes on at all, taking a leading part in a water fight which ranged up and down the staircase of the house that we occupied.[15]

Vischer was at Ridley Hall at the time, studying Divinity and proving unorthodox even there. His principal 'good work' was to organise meals for itinerant Italian musicians, including the organ grinders to be found in Cambridge. He called it his Macaroni Club, and the enjoyment with which he ran it added a touch of light-hearted revelry to the meals.[16] If love of his fellow-men expressed in action is the hall-mark of one category of Christians, Vischer was stamped with it.

Howell had recognised — and later wrote — that Vischer, 'had great courage, gaiety and charm and was always ready for a rag. But with it all he was a sincere and devout Christian and lived up to his principles'. Howell, however, had been privileged to see beneath the surface. Richardson, one of the five men who formed the pioneering advance party for the Church Missionary Society's Hausaland Mission, had also done so, and wrote from the ship taking the group out to West Africa in 1899:

> By the way, with regard to Vischer — We hope nothing will hinder his coming out speedily. I mention this because he may not be appreciated at his right value. As an Undergrad., I think, he in no way identified himself with Christian work at the Varsity, and being full of energy and mirth earned the character of a 'rotter' (If I may use an expressive term.) But Miller and I have no doubt at all about his worth.[17]

Vischer certainly prepared himself seriously for his role as a lay missionary, continuing his Biblical studies with his father and taking a medical course at a hospital in Switzerland before sailing in November

1900. Yet he remained a missionary for only two years serving for most of the time at Loko. The troubled story of how relations between the Northern Nigerian Administration and the missionary societies developed has been dealt with at length elsewhere and is not relevant to this study. Dr Walter Miller, who was Vischer's immediate superior, found the young Swiss complex, extremely clever, with no limit to his resourcefulness and initiative, 'a most loveable fellow and a true friend', but he saw Vischer as an ideas man producing possibly worthwhile schemes, such as a farming project, but not methodical enough to be put in charge of their development.

> He is a dear, true, whole-hearted fellow whose faith and simple trust are most inspiring; but he needs some gentle handling for he is inclined to be very independent and on any suggestion of limitations speaks of working independent of the Society. I think I have talked him out of this, but if he grips an idea it is very hard to get him off it.[18]

Stationed at Loko on the Benue river on the southern edge of Nassarawa, Vischer saw the opportunities as immense and was as keen as Miller to press forward into the Moslem north. He believed that the Hausa needed agricultural, medical and educational aid and began to think that a Christian might accomplish more in Africa if not labelled a missionary. He experienced the loneliness and all the dangers inseparable from pioneer service in a country which had been declared a Protectorate only in 1900, and which was going to take Sir Frederick Lugard three years to subdue. With a total disregard for self, Vischer forbade his colleague, The Rev. G. P. Bargery, to tell their Superintendent of his recurring bouts of fever, of which Miller had been unaware when criticising him for being unmethodical. On one occasion Vischer was discovered by a pagan African chief alone on the bank of the Benue river, seriously ill with malaria and dysentery. The African considered whether to let this unwanted intruder die, but fortunately decided to give him shelter and aid. Vischer had the gift of making friends and when they parted the chief insisted on presenting him with a carved ceremonial spoon which the family still has. Capt U. F. Ruxton came upon the sick man by accident and nursed him back to health. Ruxton was then the Resident at Ibi and later became Lieutenant Governor of the Southern Provinces, Nigeria. It was the start of a life-long friendship. Ruxton talked to Vischer about the possibility of his entering the Colonial Service and when Vischer was subsequently sent home on six months' sick leave in January 1902, the seed was ready to germinate. Before returning home the young Swiss obtained an interview with the High Commissioner and asked how he could qualify for the British Colonial Service to serve under Sir Frederick Lugard in Northern Nigeria. Vischer was still in Switzerland when his father and young brother died within a week of each other in June 1902 and so he postponed his return to be with his mother. His resignation from the CMS 'in these very altered circumstances' occurred in the following December when he notified the Society that, 'In order that I might be able to keep in touch with the country where I feel that lies the work of my life I have applied for a post of Resident in Northern Nigeria'.[19]

The change was not an easy option. Lugard had told Vischer that he could apply to join the British Colonial Service once he had become a British national, obtained the Royal Geographical Society's surveying diploma, learned the Hausa language and acquired a working knowledge of Maliki Muslim law. It says much for Vischer's quality and perseverance that, to Lugard's surprise, he had achieved all these conditions by 1903, displaying a methodical approach that gainsays Miller's judgement of him. He was accepted into the Service and posted in September of that year as Assistant Resident, Northern Nigeria, joining Lugard's little band of some forty-odd officers.[20] There followed five years of service, mostly in Bornu Province under W. P. Hewby, during which Vischer 'lived down the objections to employing him which his name at first excited'.[21]

He was happy with his choice, writing to his brother, 'Ich figuriere in keinem Missionsblatte mehr als Missionar und finde dabei noch tausendmal mehr Gelegenheit, die richtige Missionsarbeit zu thun'.[22] Three years later he confirmed his view: 'Ich bin vollständig überzeugt, dass das grösste Hindernis für Mission in kirchlichen Formen liegt. Wie oft wird Kirche und nicht Evangelium gepredigt! Um in Afrika vollständig einzudringen muss das Evangelium rein von allem Europäischen gepredigt werden.'[23]

Conditions were still unsettled and within six months of his appointment Vischer was attached as the political officer to a military expedition sent to make safe the trade routes which converged on Wase in Muri Province after the murder of six traders by restive pagans and the disappearance of a government messenger. The operations lasted a month during which two skirmishes occurred. Vischer saved the life of one of the African soldiers by sucking the poison from his arrow wound, a feat which was subsequently noted in the Annual Report.

Above all, he was fascinated by the peoples among whom he was living. He wanted to understand them and that required knowledge of their languages, their social structures, laws and traditions, knowledge which in fact the Administration encouraged its political officers to acquire. So Vischer added Kanuri to his languages and produced a Kanuri grammar for others' use. He also obtained permission in 1905 to return from his leave in Europe by following the old trade route across the Sahara from Tripoli south to Bornu. 'Now that the new routes down to the west coast and so to Europe have been opened, it is not likely that the old trans Saharan trade will ever regain its former proportions', he explained in the book he published four years later, which earned him the Back Grant of the Royal Geographical Society: 'but the spiritual influence which has given the Hausa his religion, his art and culture will still continue to penetrate from the north. By planning a journey over the desert, by the monument of the people's early history, through tribes who had contributed towards the formation of the present day Kanuri, I hoped to better understand those people among whom my life-work lay.'[24] It took months for him to gain permission for his journey from the Turkish authorities and to gather and provision a caravan of those prepared to undertake the dangerous venture alongside one Christian European. He was in almost as much danger from the enmity between the black freed slaves and the Arabs of the caravan in the early stages of the expedition as from attacks by the Touaregs and Tubbus later. Yet he collected information about the Senussi sect, the Turkish settlements, the condition of the oases, together with geological data and ancient artefacts and made many sketches.

Vischer's book about the journey is filled with the characters who became his good friends along the road, the men and women of his caravan, the Arabs, Berbers, Tuaregs and Tubbus whose salt he ate, and the Turkish and French officers he met. Something of the impact his personality had on them can be gleaned from his stay at Murzuk, the southernmost Turkish outpost in the Fezzan where he spent over a month preparing for the second and most severe stage of the journey. Everyone of note visited him, first the Turkish governor and other officials, then the wealthy Arab traders. Turks, Arabs and Fezzanis called every morning. 'There was scarcely a house to which I was not asked, and none that did not send someone to see me.'[25] On the morning he left he was astounded for, 'Scarcely a month before I had arrived, a stranger, not knowing a soul, and here was half the town around me praying for a good journey', — Moslem prayers for a man they knew to be Christian.[26]

Vischer arrived back at Lake Chad together with his freed slaves in December 1906, but as he had been due back months earlier some in authority were more annoyed than impressed. That did not stop the irrepressible Vischer from trying, though without success, to obtain permission from Lugard's successor to tackle the route from the opposite direction in company with Hubert Huddleston, then commanding the Mounted Infantry in Bornu.[27]

Vischer's career took another abrupt turn in 1908 when, through no desire of his, he was seconded from the political service to devise and put into effect the start of educational work by the Administration in the Moslem Emirates, from which missionary societies were now almost excluded. Yet this change did have some connection with that earlier trans-Saharan adventure.

His selection came about against his own wishes as he initially doubted his own capabilities for the work. In 1907 the Governor, Sir Percy Girouard, set out his own view of the necessity for the Administration to offer education in the Emirates from which it was excluding the voluntary agencies. He made certain outline proposals and asked for comments from his Residents. W. P. Hewby, Resident for Bornu, replied not only suggesting starting with a government school in Kano but recommending Vischer as the man to run it. Hewby supported his case by reference to a report on the Turkish Industrial School at Tripoli written by Vischer while there making preparations for his journey across the Sahara. So a report that was incidental to Vischer's preoccupations at the time of writing had a major impact on his career. Hewby also enclosed brief notes by Vischer in reply to Sir Percy Girouard's suggestions. These amounted to a diffident proposal for an Industrial school adapted to local handicrafts which would produce local craftsmen but introduce European improvements in their traditional methods. On the question of possible government encouragement of Moslem schools Vischer was not sanguine. He recognised the 'great work of civilisation done by the teaching of Islam in Africa'[28] but doubted whether capable mallams would collaborate with the Administration or teach the idea of a free labour market enthusiastically. The moral justification for Lugard's conquest of the Northern Emirates which had probably appealed to this ex-missionary in 1902 was the need to abolish the slave trade within the Protectorate and then ultimately domestic slavery. No one who reads in Vischer's book his description of the bones of child slaves polished by the blown sand and lining the approach to a Saharan oasis, can doubt the depths of his compassion and revulsion, but this wry understatement was typical of the man.

Also typical of the man was that, having been appointed, he devoted himself to the task with what Majorie Perham later termed his 'enthusiastic idealism'.[29] The details of his work at Nassarawa near Kano and the gradual extension of the system to other Emirates is not the concern of this study,[30] but in view of Vischer's later position as Secretary to the Advisory Committee, the principles which he formulated and acted on are important. He began by visiting Egypt, the Sudan, the Gold Coast and Southern Nigeria to study their education systems, and found most to approve in the work being done under James Currie in the Sudan. Later, Sir James was to be a fellow-member of the Advisory Committee and one who always sought recognition of the strength and value of Islam in Africa. Vischer was by nature and personal experience pre-disposed to respect the cultures of other peoples. His initial report showed some awareness of a requirement to balance the needs of the Hausa and those of the Administration, but put the former first. Education should 'Develop the national and racial characteristics of the natives on such lines that will enable them to use their own moral and physical forces to the best advantage. Widen their mental horizon without destroying their respect for race and parentage.'[31] The emphasis was on preservation at that crucial time of initial culture clash but there was a greater vision behind it than some critics have allowed. Vischer was always aware that he was working in a changing environment and he stressed the fluidity of his plans since 'the best way of filling in the details must be indicated by the natives themselves'.[32]

In September 1909 Vischer began his work with a teacher training class for mallams so that the first indigenous teachers for his planned elementary school should be men respected for their Koranic learning.

Moreover, Isabelle Vischer, writing from Kano in 1912 about her husband's work, declared:

> La surveillance et la direction du blanc sont encore indispensables à l'heure qu'il est. C'est à lui qu'incombe le travail de discernement et de l'adaptation .... Le jour reviendra où les écoles n'auront plus besoin d'être dirigées par le Blanc. Avec la bénédiction d'Allah, la génération future verra l'oeuvre continuée par le corps enseignant purement indigène, qu'aura formé une université nigérienne.[33]

This was not a visionary's picture of a future so remote as to be dateless. By the end of his missionary service, Vischer had already decided that the European colonies in Africa had only some 80 years ahead of them and he was therefore opposed from 1902 onwards to further European settlement in tropical Africa.[34] His concern that the ultimate objective of education had to be defined as well as its aims and goals is also illustrated by his reaction to his American experiences.

Immediately on his appointment as Secretary of the Advisory Committee in 1923 he was sent, largely at Oldham's instigation, to America to get first hand knowledge of what was being accomplished at Hamilton and Tuskegee for the education of black Americans. As guest of honour at a luncheon, he listened to the conversation about what was being achieved and then turned to his hosts and asked what was the ultimate end they had in view for the black American. His shock that they apparently did not comprehend what he meant was recalled by his wife in conversation with the writer years afterwards. This may well have been the same luncheon at which Vischer himself spoke on the need to develop an educational system in the interests of the Africans themselves 'and not, as has so often been done, for our own sake'.[35] If there is some truth in Kenneth King's and Udo Bude's assessments that the function of education was seen as an improvement in the material situation of the black American in order to prevent his political activation,[36] Vischer's approach may well have struck some of his hosts as more idealistic than practical. Interestingly, in view of the influence American ideas are held to have had on British colonial educational debates in the 1920s and 1930s, the writer has found no comments about Hampton or Tuskegee in Vischer's personal papers.

Although Vischer always rejected the description of educationist, he was a better one than he would ever acknowledge. In 1933 when Joint-Secretary with Arthur Mayhew of the enlarged Advisory Committee, Vischer wrote to his uncle, Fritz Sarasin:

> Was die Afrikaner anbelangt reifen die Kolonien dort als solche ihrem Ende entgegen. Die heutige Wirtschaftlage hat den Prozess beschleunigt. Was die nächste Entwicklung sein wird ist kaum vorauszusagen, aber mehr und mehr beginnen die Leute

ihre eignen Wunsche und Hoffnungen zu formulieren und auszusprechen. Im Erziehungswesen ist das besonders bemerkenswert und ich begrüsse es sehr. Erstens wissen sie ja viel besser als wir, was sie lernen können und wollen, und zweitens zeigt dies, dass unsere Versuche, mit unseren Schulen die Leute zum Selbstvertrauen und zur Selbständigkeit zu erziehen, nicht ganz verfehlt haben.[37]

To widen the horizons of one's pupils minds, to try to develop their intelligence and moral character and then stand back and let them make their own choices may stem from a benevolent paternalism, but is certainly a far cry from cultural imperialism. One could almost say that to some degree a process of assimilation was taking place in reverse in the years 1910–14 at Kano, for Vischer was known to the Hausa as Dan Hausa (Son of Hausa), probably the most complimentary nickname they ever bestowed on a European. It was a recognition not only of his linguistic skill but also of his empathy with the Hausa people, their traditions and culture. He and Isabelle made their home in a large, rambling mud-brick house in Kano, made available by the Emir, and lived surrounded by examples of local arts and crafts. Vischer who was himself a competent carpenter as well as an artist, valued the local crafts and hoped to reach out to the Hausa artisan class through his technical class at Nassarawa. His home was still known as Gidan dan Hausa in 1962 and when Arthur Foss was then visiting Kano and confessed to having known Hanns Vischer, he was immediately taken to view the outside of the house, 'my stock having risen considerably as a result'.[38] When Hanns' youngest son, Peter, joined the Colonial Service after the Second World War, he was recognised as Dan Hausa's son by the way he walked, and when his daughter, Annabel, visited Zaria in 1975 she was addressed as 'Jinkanya Dan Hausa' (grand-daughter of Dan Hausa) by locals in the market. The memory of, and respect for, Vischer were still alive.

Unfortunately the outbreak of war in 1914 cut short his work in Nigeria and he never returned to build on the educational foundations he had laid. The planned teachers' training college was postponed and with 'the directing influence' gone and 'a staff which dwindled year by year, all that could be done was to keep the torch, so difficult to kindle, just flickering'.[39] From 1915 to 1919 Vischer served his adopted country in Military Intelligence using his linguistic skills in various parts of Europe. Promotion was rapid, from Staff Lieutenant in November 1915 to Captain and General Staff Officer the next year, and then to Commands and Staff, Special Appointments Major in May 1917.[40] He was then attached to the British Embassy in Bern but he was in charge of the military work of the Secret Intelligence Service throughout Switzerland, and 'official archive material reveals that secret reporting from the Swiss stations during that period was impressively comprehensive. Indeed, Sir Claude Dansey, who became deputy head of MI6 during the Second World War and was a man who did not use words lightly, described

Vischer as a very brave man.'[41] He emerged from the war with the CBE (Military Division), as a Chevalier of the French Legion of Honour and of the Spanish, Belgian and Italian Orders of the Crown, and also as an Officer of the French Order of the Black Star of Benin. His linguistic and diplomatic skills had taken him to the opening of the Polish Diet and to talks with Masaryk, the President of newly-created Czechoslovakia. Sometimes Isabelle was able to join him, as she did when he served in Madrid and Bern. When in 1919 he was informed that the Nigerian Administration required his return, his immediate reaction was that he would resign if the Army would keep him. He was 43 years old and wanted time with his wife and to see his boys growing up.[42] In the event the decision was made for him, for his health had been adversely affected by his experiences and he failed his medical to return to West Africa. His appointment was therefore terminated on 22 December 1919 in a letter conveying the Secretary of State's 'warm appreciation of the very valuable work performed by you in Nigeria .... The loss of your services as DE in the Northern Provinces is, he feels, a misfortune for Nigeria.'[43]

In 1920 the Vischers bought Charlwood Park near Horley in Surrey which had a small farm. Soon, however, Hanns suffered serious financial losses from European investments and appears to have spent a brief period attached to the British Embassy in Vienna. He was looking for some sort of employment in Britain when he was approached about the Secretaryship of the Advisory Committee on Native Education in the British Tropical African Dependencies which was being set up in London. The impetus for this development came from the mission societies and was directed by J. H. Oldham, Secretary of the International Missionary Council since 1910. Oldham was deeply concerned to protect the mission societies' role as voluntary education agencies in a post-war Empire in which he anticipated colonial governments would be taking a greater interest in the provision of education than hitherto. He was also hoping to widen the societies' vision and improve the standards of their educational work. An Advisory Committee was usually regarded as an unnecessary complication by the permanent civil servants of the department to which it was attached. The Colonial Office staff seem to have simply watched Oldham's initiatives as he successfully lobbied the Parliamentary Under-Secretary of State for the Colonies, W. G. A. Ormsby-Gore, by-passed the Imperial Education Conference, and won not only the support of the Education Committee of the Conference of British Missionary Societies but also that of the colonial Governors attending a London conference in June 1923.

Oldham's indefatigable if somewhat tortuous course has been charted in some detail.[44] He ran into difficulties over the appointment of the Secretary to the Advisory Committee. He would have liked Dr Jesse Jones, the chairman of the Phelps-Stokes Commission which had recently reported on education in West, South and parts of Equatorial Africa, but Ormsby-Gore pointed out that this idea was not feasible because Jones was an American citizen.[45] Oldham then supported an approach to

Dr Loram of South Africa, but no acceptable financial arrangements for his appointment were agreed. Time was running out, for the Phelps-Stokes Trust was sending out another commission under Jones early in 1924, this time to report on education in East Africa. The Americans had agreed to include the British dependencies in their survey but only if the Secretary of the Advisory Committee was appointed in time to accompany them. While Oldham was considering H. S. Scott of the Transvaal as a possible appointee, he had a discussion at the Colonial Office at which the permanent officials took the positive step of putting forward Vischer's name.[46] That he was their suggestion for the post is important for the Secretary would work from an office provided by the Colonial Office and in effect liaise between the permanent officials and the new advisers.

Why was Vischer the Office's nominee? They told Oldham 'that he is a man whom everyone likes and that he got on well with other people in Nigeria'.[47] It is clear he had made a favourable impression at the Office during his years in Northern Nigeria, particularly on Charles Strachey. The latter had gone so far in 1910 as to minute on the outlines of Vischer's education plans that he would like some appreciative remarks to be made about Mr. Vischer. 'He is a rather remarkable young man. It was he, you may remember, who got leave to go to his post across the desert via Tripoli, with a caravan of traders, and did so after many adventures. He is a great linguist and full of ideas.'[48] Then in November 1914 the Colonial Office received Lugard's draft Education Ordinance which he intended to apply to both Northern and Southern Nigeria, amalgamated in 1912 under him as Governor-General. Surprise was expressed that Lugard had not consulted Vischer, and ultimately Baynes, Harding, Strachey and Fiddes all came out in favour of excluding the Northern Provinces in order to protect 'the scheme of native education on native lines which Mr Vischer has been working out in Northern Nigeria since 1909, and which, though not at present fully developed, is certainly the most promising new departure in West Africa'.[49] Possibly some of Vischer's support from the Office had been reinforced by the long-running, strong differences of opinion between certain permanent officials and Lugard, which Margery Perham's biography of the latter first disclosed. However, Vischer's stock stood high. In 1917 the Under-Secretary of State for the Colonies told the House of Commons, 'If honourable members look to the system of education like that of Northern Nigeria, they will find one of the most remarkable developments that has ever taken place under British rule. An attempt has been made there, where you have a black population, to get inside the native mind and to develop their own system of local education .... There is an extraordinarily interesting development taking place in Northern Nigeria.'[50] Given that Vischer was available, once Oldham's plans were at a standstill and the Office became involved constructively, his name was bound to occur to the officials.

Vischer was unknown to Oldham who immediately made enquiries about him. The responses led him to believe that Vischer had left the CMS for financial reasons but that he was 'in thorough sympathy with missionary work. This is a necessary qualification if we are to bring about effective co-operation between government and missions in Education.'[51] Oldham was therefore suffering a basic misconception before meeting Vischer. After the meeting Oldham reported to Jesse Jones that Vischer, 'is keen, open-minded, has the right spirit and I should imagine gets on well with people — that is his record. He probably has a good deal to learn about education. Much depends on how far he will go in that respect.'[52] It was an extraordinary judgement in the circumstances and suggests Oldham had not penetrated Vischer's reticence. One suspects that Vischer's view that, 'Nobody knows exactly what education is and because nobody knows what it is nearly every fool thinks he knows all about it', would have finished him with Oldham at this time, but its expression was reserved for one of his circular letters to his sons at school.[53] As it was, Oldham recommended appointment of Vischer to the fellow members of the Committee who were his correspondents simply because there was no time to pursue the appointment of Scott.

At this stage, Lugard raised objections to Vischer's appointment which Oldham managed to overcome. Vischer was totally surprised by Lugard's reaction. He had actually just written to his former chief asking for advice about possible employment in Britain.[54] Lugard may well have resented Vischer being consulted by the Office over the Education Ordinance, resentment strengthened by the final decision taken. Moreover, while Vischer was serving in Madrid in 1916, he responded to a copy of Lugard's Memorandum on Education by a letter to the Under-Secretary of State which, despite a most careful preface and the tactful assumption that he and the Governor-General shared 'the same educational ideal', opposed changes that Vischer felt were being proposed 'under pressure of the very urgent need for clerks and minor officials required by the Administration of the country'.[55] He also condemned Lugard's suggestion of Moral Education in schools based on the ideas of the Moral Education League, for 'in a Mohammedan country no other form of teaching can replace religious instruction'. Lady Vischer once admitted to the writer that her husband had had a terrible disagreement with Lugard, but she refused to give any details about the occasion unless positive written evidence of it was uncovered. Her reason was that her husband had had such an admiration for Lugard, and later such a close friendship with 'the Chief', that she felt he would consider her talking about the matter disloyal and dishonourable, an interpretation which suggests that Vischer felt he had been right, though he regretted the occasion. It also indicates something about his own standards of conduct.

While Oldham persuaded Lugard to withdraw his objections, Vischer went to see Strachey at the Office and then to Switzerland to discuss the proposals with his wife, and his appointment as both a member and the Secretary of the Committee was formally made on 23 November 1923.[56] The appointment was for three years, the initial life-span of the Committee, at a salary of £1500 p.a.

Devonshire's circular letter to the Governors in December[57] set out the Committee's terms of reference: 'to advise the Secretary of State on any matters of native education in the British Colonies and Protectorates in British Tropical Africa which he may from time to time refer to them and to assist him in advancing the progress of education in those Colonies and Protectorates'. The Secretary's duties would include 'the paying of visits to furnish the Committee with first hand information regarding conditions in Africa, and to keep in touch with the education authorities in the Dependencies'. Vischer was a perfect choice as the official through whom information could be gathered and disseminated. He believed almost passionately that there was no substitute for personal contact,[58] and established a web of relationships throughout the tropical dependencies, with his office in London becoming a welcome port of call for men on leave.

The first six months of Vischer's appointment were hectic. He left London on 24 November 1923, reached New York on 3 December, had 12 days in America of which six were spent in trains, sailed from New York on 15 December and was back in London reporting to the Office on 21 December. The tour included the Hampton Institute in Virginia, the Tuskegee Institute in Alabama, a Teachers' Conference at Montgomery, and also five schools which were supervised by teachers from the two Institutes and which catered solely for American blacks. He had also met representatives of the Phelps Stokes Trust (including two of the family), of the Carnegie and the Rockefeller Foundations, and of the International Council of Missions, as well as a number of academics interested in education and sociology. He notified the Under-Secretary of State that because his wife had accompanied him, 'this made it possible to see twice as much of the work at Tuskegee and Hampton than I would have been able to do alone'.[59] Hanns and Isabelle's marriage was a true partnership. For years Vischer had said he would not marry because he could not ask a woman to share the conditions of his life in Africa, but from the time of their marriage in 1911, Isabelle not only created a home at Gidan dan Hausa, but entered fully into her husband's hopes and plans, as her published letters to her parents testify.[60] Vischer valued her opinion so highly that he told Oldham, 'I know that if I take up the Secretaryship she will share the work with me.'[61] It was perhaps a rather more modern view of marriage than one might have expected from a man born in 1876.

Vischer spent the morning after his return at the Colonial Office seeing Sir Herbert Read, A. J. Harding, C. Bottomley and Charles Strachey. Then after Christmas he spent a day with Oldham because Oldham wanted to discuss what he saw as the many danger points which would have to be guarded against when the Committee met on 9 January for the first time. He also thought Vischer, 'would be able, when we have surveyed the ground, to use the next couple of days in seeing people who ought to be seen'.[62] Vischer went to Switzerland for the New Year which must have provided a break from Oldham's pressure. Yet he took time to express strongly his view that the Chairmanship of the Advisory

Committee must pass to the Parliamentary Under-Secretary of State whatever party was in power. If the Conservatives lost the next election, then by all means ask Ormbsy-Gore to become a private member, but 'the whole aspect of our task and its nature makes it one which can be made to appeal to any political party'.[63]

Then came the return to England and the first meeting of the Advisory Committee on 9 January, the agenda for which had been prepared jointly by Vischer and Oldham. As Chairman, the Parliamentary Under-Secretary, Ormsby-Gore, gave his interpretation of the Committee's purpose, and indicated two areas for concern, the financing of native education and the relationship of mission societies and colonial governments. After some discussion, the meeting went on to more concrete issues, including the instructions for the Secretary in relation to his forthcoming visit to East and South Africa. Vischer was to collect Education reports and summarise the interesting data for the Committee, to suggest to the Directors that in future all use a model form for these reports, and also to obtain the answers to a questionnaire prepared by Lugard which the latter had wished to be sent to the Directors but was persuaded to leave in Vischer's hands. Vischer gave a brief report on his visit to America, and Dr Jesse Jones then joined the Committee for a discussion of his Commission's proposed journey and work.[64]

Four days later Vischer and his wife left London and he did not return until 14 July. Although he accompanied the Phelps Stokes Commission to Kenya, Uganda, Tanganyika Territory and Zanzibar, he was not a member of it, and his duty was to report to the Colonial Office. When the Commission's itinerary was completed, Vischer went on to South Africa, visiting schools in Bechuanaland and Basutoland in accordance with his instructions. His private letters to Oldham illustrate his ability to sit back and observe his fellow men in action, while reserving his intervention for whatever issue he believed crucial.

I feel that the Commission has fairly settled down and that each member contributes his share of useful information and works for the same object. But we are a queer team. Jones with his nerves and his sudden and unexpected impressions which he insists on writing down in fits of temper, Garfield Williams with his theological urbanity, Jock who suffers impatience and sums up the position in Latin, which makes Jones climb walls, Shantz who collects samples of soil and weeds. Father Dillard who browses around and gives 'reactions' over a whiskey and soda, George Dillard who disguises himself as a baseball player and valets his father with resignation, and over all brother Aggrey who brings up the rear with a flash of his gold teeth and 'wall, wall, wall.' My wife sobers us all down with her independent criticism and I just sit and learn. Sometimes I give tongue however when they lack respect for my African and want to force him to become white.[65]

None of this objective appraisal prevented him hoping to travel home on the same ship as Jones and Aggrey for, 'Jones' way of finding out facts and looking at Education and Aggrey's quiet manner in getting into personal touch with everybody are an education which I would not have missed for the world'.[66] He admired, too, the way Jones avoided being drawn into local controversies, missionary or political.[67] However, in view of Oldham's original preference for Jones as Secretary to the Advisory Committee, it is interesting that Vischer criticised Jones' failure to embody the views and observations of other members of the Commission, particularly those of Garfield Williams of the CMS and of the American government agricultural specialist, Dr Shantz. Why have a team if one did not use it?[68] Vischer's solution was to obtain promises of special reports from Aggrey on the native point of view, Garfield Williams on mission schools and Shantz on agriculture. To these he added one from his wife on the education of African women, and he ensured that all four were later presented to the Advisory Committee, incorporated in his own report. Awareness of the questions raised by any consideration of education for African girls influenced the appointment to the Committee of its first female member in May 1925, Dr Sarah Burstall of Manchester High School for Girls, who impressed Vischer when they first met at his office. While in East Africa Vischer also obtained the statistics Lugard had wanted on matters including school text-books, but supplemented the information by collecting copies of the books themselves for future use in London.[69] Back in London and finding the Emir of Kano there at the same time as Jones, Vischer arranged a meeting between them because 'the more the African knows about the work of Jones and the work of our Committee the better'.[70]

During his absence abroad, Vischer had missed the second and third meetings of the Advisory Committee. He therefore came back to a group which had already begun to form its patterns of work. It was also a group composed of eminent men used to leading in their own spheres. Besides Oldham, the mission societies' interests could be said to be represented by The Rt. Rev. A. A. David, Anglican Bishop of Liverpool, who had been headmaster of Clifton College and then of Rugby, and The Rt. Rev. Monsignor M. J. Bidwell, Chancellor of the Catholic Diocese of Westminster. Lord Lugard had experience of East and West Africa and had been Governor of Hong Kong as well as Governor-General of Nigeria. He was at the height of his public acclaim, having just published *The Dual Mandate in British Tropical Africa*, 'unquestionably the most influential book on British colonial policy in the 1920s'.[71] He was also British Representative on the Permanent Mandates Commission. Sir James Currie had been DE in the Sudan and headmaster of Gordon College, Khartoum, and an influence on Vischer's Nigerian work. Currie was also a Director of the Empire Cotton Growing Corporation with an interest in tropical agriculture. Sir Michael Sadler had served on the Royal Commission on Secondary Education (1893–5), presided over the Calcutta University Commission (1917–19), and in 1923 moved from the Vice-Chancellorship of Leeds University to the Mastership of University College, Oxford. Sir Herbert Read was Deputy Permanent Under-Secretary at the Colonial Office and had chaired both the Colonial Survey and the Colonial Advisory Medical and Sanitary Committees. Ormsby-Gore had entered Parliament at the age of 25 years, served in Egypt during the War and then become Private Secretary to Lord Milner in 1917, gone on to be a delegate to the Permanent Mandates Commission, and been appointed Parliamentary Under-Secretary at the Colonial Office at the age of 38 years, after completing a tour of the West Indies. This was a Committee of distinguished men but several had no personal experience of Africa. Ormsby-Gore described the Committee's purpose as being 'to avoid a repetition of the mistakes made in India and see that Africa benefited from the fruits of experience from all over the world. If a sounder system of education developed it would be less productive of causes of legitimate discontent.'[72] The political implications were clearly important to the politician. Each member probably had his own priorities: Oldham hoped to benefit Africa by raising the standard of mission education while protecting the role of the mission societies: Lugard was viewing Africa in the terms of the Dual Mandate and trusteeship: Currie hoped to advance the standard of living of Africans for, 'the great enemy of the African in the main is his poverty, and so long as he as a man can care for nothing but his belly's need, you will not get the social and moral advance you desiderate'.[73] How did Vischer see his own work and post in relation to this Committee, of which he was a member as well as the paid Secretary? He did not see it as a task to be undertaken lightly, but:

> although I feel the heavy responsibility I think I could undertake it wholeheartedly and with the feeling that my previous experience in Africa and the sympathy Africans with whom I had to deal always brought me would help me to do the work well. I say this without any great opinion of my qualifications but rather feeling that I could scarcely find any activity which would appeal to me more.[74]

The African was, as ever, uppermost in Vischer's mind. He believed that Africans were fundamentally religious, whether animist, Moslem or Christian, and that any education offered must be based on this premise. He brought to his post the philosophy that all men, irrespective of creed, colour or class, were born equal in the sight of God and created their own inequalities in His eyes by the use or misuse of their talents in their own situations.[75] The fact that African peoples other than those affected by Islam lived by oral traditions rather than literary ones did not mean an absence of culture to Vischer, but rather that when education produced a shift to literacy, both other African tribes and Europeans would then be able to appreciate what had been hidden from them. This idea of mutual enrichment was one he returned to in speeches to both Africans and

Europeans in the 1920s and 1930s.[76] This was not a widespread view in his day, most men of his generation reflecting — if unconsciously — the Hegelian concept that Africa was no historical part of the world, having no movement or development to exhibit, but Vischer had a respect for African art, music and crafts and first-hand knowledge of African story-telling. In practice his attitude meant that the new Secretary would support strongly the study and use of vernaculars once the Committee considered the vehicle for African education.

Vischer's initial moves, however, were the result of understanding the need to establish a good working relationship with the wary permanent officials in Whitehall. After he had been approached by Oldham, Vischer had not only arranged to see Strachey at once but had written to Lugard, 'who has perhaps a better idea of the official side of the matter than most men'.[77] He was well aware from the first that Oldham's view of the Committee's potential was far wider than anything envisaged at the Colonial Office. Yet when Vischer wrote to Oldham after spending a morning with Read, Harding, Bottomley and Strachey at the Office that, 'They are really keen', he added in his typical fashion, 'I could see the effects of your good work'.[78] In fact the degree of willing collaboration achieved owed much to the respect and liking Vischer aroused. Possibly Oldham never appreciated this fully. He had 'a system of working on anyone whom he considered a key man for his present purpose'[79] and had therefore established a personal working relationship with the current Parliamentary Under-Secretary. While he was fortunate that Ormsby-Gore was out of office only briefly from 1923 to 1929, the relationship may well have prevented Oldham fully realising the ability to aid or obstruct that the permanent civil servants possessed. Indeed, Furse gives an illustration of how Harding thwarted a scheme devised by Oldham together with Sir Hugh Clifford, then Governor of Nigeria. Harding thought the proposals disastrous and outmaneouvered the authors, leaving Oldham unable to find out just what had happened.[80]

Clatworthy considers that Vischer's indoctrination by Oldham began in November 1923,[81] but attempted indoctrination is more correct. One has to bear in mind the complexity of Vischer's character, his habit of self-negation and the courtesy with which he always expressed disagreement contrasting with the inner certainty of an independent spirit. Since Oldham's activities are well documented within the International Missionary Council's archives, the perspective they afford alone can be misleading. Certainly, given Oldham's key role in initiating the Committee, the weight he carried as an international representative of Protestant Mission Societies and the web of correspondence Oldham had already established with other members of the Committee such as Lugard, a Secretary who had not been prepared to collaborate with Oldham could have achieved little. Vischer, respecting the other man's intelligence, knowledge and sincerity, hoped to follow a common line of action[82] and to this end accepted — and indeed at first sought — constant suggestions and instructions from one whom Furse was to describe neatly as a 'busybody of genius'. Vischer was happy to collaborate with the influential Oldham so long as he believed that what Oldham was suggesting would benefit African education and so serve Africans. Smaller men might have resented receiving a message from Oldham, 'my suggestion for the record in the Minutes of the resolutions which I proposed at the meeting today is as follows ...'.[83] Vischer, however, had deep reserves to draw on and even three years later could still write politely, 'Thank you very much for your note reminding me of various things. The Board of Education have already been written to ....'.[84] Not for him was the expression of exasperation found in one civil servant's minute that, 'Mr J. H. Oldham is one of the people who love to interfere with and regulate other peoples' affairs'.[85] The consequence was that Oldham underestimated Vischer as a person who did not take 'any strong line of his own'.[86] Even when areas of disagreement appeared between the two, Vischer's sons never heard their father denigrate Oldham.

Much of the Advisory Committee's work was done outside its formal meetings. In some cases members appear to have written memoranda before the subject was officially taken up. Those who knew that they would miss a meeting tended to send in their observations in writing or to offer notes on matters arising, some of which notes appear to have been circulated previously to other members and acquired added comments on the way. Oldham early expressed a desire to curb Lugard's and Currie's tendency to circulate memoranda before meetings,[87] which is slightly amusing coming from the man who later admitted to Lugard that he was in the habit of drafting his own 'first rude sketch into the form it may ultimately take', i.e., a memorandum of the Advisory Committee, before showing it to others.[88] Vischer would have known from his Nigerian experience of Lugard's tendency to write lengthy despatches, and Oldham soon learned to work with Lugard on the preparation of documents, including the statement of principles which was adopted by the Committee, accepted by the Secretary of State and published in 1925 as Cmd 2374, *Education Policy in British Tropical Africa*. As Whitehead has stated, in this Oldham clearly got on paper what he had sought for the missions at the outset, official recognition of the mission societies as partners with colonial administrations in the provision of education.[89] However, Vischer got all he wanted too, for he had advocated the government inspection of mission schools in Northern Nigeria linked with the provision of grants in aid as a means to raise standards, and the principles of adaptation enshrined in the Memorandum were those on which he had based his Department's work.

The activities of the Committee and the memoranda produced between 1923 and 1929 are well known and have been considered in detail elsewhere.[90] Early on, Vischer picked up issues that concerned educationists in the dependencies, such as the provision of text-books, and the selection and training of men for educational work in Africa. Such issues were outside the Committee's scope when he first enumerated them in 1924[91] but all had received attention before the Committee was enlarged in 1929. He was particularly concerned at the inadequate provision made for training men and women for the education service and stressed in his Report on his tour of French West Africa of 1926 the contrast of the professionalism of the French teachers. Despite his doubts about the probable consequences of the French school system of assimilation, Vischer suggested that British education officers, teachers or inspectors, would benefit in West Africa by keeping in touch with their French colleagues.[92] One advantage of having a cosmopolitan European as Secretary was undoubtedly his lack of British insularity. Initially the Committee circulated to the colonial governments in November 1925 a *Memorandum on Education Staff in Africa* recommending certain changes in the recruitment, training and conditions of employment of Education Officers. Practical steps followed as a result. First a new special training course for missionaries was set up in 1927, and the next year annual courses for newly recruited Education Officers began at the London Day Training Centre whose Principal, Sir Percy Nunn, was co-opted onto the Committee. Vischer maintained personal contact particularly with his old University, seeing Cambridge as a potential area for recruitment and training.

His tour of East Africa had made Vischer deeply concerned about future developments in Kenya and also perturbed at the limited educational provision in Uganda.[93] Once E. J. R. Hussey was seconded from the Sudan Service to report on education in Uganda, Vischer encouraged him to use Vischer's office in Richmond Terrace as his London base. The scheme Hussey devised, which was submitted to the Advisory Committee by the government of Uganda and approved, proposed transforming the technical school at Makerere into a central training college 'to provide in the country such higher education as will fit students for careers in it'.[94] Rivers-Smith, in charge of the Education Department of the newly-mandated Tanganyika Territory, was also frequently to be found at Richmond Terrace at this time, beginning a productive friendship with 'Swissie'. Such informal working contacts formed an essential supplement to the formal interviewing of education officials by the Advisory Committee, and when Mayhew joined Vischer in 1929 as Joint Secretary to the enlarged Advisory Committee on Education in the Colonies, he was to adopt the same practice.

Probably the memorandum with whose preparation Vischer was most intimately concerned was that on *The Place of the Vernacular in Native Education*. The draft was circulated to all British African dependencies in July 1925 for informed comment. It included references to a number of official sources which had already touched on this difficult question, but also to work by Professor Dieterich Westermann of Berlin University, whom Vischer revered as the leading authority on philology, and interestingly, to *The Bi-lingual Problem: a study based on experiments and observations in Wales* by Dr Saer, Frank Smith and John Hughes. The Committee's provisional recommendations were that all elementary teaching should be in the vernacular, with English taught well by fully-trained teachers as a second language in the secondary stage, where it should be used as a vehicle for education only in the highest grades. The draft recognised that not every minority vernacular could be used and that choice would have to be made in multi-tribal areas. Moreover, it might prove necessary to teach mathematics and sciences in English. The recommendations tried to straddle the gap between the concept that a child benefited most from early education in its mother tongue and the recognition that 'by means of languages learned at school or later, an educated man or woman should have at least the chief keys to the world's culture'. Vischer's voice is clearly audible in certain phrases, such as when, under the heading *The linguistic Talent of the African*, the draft stated that, 'to hear an African telling a story gives one the impression of an artist who expresses himself in music, or colour, or in plastic form'. Such touches did not survive in the formal memorandum adopted in 1927 after a flood of reactions from government and missionary sources, some highly critical, had been digested.[95]

Vischer was in West Africa in 1926, and so saw for himself the popular rejection of the proposals in the Gold Coast, where the coastal Africans interpreted them as a denial of their right of access to the English language and the wealth, power and status which it could confer. On his return to London, Vischer reported that he felt no general rule could be made concerning the use of the vernacular in primary education because the coastal areas of British West Africa differed so from up-country regions or from East Africa. 'The greater part of the natives living in the coast towns spoke English and had an entirely English outlook and English ideas.'[96] English had become, in effect, the vernacular, and Vischer was not doctrinaire, even about the belief he held so deeply, that language was the essential key to a people's culture.

It was this belief that made him a founder and devoted servant of the International Institute of African Languages and Cultures. As an erstwhile DE he understood the weakness of the Advisory Committee. It dealt with subjects referred to it, could after much work then arrive at advice on a topic to present to the Secretary of State, who then chose whether or not to accept it. If he did, and the recommendations were circulated to the relevant dependencies in the form of a memorandum, that memorandum still had only advisory weight, being in no way prescriptive. This crucial factor has not always been fully appreciated by historians.[97] Vischer, however, knew from personal experience that everything depended on the reactions of individuals from the Governor downwards, and on the economic, social and political priorities within a particular colony. Above all, the doctrine that each colony had to aim at self-sufficiency meant economic restraints on educational provision. For Vischer the International Institute was to be the practical means to gain what he basically desired, an orthography for African languages accepted throughout that continent, by which the oral African cultures could be transformed into literary ones and so reach a footing equivalent to the western world's literary culture, at which stage mutual enrichment could occur.

It has been incorrectly said that the British government inspired the formation of the International Institute of African Languages and Cultures.[98] In fact 'the necessity for establishing somehow and somewhere a general clearing house for all that concerned African study and research'[99] was pressed by the American Secretary of the International Missionary Council, Dr Warnshuis, at a luncheon when Vischer was present in New York in 1923. Vischer was greatly taken with the idea which the two men appear to have discussed further, and he always thought of Warnshuis as the father of the enterprise, writing happily to him three years later that, 'In spite of various misfortunes, let me tell you that your child is doing well, beginning to stand on its legs and give speech'.[100]

Vischer was actively involved in the foundation of the Institute once the idea had been given formal structure by the missionary conference at Holm Leigh in the autumn of 1924, which he attended. He worked closely with The Rev. Edwin Smith on a provisional constitution, made contact with Sir Denison Ross at the School of Oriental and African Studies, University of London, and travelled to Paris to seek the support of leading French Africanists in what had to be an international venture involving all the current colonial countries if it was to be a worthwhile project. From September 1925 Vischer established a typical network, working through Father Schebesta in Vienna, Professor Westermann in Germany, Professors Labouret and Delafosse in France and Dr Warnshuis in America, seeking members and financial support. A total of 23 institutions and missionary societies sent representatives to a meeting in London in July 1926. They came from America, Austria, Belgium, Britain, Egypt, France, Germany and South Africa. Vischer even took personal responsibility for all the initial financial expenses of the nascent Institution up to the first meeting of its Executive Council in October 1926, working out of a room temporarily loaned by the African and Eastern Trading Co., who also gave the services of secretarial staff free of charge.[101]

Later, Margaret Read was to point out[102] that the British policy of deliberately fostering 'in certain areas, some elements in the local traditional culture, notably languages, and where the people are Muslims, the Islamic faith and pattern of living' had resulted in the accumulation of formidable problems: that the authors of the 1925 White paper, Cmd 2374, had apparently believed that an intellectual and ethical sieve could be used in schools to build on the good and reject the bad in local indigenous culture, whereas systematic studies in parallel of both the indigenous and English education and cultural traditions were prerequisites for the success of their recommendations. She did however admit that 'the studies made in Africa have been assisted greatly by the policy of the International African Institute to promote and publish studies in aspects of inter-cultural contact between European governments and missions on the one hand and African tribal peoples on the other'. Certainly for Vischer the Institute was a practical means towards achieving some of the Advisory Committee's recommendations. It was he who spoke to a statement laid before that Committee in December 1925 explaining that, 'It was felt that in order to successfully carry out Native Education on the lines indicated by the Advisory Committee at the Colonial Office and in Dr Jesse Jones' Reports, every encouragement should be given to the study of African languages and tribal cultures, and the knowledge and the advice of leading authorities in Europe and elsewhere, as well as the information collected in Africa, should be made available to those who are in charge of African education'.[103] In pressing the need for such an organisation, Vischer referred to the inability of the Directors of Education to provide the vernacular textbooks required if they were to follow the Advisory Committee's advice. He pointed out that administrations were choosing *lingua francas* but as yet major questions of orthography were unsettled: the Institute would act as a clearing house making Africanists' work available internationally.

The Advisory Committee expressed its approval by appointing Lugard as its representative on the Institute's governing body. The initial governing body had 40 members from leading academic and interested institutions in 11 countries, Belgium, Egypt, France, Germany, Great Britain, Holland, Italy, Portugal, Sweden, the Union of South Africa and the United States of America. Lugard became Chairman of the Executive Council which comprised four British members, three French, a Belgian, an Austrian and a German. The aim was to hold Council meetings in various European capitals. Under the direction of the Executive Council, the work of the Institute was run by two Directors, one German and one French, together with Vischer, first designated Vice-Director and later, Secretary General. Headquarters were in London, and known as the Bureau. It was the Secretary General's 'special duty ... to establish and maintain international connections and contacts',[104] a duty for which Vischer was peculiarly fitted. In fact his formal post at the Colonial Office and his voluntary work for the Institute simply meshed in his eyes, as he nurtured a symbiotic relationship between the two.

This began with the Secretary of State, Amery, accepting an invitation to preside over the inaugural meeting of the International Institute in London in June, 1926. Vischer was delighted at the precedent set by the invitation to the Institute's German Director, Professor Westermann, from Guggisberg as Governor of the Gold Coast to visit the colony and advise on the adoption of a suitable orthography. Then, during the planning stages of the 1927 Imperial Education Conference, the Advisory Committee asked the Institute to provide a memorandum on its aims and work to be distributed to each member of the Conference.[105] Later that year both Vischer and Oldham (also a founder member of the Institute and on its Executive Council) drew the Advisory Committee's attention to the criticisms that some of the Institute's phonetics experts

had expressed of the script for Swahili adopted for use in the schools
of the Tanganyika Territory. The DE, Rivers Smith, who was present, said
he would be glad to receive their suggestions. Moreover at the same
meeting, 'Sir Edward Grigg stated that the Kenya government would
accept the rulings of the International Institute .... Mr Vischer undertook
to bring the matter to the notice of the Institute and to ask for
suggestions'.[106] Next year, after a long discussion about the possible use
of Swahili as a *lingua franca* for Uganda, Lugard offered, in his capacity as
Chairman of the Institute's Executive Council, to obtain the advice of
Westermann. The offer to consult this expert was accepted.[107] By 1934
Vischer could write delightedly that, 'At the Colonial Office, for instance,
I have no more to suggest that such and such a matter be referred to the
Institute. The Departments and the Assistant Under-Secretaries now do
that for themselves, and in an increasing degree that also applies to the
various administrations in Africa'.[108]

Much of the credit for this situation must go to him, but he never
lost sight of the international character of the Institute's work 'brought
about and maintained with the idea that we wanted to work for all
Africans, whatever nation happened to be in charge of them at the present
moment'.[109] To this end part of his skill went into arranging the annual
Executive Council meetings at different capitals and ensuring that they
presented a high profile. On each occasion the Council was provided with
a conference room by the host country. Always there was recognition at
the highest level, whether the Council were received by a Minister for the
Colonies, or a head of state, such as King Albert in Belgium, Mussolini
in Rome and the Pope in the Vatican.[110] Often there were ruffled feathers
to smooth, as in the five months of difficult negotiations with one
German professor whom the Institute was sending out to Tanganyika, at
one point in which Vischer offered to go to Berlin over a weekend if that
would help.[111] There were papers to be written about the Institute, such
as *'Die Völkerprobleme in Afrika und das Internationale Institut für afrikanische
Sprachen und Kulturen'* which appeared in the *Verhandlungen der Schweizerischen
Naturforschenden Gesellschaft* in 1929. Despite the stress Vischer laid on the
use of the vernacular in the early stages of education, there was also
recognition that the teaching of English at higher levels offered a key to
a wider intellectual life. In whatever capital Vischer made a speech
concerning *'L'Enseignment en Afrique Tropicale Anglaise'* as Secretary-General
of the Institute, his words had the added weight of coming from one
known to be an official of the British Colonial Office. Tension could have
resulted between the demands of his two roles but for the symbiotic
relationship he was fostering between the Institute and the Office.

In London Vischer played a part in running the Institute's Bureau.
Not only did it produce a quarterly Journal, *Africa*, but also various
memoranda, such as the 1928 *Textbooks for African Schools* and *African
Native Music*, both topics Vischer had insisted were specified as within the
Institute's remit.[112] As the work of both the Institute and Advisory
Committee increased in scope, so did the demands on Vischer.

Margery Perham, who later sat on the expanded Advisory Committee on Education in the Colonies, suggested that, 'Perhaps the Committee was never so creative as in the first five years when it dealt solely with African affairs .... It could claim to be the most effective of the Colonial Advisory Committees'.[113] In fact, the Secretary of State was so satisfied that as early as November 1926 — well before the Imperial Education Conference of 1927 — Vischer knew he intended expanding its terms of reference to cover all British colonies. To someone of Vischer's religious beliefs the developments taking place 'showed the great extent and importance of the work to be done and the great driving force behind it all'.[114] When the new Committee came into being in 1929 some colonies preferred to remain outside its scope, but the expanded workload required the appointment of Joint-Secretaries and Arthur Mayhew was appointed alongside Vischer. Mayhew, a Wykehamist with a First from New College, Oxford, had been Director of Public Instruction in the Central Provinces of India before becoming a master at Eton. He had recently published a highly acclaimed book, *The Education of India: a Study of British Educational Policy in India, 1835–1920*. While they were to share the general responsibilities, the idea was that Vischer would retain his interest in African education while Mayhew's particular area would be the East. Mayhew also took on the editorship of the Committee's new journal, *Overseas Education*. Oldham had seen Mayhew as a potential candidate as early as 1927, and after an initial disappointment when he heard that the post had been offered to Dr Winstedt from the Straits Settlements, Oldham's planning again succeeded. Although very different in character, there is no evidence that the two Secretaries had any difficulties working together and they made an excellent team because their gifts were complementary.[115]

Vischer's next fact-finding visit was to the Sudan in 1929. He had already begun in 1927 his investigation into the position of African students sent to the United Kingdom to complete their education, which developed into a commitment lasting years. Given also his work for the Institute and the economic anxieties which the depression brought, it is not surprising that Vischer's health, already undermined by his African service, gave way in 1931. In the spring of the previous year he had expended considerable effort to bring Italy closer to the Institute. His schedule began with nine days in Tripoli, where he talked not only to the Governor-General, Field Marshall Badoglio, the Chief Secretary and the Heads of both the Education Department and the Department of Excavations and Historical Research, but also to Italian military and naval officers, Berbers, Arabs, some Africans from Nigeria and from the neighbouring French colonies. Having known Tripoli as part of the Turkish empire, he wanted to see the position now that it was an Italian colony before he went on to spend a further five days in Italy itself. In Rome he had to visit the British Embassy, meet Father Dubois and Professor Conti Rossini of the Institute's Executive Council, and also the Minister for the Colonies, an Under-Secretary for Foreign Affairs, the Head of Propaganda Fide and both the Pope and the Duce. All this was ostensibly to make arrangements for the Institute's Executive meeting in Rome later that year, but he was also producing a report for the Advisory Committee at the Colonial Office on conditions in Tripoli and the general policy of the Italian government.[116] The Rome meeting of the Institute produced the Resolution which embodied Vischer's creed. Forty-six years later, at the Golden Jubilee of the Institute, Professor Onukwa Dike said that 'the Rome Resolution, as it came to be called, can still guide the thinking of African states on the vital question of language in education', and he therefore quoted it in full:

> The child should learn to love and respect the mental heritage of his own people, and the natural and necessary expression of this heritage is the language. We are of the opinion that no education which leads to the alienation of the child from his ancestral environment can be right, nor can it achieve the most important aim of education, which consists in developing the powers and character of the pupil. Neglect of the vernacular involves the danger of crippling and destroying the pupil's productive powers by forcing him to express himself in a language foreign both to himself and to the genius of his race.[117]

The Rome Resolution of 1930 thus marked international support for the position already taken by the British Advisory Committee, but Vischer paid for his efforts in ill health.

Repeated angina attacks led his doctors to order a complete rest in the autumn of 1931, and he and Isabelle went to Italy for his convalescence. He was deeply worried because he felt that the Bureau in London was failing to cope with the growing volume of the Institute's work and needed reorganisation and a larger secretarial staff. Although he was not supposed to read or write, Isabelle took his paper to Paris to be read to the Institute's Executive Council's meeting there in October. Changes were even more essential as the Institute was developing a program of anthropological and social studies funded by the Rockefeller Institute, and, happily, reorganisation did take place. Vischer supported the appointment of Oldham to be Director of the study program while stressing that, 'if we are to be true to our ideal these studies must further a practical and human cause, the progress of the African'.[118]

He was unaware that Oldham had just launched an attack on him in correspondence with Ormsby-Gore. Worried that the economic depression threatened the existence of the Advisory Committee, and that if the Colonial Office insisted that one of the Joint-Secretaries must go then Mayhew would be selected on the principle 'last in, first out', Oldham appears to have raised the issue with Ormsby-Gore. Ormsby-Gore, who became Post Master General in the National government of 1931 and was to become Colonial Secretary after the October election, replied: 'It would be quite terrible to lose either Hanns Vischer or Mayhew. I have an equal admiration for them both. The former is not so clever, but he has *an admirable judgement, real knowledge of African conditions and how it all looks from the African end of the telescope'* (writer's italics).[119] Oldham cannot have rated these attributes highly, for he returned to the attack:

> I heard a rumour before I went away in the summer that the question of having only one Secretary for the Advisory Committee was being considered. I agree with everything you say about Vischer. He has many admirable and valuable qualities. I have, however, worked closely with him on the Advisory Committee for a good many years and been even more closely associated with him in the work of the International Institute of African Languages and Cultures. He has an entirely unsystematic mind and scarcely does a stroke of the kind of work that needs to be done. The plain fact is that with you gone, if Vischer is the sole Secretary of the Committee, the work of which has considerably increased because of its functions, the Committee will sooner or later fall to pieces. In Mayhew's hands the future is secure. While I am equally fond of both Vischer and Mayhew I cannot get away from the fact that in the interests of education in the colonies it is in the public interest that the Committee should have a Secretary who does its work efficiently.[120]

If Vischer had ever been aware of Oldham's attack, he would undoubtedly have challenged Oldham to substantiate it,[121] but Oldham was working behind the scenes as usual, and when he realised that Ormsby-Gore was not sympathetic, he set to work to ensure a supply of money from America which enabled the reduced salaries of both the Secretaries to be continued.

Unfortunately Vischer has left no record of his opinion of Oldham whereas Oldham's of Vischer is known. In 1923 Oldham had wanted a man who would lead the Committee: Vischer saw himself as its servant. Mayhew with his meticulous mastery of paperwork was undoubtedly nearer Oldham's ideal as Secretary than Vischer was. Vischer laid more emphasis on the establishment of beneficial personal relationships, work which was actually written into the job descriptions of both his posts and which was his forte. His priorities perhaps irritated Oldham. Once Vischer missed a meeting of the Bureau in London because he had gone to Folkestone. He had earlier met some Italian cavalry officers who had been buying horses in America and had promised to help them with the loading formalities when they arrived at Folkestone *en route* for Italy. Because of bad weather in the Atlantic, their arrival was delayed until it coincided with the meeting.

Vischer's apologies to Lugard were made in the confident expectation that Lugard would understand that not only had Vischer to keep his word, but that his action might ultimately benefit the Institute since Mussolini took a personal interest in such matters.[122] Lugard probably understood, because his liking for, and trust in, Vischer, were growing. Possibly Oldham did not appreciate the choice Vischer had made.

The Advisory Committee might well have 'collapsed' in the early 'thirties through lack of funds, but Oldham's fear that Vischer would fail to sustain it if sole Secretary underestimated the man. One doubts if a 'totally unsystematic mind' could have run successful military Intelligence operations in the First World War. Moreover Vischer's actions during the Second World War prove how capable and determined he was in preserving through the most adverse conditions an institution which he felt of benefit to Africa.

In 1940 a meeting in London agreed that the Institute of African Languages and Cultures must suspend its activities at a time when Europe was dominated by Germany's success, international co-operation was almost impossible and invasion of Britain seemed imminent. Vischer pointed out that since they were unlikely to be able to sell the lease of their offices in London, he might as well look in from time to time to keep an eye on matters. In effect, he refused to let the Institute close, and supported by Lugard he maintained contact with members in countries such as Portugal, Sweden and the Vatican. He ensured that while the quarterly journal *Africa* could not be printed, at least short notes appeared in the *Journal of the Royal African Society*. Soon he formed what he called an Interim Committee. This then oversaw, through three sub-committees, the production of *Africa*, the printing of books already in the pipe-line, and the continuation of the Vernacular Prize Essay Competition. The international nature of the Interim Committee was ensured by co-opting qualified members of various Allied governments in London, so that by 1943 it included a Frenchman, a Belgian, a Dutchman, a Pole, an American and a West African. Links with America were maintained throughout, and from the time in 1941 that Vischer heard privately that applications for financial assistance under the Colonial Development Fund were being received at the Colonial Office, he and Lugard bore that source of funds in mind.[123] Vischer was eager that the Institute should resume its full activities from 1 January 1943, and Lugard agreed somewhat reluctantly as he feared Vischer might be over-taxing his strength.[124] The successful emergence of the Institute into the post-war world was largely due to Vischer's determination that it should not die, even though he served once again in British Intelligence.

Oldham was never specific when he wrote to his correspondents of his fears of missed opportunities, but some of these could have been schemes of which Vischer disapproved, just as Harding had done of that joint plan of Clifford and Oldham. The vehemence of Oldham's attack on Vischer — not withstanding his protestations of liking the man — makes one wonder if Oldham had discovered by 1931 just how quietly but determinedly independent Vischer could be. Oldham's primary concern was the status and work of the Protestant Missions. As early as the fourth meeting of the Committee Vischer had spoken up for the Moslems of Uganda who 'tended to feel neglected because the Christians had their white missionaries who shared with the government officials the prestige of belonging to the ruling race'. As late as 1927 Oldham defended Vischer against attack by Alec Fraser, 'I have tested him over a number of years and he is unfailingly friendly to missionary work.'[125] Fraser, Principal of Achimota College and Oldham's brother-in-law, had recently toured Nigeria at the request of its government to report on education there. Fraser thought education in the North thinly-spread, backward-looking and undemocratic, and blamed Vischer as 'responsible more than any other individual for the state of matters in the North and for this anti-mission policy'.[126] He had therefore sent Vischer a letter[127] which was 'little less than a declaration of war'. Oldham's temperate reply was based on his theory that Vischer had probably been carrying out instructions. However, the intensity of the repeated attack in Oldham's reply to Ormsby-Gore suggests at least a possibility that by 1931 he saw Vischer in a different light. Interestingly, it is in late 1927 that we first find Oldham expressing privately to Mayhew his fears that the Advisory Committee's potential might not be realised unless Mayhew became one of its Joint-Secretaries.

Margery Perham gave a glimpse of these men as she saw them in the 'thirties when she first became involved in the Institute's affairs as a young researcher.

> It was a joy to see them at any of the larger functions of the Institute — Lugard, a little shy, a little aloof, combining courtesy with dignity and quite unconscious of the reputation which gave him the primacy: Oldham, far-sighted, sharing, perhaps, with some eminent continental in a quite corner his understanding of the depths of Africa's problems: Vischer, handsome, witty, cosmopolitan, circulating confidently in three languages amongst the mixed company and making everyone feel happier and more intelligent as they sparkled in the glow of his humanity.[128]

Vischer's humanity is shown clearly in his concern for African students in the United Kingdom. His initial brief after the Imperial Education Conference of 1927 was to collect information concerning the experiences and needs of the growing number of Africans seeking education in Britain. He decided that schools, commercial firms and hospitals looked after young African pupils, apprentices and student nurses, but that African university students suffered great social difficulties. In 1925 Ladipo Solanke had managed to persuade fellow law students that the four existing organisations of African students in Britain were inadequate and that one was needed to represent all students from West Africa.[129] The West African Students' Union which resulted interested Vischer and he took pains to become acquainted with its officials and was in turn invited to some of its meetings. Indeed, when the Union held a dinner for

Nana Sir Ofori Atta at a restaurant in High Holborn in 1927, it was
Vischer, one of the two non-Africans present, who proposed the toast
of the West African Students' Union.[130] His contacts and enquiries at
various British Universities gave him the insight he needed into the culture
shock these intelligent, successful men suffered when they, justly proud of
their educational achievements at home, reached their goal of higher
education in Britain only to find themselves facing a colour bar which
differentiated particularly against blacks. 'In the majority of cases', he
warned, 'they feel very bitter against us as a result of their experiences in
England'. He suggested that an idea for a central Club House in London
put forward by the West African Students Union should be supported.
'Since the African has not the entry into the English home, he should
have a home of his own in England.' He warned that 'The Africans
themselves are suspicious of official control and mistrust philanthropic
effort', and he advocated a hostel or club for West Africans to be run by
the students themselves under a Manager and his wife appointed by
whatever Trust had to be created to raise the necessary money. He hoped
that his friend Ruxton, now retired from the Colonial Service, would
become Manager and live at the Club with his French wife, Geneviève,
and he suggested Ruxton be empowered to discuss the issue with WASU.
Ruxton's comments were enclosed and they included a blunt warning of
the effects of the colour bar on the African intelligentsia. 'It is not natural
to the African and can, even yet, be generally allayed, but it certainly
makes for increasing tension and suspicion between African and
Englishman, the blame resting entirely with the latter.'[131]

Vischer was authorised to form a Committee. His plan was
to form a Committee of influential people representing commercial firms
and other interests with one or two of the African students. The
Committee would formulate proposals to be submitted to the Secretary of
State with a view to inviting the various African governments to co-
operate.[132] Azikiwe later wrote, 'To some African students the role
of Major Vischer was one that should be carefully scrutinised. To others
he was a friend whose acquaintance should be cultivated.'[133] On this
occasion he was certainly the best friend they had, but WASU decided to
maintain its independence of control by raising the money for the Club
without assistance, and Vischer returned from a holiday in Switzerland
(from where, characteristically, he had sent Solanke a postcard) to a letter
from the latter informing him that the students had delegated Solanke to
collect funds in West Africa. Vischer was in accord with Colonial Office
opinion that WASU would not be able to maintain a Club even if Solanke
collected enough to lease a suitable building, but was sympathetic to their
efforts. He tried to constitute a link between Solanke and the official
proposals, and on his advice the colonial administrations were told that
although Solanke's initiative had no official standing, he had been
extremely helpful and had considerable influence, so that great tact should
be exercised and repudiation of him avoided. It was the beginning of a
lengthy process[134] which resulted in the early 'thirties with the establish-

ment of the officially-backed Aggrey House confronting WASU's hostel in Camden, months of tension, angry articles in West African papers and divisions among the students themselves. Throughout it all, Vischer tried to maintain contact with WASU, visiting the new hostel, Africa House, and congratulating the members on their great achievement in 1933.[135] He was undoubtedly glad when the Colonial Office came to the assistance of maintenance costs for Africa House in 1938.

Oldham's involvement in the hostel issue began with a letter to Ormsby-Gore in 1929[136] in which he proposed what he termed a Committee of control, including representatives of the Protestant and Catholic missionary societies and the Student Christian Movement. He was aware at the time that Vischer advised against any such voluntary associations being involved, and it seems at least possible that his criticisms of Vischer to Ormsby-Gore in 1931 were coloured, perhaps unconsciously, by his opposition to a Secretary who had urged that the hostel or club should be, 'their place to which they, as Africans, have the first right of entry, and to which they are not asked to come for any philanthropic motive'. While Vischer was protective towards Solanke, Oldham was expressing doubts to Ruxton as to whether Solanke had the full confidence of the students.[137] Lionel Aird, Secretary of the East West Friendship Committee which Oldham had involved in the matter, had written to warn Oldham that although he hoped to bring Solanke and one or two others into friendly relations with missionary headquarters in England, he doubted the outcome and, 'Unless greater confidence can be created, little that is useful can be done'.[138] Unfortunately, not only did the Africans mistrust the motives of the voluntary associations and of the Colonial Office, but few on that side seemed ready to go as far as Vischer in trusting the Africans students to participate sensibly in organising their own affairs. In 1930 Oldham could write that, 'A very real snag in connection with the Hostel is African opinion. It may quite easily wreck any scheme. It would be a great advantage to have a good African on the consideration of the matter for a start. In the various meetings [where] we have considered the matter before we have always wanted to have an African with us, but have never been able to find the right person.'[139] Presumably a good African was one who was totally co-operative. It was all a far cry from Vischer's original appeal for a place that Africans could call their own home in London and undoubtedly another issue over which he and Oldham held differing views from 1929 onwards.

Azikiwe recognised that Vischer hoped to be accepted as a friend of the African students and considered him a conscientious liaison official in all his dealings with them. After nine years' studying and teaching in America, Azikiwe passed through London on the way home in the summer of 1934. He was asked to call at Richmond Terrace where he was able to protest to Vischer about the lack of opportunities for educated Africans in the higher grades of the civil service in British tropical Africa and explain the humiliation they felt when posts were labelled 'African' or 'Assistant' and carried lower salaries than were paid to Europeans doing the same work. It was typical of Vischer's genuine interest that he issued a private invitation to Azikiwe to lunch with him at the Royal Societies Club and that when the African arrived, he found a luncheon party of what he termed British savants arranged to meet him. Moreover, next morning Vischer was at Euston station to see him off on his return journey to West Africa, alongside some half a dozen members of WASU.[140] This personal touch was central to Vischer's work, but there is no easy formula by which its consequences can be assessed.[141]

Meanwhile collaboration continued between himself and Oldham on other matters. They were in agreement on the importance of the Advisory Committee's *Memorandum on the Education of African Communities* of 1935. Oldham's initial draft, which related to African rural communities, produced a lengthy critique[142] from Vischer beginning tactfully with an agreement with what Oldham was proposing, but suggesting that changes in presentation might facilitate its acceptance. 'Since our Committee has come into existence we have seen one country after another, Russia, Italy and now Germany evolve national systems of education in order to effect a policy of national development and so perhaps we have a chance now to convince the Office and the various governments that their conceptions of Education as a departmental affair purely is slightly behind the times. If we succeed it will be the biggest thing we have done.' He did not want the proposed title which related only to rural communities since 'I think we can take it for granted that even the CO realises that with the exception of a few thousands the Africans are pastoral and agricultural people' and its omission would prevent departments viewing the advice as something applying to only a section of the population in each dependency. If the memorandum accepted that the economic development of natural resources was desirable then the Committee might proceed to show how the policy should be implemented. 'It would then follow quite naturally that such a plan of education concerns all the various departments, health, agriculture, forestry and administration and that the moral and religious side must be attended to with special care.' For Vischer the idea that they were trying to rejuvenate traditional society by the creation of a healthy and prosperous peasant class,[143] was apparently not so revolutionary as the fact that they were 'aiming at changing completely the present official concept of education'.

Vischer knew enough about the official machine to 'treacherously forestall it', as he put it, from time to time. A very important sub-committee was that chaired by Currie on Higher Education. Vischer was probably responsible for ensuring that in London the sub-committee interviewed not only Sir Edgar Bonham Carter formerly of the Sudan administration, the Principal of Fourah Bay College and S. J. Hogben of the Nigerian Education department, but also a number of African graduates and students studying in Britain, including Ladipo Solanke. The Currie draft report, in which Oldham undoubtedly had a share, recommended the creation of regional universities in the colonies.

Although Vischer connived with Currie in a practice which the Colonial Office deplored — that is, communicating the draft's contents to various directors of education and governors ahead of any official acceptance — he was proved right in his fears as to its reception.[144] It was never printed. It was too radical for the economically-restricted administrations of 1933, and its only practical result was the commission appointed in 1936 to advise on the development of Makerere College in Uganda.

As a member of that commission, Vischer was present at the preliminary hearings in London, but ill-health prevented him accompanying the commission to Uganda. He was happy however to associate himself with a report which recognised that, 'The African background today comprises not the native alone, and not the European alone, but the interaction between the African theory of traditionalism and the European theory of progress' and which advocated among other subjects the setting up of African Studies at the College.[145] Once again, however, this was a case when advice from London was only partially acceptable. Makerere was to concentrate on vocational rather than academic courses and the African Studies course was not adopted.[146]

Vischer was well enough to take part in the quinquennial inspection of Achimota College in 1938. In addition to the standard inspection, the four-man team under Dr Pickard-Cambridge was asked to consider the contribution of Achimota to education in the whole of British West Africa, not just the Gold Coast, and whether the time had come to introduce a BA pass degree. The report was termed unexpectedly timorous by Eric Ashby since for a variety of reasons it rejected both the establishment of an African University at that time and the introduction at Achimota of the BA pass degree. Yet he considered that there was a strong liberal purpose behind its apparently reactionary stand — 'with Hanns Vischer on the committee it would have been strange had it been otherwise'.[147] The committee was in favour of a university which would be African, with African staff to direct it, and one that was not a 'mere reproduction of an English university in its curriculum, its examinations and its methods of work'.[148] Since the body of African graduates needed as staff did not exist, such a university could not yet be established. Moreover, the committee was aware of the emphatic opposition to a West African university expressed by African members of the College Council, and perhaps its caution came partly from recognition of the suspicion of the anglicised, graduate African élite that the adaptive policy in education meant they were being offered a second-rate system. As Margaret Read said later, the British had chosen a difficult path. The report did support the setting up at Achimota of the proposed Institute of West African Culture as a preliminary step, with two main branches, Craft Industries and Social Studies, each with three functions, research, teaching and practical work for the community.[149] Possibly for Vischer this was the best outcome of all the deliberations since it was a practical step. However, planning was disrupted by the outbreak of war, and only in 1942 was it agreed to establish the West African Institute on a war-time basis. Once that Institute's London Advisory Committee was created in 1944, Vischer sat on it as representative of the International Institute of African Languages and Cultures, having retired by then from the Advisory Committee on Education in the Colonies. In February 1939 the Colonial Secretary, Malcolm MacDonald, decided to appoint a full-time Educational Adviser at the Colonial Office once Vischer's and Mayhew's annual contracts expired in the following December. A full-time Agricultural Adviser had already proved a success, and in the climate of opinion created by Lord Hailey's *African Survey*, the change was seen as a positive contribution to producing an effective colonial education policy.

Throughout the 'thirties Vischer had seen changes in the Institute's work with concentration on research into specific topics. With Oldham as Administrative Director from 1931 to 1938 and Professor Malinowski of the London School of Economics as principal adviser, 16 research Fellowships were granted for anthropological and linguistic studies in Africa. Fellows included J. P. Crazzolara, Meyer Fortes, Johannes Lukas, S. F. Nadel, Margery Perham, Margaret Read, Gunther Wagner and the first African Research Fellow, Zacharias Mathews. The annual vernacular essay competition was begun in 1930 to encourage the creation of vernacular literature and in nine years 300 manuscripts were submitted in 32 languages, some of which were published and incorporated into school text-books.[150] Its standard orthography had been adopted for 60 African languages by 1938 and in that same year the Institute published Jomo Kenyatta's *Facing Mt. Kenya*.

Vischer had few illusions in the 1930s about the international situation. In 1934 he wrote to Lugard that, 'the Italians support the Institute because other colonial powers do so, and the German government, in spite of Hitler's dislike of all that is international, are with us because we supply the only platform for German experts in linguistics or anthropology and give them an opportunity for continuing their African studies'.[151] When his post at the Advisory Committee ended in 1939, hope was expressed that at some point he might return as an ordinary member. Mayhew was in fact to do this briefly. There was also some idea of continuing to use Vischer as a link with African students in this country, but for the last four years of his life Vischer devoted himself to two war-time tasks. Mention has already been made of how he nurtured the International Institute, refusing to let it die: as a linguist he offered himself once more to Intelligence, and joined what was initially called the Department of Propaganda to Enemy Countries (later the Political Warfare Executive and then the Psychological Warfare Executive), and he became its liaison officer with MI6. The Department was housed at Woburn Abbey, eight miles from Tickford Lodge, the Vischers' country home since 1936. Vischer rapidly became known as 'Uncle Hansi' to his younger colleagues, who had little idea of his past career but thoroughly appreciated his turning up for the Christmas party in 1940 in Swiss national dress carrying his beloved concertina which had travelled miles in Africa with him. He brought the house down with his performance. Among his duties for the PWE was the vetting of staff before they were recruited and he also had responsibility for providing information from secret sources which might help those devising black or white propaganda. White propaganda was material to be used for BBC broadcasts whose origins were obvious, but black propaganda was intentionally misleading. About once a month a group would meet, usually on a Friday evening, to dream up items of misinformation for MI6 to feed into the neutral press in the hope that the enemy would pick them up. A young colleague was to recall, 'The occasional bottle of wine helped to sharpen our imagination. I well remember Hanns' infectious chuckle at some particularly outrageous innuendo about Goebbels' private life.'[152]

Vischer also broadcast on the BBC West African service in Hausa, French and English on a variety of topics, ranging from Britain's Allies to the colour bar, a subject about which he had strong feelings. By 1944 Vischer was able to revert to education, first presenting a couple of talks about Africans he had known in Africa and others he had met in England. These broadcasts were intended to create an audience which would, hopefully, listen again when he spoke in December 1944 about *Adult Education* in the context of the latest Advisory Committee recommendations about Mass Education.[153] His service was not entirely desk-bound, however. His sons remember that their father was sent on a secret mission to Nigeria, the Gold Coast, Sierra Leone and the Gambia in 1943. Because of its nature he never spoke about it, but it was important enough for him to be given VIP treatment.

Vischer was awarded the CMG in 1936, and knighted in 1940 for his services to education in Africa. Two stories have been told about this knighthood which illustrate how complex the recipient was. The day after the Honours List was announced, Vischer shared a staff car with a young cartoonist also engaged on propaganda. The cartoonist later told the story against himself, that he had inveighed against the sort of people awarded honours with Vischer heartily agreeing with him. Only next day did he discover that Vischer had been awarded a knighthood. Vischer was amused, for taking something seriously did not mean one had to be solemn about it. The second story, told by Sir Ralph Furse,[154] illustrates how seriously Vischer did take his knighthood. Furse had just become a Knight Commander of the Order of St Michael and St George, and Hanns asked his friend, 'Do you think your uncle would grant us the hospitality of his abbey for a night?' Furse's uncle was Bishop of St Albans and he understood at once that Vischer was proposing a night's vigil there. At 9 p.m. the two entered the Abbey and laid their swords and scabbards at the foot of the altar in the chapel of the Transfiguration, beginning their night watch in the darkened building lit by just one bulb in the middle of the great transept. Furse claimed that he had seldom been so happy as that night in an abbey thronged with invisible presences. At 3.30 a.m. they shared sandwiches and coffee, since medieval knights had been allowed wine and spices. 'When we had finished — "Now", he [Vischer] said with that odd little note of authority which would sometimes sidle into his voice, "now we'll salute St Alban in his tomb. Then we'll go down to hear the Roman trumpets sounding reveillé".' So they stood together, two romantics with sensitive imaginations, in the ruins of Verulamium as the rising sun dispersed the autumn mists.

By 1944 Vischer and Lugard had the satisfaction of knowing that their application on behalf of the Institute to the Colonial Development Fund had borne fruit: £900 was offered for a Language Handbook, the grant to be renewable in May 1945, £3,100 for four years' research in the Cameroons, and £14,000 for five years for an ethnographic survey.[155] Both men were dead by the time peace returned, but they had ensured the survival and potential development of an international institution which both believed of value to Africa's future. In February 1945 Vischer visited Paris by invitation to meet the Minister for the Colonies of the new French government on behalf of the Institute and renew other links with French Africanists. It was still war-time, conditions were grim, the weather was bitter and there was little heating. Vischer caught a chill which turned to pneumonia, and he died suddenly at Tickford Lodge on 19 February. In 1902 he had stated that his life's work lay in Africa and he had tried to serve Africa and Africans literally to the end of his life, making little distinction between his official and his unofficial roles.

The doctrine he constantly preached was that Europeans could not only help, but learn from, Africa.

> Après avoir énuméré les avantages que notre système [d'éducation] doit apporter à l'Africain, je ne voudrais pas terminer, sans vous inviter à considérer vous-mêmes, l'immense gagne qu'il y a pour nous, à donner à l'Africain le moyen d'exprimer sa propre pensée dans sa propre langue. Déjà nous apercevons dans les écrits d'Africain en langue indigène, les éléments d'une littérature, qui non seulement élargira notre connaissance de l'Afrique et de son histoire, mais qui contribuera à la beauté et à la richesse de la littérature du monde civilisé.[156]

It was vital that an official of the Colonial Office held this view at a time when serious British debate at the highest academic level could produce the query that, 'it was all very well to say that a rational system of education would make the African take a pride in his own culture but what could we show him in his traditional beliefs to which European ideas were not immeasurably superior?'[157] The adaptation principle in education was attacked often by African writers in the immediate post-independence decades. Now, at a greater distance, it may be easier to evaluate the work of men like Vischer in the context of their day, accepting that his role in helping form the official attitude towards educational development in the colonies was the result of a genuine concern for the future well-being of indigenous cultures, possibly even applying the counterfactual approach to consideration of the consequences? Vischer, after all, both believed and stated that it was in their oral traditions reduced to writing that Africans would find the historical background 'which any people wishing to assert itself must have'.[158] One should also not forget to turn the telescope on London, to view his liberalising influence there, remembering Furse's remarkable claim, 'The Advisory Committee gave us much help over the years. But to me — and I dare to think also to the Colonial Empire — the most valuable result of its creation was that Hanns Vischer was brought into close association with the office during the next 16 years'.[159]

NOTES ON CHAPTER

1. This article first appeared in *Education Research and Perspectives* 25/1 (1998), pp 1–45
2. Sir Ralph Furse, *Aucuparius Recollections of a Recruiting Officer,* (1962), p 126
3. *Ibid.*, p 29
4. *Ibid.*, p 131
5. H. Vischer, *Across the Sahara from Tripoli to Bornu* (1910)
6. *The Illustrated London News* 30 Jan 1909
7. Vischer Papers [VP], Account of his journey from Berne to Vienna, Prague, Warsaw and Budapest, 5 Feb to 18 Mar 1919, by Hanns Vischer. [The Vischer Papers have been augmented and catalogued since Lady Vischer's death in 1963 and are held by a family Trust. Any scholar seeking access should make a written application to the Trustees and send it to the Librarian, Rhodes House Library, Oxford.]
8. *The Road to English Stage 1*, Sudan edn., OUP 1932
9. Furse, p 131
10. VP, Peter Vischer, *The Story of the Vischers*. The information concerning Sir Hanns' family background comes either from the Vischer Papers or from oral evidence provided in the early 1950s to the writer by his widow, in 1964 by his brother, Adolf, and in the late 1990s by his sons, John and Peter.
11. Adolf was honoured by Switzerland, France, Serbia, Bavaria and Italy for his work on behalf of orphans and victims of war.
12. *Swiss Observer,* 29 Mar 1945. He was an active supporter of the *Museum für Volkerkunde* in Basle to which he presented a number of items, and he attended functions of the guild *'Zum Schlussel'* whenever he could.
13. The coat of arms of the English branch of the Vischer family was registered with the College of Arms in 1943.
14. A *Weidlig* was a long, open wooden boat with high freeboard, raised prow and stern, propelled and steered by a single long oar, built for negotiating the (then) fast currents of the Rhine.
15. Letter 12 Nov 1952, Sir Evelyn Howell to the writer. [Howell subsequently had a distinguished career in the Indian Civil Service.]
16. Oral evidence, the late Lady Vischer
17. Church Missionary Society [CMS] 1900 (Hausa Mission) Richardson, S.S. 'Bornu', 24 Dec 1899
18. CMS 1902 (Hausa) W. R. S. Miller to Salisbury Square, 22 Jan 1902
19. CMS. 1902 (Hausa) Vischer, Redhill, 6 Dec 1902
20. Vischer had also graduated MA and become an FRGS in 1902, his proposer being Ruxton
21. CO 446/74 No.30542, Minute, F. G. A. Butler, 27 Aug 1908
22. Staatsarchiv Baselstadt: Archiv der Familie Vischer, PA 511, HV to Adolf V., 22 Jan 1904 [I no longer feature as a missionary in any Missionary newsletter and thereby find a thousand more opportunities to do the real

work of the missionary.] I am indebted to Dr Stephan Winkler of Bern for drawing my attention to these papers at Basle and also to the Sarasin'sches Familienarchiv, PA 212, and for kindly providing a number of relevant extracts for me.

23. *Ibid.*, HV to Adolf V., 2 Oct 1907. [I am fully convinced that the greatest handicap facing the Missionaries is wanting to set up their Church. How often is Church given precedence over Gospel! Any message standing a chance of being accepted by the African must relate strictly to the values as defined in the Gospels and not come across as disciplines imposed from Europe.] HV remained throughout his life a member of the Swiss Evangelical Church. He sometimes attended Church of England sevices in the United Kingdom, but never took Communion

24. Vischer, *Across the Sahara* …p 3

25. *Ibid.,* p 150

26. *Ibid.*, p 170 Some explanation of this phenomenon is given in a letter of 3 Dec 1906 to Vischer's family from two Turks of Murzuk: 'En route Mr H. Vischer was attacked by Tuaregs. He repulsed the attack by making it a point of killing only their camels, thereby depriving them of their means of pursuit. This was considered a noble act by the people here who venerated him and said devout prayers for him. We need hardly tell you that the people of Murzuk adored him. Whilst here he gave medical treatment to the poor, who regarded him as their benefactor .... Finally we would add that a legend has grown up around him here which regards his presence to have been the visitation of a Saint disguised as a Roumi.' [i.e. a stranger]. VP, English translation of the original French. Vischer's trans Saharan journey was the inspiration for a recent international expedition, led by John Hare, which traversed the Sahara from Kukawa in the south to Tripoli in the north, using only camels. Restoring the memory of the remarkable Hanns Vischer was one of the main aims of the project. The story of the recent expedition appeared as an article — John Hare, Surviving the Sahara, in the Dec 2002 issue of the *National Geographic* magazine. A book about the expedition is due to be published in the United Kingdom in early 2003.

27. VP, General Sir Hubert Huddleston to Lady Vischer, 22 Feb 1945

28. CO 446/65 no.41753, enclosures, Hewby to Girouard, 30 Sep 1907; also Vischer to Hewby, 1 Aug 1907

29. M. Perham, *Lugard the Years of Authority* (1960), p 503

30. See Sonia F. Graham, *Government and Mission Education in Northern Nigeria 1900–1919*, Ibadan University Press (1966)

31. CO 446/89 no.13864, Hesketh Bell, Zungeru, 31 Mar 1910 enclosure, General Ideas, Vischer, (Sep 1909)

32. Imperial Education Conference Paper III (Northern Nigeria) 1913, p 3

33. I. Vischer, *Croquis et Souvenirs de la Nigérie du Nord* (1917), pp 116–18. [Under present conditions the white man is indispensable for supervision and guidance. On him falls the work of choosing and adapting, but the day will come when the schools will have no further need of white direction. With the blessing of Allah, a future generation will see the work carried on by a teaching body which will be completely African and which will have been trained by a University of Nigeria.]

34. Oral evidence, Dr A. L. Vischer to the writer, 19 Nov 1964

35. D. Dalby, 'The Story of the Institute,' *International African Institute Bulletin* No.1 1976

36. Ido Bude, 'The Adaptation Concept in British Colonial Education', Comparative Education, XIX/3 (1983), p 341–355: K. King, *Pan-Africanism and Education,* (1971)

37. *Staatsarchiv Baselstadt: Sarasin'sches Familienarchiv,* PA 212 Vol.XXXIX, HV to Fritz Sarasin, 14 Jul 1933. [For the African colonial rule is already

approaching the end of its effective span. The current economic situation has accelerated the process. One can hardly predict what the next development will be, but more and more the people are beginning to formulate and to express their own wishes and hopes. This is particularly noticeable in the educational field and I welcome it. Firstly they may have a far better idea then we as to what they can and want to learn, and secondly this shows that our attempts to educate the people towards self-confidence and independence with our schools have not completely missed the target.]

38. VP, An Appreciation of Hanns and Isabelle Vischer, written in 1994 by Arthur Foss, who first met Vischer through war work early in the Second World War
39. D. H. Williams, *A Short Survey of Education in Northern Nigeria,* (1960). Years later, another former DE, E. J. R. Hussey, was surprised to learn in conversation with the writer that Vischer had spent barely five years, not 11, on education in the Northern Provinces, and modified his criticism of the pace of early developments accordingly.
40. Information supplied to the writer by the Army Historical Branch, Ministry of Defence. Unfortunately Vischer's Personal File could not be found at the Army Records Centre, Hayes, and so the exact nature of his work remains unknown but it was undoubtedly operational. In 1916 he was attached to the Embassy at Madrid. When Spain later became a Republic, he returned the decoration he had received from King Alfonso, whom he liked and admired
41. VP, Arthur Foss
42. VP, Private account of his journey from Bern to Vienna, Prague and Warsaw, Feb-Mar 1919, by HV
43. VP, H. J. Read to H. Vischer, 22 Dec 1919
44. F. J. Clatworthy, *The Formulation of British Colonial Education Policy 1923–1948* (1971)
45. International Missionary Council/Council of British Missionary Societies Archives [IMC/CBMS], Box 219, Ormsby-Gore to Oldham, 9 Jun 1923
46. *Ibid.,* Oldham to the Bishop of Liverpool, 7 Nov 1923
47. *Ibid.*
48. CO 446/89 no.13864, Minutes, C. Strachey and Sir F. Hopwood, Jul 1910
49. CO583/20 No. 47052, Lugard, 7 Nov 1914, and Minutes, including Harding, 23 Mar 1915
50. Cited in D. H. Williams: *A Short Survey of Education in Northern Nigeria,* (1960)
51. IMC/CBMS Box 219, Oldham to the Bishop of Liverpool, 7 Nov 1923
52. *Ibid.,* Oldham to Jesse Jones, 15 Nov 1923
53. VP, Letters to my Boys, 7 May 1926, describing his official visit to French West Africa. and to Nigeria and the Gold Coast
54. IMC/CBMS Box 219, Vischer to Oldham, 15 Nov 1923.
55. VP, Vischer, 8 Nov 1916. F. M. Urling Smith, appointed in 1910 to assist Vischer, remembered Vischer saying, 'When you and I stand before the Great White Throne we shall not be in a good position if H.E. says to us "What about those poor Hausas you tried to turn into white collared clerks for the benefit of the government departments in Nigeria?".' [F. M. Urling Smith to the writer, 25 Feb 1951]
56. From 1924 to 1936 the Vischers lived at 237 Knightsbridge, London
57. CO879/121 African No.1100, 27–29 Dec 1923
58. VP, Letters to my Boys, 7 May 1926
59. VP, Vischer to Under Secretary of State, 21 Dec 1923, and enclosures
60. I. Vischer
61. IMC/CBMS Box 219, Vischer to Oldham, 15 Nov 1923
62. *Ibid.,* Oldham to Vischer, 27 Dec 1923
63. *Ibid.,* Vischer to Oldham, 31 Dec 1923

64. VP, Minutes of the First Meeting, A.C.N.E.T.A., 9 Jan 1924.
65. IMC/CBMS Box 219, Vischer to Oldham, 24 Mar 1926. [Garfield Williams was Educational Secretary of the Church Missionary Society: Dillard was President of the Jeanes and Slater Fund and a member of the United States General Education Board and his son, George, was a secretary to the Commission together with James Dougall i.e. 'Jock': Leroy Shantz belonged to the United States Department of Agriculture: James Aggrey was African-born and American-educated and became the Vice Principal of Achimota College.]
66. *Ibid.,* Vischer to Oldham, 4 Apr 1924
67. VP, Vischer to Strachey, Zanzibar, 14 Apr 1924
68. IMC/CBMS Box 219, Vischer to Oldham, 1 May 1924
69. VP, Vischer to Under-Secretary of State, 27 Jul 1924
70. IMC/CBMS, Box 219, Vischer to Oldham, 23 Sep 1924
71. C. Whitehead: 'The Advisory Committee on Education in the [British] Colonies', *Pedagogica Historica*, XXVII/3 (1991)
72. VP, Minutes of the Advisory Committee on Education in British Tropical Africa, 1st Meeting, 9 Jan 1924
73. IMC/CBMS Box 221, Currie to Oldham, 3 May 1934
74. *Ibid.,* Vischer to Oldham, 9 Nov 1923
75. This creed is attested to by his sons
76. VP, e.g. West Africa, 14 Jul 1928, report of speech by Major Vischer at a dinner of the West African Students' Union on 30 Jun 1928: also Hanns Vischer, 'Native Education in British Tropical Africa', Rome, Oct 1938
77. IMC/CBMS Box 219, Vischer to Oldham, 9 Nov 1923
78. *Ibid.,* Vischer to Oldham, 22 Dec 1923
79. Furse, pp 125–6
80. *Ibid.*
81. Clatworthy, p 38
82. IMC/CBMS Box 219, Vischer to Oldham, 16 Dec 1924
83. *Ibid.*, Oldham to Vischer, 6 Oct 1924
84. *Ibid.*, Vischer to Oldham, 13 Jun 1927
85. CO323/1078 no.70238, Minute, Flood, 21 Apr 1930
86. IMC/CBMS Box 237 Oldham to Alec Fraser, 4 Jul 1927
87. *Ibid.*, Box 219, Oldham to Vischer, 1 May 1924
88. *Ibid.*, Box 221, Oldham to Lugard, 26 Jan 1934
89. Whitehead, p 396
90. Clatworthy Also Clive Whitehead, 'Education Policy in British Tropical Africa: the 1925 White Paper in Retrospect', *History of Education* 10/3 (1981). and 'The Advisory Committee on Education in the Colonies', *Pedagogica Historica*, XXVII/3 (1991)
91. IMC/CBMS Box 219, Vischer to Oldham, 16 Dec 1924
92. VP, Report by Major Vischer on his Visit to French West Africa, 18 June 1926
93. IMC/CBMS Box 219, Vischer to Oldham, 24 Mar 1924
94. E. Ashby, *Universities: British, Indian, African* (1966) p 192
95. CO 879/121 African No.1100, Part II Memoranda and Reports, Part III Correspondence
96. *Ibid.,* Minutes, 27 May 1926
97. See S. Sivonen, *White-Collar or Hoe Handle. African Education under British colonial policy 1920–4.* (1995) p 123 where he refers to the instructions Vischer issued to colonial Education Departments on the subject of language policy
98. M. Omolewa, 'The Adaptation Question in Nigerian Education', *Journal of the Historical Society of Nigeria* 8/3 (1976)
99. D. Dalby, 'The Story of the Institute', *International African Institute* [IAI] *Bulletin*, No.1 1976

100. VP, Vischer to Warnshuis, 26 Nov 1926
101. IAI, 1/5, Minutes of the First Meeting of the Executive Council, London, Oct 1925. See also 1/8, Hanns Vischer's File
102. M. Read, 'Education and Cultural Tradition' (Inaugural Lecture 19 Jun 1950), *Studies in Education No.2*, Institute of Education, University of London
103. CO 879/121, African No.1100, Minutes, Dec 1925
104. VP, Memorandum, 'The International African Institute', Vischer to CO, 4 Nov 1943
105. CO 879/121 African No.1100, Minutes, Feb 1927
106. *Ibid.*, Minutes, May 1927
107. *Ibid.*, Minutes, Mar 1928
108. VP, Vischer to Lugard, 14 Feb 1934
109. *Ibid.*, Vischer to Lugard, 20 Jan 1939
110. Contemporary pictures of the inter-war period of the Institute's life can be found in 'The Human Side of African Development', *United Empire*, Jul 1928, by Lugard, and in 'The Story of the Institute', *Africa*, VII, Jan 1934, by E.W. Smith
111. VP, Vischer to Lugard, 20 Feb 1930
112. IAI, 1/5, Minutes of first meeting of the Executive Council, Oct. 1926. Vischer also successfully advocated the inclusion of novels by Africans in the Institute's survey of books available in African languages
113. Perham, p 660
114. VP, Vischer to Warnshuis, 26 Nov 1926
115. C. Whitehead, 'The Nestor of British colonial education; a portrait of Arthur Mayhew CIE, CMG (1878–1948)', *Journal of Educational Administration and History*, 29/1 (1997) pp 51–76
116. VP, Vischer to Lugard, Rome, 2 May 1930
117. IAI *Bulletin,* supplement to Africa, 46/3 (1976)
118. VP, Vischer to Lugard, Italy, 10 Oct 1931, and enclosure, English version of his paper to the Council of the International Institute
119. IMC/CBMS Box 219, Ormsby-Gore to Oldham, 1 Sep 1931
120. *Ibid.*, Oldham to Ormsby-Gore, 4 Sep 1931
121. In Nigeria in 1910 Vischer was told by The Rev. G.P. Bargery of certain statements made about Vischer by Dr Miller of the CMS. Vischer wrote at once saying he must consider their friendship at an end and would take Miller to court unless a satisfactory explanation was given. Miller apparently placated him.(CMS [Hausa] Miller to Secretary, 31 Jul 1910.) Interestingly, after years of service in the CMS, Bargery joined Vischer's Education Department
122. VP, Vischer to Lugard, 3 Dec 1929
123. *Ibid.*, Vischer to Lugard, 15 Jul 1941; also Memorandum to the CO, 4 Nov 1943
124. Lugard, 'Sir Hanns Vischer' *Africa*, XV, Apr 1945
125. IMC/CBMS Box 273, Oldham to Fraser, 4 Jul 1927
126. *Ibid.*, Fraser to Oldham, 14 Jun 1927. Fraser was apparently unaware of the circumstances of Vischer's secondment to Education
127. *Ibid.*, copy enclosed
128. Perham, *op. cit.*, p 700
129. P. Garigue, 'The West African Students' Union, a study in culture contact' *Africa,* XXIII, Jan 1953. See also the students' own journal, *WASU.*
130. *West Africa*, 14 Jul 1928
131. CO 323/1025 No.60050 Vischer, 9 Jan 1929 and enclosure, Ruxton, 5 Jan 1929. See also IMC/CBMS Box 202
132. CO 323/1025 No.60050 Vischer 15 Oct. 1929
133. N. Azikiwe, *My Odyssey*, pp 211–12
134. See also CO 554/80 No.4131 (1929), CO 554/86 No.4364 (1931),

CO 323/1126 No.80202 (1931). There is evidence that some thought students in an official hostel would be less open to subversive elements, i.e. guest speakers critical of British colonial affairs. Vischer's seems to have been happy to use any funds which that fear might generate without raising the issue initially himself

135. WASU, 2/2, (Apr-Jun 1933), p 11
136. IMC/CBMS Box 202, Oldham to Ormsby-Gore, 8 Jan 1929
137. *Ibid.*, Oldham to Ruxton, 5 Jun 1929
138. *Ibid.*, Aird to Oldham, 4 Jun 1929
139. *Ibid.*, Oldham, 10 Sep 1930
140. Azikiwe, pp 211–14
141. Vischer did not limit his interest to students. He took a group of Africans, most found by him in London's dockland, to perform in a Cambridge theatre 'sometime in 1933–36'. The acts included walking barefoot on broken glass. (Sir Evelyn Howell to the writer, 7 Nov 1952.)
142. IMC/CBMS Box 221, Vischer to Oldham, 19 Jan 1934
143. C. Whitehead, 'The Advisory Committee...' *Pedagogica Historica*, p 403
144. IMC/CBMS Box 221, Vischer to Oldham, 19 Jan 1934
145. *Higher education in East Africa: report of the commission appointed by the Secretary of State for the colonies*, Sep 1937, Colonial No.142, HMSO 1937
146. See Ashby
147. *Ibid.*, p 202.
148. *Report of the committee appointed in 1938 by the governor of the Gold Coast Colony to inspect the Prince of Wales' College, Achimota, Accra, 1939*
149. VP, Memorandum on the proposed Institute of West African Arts, Industries and Social Science, Achimota 1942
150. VP, Memorandum, The International African Institute, Vischer to CO, 4 Nov 1943
151. *Ibid.*, Vischer to Lugard, 14 Feb 1934 Frequent family visits to the continent added to Vischer's official opportunities to gauge the international situation. Also, Isabelle often visited the Ruxtons in Paris in the 'thirties, describing a stay there as 'an intellectual shampoo'
152. Foss
153. *Mass Education in African Society*, Colonial No.186, 1943
154. Furse, pp 132–3
155. VP, Notes on Colonial Office Grants by Vischer
156. *Ibid.*, 'L'Enseignement dans les Possessions Anglaises d'Afrique', 1931. [After having enumerated the advantages that our system of colonial education needs to bring to African people, I could not finish without inviting you to consider yourselves the immense gain that there would be for us if we gave African people the means to express their own thoughts in their own languages. We can already see in African peoples' writings produced in their indigenous languages that there are elements of literature which will not only widen our knowledge of Africa and its history, but which also will contribute to the beauty and richness of the civilized world's literature.]
157. Report on the British Association meeting at Leeds, *The Times*, 7 Sept. 1927
158. H. Vischer, 'Mass Education in African Society' Africa, Vol. XIV, 1943–4
159. Furse, p 125

8. Arthur Mayhew

The Nestor of British Colonial Education[1]

Paying tribute to Arthur Mayhew soon after he died in March 1948, W. E. F. (Frank) Ward, his successor as editor of the journal *Oversea Education,* wrote of him thus:

> There are probably many of us in the Colonial Education Service to whom for many years the Colonial Office meant simply Arthur Mayhew. In our timidity we never ventured to approach the frowning portals of Downing Street; but on the other side of the Cenotaph, in the sunny seclusion of Richmond Terrace, we were sure of a ready welcome from a professional colleague. Mayhew was a man of two worlds: a man of Kipling's India and, though he never served in the Colonies, a man of the Colonial Empire.[2]

Despite Ward's eulogy, Mayhew has remained a relatively obscure figure in the history of British colonial education. He left no rich repository of personal papers and correspondence to posterity and nothing of substance has been written about his life and work since his death yet, as any foray into colonial archives will readily reveal, he played a leading role both in shaping and articulating colonial education policy in the 1930s. Before that he had enjoyed an outstanding career as an educational administrator in India, followed by a spell in the 1920s as a Classics Master at Eton. Like Sir Christopher Cox, who succeeded him at the Colonial Office in 1940, Mayhew never consciously sought the limelight. His outstanding intellect was best suited to those behind-the-scenes activities traditionally associated with the drafting of important memoranda and managing the affairs of the Colonial Office Advisory Committee on Education in the Colonies. His immediate family were aware that he occupied an important position in Whitehall but they were seemingly never fully cognisant of the precise nature or significance of his educational work. It is now more than half a century since his death and the British Empire that he served is no more. It is important, nevertheless, that a new generation should know of his contribution to colonial education, one of the most enduring aspects of Britain's imperial legacy in the modern world.

Arthur Innes Mayhew was born in Oxford in September 1878, the third son and sixth child in a family of seven children. His father was The Rev. Anthony Lawson Mayhew, Chaplain of Wadham College, Oxford, and his mother, Jane, the daughter of John Griffin, a doctor in nearby Banbury.[3] Anthony Mayhew's origins are obscure but he attended Clapham Grammar School before enrolling at Wadham College, Oxford, from whence he graduated in June 1863. He was ordained a priest in 1866 and thereafter occupied a variety of clerical posts before finally settling in Oxford in 1873. He was made Chaplain of Wadham College in 1880 and retained the position until his retirement in 1912. It was during the latter part of his life that he became a leading authority on the lexicography of the English language. He worked closely with The Rev. W. W. Skeat, Professor of Anglo-Saxon at Cambridge and published extensively in the field.[4] Perhaps his most outstanding contribution was *A Concise Dictionary of Middle English from A.D. 1150 to 1580,* published by the Clarendon Press in 1888. The study was jointly authored but in the Introduction Skeat emphasised that most of the research was done by his co-author. It is not surprising, therefore, that Anthony Mayhew is best remembered as a recluse who spent much of his time working in the large library which he built on to the family home. He died in December 1916, a year after his wife.

In Oxford, the Mayhew family resided at 18 Bradmore Road, which was situated next door to the original Oxford Preparatory School in Crick Road. The 'OPS' as it was often called, was later widely known as 'Lynam's' before it became known officially as the Dragon School in 1921.[5] Arthur Mayhew and his two older brothers Charles[6] and Arnold[7], all attended the Preparatory School. Arthur, nicknamed 'Moony' on account of his round and chubby face, was a voracious reader who also excelled at the art of repartee.[8] It would seem that he retained fond memories of his early schooling. In later life he sent his own two sons to the Dragon School, frequently returned to speak at school assemblies, and made numerous literary contributions to the *Draconian*, the school magazine. From an early age Mayhew showed academic promise and in 1891 he won an open scholarship to Winchester College. His lifelong friend and admirer Sir John Hubback,[9] who spent six years with him at Winchester, recalled how they shared the thrill of the telegram which told of their election to College: 'It came as we consumed ices in Cox's tuck shop at Crick Road, while the rest of the school were more studiously employed'.[10]

Mayhew's years as a pupil at Winchester [1891–97] coincided with a decade of outstanding intellectual achievement in the history of the School under the direction of the Headmaster The Rev. W. A. Fearon, a Fellow and former Tutor of New College, Oxford.[11] In his unpublished memoirs,[12] Mayhew recalled the time he spent at Winchester with great affection, especially the atmosphere, 'the quiet appeal of its buildings', the abiding influence of the nearby Cathedral, and 'the homeliness of the watermeads'. Winchester, as he remembered it, 'was preeminently quiet, leisurely, and sheltered. It was so different', he wrote, 'from the Eton that I came to know 30 years later, fascinating and exciting but so exposed geographically and otherwise to the outside world, so lacking in repose'. Mayhew was a 14-year-old pupil at Winchester at the time of the Quincentenary Celebrations held in July 1893, to mark the 500th anniversary of the School's founding by William of Wykeham. As he later recalled, 'as a small choirboy, I looked down on the long knave of Winchester Cathedral packed with Wykehamists and heard Archbishop Benson "praise famous men and our fathers that begat us"'. Likewise in Chamber Court, he saw the Prince of Wales formally greeted, and later sang Latin Grace at the formal dinner in the School Hall. In the 1890s the Classics still ruled supreme in the public schools and Winchester was no exception. By the time that he left school, Mayhew was able to read the classical authors studied at the time with 'real pleasure'. He had also acquired a deep knowledge of classical history and culture, a growing interest in English literature, and some proficiency in German but overall he recalled an isolation from contemporary life, 'from anything indeed not firmly rooted in classical or mediaeval soil'. The clearest manifestation of this was Winchester's 'almost contemptuous treatment of science'.

Mayhew's academic promise was fulfilled in his final year at Winchester when he was awarded one of six prestigious annual scholarships to New College, Oxford, from which he subsequently graduated in 1901 with a First in both Classical Moderations and *Literae Humaniores.*. Mayhew was a student at Oxford in what has been called 'the high period of empire' when many Oxford graduates joined the elite Indian Civil Service [ICS] or sought careers as government officials in the Colonial Empire.[13] After 1892 the age of entry to the ICS was raised to 23, thereby enabling Oxford graduates to qualify. Of more immediate interest to Mayhew's subsequent career, however, was the creation in 1896–7 of the equally prestigious Indian Educational Service. The IES had its origins a decade earlier in the recommendations of the Indian Public Service Commission which highlighted the need to attract highly qualified Europeans to serve as senior educators in India.[14]

By his own admission, only one public question of the day interested him as a philosophy student at Oxford 'and that interest determined my professional career'. A brief but very fruitful contact with R. B. Haldane[15], the Liberal MP for Haddingtonshire, directed Mayhew's attention to the 'amazing treasury of educational doctrine in Plato and Aristotle, and more particularly to Plato's insistence on the State's responsibility for the education, in the broadest sense, of its citizens'. At the time Sir Robert Morant and A. J. Balfour were planning the Act which in 1902 would lay the basis for a national system of education in England and Wales. In his memoirs Mayhew recalled listening to a 'brilliant discourse on Prussian education' by Haldane which encouraged him to read the reports on various state systems of education which Michael Sadler was then producing for the Board of Education, and Matthew Arnold's essays on French education. Armed with introductions from

Haldane, Mayhew subsequently went to Berlin, together with students from all over Europe, to study the philosophy of education under Paulsen and Munch. He also visited all grades of Prussian schools before going on to Jena to study the theory and practice of teaching in Professor Rein's seminar. The German experience confirmed his wish to pursue a career in education but not like that of many of his colleagues as an academic or as a teacher in a public school.

'What attracted me' he later wrote, 'was the relation of education to the history of civilisation, its place in national life, its religious ethical and social background and aims'. Elsewhere in his memoirs he wrote: 'What really excited me ... was the general question of Imperial functions, the justification of the correct attitude of a dominant persuasive race to[wards] primitive races of other types of culture .... Comparison of our [British] aims and methods with those of Periclean Athens and Trajan's Roman Empire was fascinating.' These interests were best pursued not by classroom teaching but in administrative and inspection work which he subsequently found in India and later at the Colonial Office.

Mayhew's immediate family claim that after graduation he initially set his sights on obtaining a Fellowship at All Souls College but he was unsuccessful due to a breakdown in his health while preparing for the qualifying examination.[16] There is no mention of this in his memoirs although he does mention briefly that his father had a serious mental collapse during his [Arthur's] final year of study.

Mayhew's appointment to the Indian Educational Service as what Philip Woodruff would have termed 'one of Plato's Guardians'[17] took effect on 30th June 1903, approximately two years after he graduated from Oxford. In his memoirs he casually mentioned that his interest in the historical and ethical aspects of British imperial policy was made 'more real and fascinating by a visit to Burma and Ceylon soon after I left Oxford, in circumstances to be noted later'. Unfortunately, he never explained the reasons for his visit nor did he provide any details of where he went or what he saw. His only comment was that by then he was committed to education work and on his return to England readily accepted a post in India.

Madras, to which Mayhew was first assigned as a School Inspector in 1903, was a far cry from his beloved lilacs and laburnums of Oxford,[18] but like many others of his generation, he was doubtless motivated, to go east, in part, by the intense interest in India which was characteristic of Oxford at the turn of the century. Moreover, he went out to India as a member of an education cadre whose conditions of service and remuneration bore ample testimony to their elite status. Mayhew was to spend almost 20 years of his working life in India during which time he met his future wife, raised a family of three children, and rose to high office in the educational bureaucracy.

He arrived in India during Lord Curzon's period as Viceroy (1898–1905) when, as he later wrote, 'British administration, on paternally autocratic lines, [was] at its zenith', and subsequently served the *Raj* during two decades of growing political turbulence occasioned by the rise of militant nationalist feeling and the economic impact of the First World War. Mayhew's Indian sojourn also coincided with a period of rapid and unprecedented expansion of education at all levels during which the government, encouraged by Curzon, took a more proactive role than hitherto in a vain attempt to improve the quality of instruction in schools and colleges. It was also the heyday of the Indian Educational Service which enjoyed unparalleled prestige and influence in educational administration. Although this did not preclude education policy from being the subject of adverse criticism from both Indians and Europeans alike. Indian nationalists objected to the dominance of Western values and content in the curriculum while Europeans accused the schools and colleges of breeding disloyalty and sedition amongst educated Indians. In retrospect, Mayhew may have found life in India stressful at times but it must surely have been equally stimulating and eventful.

From the outset Mayhew clearly impressed his superiors. Within four years of arriving in India he was Deputy Director of Public Instruction in Madras (1907) and two years later Inspector of European and Teacher Training Schools. In 1909, his career took an unusual twist when he was seconded for two years as Educational Adviser to the Nizam of Hyderabad. During that time he prepared a substantial report on the future of education in that princely state. In 1914, at the age of 36, he was appointed Acting Director of Public Instruction in the Central Provinces and confirmed as Director two years later. In his capacity as Acting [Officiating] Director he presided over a Committee which reported on the prospects of establishing a university in the Central Provinces. He chaired many of the sub-committees and wrote most of the final report which led ultimately to the establishment of Nagpur University in 1923.[19] Within the space of 13 years he had reached the top echelon of the IES. His subsequent work on behalf of Indian education was duly acknowledged when was made a Companion of the Order of the Indian Empire [CIE] in 1919.[20]

In 1921 the Indian government established a Central Advisory Board of Education. Mayhew, in his capacity as Director of Public Instruction in the Central Provinces, was an inaugural member of the Board. At the Board's fourth meeting, held in Delhi in January 1922, he assumed the position of acting Chairman but only presided over two further meetings before his departure from India. Even in that short time Mayhew demonstrated his undoubted talents as an administrator and committee member. As acting Chairman he prepared a lengthy memorandum for the Board on the education of blind and deaf mute persons in India, an extended Note on the work of the Board in its first year of operation, and a statement on Adult Education in India, all of which involved lengthy and detailed preparation.[21]

Mayhew left India in 1922, probably for several reasons. His son suggested that his poor health may have been a primary consideration. Evidently Mayhew suffered from recurrent bouts of malaria throughout his adult life and there were also hints of possible kidney problems. In 1921 education had also been one of the subjects handed over to local Indian control as a consequence of the Montague-Chelmsford constitutional reforms and Mayhew was opposed to the move.[22] After almost 20 years service he was entitled to a generous retirement pension and it seemed likely that the days of the IES were numbered. There were, however, also family reasons for leaving India. In London in September 1908, Mayhew had married May Catherine, the daughter of Sir James Davies, a colourful judge of the High Court of Madras. Thereafter, they had two sons and a daughter. Their sons, born in 1909 and 1913 respectively, were sent back to Oxford, to the Dragon School, for their preparatory schooling while a daughter, born in 1915, remained in India with them. By the time that Mayhew decided to leave India his daughter was seven years old and her future schooling was an immediate consideration.[23]

Upon his return to England, Mayhew rented a house in Windsor before moving to 'Normanhurst' described by his daughter as 'a solid Victorian five bedroom house with stables and about an acre of ground' located in the picturesque village of Datchet, near Slough in Buckinghamshire.[24] He lived there until he died in 1948. In the 1930s, when Mayhew worked in Whitehall, his daughter recalls that he travelled daily to London by train and unselfishly took *The Times* newspaper of the previous day to read. Evidently he derived wry amusement from fellow passengers when they eventually conjured up the courage to point out to him that he was reading yesterday's paper.[25]

In England, Mayhew obtained a teaching position on the staff of Eton College as the result of a close friendship between the Headmaster, Dr C. A. Alington, and Mayhew's older brother The Rev. Arnold Mayhew,[26] who later became Canon of Salisbury Cathedral. Mayhew taught classics at Eton in the 'Division' immediately below the Sixth Form. To quote Sir John Hubback, he taught a course called '"Culture and Anarchy", his main duties being to provide a modicum of culture for those who had hitherto successfully avoided its infection, and to combat the anarchy which that aim tended to provoke'.[27] Mayhew's lifelong love of English literature, ready wit and gift for story-telling made him a popular teacher. In India he had been known to his friends as 'JOA' or 'Jolly old Arthur' because of his wholesome laughter and 'vivid' personality[28] but his daughter claims that it was her mother who coined the name because she thought he was sometimes too serious at picnics and parties.[29] By the same token, his daughter can still recall an occasion when he jumped off a springboard into a swimming pool dressed in fancy dress holding up an open umbrella. Mayhew was also very fond of classical music and played the violin from an early age. At Eton he played in the school orchestra. His daughter still remembers the classical music that regularly emanated from the gramaphone in his study at 'Normanhurst'. Throughout his life he was also an avid reader. Legend has it that he completed reading the whole of Gibbon's *Decline and Fall of the Roman Empire* while he shaved each morning.[30] He had no great love of sport but he derived much satisfaction from the cricketing prowess of his eldest son, who won a Blue for cricket in 1930 when he was a student at Brasenose College, Oxford. John Mayhew also recalled one occasion when his father was injured by a passing vehicle in London while reading about him in the evening newspaper instead of watching the traffic.[31]

While teaching at Eton, Mayhew wrote two books which established him as a leading scholar on British rule in India. The first, *The Education of India*,[32] published in 1926, provided a critical commentary on British education policy in India from the adoption of Macaulay's Minute in 1835, with its emphasis on the teaching of Western knowledge by means of the English language, through to the early 1920s when education passed to Indian control. Mayhew was highly critical of the way in which education had been developed and saw little prospect of any improvement as a result of its transfer to Indian control. He deplored the neglect of Indian culture, the excessive emphasis placed on passing examinations, and the direct link between an overriding academic curriculum and the creation of a 'babu' or white-collar class. His second book, *Christianity and the Government of India*,[33] was published in 1929. In it Mayhew paid a generous tribute to the work of the missionaries but he was mainly concerned with the ethical problems encountered by the British when called upon to rule over millions of Hindus and Moslems. Mayhew argued 'at the risk of embarrassing a bureaucracy unused to praise' that the principles of Christianity had largely dictated the nature of British rule. By the late 1920s Mayhew was looking for a new career opening. In private correspondence he mentioned the possibility of becoming DE in Kenya and also considered taking up an unspecified educational post with the missions but he eventually obtained an appointment in Whitehall as one of the two Joint-Secretaries of the enlarged Advisory Committee on Education in the Colonies.

It the early 1920s, prompted by strong missionary pressure, the Colonial Office began, for the first time, to take a systematic and enduring interest in the development of education within the Colonial Empire. As a consequence the Advisory Committee on Education in British Tropical Africa was established in the latter part of 1923 with Hanns Vischer as its secretary. Initially, the work of the Committee was confined to the African colonies but at the Colonial Conference of 1927 moves were set in train to extend its brief to cover all the colonies. It was agreed to enlarge the composition of the Committee and to appoint two Joint-Secretaries. One would deal with matters affecting the African colonies while the other would attend to the needs of the rest. After a long delay caused by the slow response of colonial governments to agree to finance the expanded committee and much ensuing heartache on Mayhew's part, he eventually joined Vischer in 1929 as a Joint-Secretary of the revamped Advisory Committee on Education in the Colonies. During the next 10 years of his life he was to occupy a pivotal role in colonial education both as author and critic and as a key figure on the Advisory Committee.

When The Rt. Hon. W. A. G. Ormsby-Gore, the Parliamentary Under Secretary of State for the Colonies first mooted an expansion of the Advisory Committee he had in mind the appointment of two joint-secretaries and a third official to edit a quarterly bulletin. He hoped the latter would be a first-rate journal, which would provide a forum for new ideas and a genuine medium of exchange of information on matters of common educational interest. He envisaged the editor of the proposed journal as someone with a real knowledge of education, a gift for writing, and a philosophical outlook.[34] In advocating two joint-secretaries, Ormsby-Gore thought the second secretary should be someone with Asiatic experience and he even mentioned Dr Winstedt, the DE in the Straits Settlements of Malaya, as a potential candidate.[35] Winstedt chose not to apply and when Mayhew was eventually appointed he agreed to act as both Joint-Secretary and Editor of the new journal *Oversea Education*.[36]

In part, Mayhew's appointment appears to have been linked to his strong support for the educational work of the Christian missions and more specifically to J. H. Oldham's influence in the Colonial Office.[37] Mayhew's father and one of his brothers were both Anglican clerics and Mayhew himself was a practising Anglican throughout his life. His late son and surviving daughter both recall religious services at home in their younger years when 'we children read bible passages and prayers' but his son never thought of his father as a 'strict' Anglican in any dogmatic sense, although he felt that the traditions of Anglicanism were very much a part of his father's life as a result of his upbringing: 'It was obvious to me that the Christian religion was the guiding principle in his life'.[38] The two books that Mayhew wrote in the 1920s also reflected his strong interest in the role of the Christian Church in India. He was also a founding member of the Institute of Christian Education and a member of the editorial board of the Institute's quarterly journal *Religion in Education*.[39] In 1933 he also edited *Selections [English] A Bible Treasury*, a second edition of which was published in 1939,[40] and in 1941 contributed a chapter on 'The Christian Ethic and India' to L. S. S. O'Malley's study *Modern India and the West*.[41]

The first hint of Mayhew's influential standing in British missionary circles was evident in 1923 when Oldham showed him a draft copy of the memorandum that he had prepared for the Colonial Office as part of the negotiations which led to the formation of the Advisory Committee on Native Education in British Tropical Africa. Mayhew assured Oldham that his account of the 1854 Despatch on Education in India and the sense of partnership that was then envisaged between the missions and the government in promoting education in India was an accurate interpretation.[42] Mission archives reveal no further correspondence until Mayhew wrote to Oldham some four years later. The tone of the letter does not suggest that they had maintained a close friendship in the interim but Mayhew was certainly one of Oldham's many useful 'contacts'. Mayhew told Oldham that he was provisionally a candidate for the post of DE in Kenya although he thought it highly unlikely that he would be able to accept the position if it were offered to him because of his family circumstances. [At that time he had two sons at Eton College and a 12 year old daughter to consider.] In apologetic vein Mayhew wrote: 'I have ventured to quote your name to the Colonial Office as one who might be ready to [supply] information about me .... You will understand, of course, that I have not in quoting your name relied in any way on your being able to recommend me for the particular post'. He went on to say that he had experienced a particularly busy term at Eton and apologised for not having found time to comment in detail on a preliminary statement on Religious Education that Oldham had sent to him. He had, however, read enough of it to realise that it was a very lucid and comprehensive document.[43]

Oldham replied a fortnight later, apologising for not writing sooner due to having been away from his office on holiday in Europe. Meanwhile, he had, as usual, been working behind the scenes. He expressed interest in the Kenya position but said that he wanted to talk more about it with Mayhew. He was not sure that it was the right job for him. He then referred to the projected enlargement of the Colonial Office Advisory Committee on Education and the need for additional staff and added: 'In connection with any new appointment that may be made *I have suggested your name.*'[44] He did not know whether anything would come of it but he concluded his letter by saying 'If at any time an approach should be made to you in regard to this matter, please do not turn down the proposal without having a talk with me about it first'.[45] Mayhew must have spoken to Oldham in person almost immediately afterwards because little more than a week later Oldham again wrote to say that he had seen Ormsby-Gore and Major Furse, who was in charge of the recruitment of Colonial Office staff. As a result of the meeting he believed that Mayhew would be approached regarding the new appointments for the Advisory Committee but that the Colonial Office would probably look elsewhere to fill the post of DE in Kenya.[46] Oldham hastened to add that these were no more than his inferences from the conversation and should not be regarded as definite or final.[47]

Mayhew must have contacted Oldham again almost immediately because four days later Oldham wrote saying that he saw no reason why Mayhew should not send a letter to the Colonial Office on the lines he had suggested — presumably indicating his interest in the new appointments and his qualifications for them. Oldham went on to say:

> I most earnestly desire and hope that the Colonial Office may offer you an appointment in connexion [sic] with the Advisory Committee, and that you may see your way to accept it. This would transform the situation. But the ways of the CO are mysterious, and one never knows whether they will carry out what appeared to be their intentions until the step has been actually taken.[48]

Mayhew now entered on what must have been one of the most frustrating periods of his life. On 29 November, some three weeks after receiving Oldham's letter he wrote again to Oldham:

> I have been asked by a mission to take up a post where I feel that I am really needed and to which I am strongly drawn. Whether it will financially be practicable has yet to be seen. I do not think anyhow that family considerations would justify my taking it, if the Colonial Office had any work, also of a useful nature, to offer me at home. I have till Christmas to decide. It would help me very much in my decision if I were to hear from you that there is now no chance of the Colonial Office offering me anything. If on the other hand the offer is still under consideration, it might be possible perhaps for you to let the CO know that by Christmas I may, in the absence of any information from them, have committed myself elsewhere.[49]

On 21 December Oldham replied to Mayhew's letter saying that he had seen Ormsby-Gore the day before and from what had been said, he believed that the Colonial Office would ask him to become one of the joint-secretaries. However, the Colonial Office was unable to make him an offer until replies had been received from all the colonial governments endorsing the enlargement of the Committee and agreeing to contribute to the revised budget. It was unclear when all the replies would be received. He concluded by saying:

> In the circumstances you should not commit yourself in any other direction. I am personally very much concerned about the future of the Advisory Committee at the CO. It seems to me to have extraordinary opportunities and possibilities but it would not be difficult for them to be missed. My anxieties would be largely allayed if I knew that you were appointed as one of the secretaries. If the offer should be made to you during my absence in Africa and you decide to accept, I should be grateful if you would let me know .... Please treat what I have said as confidential.[50]

Mayhew had to wait until 13 October 1928, some nine months later, before he was finally offered the post of Joint-Secretary, which he took up in January 1929.[51] The long delay was caused by the slowness of several colonies to agree to the financial implications of a revamped advisory committee and the launching of a quarterly journal. Some Colonial Officials expressed their concern lest the long delay should result in the loss of Mayhew for the post of joint-secretary and editor of the journal. One official minuted that it would be extremely difficult to get anyone else as good as him and it was freely admitted that his financial prospects were better at Eton.[52] It was Ceylon that caused the main delay to

Mayhew's appointment. The Finance Committee in Ceylon decided by a large majority not to participate in financing the new venture which included Mayhew's salary. Eventually, Ormsby-Gore agreed to proceed without Ceylon. Other colonies choosing not to participate included the Leeward and Windward Islands, Somaliland, the Bahamas and Iraq. All the other colonies agreed to contribute 1/600th of their annual government expenditure on education to finance the expanded advisory committee, including £3000 p.a. for the salaries of the two joint-secretaries, and the new journal.[53]

Oldham's expression of concern to Mayhew about the future of the Advisory Committee largely centred on his reservations about Hanns Vischer's record as secretary. Vischer was highly intelligent and he had an intimate knowledge of Africa. He was also a close colleague of Lord Lugard, a former Governor-General of Nigeria and one of the most influential members of the Advisory Committee, and directly involved in establishing the International Institute for African Languages and Culture, but Oldham always had reservations about his qualities as a secretary.

Oldham believed that the Secretary of the Advisory Committee should initiate inquiries and reports rather than follow the lead of others. He was also acutely aware that the long-term future of the Committee and its influence on colonial education policy was very dependent on the quality of leadership and organisation of its executive secretary. He was extremely concerned to ensure that an enlarged committee, which might potentially exert immense influence because its brief was to include the entire colonial empire, was administered by someone of outstanding ability who was also sympathetic to the mission cause. Mayhew was the ideal candidate. In a private letter to Ormsby-Gore he wrote: 'We are fortunate in having an exceptionally good man in Mayhew. The quality of education in the colonies in the next few years may depend to a large extent on our being able to retain him'.[54] During his time in India Mayhew had excelled in committee work, including the writing of reports and memoranda. Moreover, he was highly intelligent, and had warm personal qualities that enabled him to work amicably with others. By nature he was unassuming and modest but far from diffident while his deep Christian convictions ensured that he was acceptable to the missions and someone they could depend upon to protect their interests. As The Rev. C. A. Alington, Headmaster of Eton, remarked when highly recommending Mayhew to Ormsby-Gore for the post of joint-secretary, he would be sorry to lose him.[55]

Oldham's misgivings about Vischer continued. As late as August-September 1931 he wrote to Ormsby-Gore complaining about Vischer's 'entirely unsystematic mind' and his poor command of committee work[56] but Ormsby-Gore did not share Oldham's opinion. 'I have an equal admiration for them both', he said. He admitted that Vischer was not as 'clever' as Mayhew but he claimed that Vischer had admirable judgement and real knowledge of African conditions 'and how it all looks from the

African end of the telescope'.[57] In practice, Vischer and Mayhew worked closely and harmoniously together throughout the 1930s.

Mayhew was 50 years old when he started sharing an office with Hanns Vischer at 2 Richmond Terrace, situated on the southern side of Whitehall. During the next 10 years he would travel widely, be known personally to dozens of people serving in the CES, edit a successful journal about colonial education, be closely involved in the ever expanding activities of the Advisory Committee, attend two major overseas conferences on colonial education, lecture on British education policy in India and the Colonies at the University of London's Institute of Education, and write a third book, *Education in the Colonial Empire* (1938), based on his experiences as a joint-secretary, thereby establishing himself as the leading authority on the subject. Yet this impressive record of service and achievement might never have come to pass but for the benevolence of the Carnegie Corporation of New York.[58]

In the summer of 1931, in the wake of the Depression, and as part of wide-ranging government cost-cutting measures, it was agreed that drastic reductions should be made in the expenses of the Education Advisory Committee. The projected cuts amounted to the abolition of one of the joint secretarial positions, a saving of £1500 p.a. Vischer had served on the Advisory Committee longer than Mayhew so it looked as if it would be Mayhew's position that would be retrenched. Oldham was gravely concerned at the prospect and wrote to Ormsby-Gore stressing that Mayhew's retention was vital to the Advisory Committee's survival. Ormsby-Gore claimed that the pressure for retrenchment stemmed from within the Colonial Office and had its origins in the long-standing resentment felt by permanent staff towards advisory committees. He advised Oldham to talk to Malcolm MacDonald, the Prime Minister's son, who was tipped to become Colonial Under-Secretary and Chairman of the Advisory Committee. MacDonald didn't become Under-Secretary but Oldham received an assurance that both Vischer and Mayhew would be retained as Joint-Secretaries for at least another year.

Unfortunately, there was no improvement in the economy and by June 1933 there was renewed pressure for cuts in the Advisory Committee's finances. Precisely what transpired at this point is unclear but Mayhew appears to have suggested to Oldham the possibility of soliciting financial support for the Advisory Committee from the Carnegie Corporation. The idea was probably linked to the fact that Dr F. P. Keppel, the President of the Carnegie Corporation, was to visit Britain and planned to spend time with Oldham at his home in Chipstead. Oldham was enthusiastic about the idea and asked Mayhew to draft a memorandum for Keppel's benefit outlining the scope and functions of the Advisory Committee. Mayhew was careful to stress that the idea was his alone and not that of the Colonial Office. Writing literally to save his job, he argued that the Advisory Committee and its joint secretaries provided the nucleus of a projected bureau of research in oversea education which the London Institute of Education was not yet able to staff.[59] Keppel was supportive in principle of Carnegie funding and Oldham duly sought Colonial Office endorsement of the idea. Lord Plymouth, the Colonial Under-Secretary, was reluctant to approach the Carnegie Corporation directly but expressed strong support for any personal move that Oldham might initiate. Oldham then wrote a six page letter to Keppel requesting a grant of $5000 a year for the next three years.[60] The Carnegie Corporation duly endorsed Keppel's support, and the Advisory Committee weathered the storm. Needless to say, Mayhew also kept his job.

The Corporation agreed to make finance available expressly 'to enable the staff [of the Advisory Committee] to continue their work during a time of exceptional difficulty and not merely to reduce the charge on Colonial budgets'. An initial grant of $10,000 was given to cover 1933 and 1934, followed by a further $10,000 to cover 1935 and 1936. A final grant of $10,000 in 1939 brought the amount of American philanthropic aid given to British colonial education to $30,000 in six years.[61] In retrospect, one cannot escape the irony of the situation. On the one hand the British government readily accepted generous amounts of American financial aid to promote education in the colonies but at the same time, members of the Advisory Committee and senior Colonial Office staff were highly critical of American education and forever anxious to ensure that it did not 'contaminate' colonial students.[62]

Mayhew's first overseas trip was to the West Indies in 1931–32. Together with F. C. Marriot, the DE in Trinidad, he wrote a report on the problems of primary and secondary education in Trinidad, Barbados, and the Leeward and Windward Islands.[63] In 1932 he also visited West Africa as a member of the first inspection team of Achimota College.[64] In August-September 1934, he attended a summer seminar on the education of non-Western peoples, officially called 'Education and Cultural Contacts', held at Yale University, where he gave lectures on education policy in British colonies. This was followed by a brief visit to Cyprus in the Spring of 1935 for discussions with the Governor on proposals to widen the scope of the secondary school curriculum and its implications for elementary education and teacher training.[65] In 1936 he attended another seminar-conference on 'Education in Pacific Countries' held in Hawaii. As at the Yale conference, he gave several lectures on aspects of British colonial education.[66] After attending the Hawaii conference he proceeded immediately to Fiji where he compiled a report on education in response to growing Indian agitation for more educational opportunities, especially at the secondary level.[67] The book that he published in 1938 contained the essence of the lectures on British colonial education policy that he gave at Yale and Hawaii, together with his observations of education in British tropical Africa, Malaya, Fiji, and the West Indies.

Mayhew was invited to participate in the Yale seminar by Professor Charles T. Loram. A South African by birth but educated at Cambridge and Columbia Universities, Loram had been offered the position of Secretary, ahead of Hanns Vischer, when the Colonial Office Advisory Committee on Education was first established in 1923 but he declined for financial reasons. He had never met Mayhew when he invited him to Yale but this did not prevent them from engaging in a most interesting dialogue about the title of the conference.[68]

Loram's initial choice of a title was 'The place of education in the introduction of Western civilisation to non-Western peoples'. Mayhew wrote back saying that from what he knew of public opinion in the West Indies after his recent visit [The Carnegie Corporation had indicated its willingness to fund the attendance of several West Indians at the conference] their participation in any conference dealing with primitive (or non-Western) peoples was not likely to be popular: 'I noticed during my recent visit,' he wrote, 'what I think most visitors to the West Indies have observed, a reluctance to associate West Indian educational problems in any way with African problems.' Loram responded first with 'The place of education among underprivileged peoples', then 'Cultural Contacts and Education' and finally 'Education and Cultural Contacts'. Mayhew expressed a preference for something akin to 'Education in tropical and sub-tropical areas' or even 'Tropical Education' to assuage West African feelings but ultimately accepted Loram's final suggestion. Later he apologised for being 'such a bore in the matter' but pointed out that he had good reason to know how extremely sensitive public opinion was in the West Indies.

In his capacity as Joint-Secretary of the Advisory Committee, Mayhew had to seek permission to attend the Yale Conference and lecture on British education policy in the Colonies. This was readily granted by the Advisory Committee but only if he went in a private capacity and not as a representative of the Colonial Office. Sara Burstall, a member of the Advisory Committee and a former Headmistress of Manchester High School for Girls, expressed regret that Mayhew could not deliver a similar course of lectures at the London Institute of Education and that education officers in British colonies should have to go to America for their training. Sir Percy Nunn said that a similar course at London had been under consideration for some time but that it had been postponed on account of the financial depression. One Colonial Office official minuted his objection to British education officials being mixed up in a conference about 'under-privileged' peoples: 'If it is used as synonymous with 'non-western', it is [a] typical piece of American arrogance'.[69] In October 1933, Mayhew minuted that Professor Radcliffe Brown was unable to give the sociology lectures at the Yale Conference and that Professor Malinowski had been invited instead. This prompted Harold Beckett, the Acting Assistant Secretary in the West Indies Department, to minute 'No doubt Mr Mayhew will counteract his alleged communistic proclivities'.[70]

The 'seminar-conference' — so-called to emphasize the scholarly nature of the discussions held in Hawaii in 1936 — was jointly sponsored by the universities of Hawaii and Yale, and organised by Loram and

Professor Felix M. Keesing, the head of the Anthropology Department at Hawaii. Most of the 66 educators and social scientists who attended did so as a result of personal invitations. They came from a wide array of countries and their deliberations were spread over five weeks. Mayhew, clearly a leading figure in the proceedings, addressed the full conference on 'British Colonial Policy in its Educational Aspects' on the second day. He also gave two other lectures, one on 'Fundamentals' and an evening address which was open to the general public on 'India and its Problems'.[71]

Throughout his time as Joint-Secretary of the Advisory Committee and for several years thereafter, Mayhew edited the quarterly bulletin *Oversea Education*. The format consisted of articles of general interest mostly but not exclusively contributed by members of the CES; miscellaneous news items of people and events thought to be of interest to colonial educators; reviews of books related to both the theory and practice of education in colonial settings; and summaries of the main activities of the Advisory Committee on Education in the Colonies. Like many editors, Mayhew was always seeking more articles of general interest and additional subscribers to defray rising costs of production. When he retired from his role as Joint-Secretary in December 1939, he agreed to continue editing *Oversea Education* on a temporary basis. Due to the prolongation of the war he was destined to remain as editor for another five years until Frank Ward replaced him in 1945. The bulletin continued under Ward's equally scholarly editorship until its eventual demise in 1963. Any library possessing a full run of issues has a valuable historical archive for the study of British colonial education.

A close study of the Minutes of meetings and papers of the Advisory Committee on Education in the Colonies during the period 1929–1939 bears ample testimony to the pivotal role that Mayhew played in Colonial Education in the 'thirties. He rarely missed a meeting of the Advisory Committee and then only because he was abroad; he served on numerous sub-committees and wrote copious memoranda and reports, including the Memoranda on the Aims and Methods of Language Teaching (1930) and that on Educational Grants-in-Aid (1933); he interviewed numerous recruits for the CES and thereafter kept in regular touch with them when they were on leave; he consulted with a wide range of colonial officials on educational matters when they passed through London, and he also gave an annual course of lectures on British education policy in India and the Colonies to students in the Probationers' course in the Colonial Department at the Institute of Education. As one writer has commented, during the 1930s Mayhew was without doubt 'one of the most experienced educationists then living',[72] a fact duly acknowledged when he was awarded the CMG in 1936 for his services to colonial education. The late Sir Christopher Cox thought of Mayhew as a ready and exact draftsman who was completely at home in committee work.[73] This fact is readily apparent to anyone conversant with the Colonial Office files of the 1930s. His neat and unmistakable handwriting appears in numerous contexts. Like his successor Frank Ward, his comments were generally brief but always incisive. He forged a good understanding with Vischer, being responsible for all non-African files, and also built up a sound and very important relationship with the various Christian missions. Cox also commented on Mayhew's selfless character, his unassuming and modest but far from diffident personality, and his depth of knowledge, sanity, clarity and accuracy, to which he sometimes added irony and a salty wit. The opening paragraph of Mayhew's book on education in India was cited by Cox as a case in point:

> It is only the professional who is perplexed by educational problems. Laymen who are compelled as parents, politicians, or members of committees to consider educational aims and methods find nothing puzzling except the schoolmaster's inability to face obvious facts and apply unassailable principles. In India there has been no subject on which Viceroys and Governors have expressed their views with more ease and eloquence. Mind and pen move along well-worn grooves. The experienced Secretary, after spending his morning energy on financial and judicial files, drafts with the sinking sun his educational resolution, in which educationalists are reminded that their task is the formation of character and the training of good and productive citizens, and that their methods must be effective within the limits prescribed by economy and public opinion.[74]

A further illustration of Mayhew's penchant for the witty remark was contained in a Minute that he wrote soon after joining the Colonial Office. Dr R. O. Winstedt, the DE in the [Malayan] Straits Settlements had written to him in connection with the Malayan government's decision to subscribe for three years to the costs of the Advisory Committee. In a forthright manner he told Mayhew that the Malayan government had agreed to subscribe mainly in the hope that the Committee would be able to help overcome an acute shortage of teachers. If the Committee failed in this respect, Winstedt told Mayhew in no uncertain terms that his government would consider it had failed in its chief object. Mayhew minuted, somewhat wryly, 'The SS Government evidently believes in "payment by results"!'[75] One wonders what Mayhew may have thought privately several years later when Winstedt, by then retired and knighted for his services to education in Malaya, became a member of the Advisory Committee.

It was at the November meeting in 1939, the last for the year, that Lord Dufferin announced with regret that the services of both Vischer and Mayhew as Joint-Secretaries 'would cease' at the end of the year, although Mayhew would remain as editor of *Oversea Education* 'for a few months' longer.[76] Their retirement was due principally to Malcolm Macdonald becoming Colonial Secretary in 1938. He sought to embark upon a far-reaching reform programme in colonial policy, including the introduction of younger men into senior positions.[77] He was particularly influenced by Lord Hailey's *African Survey*, published in 1938,[78] in which Hailey strongly recommended the appointment of a full time Educational Adviser to the Colonial Office who would be expected to travel regularly around the Colonies providing advice and encouragement to officials-on-the-spot. As early as February 1939 Macdonald had discussions with his senior officials at which it was agreed to appoint an Educational Adviser as from the start of 1940.[79] Vischer and Mayhew had also both reached retirement age [Mayhew turned 61 in the September] and it was, therefore, deemed an appropriate time to appoint Christopher Cox, then DE and Principal of Gordon College in the Anglo-Egyptian Sudan, to the newly-created advisory position.[80] In announcing that Vischer and Mayhew would retire at the end of the year, Lord Dufferin expressed the hope that both men would in due course become members of the Advisory Committee in their own right. Vischer never did so — he died in 1945 — but Mayhew returned in 1946 for a brief period on the Committee before he retired at the end of 1947.

Mayhew clearly played a pivotal role in maintaining and extending the influence of the Advisory Committee throughout the colonies in the 1930s but one inevitably wonders how he would have handled the rapid pace of change that was ushered in by the onset of war in 1939. The decade that he spent in Whitehall was not a propitious time for educational expansion and reform. The crippling impact of the Wall Street Stock Market crash in October 1929 had a severe and long-term impact on government spending both in Britain and the colonial empire. Throughout the period there was also a widespread belief that there was no great urgency to reform the nature and essence of colonial administration or to increase significantly the welfare role of government. Likewise, few, if any, of the Empire's critics envisaged that what are now thought of as the halcyon days of empire were soon to disappear for ever. Throughout the 1930s education was still universally viewed as an item of consumption — a financial burden on the taxpayer — rather than a vital investment in a nation's future socio-economic wellbeing. The Indian educational legacy still exerted a strong influence on colonial thought. Educational expansion had to be treated with great caution otherwise it might get out of control and generate political unrest. Members of the Education Advisory Committee frequently endorsed the need for new initiatives but it must be remembered that their role was purely advisory and that most of them were locked into the same mindset as their contemporaries. Mayhew, a late Victorian by education and upbringing, managed to combine the characteristic detachment of the scholar with the qualities of an outstanding administrator thereby giving him the edge on many of his contemporaries. A lifetime spent in administration and teaching likewise enabled him to acquire an extensive and unique fund of practical knowledge about education which he put to good effect as an educational adviser.

The onset of war gave Mayhew few opportunities to enjoy retirement although he continued to enjoy his long-standing membership of the Authors' Club.[81] Besides editing *Oversea Education*, he was also engaged in war work of a non-educational kind at the Colonial Office and later at the War Office. In 1941 he was included as a member of an important sub-committee of the Advisory Committee on Education in the Colonies which examined Adult and Mass Education. The sub-committee's report *Mass Education in African Society* figured prominently in reshaping post-war educational priorities in the colonies. Mayhew also served on the Council of Radley College, near Oxford, continuously from 1929 until his death.[82] In 1940, *The Times Educational Supplement* also published a series of 10 articles by him entitled 'Educating the Colonies'.[83] After the war he also did some relief teaching in a nearby secondary school but by then his health was fast deteriorating. He had been a heavy smoker throughout his life, a habit he claimed to have acquired when he was a pupil at Winchester College in the 1890s, and although he gave up smoking towards the end of his life he appears to have suffered increasingly in his latter years from chronic emphysema.[84] He died unexpectedly in his sleep on 16 March 1948.[85]

In his history of Winchester College, J. D'E Firth remarked on the fact that no other public school had been quite so fully represented as Winchester in the higher administrative ranks of the public service at home and in India. The close integration of Winchester and the Universities with the public service was comparable with the Platonic ideal. Boys of high promise, he claimed, found in Winchester the 'fair meadow' in which Plato desired his future rulers to browse during their earlier years. Thereafter, at the University, they were trained to be Guardians of the Republic, spending their working lifetime in the higher ranks of governmental administration. Mayhew's life epitomized that ideal — 'not to get on in the world, not to compete in separate rivalries for honour or riches, but to be the faithful soldiers and servants of God and their Country'.[86] Frank Ward, who succeeded Mayhew as editor of *Oversea Education* and who was also, like him, an outstanding teacher, a distinguished author and a significant but hitherto largely unheralded influence on British colonial education policy in the corridors of Whitehall, described Mayhew's greatness as that of a 'born schoolteacher' whose gentle nature did not covet honours but whose memory would be preserved in the minds of countless pupils that had passed through his hands and who were 'proud to own him as master'.[87] There is a touch of irony in this last statement. Mayhew never set out to be a teacher in the conventional sense and one suspects that he probably derived most satisfaction from being widely acknowledged in his lifetime as the leading scholarly authority on the broad aspects of British education policy both in India and the Colonial Empire. It was a Platonic image nurtured in the Wykehamist tradition to which he truly belonged.

NOTES ON CHAPTER

1. This essay first appeared as 'The Nestor of British Colonial Education: a portrait of Arthur Mayhew CIE, CMG (1878–1948) in the *Journal of Educational Administration and History*, 29.1 (1997) pp 51–76 Mayhew left no personal papers apart from an unpublished memoir of his early childhood years and his time at Winchester and New College so the story of most of his adult life must necessarily be reconstructed from miscellaneous official and semi-official sources and from the memories of his surviving family. I am, accordingly, much indebted to the late Mr John Mayhew and Mrs Felicity Harlow, Mayhew's son and surviving daughter, and to Rear Admiral (Ret.) Anthony Davies, Mayhew's nephew, for so readily supplying me with information about Mayhew's immediate family, family background and those all too rare glimpses into his private life.

2. *Oversea Education*, XIX /4 (1948), p 755

3. Information about Arthur Mayhew's paternal background was provided by his daughter Mrs Felicity Harlow.

4. For a list of Anthony Mayhew's publications see *British Museum General Catalogue of Printed Books to 1955*, London, 1964

5. For a history of the school see C. H. Jaques, *A Dragon Century 1877–1977*, Oxford, Blackwell's, 1977

6. Charles Lawson Mayhew was born in 1874 and spent his adult life in the Royal Marines rising to the rank of Major General. He saw action in the Boxer Rebellion in 1900. He never married and died in 1929.

7. Anthony Arnold Mayhew was born in 1873 and entered The Church of England where he eventually became Canon of St Albans Cathedral and later of Salisbury Cathedral, where he died in 1939. He never married.

8. Obituary of Arthur Mayhew by A. E. Lynam, *The Dragonian*, Easter 1948, p 10943

9. Sir John Austen Hubback, b28 Feb 1878. Ed Winchester and King's College, Camb. Entered ICS 1902 Governor of Orissa 1936–41 Retired 1941

10. *The Dragonian, p 10944*

11. J. D'E. Firth, *Winchester College,* London, Winchester Publications Ltd., 1949, p 201

12. The original rough typescript copy of Mayhew's unpublished memoirs of his youth are in the possession of his daughter Mrs Felicity Harlow. The manuscript is not dated but appears to have been written a year or two before Mayhew died in 1948. It has since been published as 'My Early Life – a Personal Memoir' with an introduction by the author in *Education Research and Perspectives,* 25/1 (1998) pp 46–104

13. Richard Symonds, *Oxford and Empire The Last Lost Cause*, London, Macmillan, 1968

14. For greater detail on the establishment of the IES see chap 1 of this study.

15. Mayhew met Haldane probably in the summer of 1901 at Mells Park in Somerset where he was coaching Edward Horner, the son of Sir John Horner and brother-in-law of Raymond Asquith. Haldane, later Viscount Haldane, was educated at Edinburgh Academy and Edinburgh and Gottingen Universities. He obtained an MA degree with First Class Hons. from Edinburgh University and later qualified for the Bar. He entered politics as the Liberal Member for Haddingtonshire in 1885 and was later Secretary of State for War (1905–12) and Lord High Chancellor (1912–15). He also became a QC in 1890.

16. John Mayhew to the author, 4 Jul 1995

17. Symonds, p 32 See also P. Woodruff, *The Men Who Ruled India*, London, 1953

18.Recollections of Arthur Mayhew by Sir John Hubback, *The Draconian*,
Easter 1948, p 10944
19.*Report of the Central Provinces and Berar University Committee,* Nagpur, 1915
20.For a brief summary of Mayhew's Indian career see various editions of the
India Office List.
21.Minutes of the Central Advisory Committee of the Board of Education,
P. J. Hartog Papers, Mss Eur E 221/60, India Office Library, London
22.Sir John Hubback's notes on Mayhew, *The Times,* 30 Mar 1948
23.The circumstances in which Mayhew met his wife are worth recording for
posterity. Mayhew and Arthur Davies, the son of Sir James Davies, a High
Court judge in Madras, shared bachelor living quarters — *a chummerie* — in
Madras, probably about 1906–7, and agreed to write to their respective
sisters suggesting that they go out to India to keep house for them. The
girls did so and two marriages eventuated. Mayhew married May Catherine
(1882– S1954), the youngest daughter and a twin of Sir James Davies in
South Norwood, London, in September 1908. Her daughter Felicity
Harlow describes her as 'not academic but very attractive, lively, interesting
and amusing, a perfect hostess and much loved and appreciated by my
father'. Evidently she greatly enjoyed the club and social life in India and
subsequently found life in suburban England rather dull by contrast. Her
eldest son John Mayhew recalls her strong personality and the efficient way
in which she organised family life but claims that she and Arthur Mayhew
had little in common. They both delighted in their children, however, and
he retains warm memories of a close-knit family and annual holidays,
sometimes to Europe, well organised by his father. Arthur Mayhew's
nephew Anthony Davies recalls Aunt May as an extrovert, not intellectual
or well-read but always full of fun and very kind. He claims that she
inherited many of her father's qualities. He also related to the author the
following amusing anecdote which has been handed down through the
family about May's birth in India on 27 Feb 1882. Evidently it was Sir
James Davies' practice to relax from his legal labours by taking his carriage
the short way to his Club to play whist in the early evening, and this he did
on 27 Feb. The whist four settled down to play with the *punkah wallah* using
his big toe to pull the rope as usual. There was a knock on the door and a
'boy' crept in and stood quietly near Sir James, who in due course asked
what he wanted. The 'boy' replied, 'Please Sahib, Missy have baby', to
which Sir James said, 'Oh, all right. Stop interrupting and get out', and as an
aside to his partners, 'Quite forgot she was pregnant'. Time passed, the
whist continued and there was another knock on the door; the same 'boy'
crept in and interrupted in the middle of the hand saying 'Please Sahib,
Missy have another baby'. This incensed Sir James who threw his cards on
the table and exclaimed, 'Damn it, I must go and put a stop to this'.
Arthur Mayhew's sister Margaret married Arthur Davies (1873–1939), son
of Sir James, in Oxford in 1910. Her husband had attended Rugby School
and like Arthur Mayhew, was a graduate of New College Oxford. He then
read for the Bar in London and subsequently became the Principal of the
Law College in Madras.
24.Felicity Harlow to the author 29 Jul 1995
25.*Ibid.*
26.*Ibid.* 28 Jun 1995
27.Hubback, notes
28.R. A. Wilson, *The Dragonian*, Easter 1948, p 10945
29.Felicity Harlow to the author, 29 Jul 1995
30.*Ibid.,* 28 Jun and 29 Jul 1995
31.John Mayhew to the author 7 Aug 1995
32.*The Education of India*, London, Faber and Gwyer, 1926
33.*Christianity and the Government of India*, London, Faber & Gwyer, 1929

34. Memo by Ormsby-Gore on the extension of the Advisory Committee, 4 Aug 1927. Joint International Missionary Council/Conference of British Missionary Societies Archives [IMC/CBMS] Box 223
35. Minutes of the Advisory Committee on Native Education in British Tropical Africa, 14 Sep 1927
36. For details about the history and content of the journal see the author's paper 'Centre and Periphery: the role of *Oversea Education*': *A Journal of Educational Experiment and Research in Tropical and Sub-tropical Areas' [1929–1963]* in the History of British Colonial Education presented at the Combined Conference of the Australia New Zealand and British History of Education Societies, Swansea, Dec 2002.
37. J. H. Oldham, variously described as a missionary, an ecclesiastical statesman, and a 'busy-body of genius' was the Secretary of the International Missionary Council and the chief spokesman and trusted adviser of the Protestant Missions in their dealings with the British government.
38. John Mayhew to the author 4 Jul 1995
39. Arthur Innes Mayhew *OD* by A. E. L. ['Hum' Lynam], *The Dragonian*, Easter 1948, p 10944. The work of the Institute was reported on in *Oversea Education* in the 1930s. Mayhew was Chairman of its Ovesea Committee. The Institute ran a quarterly journal *Religion in Education*. Its headquarters were at 49 Garden Square, London.
40. See *British Museum of Printed Books to 1955*, London, 1964
41. L. S. S. O'Malley (ed.), *Modern India and the West A study of the interactions of their civilisations*, OUP, 1941, pp 305–337
42. Mayhew to Oldham 20 Apr 1923 IMC/CBMS Box 219
43. *Ibid.,* 13 Aug 1927
44. Author's emphasis
45. Oldham to Mayhew 27 Sep 1927 IMC/CBMS Box 219
46. The post was filled by Herbert [later Sir Herbert] Scott. See chap 6 of this study
47. *Ibid.,* 5 Oct 1927
48. *Ibid.,* 9 Oct 1927
49. Mayhew to Oldham 29 Nov 1927 IMC/CBMS Box 219
50. *Ibid.*
51. CO 323/1008/12
52. *Ibid.*
53. *Ibid.*
54. Oldham to Ormsby-Gore 31 Aug 1931 IMC/CBMS Box 219
55. Alington to Ormsby-Gore 3 May 1928 CO 323/1008/12
56. Oldham to Ormsby-Gore 4 Sep 1931 IMC/CBMS Box 219
57. Ormsby-Gore to Oldham 1 Sep 193 IMC/CBMS Box 219
58. The details of how the Carnegie Corporation provided finance to assist the ACEC in the 1930s is derived principally from the IMC/CBMS Archives and CO files. A full account using IMC/CBMS sources is to be found in F. S. Clatworthy, *The Formulation of British Colonial Education Policy 1923–1948*, Michigan, University School of Education, 1971, pp 56–60
59. Mayhew to Dr F. P. Keppel 8 Jun 1933 IMC/CBMS Box 219
60. Oldham to Keppel, 4 Aug 1933 There is a copy of the letter in the Carnegie Corporation's Archives in New York. See Clatworthy, p 60, fn57
61. CO 859/1/1201/1D/1939
62. This attitude was evident when the Carnegie Corporation agreed to finance the attendance of West Indians at the Yale Conference in 1934. It was made clear by the Chairman of the Advisory Committee in London that there was no question of issuing a general invitation to any West Indians to attend. Instead, West Indian governments would be asked to nominate 'suitable' persons. CO 323/1208/11

63. *Report of a Commission appointed to consider problems of Secondary and Primary Education in Trinidad, Barbados, Leeward Islands and Windward Islands 1931–32,* HMSO 1933, Colonial No.79

64. For Mayhew's observations see his article 'The Prince of Wales's College and School, Achimota, *The Year Book of Education 1933,* London, Evans Bros.

65. Minutes of the Advisory Committee on Education in the Colonies, 11 Apr 1935

66. For an edited version of the conference see Felix M. Keesing, *Education in Pacific Countries,* London, OUP, 1938. Mimeographed sets of all conference papers were also deposited in selected libraries listed in the preface to Keesing's book.

67. *Report on Education in Fiji,* Suva 1937

68. CO 323/1208/11

69. *Ibid.*

70. *Ibid..* John Mayhew could not recall that his father ever expressed strong political opinions in the 1930s despite the economic depression, the Spanish Civil War, the rise of Fascism, and the glaring social inequalities of the period. Indeed, he was actively critical of his father's apparent lack of social concern, especially when, by contrast, his uncle, Arthur Davies, expressed strong left-wing sympathies. In retirement Arthur Mayhew wrote regular articles on political and semi-political issues for the local weekly Windsor newspaper but they were designed primarily to inform and clarify meaning rather than to present a partisan viewpoint. [John Mayhew to the author, 17 Aug 1995.] Mayhew's tendency to adopt a neutral stance in politics was evident even in his student days. In his memoirs he recalled that amongst the moderates of all political parties he found 'fundamentally Liberal principles. They win my sympathy, [and] make it hard to vote for or against Labour or Tory candidates, except on purely personal grounds …'

71. Keesing

72. C. Kingsley Williams, *Achimota: the Early Years 1924–1948,* Accra, Longmans, 1962, p 87

73. Draft notes on Arthur Mayhew by Cox, 3 Feb 1959 CO 1045/1483

74. *The Education of India,* p 9

75. CO 323/1028/9

76. Minutes of the Advisory Committee on Education in the Colonies, 16 Nov 1939

77. D. J. Morgan, *The Official History of Colonial Development,* 1. *The Origins of British Aid Policy 1924–1945,* London, Macmillan, 1980

78. Lord Hailey, *An African Survey,* OUP, 1938

79. Minute by Eastwood which mentioned a meeting held on 5 Feb 1939 CO 859/1/1201/1D/1939

80. For more detail on Cox as Educational Adviser to the Colonial Office see chap 10

81. John Mayhew to the author, 17 Aug 1995

82. The Council Minutes of 21 Mar 1929 reveal that the Dean of St Albans, The Rev. E. L. Henderson, who was also Chairman of the Council, was responsible for recommending Mayhew's election to the Council. [Archivist, Radley College, to the author, 21 Sep 1995.] Mayhew appears in a group photo of the College Council taken in Jun 1947 which is included between pages 352 and 353 in A. K. Boyd, *The History of Radley College 1847–1947,* Oxford, Basil Blackwell, 1948.

83. The series comprised 10 articles which appeared between 2 Mar and 6 Jul

84. John Mayhew to the author, 4 Jul 1995

85. *The Times,* 17 Mar 1948

86. Firth, pp 189–190

87. *Oversea Education,* XIX/4 (1948) p 755

9.   Eric R. J. Hussey

Olympian and Colonial Educator: 'One of the blues who ruled the blacks'

In 1899 Lord Cromer established the Sudan Political Service. From the outset he sought to recruit 'active young men, endowed with good health, high character and fair abilities' from Oxford and Cambridge in order to produce a *corps d'elite* to rival the famed Indian Civil Service.[1] A. H. M. Kirk-Greene described the ideal recruit as a modest honours graduate with a high capacity for athletics and organized games. In many cases those chosen had gained university 'Blues' for athletics or one or more of a variety of team games. As a consequence the Sudan earned the sobriquet of 'the Land of Blacks ruled by Blues'.[2] One of the earliest and most outstanding examples of the *beau idéal* was Eric Robert James Hussey, who not only ran in the 110 yards hurdles for Great Britain at the 1908 Olympic Games but also became one of the most distinguished educational administrators in British colonial Africa during the interwar years.

Eric Hussey[3] was born at Blandford in Dorset in April 1885, the eldest of two sons[4] in a family of six of The Rev. James Hussey and his wife Martha Ellen Hewitt. James Hussey had matriculated as an unattached i.e. non-collegiate student in October 1870 and then read Theology at Wadham College, Oxford, from whence he obtained a third class honours degree in 1873 and later his MA (1878). He was ordained as an Anglican priest in 1875 and thereafter held various clerical appointments in southwest England. At the time of Eric Hussey's birth he was Vicar of Durweston, Dorset. Eric Hussey's mother was one of six children whose father is thought to have been a lawyer.

Little is known of Eric Hussey's early childhood. He is presumed to have attended a preparatory school in or near Asheldon, Torquay, from whence he won a scholarship in 1899 to Repton, an Anglican Public School founded in 1557 in the ruins of a twelfth century Augustinian Priory, situated eight miles from Derby. Hussey spent five years at Repton (1899–1904) during which he displayed outstanding sporting and scholastic abilities.[5] It was at Repton that his athletic prowess first came to the fore. In his last year he won seven of the ten main athletic events and set a new school record for the 120 yards hurdles in winning the aggregate prize for the second year in succession. He was also a member of the School's first Soccer XI, the Colour Sergeant of the Rifle Corps, and Head Prefect [Head Boy] in his last two years at the school. To cap his school achievements he also won an Exhibition Scholarship to Hertford College, Oxford.

At Oxford he soon matured into one of the nation's top hurdlers. He was awarded a 'Blue' in his first year and subsequently gained a place in the Great Britain team at the 1908 Olympic Games held in London. Throughout his time at Oxford his great rival in the hurdles event was Kenneth Powell of King's College, Cambridge.[6] In 1907 and 1908 Hussey was President of the Oxford University Athletics Club.[7] When he became President he was described in *The Isis* as a lover of music, especially Handel, Wagner and Beethoven; a singer, a good talker, and someone whose handshake paralyzed the hand. Elsewhere he was described as 'by no means the formidable person his portrait would suggest. In fact he is one of the mildest of men, and one of the most encouraging of coaches, as any Fresher who frequents the running ground can testify; and this in spite of a physique and a record, which make one tremble'. The new president was also described as having a quiet demeanour and genial disposition which made him friends wherever he went. Hussey was also a very competent soccer player and played for Oxford University on various occasions, including a game in November 1905 against Brentford, a professional side, in which he scored a goal in a 2–2 draw. He never qualified for a Blue in soccer because he did not play against Cambridge. The time spent on the athletic track inevitably took its toll on Hussey's academic studies and he could only manage a Third Class Honours degree in *literae humaniores* which he completed in 1908, only weeks before running in the Olympic Games. In those days the award of honours counted for less than in the highly competitive world of the 1990s although Hussey's son, Lord Hussey of North Bradley, claims that upon hearing of his father's class of honours his grandfather did not speak to his father for a week.[8]

In memoirs written late in life[9] Hussey claimed that prior to graduation he had not the slightest idea that he would spend nearly thirty years of his life in Africa but it so happened that in 1908 the Sudan Political Service was attracting interest amongst students at Oxford and one of his friends was selected. Hussey was particularly attracted by the fact that unlike the Indian Civil Service there was no special written examination, the academic record at university taking the place of a written test. Moreover, the final selection, after some stringent elimination rounds conducted by university 'dons', was made as the result of an interview conducted by members of the Sudan Government. He might also have added the relatively good pay, the exceptionally generous leave provisions which included annual leave, the possibility of early retirement after twenty years service at an age which allowed retirees to seek another job with comparative ease, generous expenses, and service in the oppressive climatic conditions of the south of the country counting double for pension purposes. It is hardly surprising that there was never any shortage of applicants but only a minority was chosen.[10]

In the summer of 1908 Hussey accepted the offer of an appointment in the Sudan Educational Service which, he later claimed, suited him as he had been contemplating educational work in England at the time. His father had hoped that he might follow him into the Church but readily accepted education as an alternative and worthwhile service profession.[11] The Sudan Government required his services urgently so he sailed for Africa soon after being accepted thereby missing a preparatory year at university which was devoted mainly to the study of Arabic. On the eve of his departure from Tilbury he must have seemed the epitome of that class of Victorian/Edwardian Englishmen born to rule the Empire. A natural leader of men, tall of stature, of strong build, a committed Anglican of high moral character, an outstanding athlete and no mean scholar, he epitomised the ideal type of man that Cromer sought for his *corps d'elite*. As Sir Angus Gillan would later say of him, he was also a man of serious purpose, who exhibited a delightful sense of fun, an easy mixture of self-confidence and modesty, warm friendliness and deep sincerity.[12]

He began his career[13] in Khartoum as a tutor at Gordon College under the direction of James (later Sir James) Currie, initially being involved in developing primary education. One of his duties was also to act as Private Secretary to Currie from whom he claimed he learned more about educational administration than from anyone before or after. He clearly impressed his superiors because after four years he was seconded to the Administration for a period as a District Officer. In 1912 he left Khartoum to be a District Commissioner at Sennar, specialising in legal and taxation matters. By then he had sat law examinations and acquired a spoken knowledge of Arabic. Living conditions were very primitive; there were few Europeans in Sennar, and he frequently went on tour into the hinterland. When war broke out in 1914 Hussey was twenty-nine years old. In view of his age and the nature of the job that he was doing he was retained at his post and did censorship work. In 1917 he was transferred to Tokar and was in Port Sudan on Armistice Day. At about that time he accepted the post of Senior Inspector in the Education Department and returned to work in Khartoum. The job entailed much routine office work but he also went on various tours of inspection.

In November 1920, at the invitation of the Governor, Sir Geoffrey Archer, he went on a special mission to Somaliland to advise on educational development.[14] He was asked specifically to advise the Government as to the best general lines on which to construct a native school, the curriculum that should be followed, and the plan of the school buildings etc, after studying local conditions with officers on the spot. His report was not acted upon at the time due to financial problems but Archer was very impressed with it and duly informed the Colonial Office of his feelings. Four years later, Archer, who was by then Governor of Uganda, invited Hussey to visit Uganda on a similar mission to draw up a scheme for Native education in the territory. Hussey accepted the invitation but before going to Uganda, he visited Palestine briefly. On his return journey from Uganda he made a short visit to Kenya to advise on educational matters at the invitation of the Governor Sir Robert Coryndon.[15]

Hussey spent two months in Uganda compiling a comprehensive report[16] which included provision for a Department of Education, headed by a Director, and a major reshaping of the structure of schooling which had hitherto been exclusively under mission control. Faced with literally hundreds of inferior bush schools, Hussey argued that the prime requirement was to raise the standard of instruction. He believed that this could best be achieved by selecting fifty mission schools for upgrading and building a further six government schools. These four year Elementary Vernacular Schools as they were to be known, would form the base of the education system. Above them there would be a limited number of Intermediate Schools [he envisaged eight mission schools and one government school, the latter to cater for Moslem pupils] which would provide a further four years of schooling. From these a small minority of pupils would go on to the recently established Makerere College for a variety of higher education courses. Hussey was anxious to upgrade Makerere from a trade training centre to a college offering a variety of professional training courses.

He discussed his report with the Advisory Committee on Native Education in British Tropical Africa when he was on leave in London in July 1924. The Committee was most impressed with the proposals which were also strongly supported by the respective missions. In endorsing the Report, Sir Geoffrey Archer also asked the Colonial Office to approach the Sudan Government with a request that Hussey be seconded to Uganda for an initial period of two years as DE to oversee the implementation of the Report. The Sudan Government agreed to co-operate and Hussey moved to Uganda as the first DE early in 1925.[17] By then he was in his fortieth year. In July 1922 he had married Christine Morley in London. A son was born in England in August 1923 and a daughter in Uganda in April 1926.

Hussey faced a difficult task in Uganda.[18] For the first time he had to define the sphere of Government in education and suggest what part it should play in the provision of educational facilities in addition to supervising and controlling existing agencies. The Anglican and Roman Catholic missions were firmly entrenched throughout the territory and their mutual antagonism towards each other generated a constant threat to Hussey's plans. Nevertheless, he co-operated closely with both factions and successfully established an Educational Missionary Council to assist in the implementation of his report. He also formed a lasting friendship with J. H. Oldham, the highly influential Secretary of the International Missionary Council and a member of the London-based Advisory Committee on Native Education in British Tropical Africa, who visited

Uganda in 1926, and with Bishop Willis of the Church Missionary Society in Uganda. Their support was a great help to Hussey in his negotiations with the various missions.

Hussey was a firm advocate of the 'adaptation' theory of African education as outlined in a British Government 1925 White Paper.[19] He claimed that Africans should be encouraged to foster their own culture which he believed to be in no way inferior to that of the Western world. He was particularly impressed by Arthur Mayhew's contemporary critique of Indian education — Oldham had sent Hussey a copy of Mayhew's book[20] — and wished to avoid at all costs a policy of reckless Westernization accomplished through the medium of education as had occurred in India. As Hussey stated in his Ugandan Report, native educational policy should be based on 'adjustment to local conditions and an attempt to build on, without destroying the finely adjusted fabric of social life which [was] the heritage of centuries'.

The passing of the first Education Ordinance in Uganda was a major milestone in Hussey's policy. This gave legal sanction for an Advisory Council on Education, the classification of schools, the right of inspection and the revised system of government grants-in-aid, as well as the formation of local education committees and the striking of a local education rate where desired. Hussey also worked hard on the transition of Makerere from a technical college to a 'Higher College' designed to recruit boys from leading secondary or intermediate schools. At Makerere they were to receive vocational training in medicine, agriculture, vetinary science, engineering and teaching. Hussey was also anxious to promote the education of girls although progress was slow in the 1920s due to African resistance. His name was also closely linked with that of S.S. (later Sir Sidney) Abrahams, the famous ex Cambridge and British Olympic athlete who subsequently became Attorney-General in the Gold Coast. Between them they did much to encourage athletics in Uganda by starting a Ugandan Olympic Games, including a Marathon, and the Hussey Shield is still competed for annually at a major national athletics meeting. Hussey clearly impressed the Advisory Committee in London with his work in Uganda and it came as no surprise to him when he was offered and accepted the post of first overall DE in Nigeria in 1929.

The task awaiting him in Lagos was no less challenging. He had to unite the education systems of north and south by means of a new ordinance and a new grants-in-aid scheme and reorganise the structure of schooling whilst simultaneously reassuring long-established and powerful mission groups that their interests would be safeguarded. The multiple tasks inevitably generated a degree of friction with some mission groups, and especially with Victor [later Professor Victor] Murray who visited Nigeria in 1931/32 as part of a move by the Protestant missions to work out a common education policy.[21] In 1930 Hussey compiled a substantive report on education in Nigeria[22] in which he foreshadowed major structural changes to schooling based on the Hadow Report [1926] on *The Education of the Adolescent*. It was clear to him that far more pupils were likely to pass Standard VI than could be accommodated in clerical jobs. He was also critical of the way in which the Standard VI examination dominated the work of the primary schools and was pitched at a level that was not really high enough for the needs of government and commercial employers. He sought, therefore, to limit primary schools to Standard IV and to include Standards V and VI as part of post-primary education which would consist of Junior Secondary [the first four years] followed by two further years of Senior Secondary. At the same time he sought to include a practical component in the school curriculum, particularly at the secondary stage, 'so that boys and girls [would] recognise alternatives to unskilled manual labour other than in terms of typewriters and office stools'. In short, he emphasised the critical importance of forging a link between schools and the economic life of the country.[23]

The missions strongly objected to the split in primary schools at Standard IV. Traditionally mission primary schools were based on a model of two infant classes followed in a complete school by six primary standards, an eight year course in all. Most schools did not encompass the full eight years but it was the ambition of many to have a sixth standard from which pupils could sit the Standard VI examination and so qualify for clerical and a variety of public service jobs. Hussey had a reputation for being very direct and down-to-earth in his dealings with the missions, a legacy, it was suggested, from his time in the Sudan, but he was also considered a most able administrator who had the interests of the native Africans genuinely at heart. During his time in Uganda Hussey was observed by Oldham to have a passion for efficiency which tended perhaps towards autocratic tendencies, but Oldham was sure that at bottom his intentions were thoroughly sound.[24] Despite rumblings of discontent in Nigeria, Hussey retained the confidence of the Advisory Committee in Whitehall and proceeded with his plans.

Victor Murray[25], then a lecturer at Selly Oak Colleges, a major missionary teacher-training establishment in Birmingham, was the author of *The School in the Bush,* an out-spoken book about the inadequacies of colonial education policy including the alleged lack of government commitment to mission schooling.[26] Murray was especially critical of the theory of adaptation. He was convinced that rapid change was the dominating force in Africa and that education had to provide for the needs of a dynamic and not a static society. To educate a man 'along his own lines' was, he argued, meaningless. Instead, he put his faith in the often much maligned 'western educated Africans' in the belief that African society could not stand still. At a time when the principles of indirect rule were still uppermost in British colonial policy, there was no clearly defined role for the small but increasingly influential group of African 'intellectuals' that Lugard had earlier branded as conceited and often contemptuous of chiefly authority.

In a letter to Oldham, written before Murray visited Africa, Hussey commented on Murray's book:

If one were to criticize Murray's book, it would be that the problem appeared to him too easy. Anyone can find faults with any Government or Mission system [of education], but what we have to do is make the best general plan in view of all the circumstances of the case — the circumstances including money available, native prejudices (which have to be carefully analysed and not accepted as first heard, formed often by hasty judgment of ill considered facts and figures), and the country's requirements from the political standpoint and many others.

Hussey had never met Murray but he wrote saying that he knew of no reason why he should object if Murray were to be appointed as the Protestant Missions' Educational Adviser in West Africa.[27] He might have said otherwise had he known what Murray would write about him in private correspondence to Oldham both during and after his visit.

Towards the end of his stay, which lasted approximately four months [Dec 1931-Apr 1932], Murray wrote to Oldham from Lagos saying 'I'm very much embarrassed. The truth is I can see no hope whatever of co-operation between Hussey and the missions'.[28] He admitted that Hussey was very kind to him, especially when he was ill with dysentry, and that socially he was 'one of the best fellows going' but he did not think that Hussey was the man for the job. Murray claimed that colonial officials in Lagos called Hussey 'the great bluffer'; that he was very unpopular; and that he was a man of 'overweening ambition' who talked openly of leaving Nigeria in the near future:

Everybody expects (and hopes) he will get a Governership. All that agitation to get him from East Africa was a thoroughly bad thing.... If he could get a better job than his present one he'd go tomorrow'. Murray also accused Hussey of being ignorant about the job he was doing: 'With all the allowances in the world one must say that. I tried to get him to discuss [Harold] Jowitt's book on Principles of Education for African Teachers[29] but it was obvious he'd never read it and didn't want to either. And of course he *never* listens to anybody. I don't mean listen in the sense of arguing, but listen in the ordinary physical sense. He talks the *whole* time and projects his ideas on to you and goes away saying "I had a talk with Murray about this and he agrees" whereas I may never have opened my mouth! He's mad on science, knowing nothing about it ... Now all this sounds wild and exaggerated, but I've tried to think otherwise, but the evidence is too strong.

Murray then went on to criticize Hussey's grant-in-aid proposals claiming that Hussey had the face to say that "What's wrong is that the missions look at the Government's purse as bottomless". Murray asserted that no one in Lagos trusted Hussey and that this attitude was not confined to the missions. 'It's time', he wrote, that 'the missions here began co-ordinating their policy around Almighty God instead of round Hussey'. He ended his letter with a postscript saying, 'No, my views on E. R. J. H. are not the result of dysentry'.

A fortnight later Murray wrote again to Oldham from Lagos.[30] By then he had dined with Hussey and found him and his wife 'quite delightful' and admitted he had come to like Hussey 'quite a lot' but claimed that 'the only effect of this new found love (particularly after his excellent dinner) was to make him want to

> "... carve him as a fish fit for the Gods
> Not hew him as a carcase fit for hounds."

Murray's ensuing report also pulled no punches as far as Hussey was concerned but he failed to impress Oldham who knew him to be an outspoken character who readily admitted to being difficult to work with. Murray, for his part, believed in the full and frank expression of opinions and expected criticism in return but he also believed that ideas should be separated from the person expressing them.[31] At the end of May 1932, after Hussey had seen a copy of Murray's interim report, Oldham wrote to him to assure him of his continued support: 'You know him well enough to give the proper value to his digs at you *a la* Victor Murray. I need not say that they will not appear in any printed report. Murray cannot write anything without poking his stick into somebody's ribs and these excursions of his are not to be taken too seriously'.[32]

Evidently Hanns Vischer and Arthur Mayhew, the Joint Secretaries of the Advisory Committee on Education in the Colonies, were singularly unimpressed when they heard of Murray's attack on Hussey. Murray responded immediately by writing to Oldham:

> I am sorry to hear that Hanns Vischer (who told him?) and Mayhew dislike what they call my attack on Hussey. It is not anything of the kind. What I feel is that the ark of the covenant has been touched once you question those people's belief in their own freehold. I am really quite sorry that Hussey should have been so childish, especially as I carefully explained to him that I was simply sending him this thing [his interim report] as a matter of courtesy. It was not going to be published as it stood but whatever he may think about it it represented the facts of the case. You cannot deal with a disease until you diagnose it and it seems to me that this case has been diagnosed only too accurately.... I am most awfully sorry if you think that I have let the cause down. I am not really violent inside at all and I think I got on very well with the Government people in Lagos but I feel that the missions are doing a big work [sic] there and they are doing it very largely free of charge for the Government and I think the Government ought to recognise them as equal

partners in the concern. This idea of going cap in hand to Hussey is, I think, thoroughly bad, quite as bad as the opposite attitude of continual opposition.[33]

On the same day Murray wrote a long letter to Hussey explaining his actions.[34]

> What seems to me to be so unfortunate is the idea that high officials have of freehold... There seems to be no sense of responsibility to public opinion, either in the colony or at home, and yet after all, you people are only trustees and trustees for a very limited time and you are responsible for your trust to the people in this country [England] and ultimately to the people of Africa.... I am saying all this because what neither you nor the Governor seem to have realised is that the point of view which you take up is after all a matter of opinion. It is based upon a certain view of anthropology and behind that a certain view of the psychological development of primitive people. There is no orthodoxy or heterodoxy about it. Driberg says one thing, Levy-Briehl says another, and who is to decide between them?

Murray then proceeded to argue that the missions had an equally valid viewpoint and concluded by saying that 'to treat the missions as if they were somehow intruders or were there only at the grace of the high command seems to me to be a failing in understanding of what the high command is there for'. There is no record of whether Hussey ever answered Murray's letter.

Oldham's position and that of the missions at home was made clear in a letter that he wrote to The Rev. H. W. Stacey, the Joint Secretary of the Christian Council in Nigeria.[35] He was fully alive to the hardships imposed on the missions by Hussey's far reaching proposals but said that they had to accept that Hussey was specially selected for the purpose of uniting the educational systems of Northern and Southern Nigeria and laying broad foundations for the future. He had to take account not merely of educational considerations but of the larger principles of Government policy. The missions were free to express opinions on such matters where they affected mission activities but they were not competent to decide such matters. What the missions had secured was an assurance from the Colonial Office that the broad principles of educational policy in Nigeria would not be altered in the future without full consultation and ample time for discussion of matters between the missions in Nigeria and the home boards.

Reference to Murray's outspoken criticism is not intended to detract from Hussey's work in Nigeria but it does serve to highlight the problems that government education officials often experienced in their dealings with mission personnel. Missionaries had often blazed the trail long before the British assumed sovereignty over a territory and many were understandably resentful at what they perceived to be uncalled for intrusion by secular authority. It was Oldham's role as intermediary and diplomat to sooth the savage breast and to endeavour to maintain eqanimity between vested interest groups.

During his term of office in Nigeria Hussey also spent much time and energy promoting the Higher College at Yaba [near Lagos] which, like Makerere, he hoped would ultimately achieve the status of a university college. The formal opening of the College was delayed for two years until the new buildings were completed but when the Governor, Sir Donald Cameron, spoke at the opening ceremony in 1934, he gave generous praise to Hussey for initiating the idea of a higher college and for seeing it through to completion.[36] Hussey was no less enthusiastic in his efforts to expand the education of girls but, as in Uganda, the subject proved controversial amongst Africans and the necessary cultural change was slow to emerge in the 1930s. He was, however, responsible for the appointment of Miss Plummer as a Woman Inspector.[37] She was later to become assistant DE and her name is forever linked with the growth of female education in colonial Nigeria.

Another important feature of Hussey's agenda was a reorganisation of teacher training which had hitherto been conducted in numerous small mission centres. He upgraded entry requirements and consolidated training in fewer but larger training colleges. He also gave support and encouragement to the Nigerian National Union of Teachers established in 1931.[38] Even before that he had to give the Lagos Union of Teachers a representative on the Board of Education. He became Patron of the NUT and addressed teachers and contributed to debates at their 1932 Conference. It has been suggested that he courted the favour of the NUT to defer criticism from the missions but it seems more likely that he sought to encourage trade unionism in the colonies in line with official Colonial Office policy[39] and that he also genuinely wanted teachers to be partners with the Government in shaping education policy. It was, for example, well known that he often consulted with Union members before Board of Education meetings.

Hussey was also responsible for a change in the University of London matriculation requirements. In reshaping the secondary school curriculum he excluded Latin although he was aware that this would result in some pupils missing out on matriculation to the University of London. Consequently, on his first leave in England as Director, he approached Sir Percy Nunn, a member of the Advisory Committee in London and a Professor of Education at the Institute of Education, about the matter. Nunn put him in touch with Dr Dellar, the Principal of the Institute, and eventually permission was granted for Nigerian students to sit the Matriculation examination without offering a second language in addition to English.[40]

Unfortunately Hussey's Directorship in Nigeria coincided with the onset of the Great Depression and a partial failure of the cotton crop which resulted in severe and prolonged financial and staff retrenchments which delayed the full implementation of his plans. In 1931, for example, his Education Department lost 27 European and 42 African officers as a result of financial retrenchments. A year later the annual report of the Education Department stated that since 1929 there had been a loss of 42 European staff because of financial cutbacks.

In 1932 Hussey was a member of the Commission of Inspection which visited the Prince of Wales College at Achimota in the Gold Coast and in the following year he was awarded the CMG for his services to colonial education. His term of office in Nigeria ended in February 1936 and so, somewhat surprisingly, did his career in the CES. By then he had reached retirement age and although he was keen on another colonial appointment there was nothing available at the time.[41] At the age of fifty he was, therefore, faced with the need to seek alternative employment.

He found it first as Assistant Secretary [March 1936] and subsequently as Secretary [December 1936] of the National Society which was responsible for many hundreds of Anglican schools throughout England and Wales.[42] In the latter post he replaced Richard Holland who retired after having served the National Society for fifty-three years, the last eighteen as Secretary. Hussey's appointment was achieved in the face of strong competition from no less than twelve other candidates including Sir George Anderson, late Director of Public Instruction in the Punjab. For once Hussey's age was an advantage and he was the unanimous choice of the selection committee. His appointed came at a crucial time in the history of the National Society.

In April 1934 the National Society had been granted a revised or 'Supplemental' Charter. This was prompted by a recommendation from the 1929 Archbishop's Commission to the effect that a Central Council of the Church for Religious Education should be established with administrative powers for dealing with all aspects of religious education, and that the National Society should be asked to enlarge the scope of its operations and where necessary reform its constitution to enable it to act as the Central Council. By November 1931 it was agreed that the Society should continue its existing work but also extend the scope of its operations to include the encouragement of religious education amongst all classes of the people in accordance with the principles of the Church of England. In line with this proposal it was suggested that the full title of the Society should be changed from *The National Society for promoting the education of the poor in the principles of the Established Church throughout England and Wales* to *The National Society for promoting Religious Education in accordance with the principles of the Church of England*. The revised Charter also provided for much greater lay representation on the Standing [Executive] Committee and for a far more democratic format for the election of members of the Committee.

It was argued that since the original granting of a Charter to the National Society in 1817 there had been great changes in the education of the people. The Society began with elementary and Sunday schools of the simplest type but it was obliged to train teachers from the start, and soon had to extend its operations to central schools, where teachers were trained, and later still to district training colleges. By the 1930s the Society was obliged to cover the entire range of schooling including secondary schools. The Hadow Report on the education of the adolescent [1926] which had called for the reorganisation of schools and new proposals for government building grants for voluntary schools entering into new schemes of reorganisation, also highlighted the need for changes to the National Society's Constitution. Hitherto, many educational matters relating to Church of England schools had been dealt with by *ad hoc* committees appointed by the bishops at the request of the Church Assembly. In future it was envisaged that such matters would be dealt with by the National Society acting as the Central Body representing the Church officially in educational matters. Under the revised Charter the role of Secretary took on an enhanced status akin to that of the Church's Minister for Education.

Hussey was to serve the Society with distinction until June 1942 when, British troops having defeated the Italians in East Africa, he was asked by the Government to go out to Ethiopia for two years to act as the Emperor's educational adviser. At Hussey's last executive meeting, the Chairman, Lord Sankey, spoke highly of his work and then released him with great regret for other more pressing duties. The Society's annual report for 1943 referred to his work in glowing terms. It was stated that he had not only carried on the tradition and work of the Society and maintained the confidence of the Board of Education but that he had also achieved 'an administrative triumph' in shaping the affairs of the Society in order to meet new demands under the revised Charter and steered it safely through the difficult period of transition with 'unostentatious ability and faithfulness'.

In 1940 Hussey was made a member of the Advisory Committee on Education in the Colonies [ACEC] under the new direction of Christopher [later Sir Christopher] Cox, and played a leading role in its affairs until his departure for Ethiopia.[43] In May 1940 he was included on a sub-committee which was asked to examine the future of higher education in West Africa in the light of the West African Governors' Conference of 1939. In its report the sub-committee called for a major commission of inquiry into the matter similar to that which had visited East Africa in 1937.[44] This precipitated a series of moves in which Hussey was involved which eventually led to the Asquith Commission of Inquiry into higher education in the colonies in general and to a separate commission of inquiry into higher education in West Africa.[45] Hussey also served on the Joint Consultative Committee which oversaw links between the Colonial Office, the Advisory Committee and the London Institute of Education, and would have chaired it in 1942 if he had not gone to Ethiopia. In May 1941 he was also included on a sub-committee which was established to examine the problems of mass education in the colonies. He left the sub-committee before its work was completed but its deliberations subsequently resulted in a major published report.[46] The minutes of the meetings of the Advisory Committee that Hussey attended indicate that he made a useful contribution, especially on Nigerian matters.

Hussey returned to England in 1944 and took up a position on the British Council in London as Director (Middle East) in the Foreign Division.[47] His links with the British Council were forged while he was in Ethiopia. He was in Addis Ababa when the British Council opened its branch there in January 1943, and he was subsequently very friendly with Henry Littler, the Council's representative. In 1945 he also became Deputy Controller, under Sir Angus Gillan, of the Empire Division. He retired from the Council in 1949.

Between 1945 and 1947 he also served a further term on the ACEC.[48] It proved to be both a busy and a challenging time as the Advisory Committee grappled with the implications of major changes in colonial policy generated by the Colonial Development and Welfare Acts of 1940 and 1945 respectively. Throughout his time on the Committee he was a member of the Africa sub-committee which dealt with the educational content of a succession of territorial development plans. He was also a member of the Joint Consultative Committee at a time when there was a major expansion in the work of the Colonial Department at the Institute of Education under the guidance of Dr [later Professor] Margaret Read, and of the sub-committee on Education for Citizenship which was to produce a published report in 1948.[49] At the first meeting that he attended in his second term on the Advisory Committee in January 1945, he gave a short report on his work in Ethiopia in relation to mass education. In response, both Professor Ifor Evans and Christopher Cox — the latter had spent a week with Hussey in Ethiopia — agreed that he had 'achieved wonders' in the time that he was there given the complex nature and immense practical difficulties of the territory.

In 1940 Hussey also began a long association with the University of London's School of Oriental and African Studies as the Nigerian representative on the Governing Board, a position he retained until his death.[50] His last overseas mission was to Eritria in 1953, to advise on education in the territory's first year of independence. On the return journey he visited the Sudan for the last time.[51]

In the immediate post-war years Hussey was also active in the Royal Africa Society.[52] In 1947 he was a member of the Council and the Finance and General Purposes Committee. In 1949 he was elected a Vice President. A year later he represented the Society at the Solway Conference on Education in Africa held in Brussels and also delivered a lecture in French which was later published.[53] Finally, in July 1948, Hussey became a Fellow of the Woodard Corporation which owed its existence to the work of The Rev. Nathaniel Woodard, an inconspicuous and poorly educated nineteenth century curate who sought to solve the problems of middle class education of his day.[54] In the late 1940s the Corporation was responsible for a group of sixteen Anglican schools of which Lancing and Hurstpierpoint [Hurst] are perhaps the best known.

In 1951 Hussey became Chairman of the Hurst governing board and retained his close links with the Corporation until his death from heart disease, aged 73 years, at his home 'Painswold' in Broad Street, Cuckfield, East Sussex, on 19 May 1958.

In 1935 Hussey gave one of the three Joseph Paine lectures[55] at the London Institute of Education and, in 1939, the sixth of the Heath Clark lectures at the London School of Oriental and African Studies.[56] He was also a frequent contributor to the journals *African Affairs* and *African World*, especially in the post-war years,[57] and made several radio talks for the BBC in 1954 on Ethiopian affairs.[58] In 1959, a year after his death, his wife arranged for the publication and private circulation of his memoirs.

As a young man at Oxford Hussey acquired a reputation for outstanding athletic prowess which, together with his quiet demeanour and genial disposition, made him friends wherever he went. They were qualities that endured throughout his life. When Christopher Cox visited him in the Sudan in 1944 he was in his sixtieth year, nevertheless as Cox commented; 'he quite thrived on a 16-mile walk over the mountains'.[59] A Nigerian Chief Michael E. Okorodudu, proudly acclaimed Hussey as the first DE in his country to wear shorts and an open-neck shirt and eat Nigerian meals with Nigerian boys and girls in local schools.[60] Finally, it was James A. Gray in *African World* who, in calling Hussey 'an educationist of distinction', was quick to add that it was 'the man himself who made the fullest impact, the big, unruffled man with the quick smile, eager approach, and quiet chuckle, courteous and friendly to everyone ... meeting Emperor and houseboy on the same sincere, open-hearted level .... Service with him came first. He was a living example of the truth of how much a man can accomplish if he does not care who gets the credit'.[61]

Hussey was a prime example of Sir Ralph Furse's ideal Colonial Service official. As Lord Salisbury said in his *Foreword* to Furse's memoirs, what was needed most in dealing with indigenous peoples in the early decades of this century was not primarily brains, although they were obviously important, but rather personality and character.[62] Hussey had both in abundance. He was also one of the true pioneers of British colonial education playing a leading role in the creation and development of education systems in no less than three separate territories. As an educational administrator in Africa he drafted educational legislation and regulations, shaped the structure of schooling, and promoted two unique institutions of higher education. Back in England, as Secretary of the National Society for over five years, he played a leading role in ongoing negotiations over funding etc between the Church of England and the Board of Education. He also oversaw the administration of hundreds of schools throughout the length and breadth of England and Wales and successfully implemented the National Society's revised Charter. Like many of his fellow 'Blues' he devoted the greater part of his working life to African education and, despite Victor Murray's passing indignation, the weight of evidence overwhelmingly suggests that to the end of his life he remained an unstinting friend of Africa and its people.

NOTES ON CHAPTER

1. For greater detail see 'Mainly Chaps in control. Blues and Blacks in the Sudan', chap. 3 pp. 71–100 in J. A. Mangan, *The Games Ethic and Imperialism*, London, Viking Press, 1986
2. See A. H. M. Kirk-Greene, 'The Sudan Political Service: A Profile in the Sociology of Imperialism', *The International Journal of African Historical Studies*, 15/1 (1982) pp 21–48
3. The author is indebted to Eric Hussey's son, Lord Hussey of North Bradley [*Who's Who 1997*, p 985] for providing access to much of the information about his father's background and early life contained in scrapbooks and photo albums and a file of research into the Hussey family mainly compiled by Dianna Rice whose grandmother was Eric Hussey's sister.
4. Eric's brother Harold was killed fighting the Turks in Mesopotamia in 1917.
5. *Repton School Register 1557–1910*, Repton, MDCCCCX, (edited for the Old Reptonian Society by the widow of G. S. Messiter) p 410 [It is of interest to note that two years after Hussey went to Repton , The Rev. Lionel G. B. J. Ford, became Headmaster after spending many years as an assistant master at Eton. Evidently a close bond was established between the young Hussey and his headmaster, especially when Hussey was Head Boy in his last two years at Repton. Ford subsequently introduced Hussey to his future wife Christine Morley and officiated at their marriage in London in Jul 1922. Ford was the brother-in-law of Christine Morley's father. He was later Headmaster of Harrow School [1910–1925] before becoming Dean of York. He died in 1933.
    See *Who Was Who*, Vol.III, 1929–1940, Adam & Charles Black, London, 1947, p 462.]

6. In 1905 in his first inter university race in the 120 yards hurdles Hussey ran fourth behind F. Teal, the winner in 16.2/5 seconds, Powell and A. M. P.Lyle in that order. In 1906 he beat the same three men to win in 16.1/5 seconds. In 1907 and 1908 he was second being beaten on each occasion by only one foot by his great rival Powell in 15.3/5 seconds and 16 seconds respectively, the faster time creating an inter-university record,. Neither runner was placed in the Olympics, the 110 yards hurdles being won by an American. Tragically Powell was killed in the First World War.
7. Information on Hussey's time at Oxford is mainly derived from a scrapbook compiled by his sister.
8. Private communication to the author
9. E. R. J. Hussey,*Tropical Africa 1908–44 Memoirs of a Period*, St Catherine's Press, London, 1959. [Privately circulated by his wife. There is a copy in the British Museum Library.]
10. Kirk-Greene, p 34
11. Information supplied by Lord Hussey
12. Hussey, *Memoirs*, p viii
13. Details of Hussey's early career in the Sudan etc. are derived mainly from his *Memoirs*. unless otherwise stated.
14. Details of the visit and a copy of his report are to be found in the Sudan file, Box 229, in *The Joint International Missionary Council/Conference of British Missionary Societies Archives 1910–1945* [IMC/CBMS], University of London

School of Oriental and African Studies Research Library. The IMC/CBMS Archives have been microfiched by the Inter Documentation Company , Ag , Switzerland.

15. See Memorandum on certain aspects of Arab and African Education by E. R. J. Hussey. IMC/CBMS Archives, Kenya Colony Documents 1919/1926 file, Box 227.

16. Copies of the interim and final reports are included in IMC/CBMS Archives, Committee Papers — Uganda file, Box 229. See also Non-printed papers file, Box 232.

17. See IMC/CBMS Archives, Uganda Education files, Box 260.

18. Sources for Hussey's term as DE in Uganda include his *Memoirs*, IMC/CBMS Archives, and Annual Reports [1925–1930] of the Department of Education, Uganda.

19. *Education Policy in British Tropical Africa*, Cmd. 2374 (London 1925)

20. A. L. Mayhew, *The Education of India*, London, Faber & Gwyer, 1926

21. See IMC/CBMS Archives, Murray Scheme: correspondence with A. Victor Murray, Box 275

22. IMC/CBMS Archives, Committee Papers — Nigeria file, Box 230

23. These ideas were enlarged upon in Hussey's Joseph Payne Lecture 'Some Aspects of Education in Nigeria' delivered at the London Institute of Education, 28 Oct 1935. See University of London Institute of Education, *Studies and Reports Nos 1 – 14 (1933–46)* in the Hans Collection, Institute of Education Library.

24. J. H. Oldham to H. M. Grace, 24 Jun 1926, IMC/CBMS Archives, H. M. Grace file, Box 260

25. Sometime Exhibitioner of Magdalen College, Oxford and subsequently Professor of Education at University College, Hull. In 1934 Murray visited South Africa to attend the New Education Conference on Native Education.

26. *The School in the Bush*, London, Longmans Green and Co., was first published in 1929. It was based on a visit to Africa lasting eight months during which Murray travelled extensively. A second edition, with a *Foreword* by Professor Nunn was published in 1938. Nunn commented on the courage with which Murray criticized established persons and institutions, whatever their authority or prestige. He did not agree with all that Murray said but he admired his honesty of purpose.

27. Hussey to Oldham 26 Nov 1930 IMC/CBMS Archives, E. R. G. Hussey 1930–33 file, Box 274

28. Murray to Oldham 17 Mar 1932, IMC/CBMS Archives, Murray Scheme — Visitation 1930/1 file, Box 275. [Murray's visit had originally been planned to occur much earlier and no one changed the date on the office file to read 1931/2]

29. Harold Jowitt, *The Principles of Education for African Teachers in Training*, London, Longmans Green & Co., 1932. [Given the date of publication of the copy in the London Institute of Education library, it is probable that there was an earlier printing of the book otherwise it is difficult to see how Murray would have known of it or expected Hussey to have read it.]. Jowitt was educated at University College, Southampton and started his career as Headmaster of Edendale Training College in Natal. He later became a Senior Inspector of Schools there before moving to Southern Rhodesia where he was in turn Director of Native Education and Director of Native Development. In 1934 he became DE in Uganda.

30. Murray to Oldham 2 Apr 1932 IMC/CBMS Achives, Murray Scheme — Visitation 1930/31 file, Box 275

31. *Ibid.*

32. Oldham to Hussey 31 May 1932 IMC/CBMS Archives, E. R. J. Hussey 1930–3 file, Box 274

33. Murray to Oldham 12 Jul 1932, IMC/CBMS Archives, Journey 1932 and follow-up file, Box 275

34. Murray to Hussey 12 Jul 1932, IMC/CBMS Archives, Journey 1932 and follow-up file, Box 275

35. Oldham to the Rev. H. W. Stacey 12 Dec 1930, IMC/CBMS Archives, Murray Scheme — Visitation 1930/1 file, Box 275

36. *Annual Report* of the Department of Education, Nigeria, 1933

37. Hussey *Memoirs*, p 92

38. For details of Hussey's links to the NUT see A.Fajana, *Education in Nigeria 1842–1939*, Longmans Nigeria, 1978 pp 204–206

39. Lord Passfield, the Secretary of State for the Colonies, issued a directive on 17 Sep 1930 which actively encouraged the growth of trade unionism in the colonies but government officials were expected to ensure that unions emerged as constitutional organisations with legitimate aims.

40. *Memoirs*, p 92

41. Information supplied by Lord Hussey

42. Sources of information on this period of Hussey's career include the annual reports of the National Society and various Minute books of the Standing, Executive, and Finance and General Purposes Committees. These records are all kept at the Church of England Records Centre, 15 Galleywall Road, South Bermondsey, London.

43. Information on Hussey's ACEC activities is derived from the Minutes of the ACEC, see CO 987/1, 2 & 3. and also The Sir Christopher Cox Papers CO 1045/6, 7

44. *Higher Education in East Africa*, Colonial No. 142 (1937)

45. *Report of the Commission on Higher Education in the Colonies*, Cmd. 6647 (1945) and *Report of the Commission on Higher Education in West Africa*, Cmd, 6655 (1945)

46. *Mass Education in African Society*, Colonial No. 186 (1943)

47. Details of Hussey's links with the British Council are derived from *Annual Reports* of the Council and Hussey's *Memoirs*.

48. See Minutes of the ACEC, CO 987/2, 3 and CO 1045/7

49. *Education for Citizenship in Africa*, Colonial No. 216 (1948)

50. See *Annual Reports* of the University of London School of Oriental and African Studies 1940–1958

51. Hussey *Memoirs, Foreword* by Christine Hussey

52. Information on his links with the Africa Society is derived from volumes of the Society's journal *African Affairs* (1947– 1955)

53. Tendances de l'Enseignement dans les Colonies Britanniques d'Afrique, *Revue Coloniale Belge* (Brussels), No 58 Mar 1, 1948, pp 139–141

54. The story of the Woodard Schools and the Corporation is told in K. E. Kirk, *The Story of the Woodard Schools*, London, Hodder & Stoughton, 1937. Details of Hussey's links with the Corporation are derived from Minute books and the Roll of the Corporation in the Archives of the Woodard Corporation located at I Sanctuary Buildings, Westminster, London. Hussey was listed as Fellow No. 328 of the Society of SS Mary and Nicolas.

55. 'Some aspects of education in Nigeria'

56. 'The role of education in assisting the people of West Africa to adjust themselves to the changing conditions due to European contacts'

57. There is a summary of most of his published articles in his *Memoirs*

58. File of typescript talks in possession of Lord Hussey

59. Hussey *Memoirs*, p 129

60. *Ibid.*, p 155

61. *Ibid.*, pp 152–3

62. Major Sir Ralph Furse, *Aucuparius Recollections of a Recruiting Officer*, London, OUP, 1962 p vii

10. Sir Christopher Cox

An Imperial Patrician of a Different Kind[1]

During the 1930s, the British Empire exuded an imposing air of permanence and power but in reality it was a fragile structure that was destined to be transformed in scarcely more than two decades into little more than a curiosity of history. After 1945, all aspects of British colonial policy were subject to searching reappraisal and education was no exception. In the Colonial Office there was a new determination on the part of the Colonial Secretary Arthur Creech Jones, and Andrew Cohen, Under-Secretary of the African division, to provide a more positive and dynamic style of leadership in Whitehall.[2] The long-standing policy of indirect rule, whereby Britain had ruled through local indigenous leaders was abandoned, and henceforth, every effort was made to work with, rather than against, those in the indigenous population who were western-educated. Everywhere, after 1945, a major emphasis was placed on a rapid expansion of schooling, especially at the secondary level, to facilitate economic and social development. New universities were also established in Africa, Malaya, and the Caribbean, and later still in the South Pacific, to provide the elite cadre of administrators needed to sustain the new thrust towards self-government.

The granting of independence ended formal constitutional links with Britain but reliance on British technical and financial support continued unabated throughout the 1960s, as new states sought to expand and improve the quality of their educational systems. The provision of expatriate staff, financial assistance with capital projects, advanced education and training for overseas students in British tertiary institutions, and expert advice on technical matters, were all important aspects of continuing educational links between Britain and the new member of the Commonwealth.

Throughout this period of rapid post-war change there was an important, indeed, a unique element of continuity in Whitehall in the person of Sir Christopher Cox, who occupied the post of Chief Educational Adviser to the British government from 1940 through to 1970. Until 1961, he was adviser to the Secretary of State for the Colonies. He then transferred to the newly created Department of Technical Cooperation before transferring yet again, in 1964, to the Ministry of Overseas Development. Cox retired well beyond the normal retirement age partly because he expressed no wish to depart the scene but also it would seem because no one had the heart to tell him to go. When he did eventually step down at the age of 71, it was jokingly rumoured in the corridors of power that the government had been considering the passage of an Act of Parliament to remove him.

During his long tenure in office, Cox travelled repeatedly throughout the colonial territories. Wherever he went he was highly regarded for his professional knowledge and understanding while his warm and generous nature also generated legions of admirers and friends across the globe. As one New Zealander wrote to him after travelling through a variety of British colonies, 'wherever I went and your name was discussed, I found the greatest respect for your terrific energy and capacity to remember detail. You had left more than one officer completely exhausted after a visit, but none was left without admiration'.[3] Cox also came to be widely accepted throughout the colonies as a notable eccentric — an imperial patrician of a different kind — one of a small but dedicated band of British officials in Whitehall, charged with the responsibility for shaping and guiding the transition from colonies to commonwealth.

William Dodd, then an Education Officer in Tanganyika, remembers first meeting Cox on the slopes of Mount Kilimanjaro. He had been warned that Cox would quiz him about girls' education so he made sure that he was well prepared. He was duly given his cue and launched forth for about a minute before Cox tapped him on the shoulder and asked him whether he thought two nearby birds were mating. Cox had heard enough to feel confident that girls' education was in good hands.[4] In the 1960s, when Cox and Cohen were housed in the old India Office, it was common knowledge that they frequently roared at each other across the inner quadrangle from their respective study windows.[5] Who, then, was this man whose legacy is now writ large in so many parts of the Third World?

Christopher Cox was born in November 1899, the eldest of three sons of a headmaster of a preparatory school in Plymouth.[6] Later in his life, the family home was located at Yelverton on the edge of Dartmoor. It was a haven he constantly returned to until his parents died in 1947. It was there that he sought serenity and relief from the strain of what ultimately became a prodigiously active and demanding life. He won a scholarship to Clifton College, where he established a reputation as an outstanding classical scholar. He narrowly missed out on being Head of School but was Head of his House and a dutiful if unenthusiastic games player. In December 1917 he won another scholarship to Balliol College, Oxford, then widely regarded as 'the top college for brains'[7] but by then he was just old enough to join the army and eventually sailed for France as a second lieutenant on Armistice Day. During the war junior officers like Cox had seldom lasted more than a couple of months in the front line trenches. In 1919, he went to Balliol to study classics and emerged four years later with a First in *Literae Humaniores*. Then followed two years at Magdalen College on a Craven Fellowship and a Senior Demyship, before he was appointed as a Fellow and lecturer in ancient history at New College, which was to be quite literally his home for the remaining 56 years of his life.

One of Cox's former students has recalled that he was a very popular tutor but quite unlike anyone he had ever met or has met since.[8] He had a keen eye for detail and was prepared to argue everything at enormous length. Unfortunately, however, he had no sense of time and tutorials frequently ended with most of an essay unread. Nevertheless, tutorial relationships frequently led to close and lasting friendships because Cox was willing to listen to student woes and offer sympathetic guidance. In the mid-1930s, when he served a term as Dean of New College, he is said to have shown a penetrating insight into human nature and to have won praise for his sympathetic handling of disciplinary matters. As one of his contemporaries has since remarked, 'I knew no pupil and indeed no one at all who disliked him'.[9]

Academic research took him on frequent visits to Turkey and the ancient Greek world. In 1937, he co-authored the fifth volume of *Monumentia Asiae Minoris Antiqua*. The records of earlier research done in the 1920 have also come to light since Cox's death and these too have now been edited and published.[10] But people, not paper, were his passion in life.[11] There were times during his teaching years at New College when he found it impossible to answer correspondence or mark student scripts, so that he would sometimes carry bundles of unopened letters away with him on holidays. In 1929 he visited South Africa, taking with him a bundle of examination scripts, including those of the late Richard Crossman. Travelling back on the overland route to Cairo, he is reputed to have reached the Victoria Falls and been sorely tempted to throw the scripts into the Zambesi River.[12]

Cox developed an early interest in the African colonies through his lifelong friendship with C. H. Baynes, his contemporary at Balliol.[13] Thereafter, Baynes spent several years teaching at King's College, Lagos, before returning to Oxford in the 1930s as Headmaster of the New College Choir School. While in Nigeria he maintained a steady correspondence with Cox. In 1929 Cox went to South Africa as a member of the delegation of the British Association for the Advancement of Science. He chose to return overland to Cairo via Khartoum where he met and made friendships with local educators.[14]

In 1937, he received a pressing but quite unforeseen invitation 'literally out the Sudanese blue' to go back to the Sudan for two years as DE and Principal of Gordon College.[15] He leapt at the idea of initiating a new ten-year development plan. Having successfully negotiated a secondment from New College, he embarked on what proved to be the start of a second career and the two happiest years of his life.[16] He made a lasting impression in the Sudan and is still remembered for the way in which he built up Gordon College, the forerunner of the University of Khartoum. He was fortunate in taking up his appointment at the time when Lord De La Warr's Educational Commission was visiting East Africa to examine the future of higher education in the region. The Commission made a close inspection of Gordon College and Cox was specifically thanked for his valuable assistance in the ensuing report.[17]

Cox returned to England shortly before the outbreak of war and soon afterwards was appointed Educational Adviser to the Secretary of State for the Colonies, initially for three years or until the end of hostilities. This was a new post created at the insistence of Malcolm MacDonald, who had assumed office as Secretary of State for the Colonies in May 1938, determined to initiate a major shake-up in colonial policy in general.[18] Cox was appointed to replace Arthur Mayhew and Sir Hanns Vischer, the joint secretaries of the London-based Advisory Committee on Education in the Colonies, who had both reached retirement age.

Prior to accepting the Colonial Office appointment Cox was asked whether he would consider going out to the Gold Coast to replace The Rev. H. M. Grace, the retiring Headmaster of Achimota College, but he declined.[19] In 1938 he had similarly turned down an offer to go to Uganda as Principal of Makerere College.[20] On both occasions he considered that he was not the man for the job. Moreover, he felt obligated to return to New College after his term expired in the Sudan. He believed that anyone undertaking either of the jobs offered to him should not go on loan but should be prepared to commit himself for a minimum of five, if not ten years. Cox accepted the Colonial Office appointment only after New College had agreed to release him for the duration of the war.

The full story behind Cox's appointment may never be known but Major Ralph Furse, the chief recruitment officer for the Colonial Service, clearly played a key role in securing Cox's services. The post of Educational Adviser was formally authorised at a meeting held in the Colonial Office in July 1939, where it was agreed to seek the services 'of a university man of distinction'. Sir Will Spens was asked to sound out any likely candidates at Cambridge while Furse was asked to do likewise at Oxford.[21] Spens could not think of anyone but Furse immediately approached Cox. There is ample evidence in Cox's correspondence to show that both men had known each other for some years. For example, Colin Baynes had written to Cox as far back as 1931, to ask if he would approach Furse about a job as he was anxious to leave Nigeria.[22] It was also clear that Furse had discussed Cox's future career with him as late as November 1938.[23] Cox had an impeccable academic pedigree, which was invariably a necessary prior condition for recruitment into Britain's patrician class in the inter-war period. He also made a very favourable impression on Sir Douglas Newbold, the highly esteemed Sudan Civil Secretary, while he was DE in Khartoum.[24] Newbold was a close friend of Margery Perham, a prominent authority on colonial matters in the 1930s and a close confidante of the government. She became a member of the Education Advisory Committee in 1939, and was present at the meeting held in May 1939, at which Lord Hailey recommended the appointment of a full-time educational adviser at the Colonial Office.[25] Sir William McLean may also have supported Cox's appointment. He was a former colonial official who had been responsible, jointly with Sir James Currie, for establishing education in the Sudan. A former Conservative MP, he was a member of the De La Warr Commission and also a member of the Education Advisory Committee for most of the 1930s. During those years colonial education was the concern of a relatively small but highly influential group of people and informal contacts were undoubtedly important in determining many official appointments.

No one, least of all Cox himself, could have foreseen the key role he was to assume during the next 30 years as the colonial empire was dismantled and colonial education was transformed. The war and its aftermath heralded new initiatives and encouraged a spirit of optimism in colonial education — what Cox later called 'disorderly dynamism',[26] while the Colonial Development and Welfare Acts of 1940 and 1945 respectively, encouraged forward planning. Cox's role as an Educational Adviser placed him in a unique position. He was not an administrator in the conventional sense, nor did he direct a Colonial Office Department of Education. Nevertheless, he rapidly established himself as a key figure in determining the broad thrust of colonial education policy.

There is no record of his having received any formal job description when he joined the Colonial Office but he was given a statement of purpose when he made his first tour of Africa and Mauritius in 1943, which provides an idea of what was expected of him. He was instructed to acquaint himself at first hand with educational problems in the territories he visited and to have on-the-spot discussions with appropriate educational authorities so that he could, on return, tender up-to-date advice to the Secretary of State. It was stressed that his tour was not in any sense a formal visit of inspection, nor was he expected to give public addresses in his capacity as Educational Adviser.[27] In practice, Cox was given a free hand to create his own unique role. Freda Gwilliam was placed in a similar position when she was appointed as Women's Education Adviser in 1947. No one told her what to do when she reported on her first day at the Colonial Office. Instead, she was left free to determine herself how best she might function in her appointed role.[28] Clearly the success of this *laissez-faire* approach depended greatly on the calibre of the people selected. In the case of Cox and the small team of advisers that he subsequently gathered around him, it proved an unqualified success.

Cox soon showed the intellectual and diplomatic qualities that were to make him an outstanding public servant. In the early war years he played a decisive role behind the scenes in the creation of the Asquith Commission which prepared a seminal report on the future of higher education in the colonies.[29] In 1943, he was called upon to give evidence to that commission. Lord Asquith later wrote to the Secretary of State and singled Cox out for the highest praise: 'Cox's evidence, which lasted three days, was an intellectual treat of the first order'.[30] In 1944, Cox was

awarded the CMG Sir George Gater, then the Permanent Under-Secretary
at the Colonial Office, wrote to congratulate him: 'It is a great source of
pleasure and inspiration to have you as a colleague. You have been a
brilliant success'.[31] In 1945, he was also called upon to sort out a serious
difference of opinion which had arisen in The Gambia over the
governor's reorganization of education.[32] It was a delicate matter
involving a proposed government takeover of some of the existing
mission primary schools. In essence, the Anglican and Methodist schools
were to be taken over by the government while the Roman Catholic and
Moslem schools were to be allowed to remain independent. Eventually
Cox went out to Bathurst to pour oil on the troubled waters. Agreement
was finally reached and Cox delivered a special message to the people at
the conclusion of his visit to reassure them. It was the only occasion he
ever did so. During the same period he was also involved in settling
differences in Gibraltar between the government and the Roman Catholic
Church over post-war educational reorganization.[33] The government took
the opportunity, while all children had been evacuated from the territory
because of the imminent threat of invasion, to reshape education and, in
particular, to wrest control from the Roman Catholic Church. In both
instances Cox won high praise from senior Colonial Office staff.[34]

Cox was particularly adept at working behind the scenes to achieve
successful outcomes. For example, in 1953, he played a key role in the
success of talks held in London with a delegation from the Rhodesias and
Nyasaland regarding the establishment of a university college in Salisbury.
Margery Perham, who was present at the talks, joined with senior
government officials in congratulating Cox: 'I do congratulate you on the
work you have put in behind the scenes to make this affair a success.
I could not help smiling admiringly to myself as you sat silent while we all
played our parts according to your instructions.'[35] An unsigned minute in
a Colonial Office file dated 3 November 1960, further highlights the
crucial role that Cox later played in the provision of financial aid for
educational development in Britain's former colonies:[36]

> I do not myself think that it would be going too far to say that it
> is essentially his personal contacts, in London, Oxford and
> elsewhere with the very distinguished members of the various
> advisory committees that ensure that the machinery operates
> smoothly …. I would myself be doubtful whether even exactly
> the same machinery would successfully serve the same purpose
> if there were not someone playing the crucial role which Cox
> plays in all this.

At the end of the war Cox was faced with the most difficult decision of
his life, whether to accept a permanent position in Whitehall or to return
to academic life at Oxford. Eventually he decided to stay at the Colonial
Office but the strain imposed upon him by the dilemma in which he was
placed almost precipitated a nervous breakdown. W. E. F. Ward, who was

appointed as Cox's deputy in 1945, recounted how, one Friday evening at the height of the crisis, he and a colleague personally escorted Cox to Paddington station to catch his Oxford-bound train for fear that he might not make it.[37] Cox's ardent wish not to sever his ties with Oxford was ultimately met by the generosity of New College who agreed to award him a supernumerary fellowship which provided him with rooms in college on a permanent basis.[38] Earlier Gater had written to the Warden suggesting that the association of the College and the Colonial Office would be mutually advantageous. Oxford could provide Cox with relaxation from the strain attached to office work in London, and ideal conditions for the reading and thinking essential in the work of an adviser. Moreover, time spent at Oxford would not be deducted from Cox's annual leave entitlement.[39] The arrangement worked well, with Cox spending most weekends at Oxford when he was not away touring in distant colonies. After his retirement in 1970, he was made an Honorary Fellow and remained a permanent resident at New College until his death.

Unfortunately, the 1945 crisis was not the only occasion when Cox suffered from disabling depression, or 'the fumes' as he called it. Throughout much of his life he fought against periodic bouts of it with the aid of doctors, family and friends.[40] In long vacations he tried to counter it by visiting *Le Chalet des Melezes*, a property in the French Alps owned by New College, watching cricket at Lords (he was a member of the MCC and frequently watched the full five days of a Test Match — often alone!); and by hill-climbing in the Scottish highlands. After the death of his parents, still in search of a diversion from depression, he became a skilled amateur botanist and actually discovered a new plant in north-west Scotland. In the late 1940s and early 1950s, when Cox was away touring for long periods, Ward's correspondence with him often included detailed descriptions of the flowers and birds in his garden in Cheam: 'Bright sunshine, with a cold NW wind, and night frost. Daffodils at their best, chestnut leaves out of the sheath and hanging limp. My garden is a mass of red dead nettle .... Chaffinch busily nesting somewhere close to my house, but not in my garden I fear'.[41] Cox found calm and renewal of vigour amidst hills and mountains and even climbed Mount Popocatapetl in Mexico (almost 19,000 feet) during a weekend break at a Unesco conference in 1947.[42] When depressed he believed he was of no value to anyone. At such times he often sought solace from A. H. Smith, the Sub-Warden at New College who tried valiantly to reassure him of his worth.[43] In the early 1960s he spent several weeks in hospital worried about possible blindness and cancer of the heel but eventually modern drugs helped lessen the severity of the attacks.[44] In the late 1960s he also suffered from arthritis and had a hip operation in the early 1970s.

Throughout his public life Cox maintained an enormous personal workload which was compounded by the relentless travelling that he embarked upon year after year, at a time, let it be remembered, when air travel was not quite as straight-forward or as predictable as it is today.

He never enjoyed air travel but was forced to accept it on practical grounds.[45] For much of his working life he boarded during the week in central London — always, it is worth noting, with a family — returning to New College at weekends.[46] For many years he lived in St John's Wood close to the Lords cricket ground. He drove a car in the 1930s but then gave it up. In London he always walked or took a taxi. A normal working day in the early 1950s began with his arrival in mid-morning at Church House, Great Smith Street, located behind Westminster Abbey, one of the numerous annexes of the Colonial Office. He would read *The Times* and look over correspondence until midday and then retire to the *Athenaeum* for lunch. This would often include a working session with a DE home on leave from one of the colonies or some high-ranking government official. After lunch his real working day commenced. Much to the dismay of his secretarial staff he would often work solidly into the evening, long after everyone else had gone home. On many such occasions work was doubtless a refuge from himself.

He never married but he retained close links with his immediate family. Two women attracted him greatly while he was a tutor at Oxford. One was Mary Fisher, later Mrs Bennett, the daughter of H. A. L. Fisher, the Warden of New College 1928–41. She later became Principal of St Hilda's College, Oxford. The other was Sheila Grant-Duff, a brilliant and beautiful undergraduate who was 13 years younger than Cox. She subsequently fell madly in love with a young Fellow of All Souls. As Cox later told his brother David, the people he would have liked to marry would have been impossible to live with. It was his fate, he thought, never to fall in love with a girl who would have made him happy. David Cox suggested that his brother would indeed have been quite a 'demoralising' husband.[47] Those who knew Christopher well spoke of his vibrant personality but there were also times, especially in later life, when he desperately needed solace and would claim hours of attention from his colleagues without recognising that they also had lives of their own to attend to.[48]

Throughout his life he was one of the most garrulous and untidiest of men although, ironically, he shied away from public speaking whenever possible. He claimed that he was not a ready speaker in the formal sense and that public speaking engagements distracted him for days beforehand.[49] Frank Ward referred to picking his way frequently on tip-toe through piles of files and papers with which the floor of Cox's room was invariably covered to ask a question. But he was never given the opportunity. 'Christopher would talk without stopping, maybe for a full hour until I could take no more and excused myself.'[50] The chaotic disorder of his rooms in New College surpassed description. Letters were known to have been headed 'Saturday, or don't I mean Sunday,' and later in his career his style of writing became characterized by lengthy parentheses. In later life his handwriting also deteriorated so much that colonial officials or their secretaries frequently had to guess at the contents of some letters. Evidently, one secretary usually managed to extract the gist of his letters 'by taking them at a rush'.[51]

Preparations for his many trips abroad were also a regular ordeal for those involved. Packing was often left to the last minute. On one occasion Ward recalled receiving a frantic phone call from Cox's landlady to say that she had made a last minute cheek of Christopher's case and found to her dismay that he had included six pairs of dirty socks some of which had holes in them. What was she to do? Ward solved the problem by sending one of his secretarial staff out to purchase several new pairs of socks from his own pocket. To the best of his knowledge, Cox never even noticed.[52] Cox's departure for West Africa in 1947, was recorded for posterity by one of his advisory team writing to the DE in Fiji: 'though I was not associated with the preparations made by Stanley when he visited [Africa] or when Cook toured in your part of the world, I am quite sure that their preparations were as those for a half day excursion to Brighton when compared with Christopher's'.[53]

When travelling, 'our wandering boy'[54] or 'Major Irritant',[55] as he was called by some of his intimate Whitehall colleagues, was always scribbling in notebooks although those that survive in his papers are mostly illegible. But everywhere Cox went he won friends. He had a prodigious memory for detail and readily identified with individuals and their problems. As one admirer in Africa has recalled, 'Christopher's visitation was a whirlwind experience for us all. At the time he was careering all over the Colonial Empire, stimulating us, gauging our problems, encouraging the newly appointed, post-war education officials and breathing new life into Education Departments which were greatly in need of fresh air'.[56]

He had none of the routine qualities of an administrator or civil servant and probably no bureaucracy in the world save the British could have deployed him to such effect, much less tolerated him. His deputy, Frank Ward, scholarly and meticulous by nature, readily concedes that Cox was often exasperating, almost to the point of distraction, to work alongside. Indeed, he readily admitted that Cox's 'utter lack of method' precipitated his own partial retirement in 1956.[57] It was Colin Legum, the noted African correspondent, who provided perhaps the most colourful description of Cox. He portrayed him as both informal and unorthodox:[58]

> a large restless man, with an unruly mop of hair, a passion for talking and smoking and moving around. Neatly-docketed facts, tidy formulae, files, routine and formal administrative work matter as little to him as gnats to elephants. He has a bulging mind crammed with ideas that bubble over and scatter themselves profusely in a way that makes ordinary conversation dull and unprofitable.

Ward also had first hand knowledge of how Cox's garrulous nature spilled over into his writing. In 1952, Cox delivered an address at the fiftieth jubilee celebrations of the University of London's Institute of Education. Four years later he gave the presidential address at the annual conference of the British Association for the Advancement of Science. On both occasions Ward had the unenviable task of editing Cox's long rambling scripts. After reducing the British Association address from 11,000 to 7,500 words, Ward commented, 'I didn't like doing it and you won't like what I have done .... But for Pete's sake don't try to cram in any more ideas or you will over-run both your space and your audience's absorptive capacity. It is good stuff without adding any more.'[59] Ward's valiant efforts were to no avail. Both addresses ran well over the allotted time when they were presented but they were very favourably received. J. A. Perkins, the Vice-President of the Carnegie Corporation, considered Cox's address to the British Association 'one of the best statements I have read on the British view of their colonial education programme'.[60] Another insight into the relationship between Cox and his deputy Frank Ward is provided by a letter Ward wrote to Cox in January 1959 to explain why he had not shown him the typescript of his book *Educating Young Nations*, which was about to go to press:

> I hope you will not suspect that my reason for not submitting the typescript to you was that I did not know what luminous (*not* voluminous!) advice you would give me. I am fully aware of that.
>
> I did not show it to you, quite deliberately. I know how fiendishly busy you are, and also how much of a perfectionist (I have had rare experiences of the trouble you take over your own scripts!). For one thing, you — being you — could not rest until you had weighed the tense and mood of every verb and assured yourself that no further qualification was needed to any sentence. And, frankly, the book is so slight that it doesn't deserve all that trouble.[61]

An insight into Cox's passion for work, his total lack of mechanical aptitude and his lack of formality with people was provided by Mrs Ross or 'Hester', his Canadian stenographer at the Colonial Office, who wrote to him in August 1956.[62] Cox had gone to the New College Chalet in France for a few days rest and she wrote partly to reassure him that all was well back in the office. Her letter began 'Dear Major Irritant, No, Dear Sir Christopher', and continued in a highly familiar but, nevertheless, respectful vein:

> I thought I'd better let you have a note in case you thought you were gone and forgotten which is not the case for we all miss you, no fooling! Mrs. E. [Evelyn Engleback, his personal secretary[63]] asks me to tell you, if you haven't already discovered it, that the Biro is not broken but you just haven't the mechanical

mind. You press the end bit in to use it and likewise press it again to close it — with your thumb! *Voila!*

She then expressed the hope that he would really take a rest from his work and return feeling better but she doubted whether he would. 'Did you ever figure to yourself the fact that if you get your call-up papers to go and fight little old Nasser the work will get done somehow, somewhere and by someone???? So — enjoy your holiday and to heck with work.' She was fully aware of the pressures placed upon those who worked closely with Cox:

> I am going to take a week off from the 15th of August — I was going earlier but as you are coming back for a day on the 10th I thought I would stay to give you my moral support. I see the 10th is a Friday — but I hope it won't turn out to be a BLACK Friday. I shall be armed with 1 High Pressure pill, 1 Nervous Indigestion pill and a dose of Meggatone (for pep) and, putting my faith in Heaven that you don't wear out the telephone with phone conversations, hope to be able to ease you off for the Scottish interlude ....

The rest of the letter related how she got 'high' at a farewell cocktail party for Dr Harlow, an Assistant Adviser on Technical Education, and how he, a teetotaller, had kindly driven her home afterwards. She also told Cox how thankful she was that he was not a stuffed shirt like so many of 'them' around the Colonial Office. She concluded by saying that Miss Barker and Mrs. F. sent 'their most respectful salutations but I say — here's mud in your eye!'

Cox is probably best remembered for his contribution to the development of higher education in the colonies. From the moment he arrived in Whitehall he was closely involved with the work of a sub-committee of the Advisory Committee whose task was to review the future of higher education in West Africa. The sub-committee's report[64] led directly to the setting up of the Asquith Commission in August 1943. Three years later Cox played a key role in the establishment of the Inter-Universities Council (IUC). Thereafter, for many years, he and Dr Walter Adams, the Secretary of the Council, shared a heavy workload in its deliberations. In 1946, he also chaired a committee which determined the fate of the war ravaged University of Hong Kong.[65] Much of his time thereafter, was taken up with matters related to the staffing and funding of the newly created colonial university colleges in Africa, the West Indies, and the Far East. He was also deeply involved in the creation of Regional Colleges of Arts, Science and Technology. In the 1960s he confined himself almost exclusively to matters affecting higher education and growing Anglo-American co-operation in African educational development.

In the immediate post-war years Cox was also very busy dealing with the educational components of the numerous development plans which flooded into the Colonial Office in response to the Colonial Development and Welfare Acts. At the same time he also worked closely with Sir Andrew Cohen on reshaping colonial education policy.[66] In contrast to the relative inertia of the 1930s, the immediate post-war years saw a vigorous drive emanating from Whitehall to expand education in the colonies at all levels. Secondary schooling and teacher-training, in particular, were accorded top priority as an increasing number of colonies set their sights on eventual independence.[67]

Cox was also responsible for rebuilding, almost single-handedly, the CES after the severe depredations of war. During his long tenure of office he built up a remarkable network of official contacts and close personal friendships which gave him unrivalled intimate knowledge of the internal strengths and weaknesses of literally more than 40 separate Departments of Education scattered across the globe. He corresponded on a personal basis with dozens of educational administrators and teachers while colonial officials from governors downwards, wrote to him personally expressing their opinions, their hopes and their fears. He also received frank and valuable on-the-spot-comments of people and events from his small team of advisers when they went on tour. Freda Gwilliam, in particular, was an outspoken critic who rarely minced her words.[68]

Cox was not directly responsible for making CES appointments but his advice was generally followed, especially at senior level. For example, in 1957, it was Cox's minute which decided who was appointed DE in Tanganyika:[69]

> Mr Lewis-Jones has been doing splendid work in Fiji. I have recently seen for myself how he has transformed the whole educational policy and, even more important, the atmosphere there. He and his wife are first class in social leadership. They get on well with all races, and with Government colleagues ... He is intensely loyal and keen and does not spare himself.

At least one former colonial education officer thought it a pity that Lewis-Jones didn't display the same energy and devotion to his work when he was DE in Tanganyika.[70] Cox's opinion was also sought on many occasions for appointments in colonial universities. The evidence from numerous files suggests he was a frank but scrupulously fair judge of his colleagues.

He also maintained close personal links with the Colonial Department at the Institute of Education in London, and with most of the prominent educators in Britain. Professor Margaret Read, the Head of the Colonial Department at the Institute from 1940 to 1955, was a particularly close academic colleague and friend throughout the latter half of Cox's life.[71] The work of the Advisory Committee, of which Cox was an ex-officio member, also took up much of his time. It usually met on the third Thursday in the month but Cox was also closely involved in the work of various sub-committees. He was also responsible for determining the composition of the Committee and the agendas at meetings.

In November 1954, Dr G. B. Jeffery, the Director of the Institute of Education in London, approached Cox about succeeding Margaret Read as Head of the Colonial Department when she retired in 1955. Jeffery could not guarantee that he would be appointed but he did state that Cox's name would be the first choice of the Institute when applications were considered. It would be a position, he suggested, from which Cox could exercise great influence on colonial education: 'I know of no other person who could do this particular job'.[72]

Cox received Jeffery's letter while on tour in Nyasaland. Fortunately, he kept the envelope on which he made rough notes outlining the pros and cons of accepting Jeffery's offer.[73] First, he worked out details of his pension. It was clear that he would be much better off financially if he could remain working until he reached the age of 65. Then he drew up a list of the points both for and against a move to the Institute. His main reason for moving seemed to be related to the retirement age. At the Institute he would be able to work until he was 65 whereas his future at the Colonial Office was less certain. Traditionally staff retired at 60 unless, as in exceptional cases, asked to stay on for a year at a time. Cox noted that his predecessors Mayhew and Vischer, were both retired at 61 years of age. However, he noted that in recent years Colonial Office theory had changed and staff could now reasonably expect to be asked to stay on for a year at a time until they reached 65. In practice, however, this rule had yet to be applied to senior officials but Cox wondered whether he might be treated differently because, as an adviser, he was not blocking the promotion of other people. He also noted that compulsory retirement at 60 would mean giving up the sort of work he liked and needed.

His reasons for staying at the Colonial Office were both revealing and decisive. He admitted that he liked his job immensely, especially the touring aspect of it, and that he would get far fewer opportunities for overseas travel in a university and his touring role would be different. Leaving Whitehall would also mean severing his connection with New College which he was more than reluctant to contemplate. He also disliked the prospect of having to give lectures: 'Being a Professor does mean having the answers which I don't'; public speaking; running a university department with all the problems of staff relations and collegiate loyalty; and the upheaval of moving from Oxford. Foremost, however, in his decision to stay at the Colonial Office was the 'loss of power let's be honest!' — that a move to the Institute would have entailed. Cox may not have deliberately sought the limelight, but he knew that wherever he went he was accorded the red-carpet treatment befitting his senior status in the Whitehall hierarchy. After careful consideration his reply to Jeffery read simply 'Very sorry idea should be dropped'.

His unique contribution to British colonial education was first publicly recognised in 1944 when he received the award of CMG. Six years later he was knighted, largely at the behest of Arthur Creech Jones, then Colonial Secretary in Attlee's Labour government, and a close personal friend. When Cox retired in 1970 he was further elevated to GCMG. In the latter part of his public career he also received the inevitable string of honorary degrees from the universities of Belfast (1961), Hong Kong (1961), Leeds (1962), Oxford (1965), and the Chinese University of Hong Kong (1969). In May 1958 he also accepted an invitation to join the All Souls Group, which met about three times a year to discuss various proposals for the reform of education in the United Kingdom. The Group first met in 1941 under the aegis of Dr W. G. S. Adams, then Warden of All Souls College, Oxford. Little is known publicly of what transpired at meetings because proceedings were never published but administrative, philosophical and social aspects of educational reform were high on the agenda. Various subjects were discussed in relation to their influence on education. These included the 1944 Education Act, the Welfare State, New Towns, science and industry, juvenile delinquency and moral training, the role of Britain in world affairs, and the educational and political problems of the Commonwealth. The Group attracted a diverse and impressive array of talent[74] despite an annual membership fee of £1 and members being required to pay for their own dinner and accommodation before and after meetings!

When Cox finally left Whitehall, he took with him some 91 crates of papers which he planned to sort and catalogue for posterity. His efforts were intermittent but before he died he produced approximately 2,500 typed sheets listing the contents of the numerous files in his possession, which comprised all the printed material and correspondence that he amassed during the 30 years he worked in London. Unfortunately the typed sheets did not include numerous envelopes containing miscellaneous letters and papers. Since then his 'Colonial Office' papers, as distinct from the material relating to his early life, which is housed in the library at New College, have been deposited in the Public Record Office.[75]

In retirement Cox changed little. He always claimed to be busy but as Professor Hart remarked, two minutes to spare on the phone would frequently, to the despair of his listener, extend to 20 minutes or even on some occasions to an hour and a half.[76] He found satisfaction in serving on the Council of Clifton College, his *alma mater,* but he also spent much time in the last years of his life organising guest lists for visits to the New College chalet on the slopes of Mount Blanc. In his will he donated £40,000 to New College for purposes largely connected with the chalet.[77] His death in July 1982, at the age of 83, was not unexpected as he had been in poor health for some time.

Cox used to revel in claiming, with mock superiority, to being a Victorian, by virtue of the date of his birth. Perhaps there was more to his claim than he realised. He was clearly a product of his class and time, and lived much of his life in a style which has long since departed. He was also fortunate to have occupied a key role at a unique period in the history of British colonialism.

Throughout 30 years of public life he generated a deep sense of loyalty and genuine affection amongst those who worked closely with him but one wonders how much of his extrovert personality was deliberately cultivated to cloak the loneliness and personal despondency that so often seemed to threaten his well-being. The story of his life revives memories of a period in time which seems to have slipped unceremoniously into history but the legacy of his labours lives on in many of the schools and universities of the new states in the Commonwealth.

During his public life he rarely put pen to paper in the formal academic sense and left no personal revelations about his life's work for the benefit of posterity. Fortunately, however, an enterprising biographer will find a wealth of material relating to Cox's life in the extensive archive of private and official papers that 'accumulated imperceptibly year by year' around him throughout his life.[78]

Like many people destined to achieve prominence in public life, Cox was blessed with the luck to be in the right place at the right time. Had he not accepted the Sudan offer in 1937, he might never have been considered for the key advisory position in 1940. In that case he might well have lived out the rest of his life as a relatively obscure but likeable don at Oxford. It is to his lasting credit that few, if any, of those who knew and worked with him during those exciting years of decolonisation would have wished that to happen. Cox may not have been a great educator in the classical sense — he was no Dewey or Matthew Arnold — but his influence on the course of educational development in Britain's former colonies was no less profound and deserves due recognition.

<h2 style="text-align:center">NOTES ON CHAPTER</h2>

1. This essay first appeared in the *Journal of Educational Administration and History* 21/1 (1989) pp 28–42
2. Ronald Robinson, 'Sir Andrew Cohen: Proconsul of African Nationalism', in L. H. Gann and Peter Duignan (eds), *African Proconsuls: European Governors in Africa*, New York, Free Press, 1978
3. F. R. J. Davies to Cox, 14 Sep 1953, CO 1045/509 [Cox Papers]
4. Personal communication to the author from W. A. Dodd, former Chief Education Officer and Under-Secretary, Overseas Development Administration, Nov 1987
5. *Ibid.*
6. Cox's father, Arthur, was born in 1870. He obtained a third class degree from Trinity College, Cambridge, and then taught in a variety of preparatory schools before becoming headmaster of Mount House School in Plymouth (1909–27). In 1898 he married Alice Wimbush of Torrington, Yorkshire, and Christopher was born on 17 Nov 1899. Arthur Cox had a lifelong interest in language and ornithology and kept notes on birds throughout his life. Christopher's two brothers, Roger and David, were born in 1911 and 1913 respectively. The long interval between the births of Christopher and Roger was due to their mother suffering from tuberculosis.

She was eventually cured but five of her brothers and sisters died of it. Christopher's parents died within weeks of each other in 1947. He also had two uncles, Aldwyn, a long-time missionary in Nyasaland who died in 1960, and Cuthbert, who was also a teacher and later headmaster of Berkhamstead Junior School. Roger Cox went to Clifton and Peterhouse, Cambridge, where he gained an upper second in history, but thereafter his life became unconventional. He left Cambridge in 1933, rejected Christianity, and much to his parents' dismay, joined the Communist Party. He then did another degree in Egyptology at London University and worked on a site in Palestine for six months. He also worked at the Wellcome Institute Museum for 18 months, but never had a settled career. From childhood he had an obsession with numbers although he failed to get 'O' level maths when at school. In 1939 he was exempted from war service on psychiatric grounds but subsequently worked at Bletchley in the secret intelligence unit, although his younger brother had no idea how he got the job. After the war he had serious psychiatric problems and lived 'a most peculiar existence' in St Ives with 'Lizzie', a widow 20 years his senior who he had met in the 1930s. David Cox went to Clifton and Oxford, where he studied classics and later history, and won a junior fellowship at All Souls. He nearly joined the Sudan Political Service but eventually became a university lecturer at Oxford. Details of Christopher Cox's early life are derived mainly from H. L. A. Hart, 'Sir Christopher Cox', an address delivered at Cox's memorial service held in New College chapel, Oct 1982, published in *New College Record 1982*, pp 10–16, and 'Family Notes: The Coxes and the Wimbushes' by A. D. (David) M. Cox, 1981–83.

Unpublished manuscript in the Cox Archive, New College, [CANC]
7.   'Family Notes' A. D. M. Cox
8.   Hart
9.   *Ibid.*
10. C. M. Dalton, 'The Cox Archive, introduction', 20 Mar 1986; a typescript guide to the Cox Archive, New College
11. Hart
12. *Ibid.*
13. Dalton
14. Draft text of Colin Legum's article on Sir Christopher Cox for *West Africa* (1950), CO 1045/1403
15. *Ibid.*
16. A. D. M. Cox
17. Sudan Government, *Report of Lord De La Warr's Educational Commission* (1937) p 4
18. D. J. Morgan, *The Origins of British Aid Policy 1924–45,* Vol. I of the Official History of Colonial Development, London, Macmillan, 1980 p xiv
19. Cox to H. D. Hooper, 25 Oct 1939 CO 1045/1476
20. *Ibid.*
21. CO 866/35/1402 (1939)
22. CANC, Baynes to Cox 8 Dec 1931
23. CANC, Cox to Furse, 10 Nov 1939
24. Personal communication to the author, Nov 1979
25. 18 May 1939 (94th meeting) CO 1045/6
26. Hart
27. 'Statement of purpose in Cox's tour of Africa and Mauritius in 1943', CO 1045/605
28. Personal communication to the author, Jan 1984
29. *Report of the Commission on Higher Education in the Colonies,*1944–5, Cmd. 6647, HMSO, London
30. Minute (nd), which included an extract from the letter. CO 1045/1476
31. CANC, Gater to Cox, 8 Jun 1944

32.   CO 1045/169, 1045/170 and 1045/1417
33.   CO 1045/171
34.   CANC, Gater to Cox, 8 Jun 1944
35.   Margery Perham to Cox, 29 Sep 1953 CO 1045/787
36.   Minute [unsigned] 3 Nov 1960 CO 1045/1526
37.   Personal communication to the author, Nov 1983
38.   CANC, Warden [New College] to Gater, 8 May 1946
39.   *Ibid.*
40.   A. D. M. Cox
41.   W. E. F. Ward to Cox, 9 Apr 1949 CO 1045/648
42.   Hart
43.   For example, CANC, A. H. Smith to Cox, 29 May 1943, on the eve of Cox's first African tour, and Smith to Cox, 30 Oct 1947 on Cox's visit to the UNESCO conference in Mexico.
44.   A. D. M. Cox
45.   Hart
46.   Personal communication to the author from W .E. F. Ward, Nov 1983
47.   A. D. M. Cox
48.   Hart
49.   Cox to P. Donohue, Acting DE, Hong Kong, 17 Aug 1961 CO 1045/728; Cox to Howard Hayden, 17 Jun 1960 CO 1045/319
50.   Hart
51.   *Ibid.*
52.   Personal communication to the author.
53.   L. McD. Robison to Howard Hayden, 25 Jun 1949 CO 1045/166
54.   L. McD. Robison to Howard Hayden, 8 Jul 1949 CO 1045/166
55.   'Hester' to Cox, 3 Aug 1956 CO 1045/1482
56.   Hart
57.   Personal communication to the author, Nov 1987
58.   Draft text of Cohn Legum's article CO 1045/1404
59.   Minute (nd), CO 1045/1375
60.   James A. Perkins to Cox, 13 Mar 1958 CO 1045/1405
61.   Ward to Cox, 15 Jan 1959 CO 1045/702
62.   'Hester' to Cox, 3 Aug 1956 CO 1045/1482
63.   Miss Engleback was Cox's private secretary for the greater part of his working life in the Colonial Office. He left her £750 in his will.
64.   *Report of the Sub-Committee on Higher Education,* ACEC 7/43 Miscellaneous No. 507
65.   *Hong Kong. Report of the Hong Kong University Advisory Committee* CO Print ACEC 15/4
66.   For example, 'Education Policy in Africa', an unpublished paper prepared for the African Governors' Conference, Colonial Office, Nov 1947 CO 987/I See also CO 847/37/47242(47) for Cox's key role in the formulation of education policy.
67.   'Education Policy in Africa'
68.   The Cox Papers include numerous letters containing outspoken comments sent by Freda Gwillam to Cox while she was on tour, eg Gwillam to Cox, 19 Feb 1950, from Malaya, CO 1045/1478 Many letters sent by Gwillam to Cox while she was part of the Binns Commission which reported on education in East Africa in 1951 are contained in CO 1045/584 and 1045/1479
69.   Minute, 29 Aug 1957 CO 1045/366
70.   Private comment to the author
71.   The Cox Papers contain frequent correspondence between Margaret Read and Cox,. e.g. Read to Cox, 14 Apr 1956 CO 1045/1482 and Read to Cox, 20 Nov 1963 CO 1045/1000

72. G. B. Jeffery to Cox, 30 Nov 1954 CO 1045/672
73. *Ibid.*
74. The membership in 1959 comprised the following: Dr W. G. S. Adams, sometime Warden of All Souls, Oxford; Ambrose Appelbe, solicitor; Charles Batey, late Printer to the University of Oxford; R. Beloe, Secretary to the Archbishop of Canterbury; Prof Max Beloff, Gladstone Prof of Government and Public Administration, All Souls; R. Birley, Headmaster, Eton College; Sir Basil Blackwell, Publisher; J. O. Blair-Cunynghame, Member for Staff, National Coal Board; Mark Bonham Carter, Publisher; Sir Maurice Bowra, Warden, Wadham College, Oxford; Alan Bullock, Censor, St Catherine's Society, Oxford; M. H. Cadbury, Managing-Director, Cadbury Bros. Ltd; J. T. Christi, Principal, Jesus College, Oxford; J. Compton, Head of the Educational Department, The National Book League; Dr Colin Cooke, Senior Bursar, Magdalen College, Oxford; Douglas Cooke, Chief Education Officer, Buckinghamshire; Sir Christopher Cox; Geoffrey Cox, Editor, Independent T. V. News Ltd.; J. S. Cripps, Editor, *The Countryman*; Prof R. H. Dent, Prof of Education, University of Sheffield; R. D. Fairn, Commissioner of Prisons; N. G. Fisher, Principal of the Staff College, National Coal Board; F. L. Freeman, Chief Education Officer, Southampton; George Goyder, Industrialist; Sir Samuel Gurney-Dixon, Pro-Chancellor and lately Chairman of Council, University of Southampton; D. G. James, Vice-Chancellor, University of Southampton; Lord James of Rusholme, High Master of Manchester Grammar School; D. P. T. Jay, MP for North Battersea; Roy Jenkins, MP for Strechford Division of Birmingham; H. H. Keen, Secretary to the Curators of the University Chest, Oxford; W, O. Lester Smith, lately Professor of Sociology of Education, University of London; Kenneth Lindsay, formerly Parliamentary Secretary to the Board of Education; Major General C. Lloyd, Director, City and Guilds of London Institute; R. Y. Logan, laterly DE, Worcestershire; J. L. Longland, DE, Derbyshire; Alan Lubbock, Chairman, Hampshire County Council; Stuart Maclure, Editor, *Education*; R. M. Marsh, County Education Officer, Hampshire; R. S. McDougall, General Manager, Stevenage Development Corporation; L. R. Missen, Chief Education Officer, East Suffolk; Henry Morris, lately Chief Education Officer, Cambridgeshire; J. H. Newman, Director, Longmans Green and Co.; Professor W. R. Niblett, Leeds University; W. Oakshott, Rector, Lincoln College, Oxford; Lady Ogilvie, Principal, St Anne's College, Oxford; A. D. C. Peterson, Director of the Department of Education, Oxford University; W. E. Philip, Chief Education Officer, Devonshire; David Price, MP for Eastleigh Division of Hampshire; H. A. Ree, Headmaster, Watford Grammar School; M. H. Rowntree, Director and General Manager, *Oxford Mail and Times Ltd*; Sir John Sargent, former Educational Adviser to the Govt. of India; F. J. Schonell. Prof of Education, University of Queensland; Dame Evelyn Sharp, Permanent Secretary, Ministry of Housing and Local Govt.; R. Sheppard, Architect; P. S. Taylor, Chief Education Officer, Reading; E. R. Tucker, Headmaster, Royal Grammar School, High Wycombe; W. R. Watkin, Chief Education Officer, Gloucestershire; E. T. Williams, Warden, Rhodes House, Oxford; G. Wilson, Deputy Head of UK Treasury; Sir John Wolfenden, Vice-Chancellor, Reading University; J. V. Wood, Director-General of Industrial Relations, National Coal Board. CO 1045/1007
75. These were catalogued for the Public Record Office by the present author in the late 1980s. See the Sir Christopher Cox Papers, CO 1045
76. Hart
77. A. D. M. Cox
78. Dalton

11. W. E. F. (Frank) Ward

Colonial educator, administrator, diplomat and scholar[1]

During his long tenure as Chief Education Advisor in Whitehall, Sir Christopher Cox worked closely with a small but very influential team of assistant educational advisers. Mention has already been made in chapter six of Rowell, Robison, Davidson, Baldwin, Foster, Harvey and Houghton. Others included Dr F. J. Harlow, an adviser on technical education who was formerly Principal of the Chelsea Polytechnic; Freda Gwilliam, the self-styled 'Great Aunt' of British colonial education,[2] and Frank Ward, Cox's deputy from 1945 until 1955. Ward claimed that 'Tommy' Baldwin was the true scholar in their ranks — he took Vergil's *Aeneid* into hospital with him as bedside reading — but Ward's all-round qualities must surely place him in the forefront of that immensely talented team of educators that Cox assembled at the Colonial Office after 1940.

The garrulous, untidy and ebullient Cox invariably stole the limelight but it was the quietly-spoken, neat and methodical Ward, a gifted teacher, administrator, diplomat and scholar, who provided the essential behind-the-scenes support which enabled Cox to spend weeks, often months, each year travelling to the far corners of the empire offering encouragement to officials on the spot and monitoring progress. The contrast in personality between the two men couldn't have been greater but they appeared to complement each other. It was Cox who delivered a memorable address to the British Association in 1956 but it was Ward who laboured behind-the-scenes ruthlessly editing Cox's endless verbiage to ensure that he performed brilliantly on the night.[3] Likewise, it was not Cox but his deputy Ward who regularly defended British colonial education policy at annual meetings of Unesco; who addressed seemingly endless groups of people in the United Kingdom about colonial education as part of his public relations brief; and who also wrote extensively about education in the colonies.

Frank Ward, born into a lower middle-class family in Battersea, an inner south London suburb, on 24 December 1900, was the eldest of four children.[4] His father, the local Borough Treasurer, had been one of eight scholars in his year to win a scholarship to the City of London School from all the London elementary schools. He was a keen amateur photographer who regularly observed the stars from a telescope mounted in his back garden. He was also a keen bird-watcher, a lover of classical music, a flute player, and a force to be reckoned with in local borough politics. Ward's mother hailed from a small Norfolk village.

In Ward's own words he was a 'physically delicate' child who nearly died of bronchitis in infancy. His younger brother did die of it. 'One of my vivid childhood memories is of my mother sitting by the child's cot, her face set (I never saw her weep) and the bronchitis kettle hissing out clouds of steam'. By his own admission he was a weakling, despised and bullied by stronger boys of his own age so he turned in on himself and on books and music. He played the piano and his father saw to it that his music teacher introduced him to Mozart at a very early age. His father also had a good library while the local Battersea free library was one of the best in London. By the time he was 12 young Ward had read all Scott's Waverley novels. At that time he was, he confesses, a 'Swot' like Kipling's 'Beatle'. During a medical examination at the age of 11, doctors discovered that he had a heart murmur, so they forbade all strenuous exertion: 'don't *ever* run for a bus' they warned him. This eliminated all thought of participating in organised sport at secondary school:

> so the routine of bullying went on — until one day I lost my temper and flew at the ring leader. He was standing with a brick wall behind him, and it took three boys to haul me away from knocking his head against the wall with one blow after another to his face. They left me alone after that, but I was still a Swot and a loner.

Ward attended the local council elementary school where he soon showed outstanding academic ability. He was lucky because it was one of several 'higher grade' schools which offered the chance to study French and elementary science. In that school he was one of a class of 64 boys, three or four of whom regularly came to school barefoot. It was there that a Mr Foyle instilled in him a lifelong love of history; 'He simply told us history as if it were a story, and he told it so well that I hung on every word'. At the age of 11 he encountered Macaulay's essays wherein he met Clive and Warren Hastings and Edmund Burke! It is hardly surprising that young Ward won junior, intermediate and senior council scholarships which took him in turn, to Mercer's School, Dulwich College and Lincoln College, Oxford, but he had few fond memories of his schooldays: 'At Dulwich I was a nobody. Though a day-boy, I was allocated to a house, and had to stand and cheer the house rugby team. A prefect heard me grumble at this chore and told me, "The trouble with you is that you are an unsportsman-like hound".' Nevertheless, he recalls that at all stages of his schooling he had first-rate teachers. One took him to the Oval to watch Surrey play cricket. Another paid a year's subscription to enable him to become a member of the Historical Association, while another, at Dulwich, took him to Westminster Abbey to hear an organ recital which included works by Bach and Debussy.

Ward won his way to Oxford by means of a 'Senior Scholarship' which was awarded on the basis of marks gained in the 'London Matric' or School Certificate, plus an interview. He cannot remember how many scholarships were awarded in 1919 but he does recall his father's comment at the interview when asked, 'If the Council awarded your boy a scholarship would you welcome it?' His father replied, 'Mr Chairman, ever since I had a son, I hoped that one day he might go to Oxford'. Ward thought they found his reply rather moving. Why Oxford remains a mystery. 'For some reason', says Ward, 'my father was always a Dark Blue on Boat Race day.'

When Ward went up to Lincoln College, Oxford, in 1919, he was one of 160 men, of whom only eight had escaped military service. He was also the junior scholar of his year. The Dulwich authorities had thought of him as a 'high-flyer' and had entered him for the prestigious Brakenbury history scholarship at Balliol but he had only just recovered from near death in the influenza epidemic when he sat the examination. He failed but a week later he succeeded in obtaining a junior scholarship at Lincoln, one of the many coincidences which Ward firmly believed helped to shape his adult life. College rooms were allotted to scholars in order of seniority, so Ward was last in line and had no choice but to take the room that no one else wanted; 'not because it was poor, but because it was large and grand and expensive'. He could only afford the room by teaming up with a young Scot from Airdrie, near Glasgow. In the first week of term they were asked if their room could be used for a meeting of the Student Christian Movement [SCM]. They were also invited to attend the meeting 'to keep an eye on proceedings'. Neither of them wanted to attend a prayer meeting but they thought it would be courteous if one of them was present. They tossed for it and Ward lost. To his surprise he enjoyed it and became a member.

Ward did not hail from what might be termed a religious background although his parents saw to it that he attended Sunday school. They attended church frequently but not regularly. His father was an enthusiastic member of the South-West Choral Society and also sang in a church choir, so Ward 'grew up amid "Stanford in F" and similar musical settings of the Anglican service'. When he went to Oxford he was a regular communicant and played the organ in the college chapel for morning prayers but he claimed that 'religion did not go very deep' at that time in his life. Nevertheless, his chance encounter with the SCM was to have far-reaching consequences.

It was through the SCM that he had his first opportunity to travel abroad. His knowledge of German led to an invitation to go to Austria as the guest of the Austrian branch of the SCM to help restore pre-war relations. Six weeks spent mostly harvesting in various student 'holiday' camps, 'half-starved but jolly', convinced him that he should spend his future life abroad where he could be of some help. Initially, he thought of the Indian Civil Service but soon learned that entry to the ICS was fiercely competitive, needing a year's coaching on top of a first-class degree. Lack of finance ruled out that option so he next considered the Indian Education Service; 'I read books about India, made Indian friends, and generally prepared for India'.

Upon his return from Austria he was elected chairman of the college branch of the SCM. A large quadrennial conference was planned for December 1921, to be held in Glasgow, but Ward ruled out any thought of attending because of the state of his finances. Eventually, however, the college chaplain arranged a small grant for him, ostensibly for his services as college organist, which enabled him to attend. It was at that conference that he first heard an address by A. G. Fraser, then Principal of Trinity College Kandy, in Ceylon. It confirmed Ward's desire to go to India. He was unaware at the time, but Fraser was destined to be the most influential person in his life and the inspiration for what is perhaps his finest scholarly work. The conference also proved to be the major turning point in his life because it was there that he sought Divine intervention; 'it was there that I deliberately put the steering wheel into God's hands. All else … followed from that direction'.

Ward firmly believed that his life's work was chosen for and not by him, and the many coincidences in his life certainly give strength to that conviction. He read history at Oxford and was considered a likely candidate for first class honours. As his Finals drew near it was hinted that if he got a First, the Fellows of Lincoln might consider appointing him to succeed the history tutor who was on the point of retirement. The prospect of an academic career at Oxford was most attractive but what of his resolve to go to India? He prayed about it, but could get no guidance, so in the end he left it to God to decide. Eventually, after a *viva* which lasted 45 minutes, he narrowly missed a First. The Rector of Lincoln gave him a chit to say that his degree was a Second, 'which I understand to have been very nearly a First'. While awaiting his finals results he attended the annual SCM conference at Swanwick, in Derbyshire, in July 1922. It was there, Ward firmly believes, that Divine intervention determined the future course of his life.

The last meeting of the conference had just concluded and Ward was waiting outside the large meeting tent to team up with his friends. A stranger emerged from the tent and strode away downhill as if in a hurry. Ward idly watched him take a dozen or more long strides downhill before he suddenly stopped dead, waited for a moment, and then turned around and came slowly and hesitatingly back up the hill as if he were looking for someone. When he saw Ward he quickened his pace and came up to him and said 'Are you doing anything special just now?' Ward said 'No', and agreed to go for a stroll together. The stranger, who turned out to be an Anglican missionary from Japan, asked Ward about himself and his plans for the future. He strongly urged Ward to go to India as he planned and then explained his behaviour outside the tent. As Ward recalled the man said:

I was in a hurry to get away from the crowd because I was due to take prayers in my tent in half an hour's time. I heard a voice say 'STOP!' There was no one near me but I heard it as plainly as I hear you speaking. The voice then said 'GO BACK!' I came back, not knowing why or what I was to do, feeling rather like Saul of Tarsus on the Damascus road. When I saw you, the voice spoke a third time; it said, 'THAT IS THE MAN; GO AND TALK TO HIM'. I had no idea what I was to say. I can only repeat that I heard those three instructions in my ears as plainly as I have ever heard anyone.

A few days later, Ward received his finals result and immediately applied to the Church Missionary Society to be taken as a candidate. He was accepted and sent to Ridley Hall, Cambridge, for training. It was intended that he should teach English at a mission school in Gorakhpur in the United Provinces of Northern India but Fate? had not finished with Ward:

At Ridley I took a mixed course, some theology plus some education. The education course included a lecture on Thursday evenings which made me 10 minutes late for dinner in Hall. The kitchen staff arranged to keep my dinner hot. One Thursday I came in as usual late to Hall and sat down on an inner form down from the long table. A man from the inner form behind me reached over and asked if I would take the Bible class that he was responsible for on some forthcoming date, and I said I would. So for a moment our two bodies bridged the gap between the two rows of forms. Fraser, the Principal-designate of Achimota College [destined to be Britain's educational showpiece in West Africa], was dining at high table, and looking for young talent. As he himself later told me, he had just asked the Principal of Ridley if he had any suitable young men, and the Principal had said that he couldn't think of any. And then he caught sight of my face bridging the gap, and said, 'Oh yes, there is Ward; I forgot him, I think he might do very well for you'. So I was invited to coffee .... And Fraser offered me a job at Achimota.

The long chain of coincidences in Ward's life at university, not all of which are related here in detail, sealed his fate. As he later commented, he couldn't see any escape; 'it was exactly like Francis Thompson's poem *The Hound of Heaven*'. The decision to go to Africa rather than India meant resigning from the CMS and refunding the cost of the year's course at Cambridge. Ward still recalls his father's reaction when he told him that he was going to Achimota: 'I have decided not to go to India after all. I have accepted the offer of a post in West Africa, and shall be going in September [1924]'. His father was delighted; 'South Africa? I am very glad you are going there: a wonderful country, with a fine climate!' Ward hastened to correct his father; 'Not South Africa, it is West Africa, the Gold Coast'. His father gave a sinister look and said, 'Oh Lord!' and turned his head away. He was thinking, of course, of 'The White Man's Grave'.

That same summer Ward met his future wife Sylvia Vallance, through his friendship at Oxford with her eldest brother. They eventually married in September 1926, while he was on leave. Ward is convinced that meeting her was largely due to impressing her father with his ability to speak German and play the piano.

On 1 October 1924, Ward sailed from Liverpool on the Elder Demster liner *Adda*, bound for West Africa. The next 16 years of his life were to be spent mostly as a teacher at Achimota. As one of the advance party of six who landed in Accra, he was first seconded to the government teachers' training college as the method master while Achimota was being built. For six months, in 1927, he was seconded to Tamale, to take charge of education in the northern territory of the Gold Coast. In 1928 the training college was transferred to the Achimota site. Fraser then directed Ward to teach music for three years although he had nothing more than 'a certain native talent' to qualify him for the role. Thereafter, he assumed the role of senior history master in the secondary school. In the 1930s he also taught English and some religious education. During his time at Achimota Ward also acted as Bursar on two occasions and several times as Acting-Principal.

Ward was a gifted teacher with a genuine interest in African history and culture. While at Achimota he learned the Twi language and researched extensively into local oral history. During many weeks spent gathering information in the bush, he developed a close understanding of, and a deep affinity for the local African people as well as an abiding interest in their music. He also wrote the standard texts on West African history used for many years in the schools. All the more reason then to note the irony in a comment Ward made near the start of '*My Africa*'. He claimed that if he had applied for entry into the African colonial service in the ordinary way he should probably have been rejected on the grounds that he was not athletic enough: 'I was not of the stuff of which administrative officers, the real empire-builders, were made'. Fortunately for the Gold Coast, his appointment by Fraser did not depend on the traditional Colonial Office interview.

The precise course of events leading to Ward's appointment as DE in Mauritius in October 1940 may never be known but he appears to have been Arthur Mayhew's choice for the post.[5] Ward had met him once in the Colonial Office while on leave and Mayhew had also been a member of the inspection team which visited Achimota in 1932. Ward had also applied to the Colonial Office, at Fraser's suggestion, for a transfer with promotion when a suitable vacancy arose. The offer of the post in Mauritius arrived in the middle of a lesson. Stanley Dunstan, the Acting Principal, interrupted Ward's class to tell him that he was wanted on the telephone; 'H.E. [His Excellency] wants to speak to you'. On the long walk to the office telephone Ward pondered what the call was likely to be about. Dunstan had told the Governor that Ward was teaching and had offered to pass on any message but the Governor had insisted on speaking to him personally. When Ward answered the call the Governor said, 'Congratulations, Ward: I've good news for you. The Colonial Office is offering you the directorship of education in Mauritius. Lovely place, perfect climate, you'll have to pass the doctor, of course. You fix that, and let me know that you are passed as medically fit and accept the offer'. Ward did so, partly on account of the challenging nature of the job — a colleague at Achimota who had taught at the Royal College in Mauritius told him of the very old-fashioned type of education which prevailed on the island — but also because of the climate. Both he and his wife had suffered from recurrent bouts of maleria — in his case no less than 25 attacks in 16 years. Such was the unstated price often paid for a posting to West Africa in those days!

Ward arrived in Mauritius on 17 January 1941. By then the Second World War had moved into top gear. The Battle of Britain had concluded but in less than a month General Rommel would arrive in Tripoli to initiate the great tank battles in the deserts of North Africa. When Ward finally departed for London some four and a half years later, the atomic bombs had just been dropped on Japan and the war was over. Mauritius, an island situated far out in the Indian Ocean, was uninhabited until Europeans discovered it in the sixteenth century. It was occupied first by the Dutch and later by the French who established sugar plantations with the aid of slave labour imported from Africa and the island of Madagascar. Britain conquered the territory during the Napoleonic wars and retained it after the Treaty of Paris in 1814 but promised to respect the language, religion and laws of the inhabitants.

Ward was sent to Mauritius to reorganise the administration of education and to update the nature of schooling which was still to all intents and purposes trapped in a nineteenth century time warp. He was under no illusions about the difficulty of the task. He was warned before leaving Africa that most of the European population was 'defiantly French at heart, with little love for the colonial power'. The rest of the population consisted of people of African descent known as Creoles, Indians who had been introduced as indentured labourers to work the sugar plantations after the slaves were liberated in 1835, and the Chinese. Government officials like Ward, brought in from elsewhere, were often greeted with suspicion and hostility as he soon found out at first hand. Within days of arriving, one of the leading newspapers carried an editorial welcoming the new DE. 'We hope', said the editor, 'that Mr Ward will realise that he has come to a model colony, with a model education system, and that methods which might suit the savages in West Africa will not suit a civilised country like Mauritius.' Ward rapidly found otherwise. As he stated in his annual report for 1944; 'Education in Mauritius is defective in every respect'.[6]

In those days the island had a school-aged population of about 100,000 of whom about two-fifths were attending school. Many schools were poorly housed, unhygenic, situated in unhealthy surroundings, poorly equipped and grossly overcrowded; 'I remember seeing 97 small children sitting in two rows on a veranda facing the light and another dimly-lit room which held 52 children in it. These were two of the worst cases. But most of the primary schools had five or six classes being taught in one room'. At one point Ward is reported as having said, 'I am brought so low that if I were shown a rabbit-hutch and told it was a school I should believe it!'[7] The teaching was excessively formal and bookish and teachers were mostly untrained and unorganised, the training college having been closed as an austerity measure in 1932. Teachers employed in government schools were civil servants but those in private schools were 'at the mercy of school managers'. There was no commonly accepted code of regulations, nor was there a uniform language policy regarding the medium of instruction in the schools. Preparation for sitting examinations seemed to be the main concern in the schools while the conduct of examinations was fraught with a multitude of dubious practices.

Towards the end of his first year in the colony, Ward produced a comprehensive report on the education system which was sent to Whitehall for comment and also published locally.[8] It rapidly became a best-seller in the colony and the subject of much heated controversy. This is not the place to enter into a detailed analysis of the report or the history of education in Mauritius during the war years but Ward's report undoubtedly played a decisive role in furthering his career. Within Mauritius, Ward was subjected to a growing chorus of dissent, especially from the French and the Indians who objected to his advocacy of English as the chief medium of instruction. Unpopularity didn't seem to worry him unduly. As he remarked in December 1941, in one of his frequent letters to Christopher Cox, 'By the way, I have reached a definite landmark; the first demand in print for my departure!' He also drew Cox's attention to what he termed a magnificent phrase later in the same newspaper article, '... and when in due course you leave this island, a cortege of anger and hatred will accompany you'.[9]

Cox and the members of the Advisory Committee on Education in the Colonies who met monthly in London were greatly impressed by Ward's report. Cox wrote to Ward in mid 1942 expressing his 'admiration for its comprehensiveness, good tempered gusto and most courageous directness — I don't think it could have been written by one who had spent all his life as a government official!' He assured Ward that the Advisory Committee would do all in its power to 'strengthen Ward's hand' in dealing with the implementation of the report.[10] In reply, Ward admitted that he had been a bit anxious as to how his report would be received in London — 'One never knows how a thing will strike other people, so I was a bit anxious, I admit.' He went on to say that most whites in Mauritius didn't want Indians educated. The Indians, on the other hand, wanted education but not from Ward 'because I am trying to drive them back to be slaves on the land'.[11] Throughout Ward's stay in Mauritius he kept Cox regularly and fully informed on developments in a series of very full and frank private letters; 'please do just as you like with my letters: in these I write with complete freedom to give you the best idea I can of circumstances here'.[12]

Ward was determined to rid the school examination system of systematic corruption and malpractice but it didn't improve his popularity with some parents. As he related to Cox: 'One indignant parent told me the other day that they had looked forward to my coming as to a Messiah, but that they were sadly disappointed in me. I suppressed the reply that came to my lips, that there was precedent for a Messiah to disappoint the public!'.[13] On the wider issue of corruption Ward suggested that Mauritius needed a lot of Englishmen to inculcate some ideas of impartiality and integrity:[14]

> It is so commonly assumed as a matter of course that everything is possible if you find the right man to bribe and the right sum to bribe him. There is no confidence in any public service ... the public regards corruption as the normal .... A man tried to bribe me in my own office! — to accept a late examination entry: and when he found that bribes wouldn't work, he threatened me with nasty articles in the press, saying he was a friend of one of the editors.

Cox expressed amazement that corruption was so wide-spread throughout the education system in Mauritius.

The open hostility expressed towards Ward, especially by some sections of the Indian community, reached a high point in 1943, when there was a walkout of Indians at a lecture given by him at the Port Louis theatre. It was reported that their hostility centred around fears that Ward's education report would keep them as backward agricultural labourers; that the use of their language would be abolished in the schools; that the government intended to Christianize them; that Indians were not to be appointed as inspectors of schools; and that Indians were to be excluded as candidates for scholarships and teacher training. Their fears were groundless and as Cox was duly informed by one of his assistant advisers in Whitehall, the trouble was probably instigated by two Indian brothers whose surname was Bissoondoyal. The younger made a large income from private tuition for teachers' certificate examinations which Ward proposed to abolish. Most Indian teachers were reported to disclaim any connection with or support for the Bissoondoyal brothers in their attempts to whip up opposition to Ward.[15]

The Governor and the island's teachers were firm supporters of Ward's report from the outset. After protracted debates in a Select Committee, the Legislative Council likewise gave its approval to all but two of the 52 recommendations made in Ward's report. Ward duly reported to Cox on the gradual change in attitude towards him:[16]

Some of my bitterest critics are now taking the line, 'Well, I don't agree with all of Ward's scheme, but at least it is a scheme, so let's push ahead with it'. A few days ago [August 1943], the [Legislative] Council unanimously asked me to stay here for another three years, and asked it very nicely too with flowers. All of which is gratifying to one who is no Stoic.

Ward's eventual success in Mauritius was clearly related to his unfailing tact, diplomacy, and good humour, qualities which were to serve him well in his later role as a British representative at meetings of the United Nations and Unesco. One incident, in particular, highlighted his ability to overcome potentially difficult situations. Ward was keen to provide the same protection from unfair dismissal for teachers in private schools as was accorded to teachers in government schools. To achieve this meant reaching an agreement with the Roman Catholic and Anglican bishops. Ward arranged a meeting with them in the crypt of the Anglican cathedral. What transpired is best conveyed in Ward's own words.[17]

We spent a few moments in small talk, but I could feel that the atmosphere was electric. The Catholic Archbishop opened the discussion. Speaking through very thin lips, he said coldly, "Well, Director, we are here to listen to your proposals". I thought, "We cannot go on like this, with fixed bayonets we shall get nowhere". So I said, "Well, you may perhaps think this a strange thing for a layman to say to two Right Reverend Fathers in God. But here in Mauritius we have 40,000 children in school, and as many more who ought to be in school but are not. You regard all these as children of God, and so do I, and you and I are responsible to God for them. Now, it will make a great deal of difference to these children if we three who are here this morning can work together in harmony, or disagree and pull apart. Do you think it would be a good thing if we all three prayed to God to guide our discussion?" There was a moment of silence. Then the Anglican said to his colleague, "Well, what do you make of that?" The Catholic bishop replied, "Well, I don't see how we can very well decline a challenge like that, do you?" "Well, will you lead us?" asked the Anglican. "We are in *your* cathedral!", said the Catholic. "Well, what could we say?", asked the Anglican. "I don't think we could improve on the prayer which Our Lord himself taught us, do you?", said the Catholic bishop. So we all knelt down and said the Lord's Prayer, and then the Anglican plucked up his courage and added a prayer from Cranmer's prayer-book: "O God, for as much as without Thee we are not able to please Thee; mercifully grant that thy Holy Spirit may in all things direct and rule our hearts, through

Jesus Christ our Lord, Amen". So we rose from our knees, feeling better, and I explained my scheme ...

The rest of the proceedings passed off without incident and Ward got the co-operation that he sought. Ward's religious predilections were an obvious asset in his educational negotiations with church leaders. They were similarly put to good use in 1944, when Ward was asked to go to the Seychelles to sort out problems with religious schools.[18]

Ward's firm belief that his life was in God's hands was well illustrated by a conversation that he had with the Anglican Bishop in Mauritius after he had been there for about three years. The Bishop told him that he hoped he would not apply for promotion to another colony just when the local people had got to know him and learned to trust him as so many British officials did after a couple of years. Ward replied that he would never apply for a transfer but that if one were offered to him he would not refuse it. The Bishop asked why? 'Because', replied Ward, 'I believe in doing whatever job God sets me to do. He put me here, and if he wants me to stay here, he can just leave me. But if he wants me somewhere else, or wants some other man to take over from me, he will presumably put a thought to that effect in the mind of the Secretary of State in London'. The Bishop, in reply, said that he had heard that the voice of the people might be interpreted as the voice of God but he had never heard that the voice of the Secretary of State might also be the voice of God. He did, however, see what Ward meant.[19]

The call from London did come eventually but not before Ward had served briefly as Acting Colonial Secretary. It was a new and interesting experience but not one, as he told Cox, that he relished. He found it very tiring and preferred working on education to dealing with miscellaneous stuff he knew nothing about.[20] When he received the invitation to return to London as Cox's deputy, he remembered his talk with the Bishop but the Governor insisted that he should accept the offer. Why was Ward chosen to be Cox's deputy? Ward certainly had no idea of entering the Colonial Office when he went to Mauritius: 'I expected that if I did well in Mauritius I might be offered promotion in my own service, i.e. to a bigger directorship'.[21] But Cox had visited Mauritius in 1943, and stayed with Ward for three weeks: 'He seemed to approve of what he saw me doing, and if he talked to the Governor about me, as he would have done, he would have found H. E. full of my praises'. There was no prior warning about an impending offer, simply a cable — 'Offer Ward appointment deputy educational adviser, salary £1,400 ....'

The Colonial Office was very impressed with Ward's work in Mauritius and duly rewarded him with a CMG in 1945 for his efforts. In a letter to Dr Audrey Richards, Cox sought here opinion of C. J. Opper, Ward's eventual successor in Mauritius. Cox asked whether he would be able to succeed 'the admirable Ward in the very tricky job in Mauritius'. He went on to explain how Ward had put through an excellent Education Act which had thoroughly overhauled the school system and how Ward had, after much initial unpopularity, 'won the confidence of all elements of the population that matter'.[22]

Ward left Mauritius in August 1945. After several weeks leave he took up his new duties in Whitehall on 15 October, 21 years to the day since he had first landed in Accra to begin his work at Achimota. He was keen to take up his new appointment but he had no illusions about his capacity to work with Cox. Several months earlier he had written to Cox about his new appointment:[23]

> Now about my job in London. I am looking forward to it greatly and what you say about it relieves me of one fear, viz that it was going to be all paper work; writing minutes to you on the wild-cat schemes of the DE in South Georgia. I shall enjoy getting to know something about English education, and 'selling' colonial education to young England.

He sought, however, to issue a few warnings. The first was that he was rusty on educational theory — in Mauritius he claimed to have worked 'by the light of nature'. The second was that 'I cannot work the way you can. I have twice nearly cracked up through overwork, and I know how far I can go. I shan't be able to keep up more than a 7 hour day average; it's no use promising what I know I couldn't perform. Though [sic] I think I am a reasonably quick worker'. The third warning was that he would need time to look closely at French, Dutch, Portuguese, and United States colonial education. He thought he might be of some use in this area on his second five-year term. Overall, however, he repeated how much he was looking forward to working 'in harness' with Cox and thanked him for the invitation.

Ward entered the Colonial Office at a propitious time. After the inertia of the inter-war years colonial policy was entering upon a new and potentially exciting phase with the advent of colonial development and welfare aid stemming from both the 1940 and 1945 acts. As Ward subsequently remarked, the act of 1945 in particular, was a real breakthrough in policy. It 'brought new life to the men in the Colonial Office. For the first time, they had substantial sums of money to administer, and the status of the Secretary of State was considerably enhanced'.[24] Colonial governments were invited to draw up 10 year plans of economic and social development and to submit them to Whitehall for approval. The anticipated need for additional administrative staff to cope with the increased work load was partly the reason for Ward's appointment.

The post of Deputy Educational Adviser was new and Ward's specific responsibilities were at best only vaguely defined when he started working alongside Cox. In due course he was to be associated with three main areas of concern. These included the varied activities associated with the daily routine of the Colonial Office; his close links with the United Nations and its subsidiary Unesco; and editorship of the journal *Oversea*

Education, together with various other miscellaneous publishing activities. At the outset, however, he had to establish a working relationship with Cox. This was not a straightforward matter because both in temperament and work habits the two men were poles apart. Cox had a brilliant intellect but he was also unorthodox. He has also been described as one of the most untidiest men in history.[25] Ward also had a keen and discerning intellect but his work habits reflected his essentially disciplined and orderly approach to life in general. Cox's office was usually a picture of disorganised chaos with piles of papers and files occupying any and every available flat space including the floor; Ward's, by contrast, was organised and tidy and at the end of a working day his desk was usually left relatively clear of papers and files. Ward spoke freely of his warm regard for Cox and it is clear from their correspondence that Cox felt similarly towards Ward, but Ward also admitted that working alongside Cox often caused him a great deal of frustration and tension.[26] When he first arrived at the Colonial Office he was told that brilliant though Cox was, he was not good at the routine of keeping office files moving: 'He was a perfectionist, and could not be hurried. Now that the war was over, we should soon be receiving a flood of 10 year education schemes coming from all round the globe. My job, I was informed, was to take as much of the load as possible off Cox's shoulders, so as to set him free for thinking and for travelling'. Unfortunately, Cox disliked delegating work to his deputy.

According to Ward, 'He [Cox] worked tremendously hard, and took bundles of office papers home every night. But, being a perfectionist, he was more keenly aware of the harm that might be done by allowing a scheme to pass on with a flaw in it, than of the harm done by detaining the scheme to make sure that all the flaws had been removed.' Eventually Ward took matters into his own hands:[27]

> I used to take from his desk files that he had not seen, and dispose of them myself, unless I felt that his personal eye should deal with them. As time went on, the load became heavier and heavier, and there arrived a new load of files dealing with universities and technical colleges; so Cox himself was kept busy on this extremely congenial subject. Whether or not he guessed at my surreptitious handiwork, I never knew. He never alluded to it, and was far too busy with universities to bother about my doings or misdoings. The office never troubled if a file came in marked 'Mr Cox' and went out with a minute signed 'Ward', it was all one … When Cox departed on one of his overseas tours, I would go into his room and clear up the mess. I always found several untouched files, some of which he had kept with him for weeks. My first business was to break the log-jam and send files on their way.

Anyone familiar with the Cox Papers [CO 1045] and other Colonial Office files related to educational matters in the post-war years frequently encounters the often brief but always insightful and always legible minutes written by Ward. He was clearly at the heart of the policy-making process in those important years immediately after the war.[28] For example, he wrote the first draft of the education policy paper subsequently presented at the conference of African governors held in London in November 1947, and he was also a member of the *ad hoc* committee that was responsible for the final draft. He likewise, introduced the paper at the conference and answered questions from those present. He was also responsible for a lengthy and important minute addressed to Creech-Jones, the newly appointed Colonial Secretary, on educational developments planned or in progress throughout the colonies at the start of 1947. In later years Ward also established himself as a leading exponent of British colonial education policy both at international forums and in print.[29] It should also be mentioned that when Cox was desperately trying to head off a Conservative move to establish a Royal Commission to examine colonial education in 1949, it was Ward who came up with the alternative suggestion of a conference of African colonies to exchange information.[30] The idea won widespread approval and resulted in the large and memorable gathering of colonial educators held at Cambridge in 1952. As might be expected, it was Ward who edited the proceedings.[31] Mention has already been made of the contribution that Ward made behind the scenes to ensure the success of Cox's memorable address to the British Association for the Advancement of Science in 1956. What is also not generally known is how Ward provided similar editorial assistance prior to Cox's equally memorable address delivered at the fiftieth jubilee celebrations of the University of London's Institute of Education in 1952.

The activities of the Colonial Office Advisory Committee on Education in the Colonies took up much of Ward's time. He regularly attended its meetings and, although he left the running of the two main geographical sub committees to Baldwin and Robison, he was closely involved with the work of two important *ad hoc* sub committees. The first attempted unsuccessfully to prepare a general statement on secondary education in the colonies. The second, produced the report *Education for Citizenship in Africa*. As the chairman of the committee, it was Ward's task to write most of the 40 pages of text.[32]

The recruitment of staff for schools in the colonies was another of Ward's many responsibilities. He was particularly concerned about the difficulties experienced by many Christian schools in attracting staff in the post-war period. To overcome the problem, he and R. J. Harvey, a former DE in Zanzibar, supervised the establishment of an Overseas Appointments Bureau aided by a grant of £3000 from the Colonial Office for office accommodation and equipment. The venture proved a great success and outlived the Colonial Office to become the Christian Education Movement.

Public relations was another important aspect of Ward's work. After the war public interest in colonial affairs grew and Cox received a growing number of invitations to address interested groups but it was a duty that he disliked and avoided whenever possible. The solution to his dilemma presented itself early in Ward's career in Whitehall.

Ward received a letter from a local branch of the Labour Party in one of the London boroughs. It contained a resolution calling on the Secretary of State to introduce universal primary schooling in all the colonies as soon as possible. Ward's immediate reaction was to offer to visit the branch to explain why their resolution was impracticable but he was told that civil servants were not permitted to enter into any kind of relations with party political organisations. He then asked if he might invite a deputation to call on him at his office. He was told that if he wanted to waste his time in that way, there would be no official objection. The secretary of the branch, an intelligent young lady, accepted his invitation and he explained to her why Britain did not give orders to the colonies or pay for their administration. As she rose to leave she said;[33]

> We in our branch are very ignorant. I am the only one who has had secondary education, and I am only in my second year at college. But we *are* interested. And you will be interested to hear that we have passed all sorts of resolutions, and sent them to various Government departments, and this is the first constructive reply we have had from any of them.

This incident gave Cox the idea of delegating responsibility for public relations to Ward. Thus it was, that Ward began addressing a wide array of audiences including numerous school and university student groups, the Central Council of the Mothers' Union, the Royal Society of Arts, The British Association, various local branches of the United Nations, Rotary clubs, the Institute of Christian Education, and the English-speaking Union, to name but a few. He was also called upon to do broadcast talks on the Home Service of the BBC; lectured to students in the Colonial Department of the University of London's Institute of Education; 'And, most strange for a civil servant, I was invited to contribute an essay on African education problems to a new book of Fabian Essays'.

Soon after Ward joined the Colonial Office it was announced that one of the 'specialised agencies' of the United Nations — subsequently known as Unesco — was to meet in London to devise its constitution and set itself to work. The Colonial Secretary, Creech Jones, announced that he would attend to watch over Britain's colonial interests but he was a busy man, liable to be called away by government or parliamentary business, so he needed support from someone in the Colonial Office. To quote Ward, 'I, being the new boy in the office, was naturally detailed for this duty'. This fortuitous act was to have important long-term implications for Ward. His first-hand experience of colonial conditions, coupled with his tact and scholarly disposition, made him an admirable advocate for British colonial policy at a time when colonialism was increasingly subjected to a gathering chorus of world criticism. The Colonial Office was particularly sensitive to the widespread belief amongst most permanent Unesco officials that all 'non-self-governing territories' were sadly oppressed and that Unesco must do what it could to lighten their load. Between 1945 and 1956, Ward attended most annual conferences of Unesco as a member of British delegations and acquired a certain standing in his own right for honesty and fair-mindedness. He likewise attended meetings in New York in 1950, 1953 and 1956, of the special committee of the United Nations set up under Article 73(e) of its Charter, to discuss reports on colonies compiled by the UN Secretariat, which were based on information supplied by the colonial powers in response to UN questionnaires. In 1948 and 1949, the UN produced reports that the British government flatly refused to sign. It then occurred to the Colonial Office to send a professional educator, in this instance Ward, to strengthen the British delegation. Ward was to deal with specific criticism of education while the head of the delegation was to tackle any serious political matters. The arrangement worked well and after the 1950 meeting other countries with colonial responsibilities followed Britain's example. It would seem that Ward 'roared for the British lion' to good effect. In 1950, he found the Secretariat's draft wide open to criticism and pulled no punches in saying so. Having taken a major role in the discussion of several sections of the report, he sat silent to allow other delegations a chance to speak:[34]

> There was dead silence, everyone looking at me. Presently the chairman, who was an Indian, said, 'Has the United Kingdom delegation no guidance to offer the committee on this section?' I replied, 'Mr Chairman, I don't want to do all the talking on this committee'. The chairman said that he was sure that every delegation would welcome the British view, and a gruff mutter came from the United States delegate sitting next to me: 'Go on, brother, tell 'em!' So I did. They took it all, and we got the Secretariat's draft thoroughly amended, so that the British delegation was happy to sign the report.

There was one further important aspect of Ward's activities as deputy to Cox; his editorship of the journal *Oversea Education*. For many years the journal had been edited by Arthur Mayhew but in 1946 he was replaced by Ward who continued as editor until the journal's demise in 1963.

It was to be a sign of things to come that when Ward assumed the editorship the veil of anonymity which had traditionally covered the editor of *Oversea Education* was lifted. Henceforth, Ward included editorials in each issue. His provocative editorial style was closely akin to that of a journalist rather than a learned academic and some of his turns of phrase were especially memorable. In commenting, for example, on the first meeting of Unesco in Paris in November 1946, he wrote: 'The cynic or the pessimist may be tempted to remark that the piers of the new bridge are being build within sight of the ruins of earlier structures which have been swept away by the floods'.[35] After the conference he remarked that

'It seems as if the conscience of mankind has awakened to the evil of ignorance as it awoke a century ago to the evil of slavery'.[36]

The main function of the journal was to keep colonial educators abreast of developments in other colonies and in the United Kingdom. It did this through articles on a wide array of subjects, miscellaneous news items and numerous book reviews. By the late 1950s education was being administered throughout the colonies by experienced and trained staff and the need for a journal like *Oversea Education* was fast receding. In short, the pioneering stage of colonial education which marked the inter-war years was long gone and with it the need for a journal to keep the centre and the periphery in touch with one another. As Ward aptly commented in the penultimate issue, the journal 'dies with the age that is dying: the age that is coming to birth will require a different kind of paper'.[37] Nowadays, the journal provides a rich historical source of information on education in the colonial period not readily available elsewhere. In 1956, Ward retired from full-time employment but stayed on in the Colonial Office on a half-time basis until 1963, principally to continue to edit the journal.

Throughout most of his life Ward was a prolific writer. He wrote 21 books together with a wide variety of journal articles.[38] He started when he was a teacher at Achimota writing a variety of history texts designed for use in African schools. In 1935, he produced his first best-seller *A Short History of the Gold Coast*. This was followed after the war by the more substantial *History of the Gold Coast* (1948). Both books have since appeared in numerous revised editions. In 1959, Ward's extensive knowledge of colonial education was encapsulated in *Educating Young Nations*. The 1960s proved to be an especially prolific period largely because Ward was free for much of that period to work full-time on his writing and research. In 1965 he produced his celebrated biography *Fraser of Trinity and Achimota*. At the end of the decade he produced yet another important study *The Royal Navy and the Slavers*, which was based on primary sources in the Public Record Office. The 1960s also saw him publish another substantial text widely used in African schools called *Government in West Africa*, which went through several reprints. Likewise, in the mid 1960s, he edited and wrote introductions to three facsimile editions of early works on West Africa. He also wrote a history of Mercer's School, his old grammar school. At the start of the 1970s he wrote two further books *The World Today* and *East Africa: a century of change* but thereafter 'my writing was unsuccessful'. One further study must be mentioned however — 'My Africa'. This manuscript, which was published by Ghana Universities Press in 1991, constitutes an important social commentary on the Africa that Ward was familiar with when he was at Achimota in the inter-war years. It also provides both a refreshing and challenging response to the flood of anti-colonial sentiment which has emanated from African sources in recent decades.

Even in the twilight years of his life Frank Ward could not resist the urge to write. In late 1991, the present author prevailed upon him to recount more of his experiences in Mauritius, the Colonial Office and the

United Nations. These manuscripts, together with private correspondence with the author, have been used extensively in this brief account of his life and work.

Frank Ward died in the summer of 1997 in his ninety-seventh year. A Londoner, both by birth and upbringing, he spent his final years in a nursing home in Banstead, a picturesque part of Surrey within a 30 minute train journey of Victoria station and the Whitehall offices where he spent many stimulating years of his illustrious career as an educational administrator, diplomat and scholar. Sadly, his wife and constant companion throughout most of his life, died in March 1992. They had no children. Always happiest when he had a piece of chalk in his hand and eager young faces before him, he looked back on his years in the Gold Coast as the most interesting time in his life because of the many people that he met ranging from African children to their elders and tribal chiefs 'who admitted me into their confidence'. He was deeply disappointed when he narrowly missed out on a First at Oxford but his tutor consoled him by saying; 'Just now you are feeling that this examination result is the end of the world. It isn't. Five years from now, nobody will care what your class was in finals; they will be judging you on your work and your personality'. His tutor could never have known just how prophetic his words were to prove.

Anyone who reads Wards numerous published works cannot fail to be impressed by the clarity and conciseness of his literary style. Nowhere was this more evident than in the numerous editorials that he wrote for *Oversea Education*. Who but Ward could have written:

> For some years past, the Colonial Office has been dwindling like an ice-floe caught in the Gulf Stream drift. One colony after another gains independence. Its department in Great Smith Street is closed, and its files are handed over to the Commonwealth Relations Office; and its new national flag flies on the High Commissioner's car to bewilder the crowds along Whitehall.[39]

Likewise, Ward used his last editorial to highlight the darker side of colonialism and to exhort young British teachers to serve as volunteers abroad:

> Even if we make allowance for the idealism of individuals, the moral account of Europe and those of European race is still heavily in the red. The work of some thousands of young teachers over the next 20 years would do something to lesson the debt .... Among the chaos of traffic jams, horror films, redundancies and wild cat strikes, expense account rackets and take over bids, the British people is seeking for its soul .... Britain has ruled many peoples; let us now learn to serve them

without ruling, and win a new Empire over mens' hearts. That would be an imperialism for which no-one need blush.[40]

After 34 years of continuous publication Ward brought down the curtain on *Oversea Education* in January 1963 with a simple but memorable sentence: 'This station is now closing down. Over – and out!'[41]

By any standards Ward was an outstanding teacher and scholar. In concluding his biography of Alek Fraser, he claimed that at the heart of Fraser's teaching was one of his favourite New Testament quotations: 'I am come that they might have life, and that they might have it more abundantly'. Evidently, Fraser used to say that every teacher ought to be able to echo those words and take them as the motto for his life and his teaching. Were Fraser alive today, he would surely be well pleased with the young history graduate he recruited at Ridley Hall in 1923, to accompany him to West Africa. For his part, Ward hoped that if he ever got to heaven, he would be greeted by his 'chief' in his characteristic way: 'Hallow, young fellow, so you've come! Now look here, I've a little job I want you to do for me …'.

It was no less a person than Professor Lionel Elvin, then Principal of the London Institute of Education, who perhaps best described Ward's virtues. He had, wrote Elvin, 'been through it all, from the village classroom of the Gold Coast to the councils of Unesco by way of educational administration in Mauritius and advising on education at the Colonial Office. He was an enthusiast with a clear head; an idealist with a zest for facts and his style was direct and vigorous. In his writing there were no windy generalisations or bloodless abstractions but a wealth of particular instance and concrete evidence to back his case'.[42]

In the Forward to *Educating Young Nations*, written in 1959, Lionel Elvin suggested that Ward's book was a modest and moving memorial to the many men and women who had gone out to the colonies as teachers. They went about their work unobtrusively and sought no special praise for what they did but in disseminating western education they sowed the seeds of a profound social and economic transformation which continues to the present day.[43] No one was more aware of that legacy than Frank Ward.

NOTES ON CHAPTER

1. This essay first appeared as 'The Admirable Ward': a portrait of W. E. F. (Frank) Ward CMG, colonial educator, administrator, diplomat and scholar' in the *Journal of Education Administration and History* 25/2 (1993) pp 138–160
2. See chap.13
3. The revisions to the original draft are included in the Cox Papers CO 1045/1375
4. Much of the biographical data on Ward and his family background is derived from personal correspondence (1991–1992) with the author. Details of Ward's years spent as a teacher at Achimota are largely derived from his manuscript 'My Africa' subsequently published as *My Africa* by

Ghana Universities Press, Accra, 1991. Information on his experiences in Mauritius and the Colonial Office are contained in the following typescripts; 'Education in Mauritius 1941–45'; 'The Colonial Office 1945–56'; and 'Early Days in Unesco and the United Nations 1945–57'. Copies of these, and the manuscript 'My Africa', together with an earlier aide-memoire (Mss Afrs 1755(27)) are to be found in the Rhodes House library, Oxford.

5.   Cox to Mayhew, 26 Apr 1941 CO 1045/103
6.   Colony of Mauritius, *Annual Report of the Education Department for the Year ending 30 June 1944* p 1
7.   R. D. Ramdoyal, *The Development of Education in Mauritius 1710–1976*, The Mauritius Institute of Education, Reduit, 1977, p 117
8.   Report on Education in Mauritius, Reduit, 1941
9.   Ward to Cox, 5 Dec 1941 CO 1045/612
10. Cox to Ward, 31 Jul 1942 CO 1045/612.
11. Ward to Cox, 3 Oct 1942 CO 1045/612 This comment was in response to Ward's attempt to make the school curriculum more 'vocational' and less academic.
12. Ward to Cox, 9 Mar 1942 CO 1045/612
13. *Ibid.*
14. *Ibid.*
15. T. R. Rowell to Cox, 24 Aug 1943 CO 1045/605
16. Ward to Cox, 5 Aug 1943 CO 1045/612
17. 'Education in Mauritius 1941–45' pp 16–17
18. Report on Education in the Seychelles (1944) See Box 248, Combined British Missionaries Societies Archives, School of African and Oriental Studies library, University of London.
19. 'Education in Mauritius 1941–45', p 26
20. Ward to Cox, 5 May 1945 CO 1045/103
21. During his term as Deputy to Cox, Ward was offered the prestigious Directorship of Hong Kong but he declined. It was also hinted that he would have been favourably considered for the Director's job in Tanganyika if he been interested. He remained in London 'as much for Sylvia's sake as anything'. Her health had suffered in Mauritius due to wartime shortages of drugs.
22. Cox to Dr Audrey Richards, 30 May 1945 CO 1045/503
23. Ward to Cox, 13 Mar 1945 CO 1045/103
24. 'The Colonial Office 1945–56' p 3
25. Obituary, *The Times*, 7 Jul 1982
26. Private correspondence with the author
27. 'The Colonial Office 1945–56' p 8
28. For more detail of Ward's role in the shaping of post-war colonial education policy see the author's article 'The impact of the second world war on British colonial education policy' in *History of Education*, 18/3 (1989) pp 267–293
29. See for example *Educating Young Nations*, Allen & Unwin, 1959; and 'Education in the Colonies' in *New Fabian Colonial Essays*, Hogarth Press, 1959
30. 'The impact of the Second World War ....' p 285
31. *African Education A Study of Educational Policy and Practice in British Tropical Africa*, Nuffield Foundation/Colonial Office, 1953
32. *Education for Citizenship in Africa*, Colonial No. 216 HMSO, 1948
33. 'The Colonial Office 1945–56' p 17
34. 'Early Days in Unesco and the United Nations' p 13
35. *Oversea Education* XVIII/2 (1947) p 437
36. *Ibid.* XVIII/3 (1947) p 487
37. *Ibid.* XXXIV/3(1962) p 140

38.		Ward's main published works include — *A History of Africa*, in three volumes. Vol.I (1934), Vol.2 (1939), & Vol.3 (1960), Longmans
A Short History of the Gold Coast, Longmans,1935. Many reprints.
A History of the Gold Coast, Allen & Unwin, 1948. Later retitled *A History of Ghana*.
Educating Young Nations, Allen & Unwin, 1959
Government in West Africa, Allen & Unwin, 1960. Many reprints
Fraser of Trinity and Achimota, Ghana Universities Press, 1965
The Royal Navy and the Slavers, Allen & Unwin, 1969
'My Africa', Ghana Universities Press, 1991
39.		*Oversea Education* XXXIII/3, (1961), p 105
40.		*Ibid.*, XXXIII/4 (1963) p 146
41.		*Ibid.*
42.		*Ibid.* XXXI/4 (1960) pp 182–3
43.		*Educating Young Nations* p 8

12. Margaret Read

Social Anthropologist turned Colonial Educator

Some 18 months after the newly formed Colonial Office Advisory Committee on Native Education in British Tropical Africa began its deliberations, C. G. Seligman, then President of the Council of the Royal Anthropological Institute and Professor of Ethnology at the University of London, wrote to The Rt Hon W. G. A. Ormsby-Gore, the Parliamentary Under Secretary of State for the Colonies and the Committee's Chairman, expressing the interest of his Institute in the future education of the African 'natives'.[1] He stressed two main points in his letter. The first, was 'the very great harm that must be done by anything approaching a rapid detribalisation of the natives of East Africa, as appeared to be demanded by some white settlers'. The second point was that while it seemed that there was general agreement that no scheme of education which could be applied to the natives of Africa would be of any real benefit if modelled on purely European lines, there did not seem to be any general conviction of what should be equally obvious, that it was hopeless to try to prepare a scheme suited to native mentality unless the body responsible for the scheme had a real knowledge, not only of native habit and custom, but also of native modes of thought. Seligman went on to say that his Council was of the view that the only way for the responsible body to attain such knowledge was for it to have amongst its members an anthropologist whose knowledge of the natives was derived from field work 'for experience suggests that there are very considerable differences of outlook and of mental development between the various groups of black men'. He then offered the Advisory Committee the expertise officially or unofficially of Institute members with first hand field experience.

The offer was not taken up partly because the Colonial Office wished to minimalize the presence of sectional interests on the Committee but also because the discipline of social anthropology was still in its infancy in Britain and Colonial officials both in Whitehall and the colonies were sceptical of its value as an aid in shaping colonial education policy.[2] This scepticism was to be maintained throughout the inter-war years. After years of field experience many colonial officials were convinced that they 'knew their natives' better than most anthropologists. The latter were frequently accused of hob-nobbing with the natives and many were thought of as little more than 'romantic reactionaries' or 'do-gooders' who wished to preserve indigenous peoples from any contact with the outside world. It was, therefore, somewhat ironic when Margaret Read, a leading social anthropologist, who had trained under Bronislaw Malinowski at the London School of Economics in the 1930s, was appointed acting Head of the Colonial Department at the London Institute of Education in 1940. Equally ironic was the fact that during the war years and thereafter, she was destined to make a significant contribution to the revamping of British colonial education policy.

Margaret Helen Read[3] was born at Battersea, a south London suburb, on 5th August 1889. She was the first of two children [a son was born in 1892] of Mabyn Read, a doctor and later a medical officer of health, and his wife Isabelle [nee Lawford]. Margaret was christened in the Unitarian Church in Wandsworth, which the Lawfords attended and where Mabyn and Isabel were married. When Margaret was 15 months old the family moved to Worcester where her father was a practising physician and part time medical officer of health. In 1912 he became Worcester's first full time medical health officer.[4] Despite some financial problems when her father first set up in medical practice,[5] it is clear that Margaret was reared in comfortable middle class surroundings. In later life she recalled domestic servants and a house full of books and the sounds of music. Her mother, who died in 1904 when Margaret was only 15 years old, was very musical having studied the piano in her youth in Heidelberg.

Initially, Margaret Read was educated at home. When she was nine she went to the local high school. Four years later she won a Scholarship to Roedean, the prestigious girls' public school situated near Brighton. Two daughters of her mother's elder sister had already gone there. From Roedean she progressed, in 1908, to Newnham College, Cambridge, where she studied history and completed her degree studies in 1911, followed by a diploma in geography a year later.[6] In those days women were not awarded degrees at Cambridge! Her nephew has claimed that in later life she was offered her degree in retrospect but that she politely declined 'as she had managed very well without it, having received a PhD and CBE!'[7] There appears to be no record of her activities from the time of her departure from Cambridge in 1912 or thereabouts until 1919 when she embarked on five years of social work in the villages of India. The period coincided with the First World War and she may have spent much of that time in voluntary social work. Prior to going to Cambridge she had spent a year keeping house for her father and at his suggestion she had done charity work for what later became known as the Family Welfare Association. She first went to India as a missionary but soon developed what was to prove a lifelong interest in social anthropology. She spent much of her time in India studying the problems of migrant labour and later claimed that it was this experience which led her to study anthropology in the hope of finding guidelines and techniques for under-standing the intricate problems of Indian peasants turned factory workers.[8] In 1924 she returned to England and for the next five years she engaged in what has briefly been described as International student work. This involved lecturing on international affairs both in Britain and the United States, but there appear to be few surviving details of this part of her life.

Her career in the 1930s is based on firmer ground. In 1930 she enrolled as a PhD student in anthropology at the London School of Economics [LSE]. At the time Malinowski held centre stage with his emphasis on 'functionalism' and especially the study of the 'culture of primitive man' and his thirst for facts derived from participant observation. Despite his controversial nature — some people found him bewitching, others found him rude and intolerant, and his overpowering personality oppressive — he attracted many mature scholars, especially women, who were already experts in other fields, and undoubtedly exerted a profound impact on the emerging discipline of anthropology.[9] During her doctoral studies, Margaret Read gave occasional lectures at the LSE. In 1934, at the conclusion of her doctoral work,[10] she was awarded a Research Fellowship by the International African Institute to study the effects of migratory labour on village life in Nyasaland.

The International African Institute had been established in 1926 to study African languages and culture. The leading figures in the early years of its existence included Dr Warnshuis, the American Secretary of the International Missionary Council, Hanns Vischer, the Secretary of the Colonial Office Advisory Committee on Native Education in British Tropical Africa, Professor Malinowski, Lord Lugard, the former Governor-General of Nigeria, and J. H. Oldham, the Secretary of the International Missionary Council. At the start of the 1930s the Institute succeeded in attracting Rockefeller research funds and a five-year research plan was published in 1932. Oldham subsequently approached Margaret Read about the possibility of doing fieldwork in Africa when he invited her to lunch in 1933. At the time she had no intention of going to Africa — India was her stomping ground — but she left the lunch table committed to applying for an IAI Fellowship.[11] At the time the main research focus of the IAI was on promoting a deeper understanding of the forces of social cohesion in original African societies in order that they might be better equipped to adjust to western influences.

Margaret Read was a Research Fellow of the IAI for five years [1934–39] during which time she did extensive field work in Northern Rhodesia and Nyasaland amongst the Ngoni people.[12] In 1937 she was appointed as an assistant lecturer in social anthropology at the London School of Economics. She had also given occasional lectures to students in the recently established Colonial Department of the London Institute of Education as far back as 1934 but her formal links with education only began in 1940 when, due to the exigencies of war, she was asked if she would take over as temporary part-time head of the Colonial Department. She accepted the offer and a year later she joined the full-time staff of the Institute. The change in direction in her academic career was largely due to the influence of Sir Fred Clarke, the Director of the Institute of Education. He had formerly overseen the work of the recently established Colonial Department and was most impressed with her contribution as an occasional lecturer. Clarke, who had held professorial appointments in South Africa and Canada before coming to London, had an international perspective in his thinking about education which enabled him to appreciate the problem of culture clash in the colonial setting.[13]

The Colonial Department[14] in the Institute of Education had its origins in the late 1920s when a training course was first established in what was then the London Day Training Centre, for probationary teachers who were destined for service in the colonies. In 1932 the Day Training Centre was absorbed by the University of London and renamed the Institute of Education. Thereafter, a Department for Colonial Studies [the Colonial Dept.] was formally established within the Division for Overseas Students, which was then under the direction of Professor Fred Clarke. In the late 1930s the Colonial Dept. was administered by Dr W. B. Mumford, a senior lecturer in comparative education with special reference to 'primitive peoples'. After war broke out in September 1939, Mumford spent much of his time working in Iraq for the British Council. In early June 1940 he returned but left for New York with his American-born wife within a month to undertake voluntary work for the British Library in New York. He later claimed that his hurried departure for the United States was linked to his wife's wish to avoid double taxation.[15] He was granted leave of absence for the duration of the war but by 1944, when the tide of war had turned, the Institute of Education put pressure on him to return or to resign. He did return, briefly, in July 1944, but resigned and returned to New York where he later took up a position with the United Nations.[16]

Meanwhile Margaret Read was approached by Clarke, who had replaced Sir Percy Nunn as Director of the Institute in 1936, to take Mumford's place as head of the Colonial Department on a temporary basis. She accepted the offer but remained in an acting capacity until 1945 when, following Mumford's resignation, she was appointed permanent head of the Colonial Department with the status of Reader. Four years later, as head of a thriving department, she was appointed Professor of Education 'with special reference to colonial areas'. She retired in 1956, aged 66, and immediately took up a position as Visiting Professor of Education at the University of Ibadan in Lagos, Nigeria. She went to Ibadan ostensibly to establish an Institute of Education but soon found the two-year appointment was not what she had expected and left after a year. Thereafter she concentrated mainly on anthropological work, including community development, with frequent overseas trips to American universities and to various United Nations food and agriculture conferences where she spoke on nuitritional problems. She remained remarkably active until the early 1970s, by which time she had reached her eightieth birthday. She was destined to live on in retirement in her small house in Paradise Walk, near the river Thames in Chelsea, until her death on 19 May 1991, by which time she was in her 102nd year. She never married.

Margaret Read's appointment as acting and later permanent head of the Colonial Department was unique. She never applied for the position, she had received no formal training as a teacher or educationist, and she was primarily a social anthropologist not an educator. Given the ambivalent, even hostile, attitude displayed by many colonial officials towards anthropologists during the inter-war years, Read's appointment may well have been a surprise to many people although it passed largely unnoticed at the time due to the imminent threat of a German invasion. In hindsight it proved to be a stroke of genius on Clarke's part, in keeping with the new and more dynamic approach to colonial policy ushered in with the appointment of Malcolm MacDonald as Colonial Secretary in 1938, and the close links established in the late 1930s between senior Colonial Office staff like Hanns Vischer and Arthur Mayhew, the Joint Secretaries of the Advisory Committee on Education in the Colonies, and Professor Clarke.

When Margaret Read took over responsibility for the Colonial Department in 1940 the Battle of Britain was about to begin and there were very few students. The buildings of the Institute were commandeered for war purposes in July and staff and students were transferred to Nottingham. Margaret Read lectured in Nottingham and London when necessary but continued to reside in London to provide research and information services for the intelligence section of the Ministry of Information. She also organized a variety of *ad hoc* courses, including some entirely in the French language for Free French personnel who were destined for West Africa, and continued to lecture in social anthropology at the LSE.[17] Increasingly, however, she became closely linked with activities undertaken on behalf of the Colonial Office. It was this work that was to establish her reputation as a leading authority on what was variously called mass education, fundamental education, and community development. She appears to have gained initial entry to the inner counsels of the Colonial Office through her close professional links to Professor Clarke, who was also a trusted colleague of Christopher [later Sir Christopher] Cox, who was appointed Educational Adviser to the Colonial Office in 1940.[18] In 1943 Margaret Read was appointed to the Advisory Committee on Education in the Colonies. By then she already enjoyed a close working relationship with Cox which subsequently developed into a close personal friendship which lasted until Cox's death in 1982.[19] During the war years she still retained a foothold at the LSE but Clarke was most anxious to retain her as Acting-Head of the Colonial Department. In a letter to Alexander [later Sir Alexander] Carr-Saunders, the Director of the LSE, Clarke claimed that a great change had taken place since she had taken over and that the Department was now related to the Colonial Office itself more intimately than at any time in its history. This, he accepted, was partly due to the war 'but very much more, I think, to the way in which the work has been managed by Dr Read'.[20] Her high standing within the Colonial Office during the war years was highlighted in a minute addressed to Cox in which it was suggested that if Mumford did return perhaps she could head up a Colonial Department at Oxford?[21]

Margaret Read's move to the Institute of Education in 1940 was opportune. The 1930s witnessed a gathering chorus of criticism of British colonial rule including the alleged neglect of indigenous peoples and the vagueness of British policy objectives,[22] but the publication of Lord Hailey's *African Survey* in 1938 coupled with Malcolm MacDonald's appointment as Colonial Secretary in the same year prepared the way for fresh initiatives. In particular, Lord Hailey's insistence on an extension of social services in the colonies and the need to combat endemic poverty led to the first Colonial Development and Welfare Act passed in 1940. The climate of change infiltrating the corridors of Whitehall generated a more positive outlook on colonial policy. Henceforth struggling colonial economies were to be helped financially and policies of active social development were to be encouraged. This meant, in effect, that the traditional concern for the preservation of African culture was replaced by an equally strong conviction that change should be hastened by all possible means including both formal and non-formal education. For a social anthropologist like Margaret Read the clash of indigenous and western cultures, especially in Africa, and the role that education should play in future policy was an especially fertile field for research and debate and a vital area for study by prospective teachers and educational administrators in British colonies. In hindsight, as Professor Angela Little has remarked, she was clearly one of the first British academics to combine the concerns of anthropology with those of education.[23]

It was in May 1940 that Arthur Creech Jones, who later became Colonial Secretary, first raised the subject of non-formal education at a meeting of the ACEC.[24] He had adult education specifically in mind and argued that its expansion would be vital if indigenous people were to be able to cope with rapid socio-economic change, including industrialisation and the growth of democratic government. His understanding of the term adult education included not only economic and political issues but also health, food, social issues and community life in general. This was clearly a field in which social anthropologists like Margaret Read had something to offer. The fall of France and the Dunkirk evacuation precluded any action until a year later when Cox succeeded in establishing a sub-committee to look into the matter.

The high-powered sub-committee reflected the new importance attached to non-formal education in the Colonial Office. It included Professor Clarke and Margaret Read, who was one of three co-opted members. The ensuing report was accompanied by a memorandum on mass education prepared by Clarke, and a manual of guidance written by Margaret Read. Thereafter, she was a key figure in a series of moves which culminated in 1948 in a despatch from the Secretary of State which made it clear to all colonial governments that mass education was to be considered an integral feature of colonial policy. Her close involvement with mass education also resulted in her attendance as a member of the British delegation at the first Unesco conference in Paris in 1946. A paper[25] she had written beforehand formed the basis of the main Unesco document on Fundamental Education discussed at the conference. Thereafter, she was widely acknowledged as a world expert in the field. The Colonial Office consulted with her over training courses for prospective community development personnel; she was a founding member of the Mass Education Standing Committee established by the Colonial Office in 1949; she succeeded in the same year in persuading the Colonial Office to establish a Community Development Clearing House at the Institute of Education in London, and soon afterwards regular training courses were started for community developers in the Colonial Department of the Institute. In the early 1950s she also helped organise and conduct a variety of conferences on community development, for example, at Eastbourne [1950], Kingston (Jamaica) [1950], Crowhurst and Dorking [1951] and Ashridge [1954]. Several of these conferences arose from the recommendations of the Cambridge Summer School of 1948 with which Margaret Read was associated, and which focussed on mass education and community development.

In July 1943, Margaret Read attended her first meeting of the ACEC as a full member although, as the Chairman remarked in his introductory remarks, she had already given the Committee much assistance.[26] Thereafter, apart from a brief absence in 1947, she served continuously on the Committee until June 1955. In her early years on the committee especially, she was heavily involved in sub-committee work. In her first three year term she not only served on all three standing sub-committees — African, non-African, and West Indies — but was also a member of the mass education sub-committee and other sub-committees on the recruitment and training of women for the CES, educational development in Bechuanaland, The Gambia, Gibraltar and Cyprus respectively, as well as the joint Colonial Office, ACEC, Institute of Education Consultative Committee. Even allowing for the fact that many committee members were heavily involved in essential war work, her contribution was quite extraordinary. Her valuable contribution to colonial education was duly acknowledged when she was chosen in June 1943 as a member of the Elliot Commission, one of three commissions established to examine the future of university education in the colonies. The Elliot Commission spent some ten and a half weeks in West Africa before becoming irrevocably split over whether to recommend one university for the whole of the region located at Ibadan in Nigeria or to bow to local pressure and recommend two universities — one in Nigeria and another at Lagos in the Gold Coast. The crux of the argument within the committee centred on whether the existing secondary schools could provide an adequate pool of talent of sufficiently high calibre to merit two universities. The committee remained deadlocked to the end and produced both majority and minority reports.[27] The majority, undoubtedly influenced in part by the strong and persistent political agitation for a second university in The Gold Coast, recommended two universities. Five of the 14 committee members, including Margaret Read, remained unconvinced and opted for a single regional university. Initially, the Colonial Office favoured the minority view but public pressure in The Gold Coast, The Gambia and Sierra Leone eventually forced the Colonial Office to change its mind.[28]

In the aftermath of war Margaret Read 'enjoyed the confidence of the Colonial Office to a remarkable degree'.[29] She was a British delegate to Unesco General Conferences in both Paris [1946] and Mexico City [1947]. In 1947 she was made a member of the newly created Social Science Research Council which was responsible for allocating funds made available by the Colonial Welfare and Development Act of 1945. Again in 1947, in August and September, she and Freda Gwilliam, the recently appointed Woman Educational Adviser at the Colonial Office, visited Northern Rhodesia and Nyasaland to report on the education of women and girls.[30] In 1949 she was appointed a foundation member of the Colonial Office Advisory Committee on Colonial Colleges of Arts, Science and Technology which took the place of a joint standing committee with the Inter-University Council. In recognition of her services to colonial education she was awarded the CBE in the New Year's Honours List for 1949. In the same year she was also appointed as the first professor of education in the Institute of Education 'with special reference to colonial areas'.

Perhaps the most significant evidence of the unique position she occupied in relation to the shaping of colonial education policy is provided by her presence, together with seven others, at a special meeting held in the office of Sir Andrew Cohen, then an Assistant Under-Secretary in the Colonial Office, on the evening of 22 June 1950.[31] The meeting, referred to thereafter as the midnight meeting, although it started at 8.45 pm, had been called to decide how best to head off a demand from the ruling Conservative Party that there should be a Commission established to report on the future of colonial education. It was a crucial point in the post-war history of colonial education and Margaret Read was at the heart of Whitehall policy discussion. At the meeting there was a general concensus that a royal commission would serve no useful purpose. Instead, it was agreed to push for two separate missions to visit and report on education in east and west Africa respectively, and thereafter to convene an education conference to discuss major issues raised by the reports. As Margaret Read wrote in a private note to Cox several months later, she had been thinking for some time that there was a need for an enquiry into the content of education in Africa: 'I have been aware often in discussing 10 Year Plans [of Colonial Development] of how mechanical they all seemed, without a full knowledge of changing needs and emphases'. She went on to say that it was inevitable that modern education should be a disruptive force socially, economically and politically in Africa: 'The need to think out how to put the pieces together in a new form is a sociological and educational task which I have been trying to formulate for some time. Maybe this and other disturbing truths had better be dragged into the daylight'.[32] The policy agreed to in Cohen's office was duly implemented and Margaret Read was one of the principal speakers at the ensuing conference held at Cambridge in the summer of 1952.[33] Two years later she was an obvious choice for membership of the newly formed Colonial Office Advisory Committee on Social Development which replaced the Mass Education Standing Committee.

The cultivation of closer links with the United States was an important feature of her work in the immediate post war years. She was no stranger to North America having lectured there on international affairs in the 1920s. It was also Rockefeller money that had funded her anthropological research in East Africa in the 1930s. In the post-war years she made frequent visits partly because of Carnegie funding which made it possible for an interchange of staff between American universities and the Colonial Department of the London Institute of Education. For part of 1951 she was Visiting Professor of Social Anthropology at Cornell University; in 1954 she was likewise Visiting Professor of Education in Africa at The North West University of Illinois, and in 1960 she was again Visiting Professor of Social Anthropology, this time at Michigan State University. Her close friendship with Sir Christopher Cox clearly gave these visits an enhanced importance. In the early 1950s the Americans were beginning to take a closer interest in education on the African continent. The Colonial Office was anxious lest American influence was unduly felt in Britain's colonial territories but at the same time anxious to tap the potentially vast financial resources which might be made available by large American philanthropic organisations. The latter aim was clearly uppermost in a confidential memorandum[34] which Margaret Read attached to a report of her visit to Cornell from September 1951 through to January 1952. She claimed that the Ford Foundation was just turning its attention to Africa and was a possible source of funds like Carnegie. She had met various people and 'left' a trail to maintain contacts. 'The important thing', she said, '[was] not to ask for help. Until a considerable exchange of views and personnel had taken place, and the rather slow process of "education" had developed.'

The close relations she enjoyed with senior Carnegie staff were evident in a letter she wrote to Cox in October 1951.[35] John Gardner, the Vice-President of the Carnegie Corporation, had expressed doubts to her about the educational extension work being carried out in Africa. He wondered whether it was playing into the hands of the Communists because it improved people's economic position without giving them any political foundation or outlet. 'That', she told Cox, 'is putting it very crudely, so *please* don't quote me or John Gardner on that theme.' It is clear that Margaret Read was one of a small intimate circle of people who quietly fostered Anglo-American relations in African education which eventually led to the Greenbrier meeting in West Virginia in 1958, the follow-up meeting a year later at Cumberland Lodge in Windsor, and the combined Anglo-American African co-operation in education which

blossomed in the 1960s.[36] Her pro-American views also extended
to Unesco. She was critical of the scepticism often voiced in Britain of
America's role in the United Nations and argued forcefully for
a strengthening of Anglo-American links, especially in international
education.

Margaret Read's work on behalf of the Colonial Office was
performed against a backdrop of a rapidly expanding Colonial
Department in the Institute of Education. She was fortunate in having as
her deputy, A. S. Harrison, formerly of the Ceylon Education
Department, who shouldered most of the day-to-day administrative
burden of running the Department thereby enabling Margaret to work
closely with the Colonial Office. Some indication of the extent to which
she was involved in activities outside her department is provided by the
fact that in the 1944–45 academic year she attended no less than 44 half
day meetings on ACEC affairs and 18 whole day meetings of the Elliot
Commission.[37] In the same year the Colonial Department had a mere
12 students. A year later, at war's end, the number rose to 66; a portent of
the growth that was to come. By the 1950–51 academic year, student
numbers had risen to close on 200 and remained buoyant thereafter.

Margaret Read's career in education came about more by luck than
any deliberate planning. When Mumford left the Institute in 1940 she
took over responsibility for the Colonial Department on a temporary
basis. She had no formal qualifications in education or teaching and
in peacetime it is most unlikely that she would have been appointed as
anything other than a part-time occasional lecturer. To her credit she
seized the opportunity and carved out for herself a unique role. It was
only after she retired in 1955 and accepted a two-year appointment as
Professor of Education at the University of Ibadan in Nigeria that her lack
of formal educational training caught up with her. She went out to Ibadan
to help establish an Institute of Education but the venture went sour from
the outset resulting in what Cox subsequently called 'the MR fiasco'.[38] It
would seem that there was a major misunderstanding between
J. T. Saunders, the Principal of Ibadan, and Margaret Read as to the
meaning and purpose of an Institute of Education. The Nigerians viewed
it primarily as a teacher training establishment whereas Margaret Read
thought of it more in terms of the London model which included a strong
academic emphasis on the study of education in all its varied aspects. To
make matters worse, the opening of the Institute was delayed for a year by
building problems. As a result, after spending a most unhappy year in
Nigeria she decided to terminate her contract. She poured out her feelings
in a letter to Cox in which she said that she couldn't contemplate another
year of sitting around with no students, no colleagues and no place to
work in. She also emphasized the need at Ibadan for 'an *orthodox*
educationist':

> My fancy qualifications, such as they are, just have no place here
> at the present time. I blame myself for not having realised this

before I agreed to come here. I have at times felt the most awful fool, because people are always asking me questions which I can't answer, and for the sake of the college they must have someone whom they have confidence in as an educationist. I am sure many of them think I am completely phoney, and indeed I feel so very often.[39]

The Nigerian experience appeared to have a profound impact on her and effectively ended her close involvement in education *per se*. Thereafter, aged 67, and at a time when most people are happy to retire, she reverted to her original role as a social anthropologist and went on to enjoy another 15 productive years in her capacity as a consultant to the United Nations World Health and Food and Agriculture Organizations in health education, nursing, the training of health auxiliaries, and community development.[40] Despite her advancing years she travelled widely to conferences and on consultancies. For example, in 1959 she spent three months in India travelling and advising on community development. In the following year she was Visiting Professor in Applied Anthropology at Michigan State University. In 1961 she was appointed Chairman of the World Health Organsation's Committee of experts on the training of medical auxiliary staff. This inevitably involved still more travel. In 1963 she visited Rome, Egypt, the Lebanon, Mexico and the United States; in 1964 she was in Uganda, Colombia, Malawi and Zambia; in 1965 she visited Nairobi and Egypt; in 1966, Delhi, and so the annual list of travel goes on. From 1965 through to 1968 she also made annual visits to Yale as a Visiting Professor in the Medical School. Between 1964 and 1969 she was also a consultant to the Millbank Memorial Fund in the United States. As late as 1967, she was still actively involved in organising a course on nutrition at the London School of Hygiene and Tropical Medicine. She made her last overseas consultancy visit when she was 81 years old and continued to lecture in the United States until she was 83 (1972). In 1971 she started work on a manuscript *Poverty, Pollution and Family Life in a Victorian Cathedral City*, in which she described her family background and the work of her father as a doctor and medical health officer in Worcester in the early years of this century. Then, at the tender age of 91 she researched and re-did her extensive family tree.[41]

Her interest in the problems generated by the clash of cultures in Africa and elsewhere readily related to a central concern of British colonial educators in the inter-war years and thereafter. She was especially interested in western influence on local cultures. As she remarked in her inaugural lecture as Professor of Education, the British, unlike the French, had not pursued a policy of political and cultural assimilation and as a result had laid up a store of trouble in the educational field. What form and content of education should be given to indigenous people had been a hotly contested field in British colonial policy since the end of the First World War. She expressed the problem in a memorable metaphor in an address to the Royal Anthropological Institute in 1951[42] when she

referred to the 'winds of educational doctrine' which had affected the type
of education given in colonial schools. The winds of doctrine blowing
from Britain to her colonies had been fitful and changeable, unlike the
steady trade winds from France and Portugal which had consistently
carried French and Portuguese culture and the orthodox methods of
teaching it to their respective colonies. She claimed that many of the more
serious mistakes made in British colonial education policy might have
been avoided if more help and advice had been accepted from social
anthropologists working in the same area.

Throughout her written work there is a constant concern with the
central problem confronting all education systems of how best to preserve
and pass on a cultural heritage to future generations while simultaneously
preparing the young for gainful participation in contemporary life and
future change. For colonial peoples the seemingly rapid transition from a
traditional to a modern lifestyle was unprecedented in human history and
gave rise to a variety of problems. It was clear to her that the tribal
background of many indigenous peoples was hardly adequate to enable
them to cope with modern civilisation. It was for this reason that she
placed such a high priority on adult education and community
development in its widest sense.

Despite her academic background she was critical of many
anthropologists. She claimed that in the inter-war years they had criticized
schools in the colonies for changing and upsetting the social systems they
were studying — 'They almost joined the ranks of settlers and traders in
their denunciation of the "mission-trained boy"'.[43] After 1945 their
criticism was directed at the failure of schools to act as a bridge between
old-established culture and the intrusive new culture. She claimed that
there was a serious lack of co-ordination between anthropologists and
educationists because neither was sufficiently aware of what the other was
doing:

> Anthropologists have had what were, to them, more interesting
> and more urgent problems in cultural change to investigate.
> Educationists, being largely ignorant of the work of
> anthropologists, have shown themselves impatient with their
> outspoken criticisms, and unwilling to revise their aims and
> methods in the light of these criticisms. Western educationists
> have found the process of teaching and of multiplying schools
> all-absorbing, and have not paused to consider the social and
> economic setting of the schools and children in the culture of the
> people, or examine the results of schooling on boys and girls
> who have to make a difficult adjustment to a changing
> environment. It is the people of the countries themselves — the
> Maori, the Malays, the Mexicans, the Africans — who are
> beginning to see the red light, and to ask whether western
> schooling must necessarily exclude all their own cultural

traditions, while at the same time seeking by its means to effect a
satisfactory transfer into a modern economic system.[44]

Within the Colonial Department she focused her teaching on both the
broad theoretical issues of cultural conflict and resolution and practical
everyday matters of education policy. These included the ownership,
administration and financing of schools, the relative emphases to be
placed on primary and secondary education, the language of instruction to
be used, the content of the curriculum and assessment procedures. In her
inaugural address in 1949, she paid tribute to three men who had greatly
influenced her educational as opposed to her anthropological thought.
They included James Fairgrieve, an outstanding geographer and teacher,
who had been responsible for initiating the Colonial Department within
the London Institute of Education; Arthur Mayhew, who had been
a leading educational administrator in India before becoming a joint-
secretary of the ACEC in the 1930s; and Sir Herbert Scott, a former DE
in the Transvaal and later Kenya, who became a leading writer and critic
of British colonial education in the late 1930s and 1940s.

Margaret Read's contribution to the thought and practice of post-
war British colonial education policy is undisputed but her volume of
published work is not great for someone of her academic rank. This fact
surfaced when she was considered for promotion to full professor in 1948
but as Dr Jeffery, the Director of the Institute of Education remarked in
support of her, she had broken new ground and achieved a genuine
advance in both the theory and practice of education. In a letter to Cox he
suggested that the fruits of her extensive field research were writ large
in Africa and not tucked away in learned journals.[45] Cox also strongly
supported her promotion. He highlighted the critical nature of the 1940s
for colonial education when policy had to be thought out afresh and 'got
across' to colonial peoples who were experiencing rapid socio-economic
change. He claimed that Margaret Read had played a leading role in that
process. Moreover, he claimed that she had brought to the Colonial
Department rich and widening contacts and the hallmark of scholarship
and authority 'which you will forgive me for saying I think it may have
lacked before'.[46] Carr-Saunders was less supportive. He expressed surprise
when she was appointed a Reader in 1945 — he thought she lacked the
academic qualifications for such a post — and claimed that she had not
been a very effective member of the Colonial Social Science Research
Council of which he was Chairman.[47]

By all accounts she was totally dedicated to her work. Clarke, who
had a deep admiration and respect for her, likened her to someone 'out
and out married' to a big idea: 'If you should be standing in the way of it,
then look out. All the resources then come into play …. I am inclined to
think it is a very good thing she never married!'[48] In any contest she was
evidently a worthy adversary. Dr Jeffery once jokingly admitted to her that
he sometimes referred to her as 'the battleaxe'.[49] Margaret Richards, who
started her long administrative career at the Institute as a young secretary

in the Colonial Department in Margaret Read's heyday, also recalled her as a somewhat fearsome and highly respected figure in the Department.[50] In her private correspondence with Cox, however, she comes across as a warm caring person although her confident outward manner may have hidden inner doubts about herself. In a letter written to Cox in 1965 from New York, she told him of the interest that American students had shown in various aspects of studies of education and social change but added 'which I always hoped to stimulate in London — and failed completely'. She went on to say that 'The sour consolation is that they continue to use (and quote) my little book '*Education and Social Change in Tropical Areas*' — published in 1955 !!!'[51]

Evidently she had a remarkable capacity for friendship and for relating to people of all ages. Soon after her death, Ruari McLean wrote to *The Independent* newspaper stating that in 1939 Margaret shared a house in North London with Canadian-born Margaret Wrong, then the Secretary to the Student Christian Movement but soon to become Secretary of the International Committee on Christian Literature for Africa.

> Both were spinsters, but utterly unspinsterish of the generation whose men had been lost in the 1914–18 war. Both had a lively sense of humour and were encouragers of the young; there was nearly always at least one young African in their house whom they were helping through London University. [In fact the house was rarely empty. Margaret Wrong had six nephews and nieces staying at different times during their school and university days and Margaret (Read) brought up my sister Joan and myself while our parents were in India][52]

When the date of Margaret Read's retirement from the Colonial Department was finally decided in late November 1954 [she was allowed to stay on for a further year after she turned 65] Freda Gwilliam wrote to Cox expressing her deep sorrow. It was, she suggested, like the passing of an age, and there was no one of Margaret's stature (in spite of occasional temperamental outbursts) to take her place that she could think of.[53] Cox, likewise, at her last ACEC meeting before she departed for Ibadan, spoke of her long service and her remarkable contribution. She had, he suggested, become part of the Advisory Committee's history.[54] During 15 years at the Institute of Education she had indeed packed in an enormous amount of effort and achievement and rightfully belongs to that group of highly talented women which includes Audrey Richards, Margery Perham, Lilian Penson, Philippa Esdaile, Camilla Wedgewood, Freda Gwilliam, Lucy Mair and Margaret Wrong, all of whom figured prominently in debate about the policy and practice of British colonial education in the middle years of the twentieth century.

NOTES ON CHAPTER

1. Seligman to Ormsby-Gore 13 May 1925 Box 223 Miscellaneous file, The
    Joint International Missionary Council/Conference of British Missionary
    Societies Archives [IMC/CBMS]
2. For more on this theme see Anthropology and Colonialism, chap. 4 in
    Adam Kuper, *Anthropologists and Anthropology The British School 1922–1972*,
    New York, Pica Press, 1973 and also the Introduction to Talal Asad,
    Anthropology and the Colonial Encounter, London, Ithaca Press, 1973
3. Details of Margaret Read's early life are derived mainly from her
    unpublished manuscript 'Poverty, Pollution and Family Life in a Victorian
    Cathedral City'. See Margaret Read Papers, University of London Institute
    of Education Archives [IOEA]
4. Margaret Read's father was the youngest in a family of 13 children of whom
    four died in infancy. When he was born his father was over 60 years of age
    and had just retired from a wholesale linen business in the town of
    Falmouth. Mabyn's mother died when he was five and he was reared by his
    father's housekeeper and later second wife. Mabyn clearly came from a
    talented family. One of his brothers was later Grote Professor of
    Philosophy at the University of London. He also had two other brothers
    who were educated at Christ's College, Cambridge and the University of
    London School of Medicine. Mabyn attended the Grammar School in
    Falmouth before he too, went to Christ's College, Cambridge in 1873 as a
    19 year old. He graduated with a BA in Natural Sciences in 1876 and then
    decided to study medicine at St Bartholomew's Hospital Medical School
    and later Cambridge University, from whence he graduated MD in 1884.
    He did his internship at Great Ormond Street Children's Hospital in
    Camden.
    Margaret's mother was born in 1863, the sixth in a family of ten. Her father
    was a partner in a firm of wool and linen merchants in the city of London.
    Her mother was the eldest daughter of Charles Bischoff, the head of the
    legal firm Bischoff Bampas & Co.
5. Soon after moving to Worcester, Mabyn's partner in the practice died
    suddenly.
6. Details of her university studies are derived from the Dr M. Read file,
    IOEA
7. The claim was made in an address by John Read at her funeral as reported
    in the *Institute of Education Society Newsletter*, Dec 1991, p 13. It may be true
    but if so it doesn't square up with a brief typed cv, dated Sep 1970, in the
    Dr M. Read file in the IOEA which states that she had an MA degree in
    history from Cambridge. Likewise, in *The World's Who's Who of Women*, she
    was listed as having an MA (1912) from Newnham College, Cambridge.
8. See her inaugural lecture as Professor — 'Education and Cultural Tradition'
    — delivered on 19 Jun 1950 and subsequently published as No. 2 in *Studies
    in Education*, Evans Bros. Ltd., for the University of London Institute of
    Education, nd
9. Kuper, *op.cit.*, chap.1.
10. The title of her thesis was 'Primitive economics with special reference to
    culture contact', See *Retrospective Index to Theses of Great Britain and Ireland
    1716–1950*.
11. See Margaret Read's handwritten copy of her Tribute to J. H. Oldham
    delivered at his memorial service 3 May 1969, and subsequently published
    in *Africa*, 1970/71 Margaret Read Papers. IOEA
12. See her *Native Standards of Living and African Culture Change*, published by
    OUP for the International Institute of African Languages and Cultures as
    Memorandum XVI, (1938). The same paper was also published as a
    Supplement to *Africa*, XI/3. See also *Migrant Labour in Africa and Its Effects*

on Tribal Life, Montreal, International Labour Office, 1943, as reprinted from the *International Labour Review*, XLV/6, Jun 1942. She subsequently published a book *The Ngoni of Nyasaland*, OUP. 1956, which was reprinted by Thomas Cass in 1970. A comprehensive holding of her published work up to Sep 1970 is to be found in the LSE Archives.

13.   See Frank W. Mitchell, *Sir Fred Clarke Master Teacher 1880–1952*, Longmans Green and Co., 1967

14.   For the history of the Colonial Department see the author's 'Not Wanted on the Voyage' (A study of the Colonial Department, ULIE 1927–1956) DICE [Dept. of International and Comparative Education] *Occasional Papers* No.11, Institute of Education, University of London, Mar 1988.

15.   Draft of a letter from Cox to Mumford [nd but drafted in reply to a letter from Mumford to Cox, dated 21 Jul 1942], Cox Papers, CO 1045/303, Public Record Office, Kew

16.   See Margaret Read's brief tribute to Mumford after his premature death in Jan 1951 in *The Times*, 7 Feb 1951

17.   Details of her wartime activities are derived principally from unpublished annual reports of the Colonial Department now kept in the IOEA

18.   The Cox Papers [CO 1045] at the Public Record Office in Kew reveal frequent and frank correspondence between Clarke and Cox during the war years.

19.   See for example the correspondence between them in the Cox Papers CO 1045/304

20.   Clarke to Carr-Saunders, 26 Mar 1943, 'Dr M. Read file', IOEA

21.   Minute from T. S. Foster to Cox, 11 Jul 1944, Cox Papers, CO 1045/1476

22.   See P. Hetherington, *British Paternalism and Africa,* 1920–1940, London, Cass, 1978

23.   See a tribute to Margaret Read by Professor Little on the occasion of her 100th birthday in the *DICE Annual Newsletter 1988–89*, Institute of Education.

24.   For details of how mass education/community development became an integral aspect of British colonial education policy and the part Margaret Read played in the process see the author's article 'When the Bush Takes Fire': A Study of the Origins and Purpose of Non-Formal Education in British Colonial Policy', chap.14 in James Lynch, Celia Modgil and Sohan Modgil (eds), *Non-formal and Non-governmental Approaches*, Vol. 4 of *Education and Development: Tradition and Innovation*, London, Cassell, 1997

25.   An Introductory Study of Fundamental Education. See Advisory Committee on Education in the Colonies Papers [ACEC] No.25/46 in CO 987/11, Public Record Office, Kew

26.   Minutes of the ACEC, CO 1045/7 Public Record Office, Kew

27.   *Report of the Commission on Higher Education in West Africa*, Cmd. 6655, HMSO, 1945

28.   See the author's article 'The "two-way pull" and the establishment of university education in British West Africa', *History of Education*, 16/2 (1987), pp 119–133

29.   Prof. Fred Clarke to the Principal, University of London 29 Jan 1945, Dr M. Read file, IOEA

30.   Report on the education of women and girls in Northern Rhodesia and Nyasaland, ACEC Papers 6/48, CO 987/13 Public Record Office, Kew.

31.   Notes of a meeting …, Cox Papers CO 1045/205 Public Record Office, Kew

32.   Read to Cox, 2 Nov 1949, Cox Papers CO 1045/304

33.   African Education and World Opinion, pp 112–130 in Margaret Read, *Education and Social Change in Tropical Areas*, London, Thos. Nelson and Sons Ltd., 1955. The proceedings of the Conference were published as *African*

Education: A study of educational policy and practice in British Tropical Africa,
Nuffield Foundation/Colonial Office, 1953
34.   Dr M. Read file, IOEA
35.   Read to Cox 22 Oct 1951 Cox Papers CO 1045/1479
36.   For more detail on this subject see E. Jefferson Murphy, *Creative
Philanthrophy Carnegie Corporation and Africa 1953–1973,* New York, Teachers'
College Press, Columbia University, 1976
37.   Reported in the Annual Report of the Colonial Department 1944–45
38.   Cox to Headmaster, Clifton College 6 Jul 1956 Cox Papers CO 1045/798
39.   Read to Cox 14 Apr 1956 Cox Papers CO 1045/304
40.   Most of the information on her activities after her retirement from the
London Institute of Education is derived from material in the IOE and/or
the LSE archives.
41.   Address by John Read at her funeral: *Institute of Education Society Newsletter*
Dec 1991
42.   Anthropology and Education, p 74 in *Education and Social Change in Tropical
Areas*
43.   The Contribution of Social Anthropologists to Educational Problems in
Underdeveloped Territories, *Fundamental and Adult Education,* Jul 1955 p 101
44.   *Ibid.,* p 102
45.   Jeffery to Cox 13 Aug 1948 Dr M. Read file, IOEA
46.   Cox to Jeffery 28 Sep 1948 Cox Papers CO 1045/409
47.   Carr-Saunders to Jeffery 19 Oct 1948 Dr M. Read file, IOEA
48.   Clarke to Jeffery 19 Aug 1948 Cox Papers CO 1045/409
49.   Jeffery to Read, 11 Mar 1953 Dr M. Read file, IOEA
50.   Private conversation with the author, late 1987
51.   Read to Cox 24 Mar 1965 Cox Papers CO 1045/1490
52.   Quoted in John Read's funeral address
53.   Gwilliam to Cox 1 Dec 1954 Cox Papers CO 1045/672
54.   218th meeting, 8 Sep 1955 ACEC Minutes CO 987/7

13. Freda Gwilliam

The 'great aunt' of British Colonial Education[1]

All the members of the original Colonial Office Advisory Committee on Education were males but it soon became clear that one of the main problems in all the colonies was the lack of education for women and girls. In April 1925, at the Advisory Committee's 13th meeting,[2] Miss Gray, the Headmistress of St Paul's School for Girls, recommended that a woman be added to the Committee to promote female education in the colonies. Sir Michael Sadler strongly supported the idea and mentioned Sara Burstall, who had recently retired as Headmistress of Manchester High School for Girls, as a likely candidate. His suggestion was acted upon and Miss Burstall joined the Committee at its 15th meeting in May 1925. At the time of her retirement due to ill-health in July 1938, she was the longest continuous serving member of the Committee. In December 1926, a second woman, Miss A. W. Whitelaw, the Headmistress of Wycombe Abbey School, also joined the Committee.

The education and welfare of women and girls was a matter of concern to the Advisory Committee throughout the 1930s, although little progress was achieved. Cultural reasons were partly responsible for the paucity of educational opportunities for girls in many territories but there was also an acute shortage of experienced ex-patriate women able to teach in and administer schools. Shortly after the outbreak of war in September 1939, the Advisory Committee established a sub-committee to re-examine the education and welfare of women and girls in Africa. The ensuing report was adopted early in 1941 but because of the war it was not published until February 1943.[3]

It was an outspoken document which highlighted just how great the disparity was between the education of boys and girls. Few girls received any schooling beyond the primary level and the majority remained at school for two or three years at most. Attendance was often very irregular and most girls barely achieved minimal literacy before they left school to marry and raise children. The report also emphasized the acute shortage of girls with adequate educational backgrounds for recruitment into the public service and the extreme reluctance of parents to let girls leave home for further schooling or professional training. The sub-committee believed that the short-term solution lay in recruiting many more European women to act as teachers and school administrators — 'we are' they stated, 'only at the beginning of the great task of providing education for women and girls in Africa'. To facilitate the task they advocated the creation of Senior Women's Education Officer posts in all territories and an on-the-spot enquiry in selected colonies to gather details of specific needs and a true understanding of the problem. The Advisory Committee was sympathetic but there was little anyone could do until the war ended.

Meanwhile, the problem of recruiting suitable women for service in colonial schools remained. In January 1941, Miss Oakden, a School Inspector and an outspoken critic of the existing system of recruitment, succeeded in persuading the Advisory Committee to set up a small sub-committee, including herself, Miss Perham and Christopher Cox, the recently appointed full time Educational Adviser to the Colonial Office, to deal separately with the recruitment and training problems of women teachers. The war delayed publication of the sub-committee's report[4] until March 1943. It recommended that the Colonial Office rather than the Board of Education should assume responsibility for appointments and that a special post of Woman's Educational Adviser should be created in the Colonial Office to deal specifically with the recruitment of female staff. The report was strongly endorsed by the Advisory Committee but further action was necessarily delayed until the end of the war.

In late 1945, Cox argued successfully for an additional advisory position on his staff.[5] He was anxious to obtain a female appointee, not just to handle female recruitment but women's educational matters in general. He emphasised the growing need for female staff in colonial schools and the fact that an additional person would greatly strengthen the advisory staff in Whitehall. Cox had hoped that Miss Oakden would accept the position but she declined and it was eventually offered to Freda Gwilliam, the Principal of the Brighton Teachers' Training College.

Freda was first suggested as a possible candidate by Mrs E. C. Mee, a Staff Inspector at the Ministry of Education, who was responsible for teacher training,[6] but it was Miss Oakden who finally persuaded Freda to visit the Colonial Office to discuss the matter at the beginning of January 1946.[7] Freda greatly impressed both Cox and his deputy Frank Ward. In a letter to his close friend Philip Morris, formerly DE in Kent and the new Vice-Chancellor of Bristol University, Cox wrote, 'I believe she has just the qualities we want, and I am not unhopeful of our being able to seduce her'.[8] Freda eventually succumbed to Cox's blandishments but her acceptance of the appointment was a far from straightforward matter. Nevertheless, her eventual arrival in Whitehall in May 1947, signalled the start of a unique partnership with Cox which was destined to last for 23 years and exert a decisive influence on the development of education in Britain's colonies.

Freda had serious misgivings about relinquishing her position at Brighton for what was initially, a temporary post with a maximum term of five years, on a substantially lower salary than she was currently receiving. She was 39 years of age, unmarried, and at a critical point in her career. She also had no love for the Civil Service or its bureaucratic processes and openly said so. This was an attitude she maintained steadfastly throughout her professional working life. As she frequently told her colleagues, she was happiest when she was away on tour in distant lands free from boring office routine. For almost two months she agonised over whether to accept the position before finally informing Cox that 'she was in his hands'.[9]

Cox was ecstatic at her decision: 'To say that Ward and I are delighted is to put it mildly'. On a more sombre note he explained that the job would have to be 'carved out', i.e. she would have to justify the position by what she made of it in the next few years. 'It would', he added, 'involve much wandering and close contacts with civil servants both in London and the Colonies and I was almost forgetting, becoming a civil servant yourself! (This is indeed for you the supreme sacrifice!)'[10] The formal offer of appointment, subject to a medical examination soon followed but what seemed like a straightforward matter soon proved otherwise.

When Freda visited London for her medical examination the doctor raised problems. As she wrote to Cox that same afternoon from Victoria Station, 'the doctor thinks my physique to be much against me'.[11] Freda was no lightweight! The doctor was also worried about her longstanding history of asthma. During the next few days she endured renewed agonies of doubt before finally writing again to Cox to tell him that she felt compelled to withdraw on medical grounds.[12]

Cox replied promptly asking her to reconsider her decision. He told her that he had consulted the doctor who was under the mistaken impression that she would need to walk miles on foot through the tropics. Had he known otherwise his advice would have been different. Cox admitted that she still had an asthma problem but he assured her that should she wish to leave the position when the initial five year term expired she would readily obtain another senior appointment. By then, he claimed, she would be a national figure in education, a view also shared by Mrs Mee. Sir Philip Morris thought it 'vital' that Freda should accept the position.[13]

There followed a further four months of agonising indecision before Freda finally wrote to Cox in July to say that she would join him in Whitehall after all. The medical problem was resolved in the short term by the doctor agreeing to pass her as fit for a five year appointment but not, as yet, for a permanent pensionable post. Her letter to Cox expressed relief now that she had made her decision, but she was clearly still annoyed at having to take a drop of some £300 in salary and highly critical of the financial discrimination then practised against women in the Civil Service. After months of thought, the wish to maintain her hard won security yielded to what she hoped was 'commonsense and a desire to do a job where you feel I can be of some use .... As to health — well, I have been singularly well for the past five years — not one day's sick leave — so perhaps I have outgrown my tendency to asthma and perhaps travelling would lead to the devoutly-to-be-desired reduction in my weight!'[14]

It was not until October that she formally signed on the dotted line. 'The deed is done' she told Cox. 'My letter of acceptance is written. The shades of the CS [Civil Service] close friendlily [sic] round me and I am looking forward to it all immensely — my letters of resignation are delivered and a great weight is lifted from me ...'.[15] It was agreed that she should take up her new appointment on 1 May 1947.

She faced an uncertain but challenging future with an understandable degree of apprehension. Three weeks before she was due to make her debut at the Colonial Office she sought some reassurance from Cox: 'I am a little apprehensive', she wrote, 'after a lifetime in educational institutions, of what happens when I come to an office instead'.[16] In conversation with the author some years ago, she recalled that Cox never did tell her what her duties were. It was not his style. Clearly she was expected to promote the education of girls and the recruitment of ex-patriate women to teach in the colonies but her brief also extended to educational development in general. In view of her immediate background as a principal in a teachers' training college, it was not surprising that she subsequently played an important role in promoting teacher-training throughout the colonies.

She quickly impressed Cox with her enthusiasm and ability. Within six weeks of her arrival at the Colonial Office, Cox suggested to Sir Thomas Lloyd, the Assistant Under-Secretary, that he should meet Miss Gwilliam as there was every sign that she was fast becoming a 'first-class' addition to the Office's advisory staff: 'She is younger than her grey hair suggests — actually only 40, I think — and broke off a rather notable career in UK education at considerable financial loss, to come to us for five years'. He added that she had poise and humour and might usefully represent the United Kingdom at the Unesco Conference in Chungking in 1948. He also noted that she kept an excellent cellar![17] Lloyd later minuted that he thoroughly enjoyed meeting her and agreed with Cox that she was an excellent addition to the staff.[18]

Freda was born at Feltham in July 1907. Her father spent his life in the prison service, first as a tutor in an approved school, later rising to the rank of a prison governor.[19] Freda was educated at Rochester Girls' Grammar School [1913–1923] and Notting Hill High School [1923–26]. She was Head Girl at the latter and a Scholar at both. In the autumn of 1926 she proceeded to Girton College, Cambridge, where she read history. She graduated BA in 1929 with a Class 2(1) in Part 2 of the Historical Tripos. Three years later she obtained her MA. She started her professional life as a teacher, first at the Falmouth County High School [1929–31] and then at the Frances Holland School in London [1931–36]. One of her former pupils recalled her outstanding ability as a teacher at her funeral service; 'She made things clear; she made them interesting; and above all she inspired her audience'.[20] Freda spent the next five years lecturing to trainee teachers at the Bishop Otter College in Chichester, including a year [1940–41] when she acted as Vice-Principal, before her appointment as the Principal of the Brighton Teachers' Training College.

Throughout her life Freda was a staunch Anglican with a strong social conscience. In the 1930s she was active in social work at the Katherine Low Settlement in Battersea and Honorary Secretary of the Women's Advisory Council on Indian Questions. During the war she was the County of Sussex youth lecturer for the British Red Cross Society, the Area Commandant of the Girls' Training Corps, Chairman of the Bishop of Chichester's Youth Council, and a member of the Chichester Diocesan Education Committee. Immediately after the war she was appointed as a Justice of the Peace for the County Borough of Brighton and also served for two years as a Member of the House of Laity of the Church Assembly. Her religious affiliations were to prove a distinct advantage in her subsequent dealings with missionary bodies in the colonies.

From the outset she proved to be 'an inveterate and indefatigable traveller'.[21] Within weeks of joining the Colonial Office she embarked on a tour of the East Africa territories which lasted until December. Her tour included a special visit to Nyasaland and Northern Rhodesia, together with Dr Margaret Read,[22] in response to the call for a detailed on-the-spot enquiry into girls' education as recommended in 1941 by the Advisory Committee on Education in the Colonies.[23] Early in 1951, she set off on yet another marathon tour lasting four months during which she visited all the British colonies in the Pacific and South East Asia as well as Australia and Ceylon. Then followed a further eight months in East and Central Africa helping prepare a report for the Cambridge Education Conference held in August 1952.[24] Air travel subsequently reduced the length of her regular trips abroad but she and Christopher Cox, long remained the best known of the Whitehall advisory staff to numerous directors of education in Britain's far-flung outposts of empire. A former DE once told the author that her visits provoked mixed feelings from colonial officials; her initial question invariably being 'Now what are you doing for the girls?' Woe betide the director who did not have a convincing answer ready to hand.[25] For her part, she revelled in occupying a front seat from which she witnessed at first hand the transition from empire to commonwealth.

Freda had to surmount one further personal crisis in her professional life before she could relax and consider herself truly one of Cox's unique advisory team. It arose when her temporary position was reviewed in late 1950 with a view to making it a permanent post. As she wrote to Cox, while he was on a tour of the South Pacific in December 1950, 'A crisis is blowing up over my very problematical future'.[26] Freda's main concern was the proposed salary scale of £800–£1200. She was on a fixed annual salary of £1050. Naturally she was anxious to secure her financial future if she stayed at the Colonial Office but she had been told that if she joined the permanent staff the Treasury would insist that she started at the bottom of the scale — 'That of course is unthinkable' she remarked, adding 'my nasty pride and passion for getting things done doesn't take kindly to the limitations of having my position as Assistant Education Adviser related to that of a Principal in the office and to the prospect of that being my fate for 17 more years'. To add to her misgivings all education salaries in the United Kingdom were then under review and there was a good chance that they would rise substantially in the near future.

Her position was complicated still further only days before she wrote to Cox when she was told that the Principal of Whitelands Teachers' Training College had resigned and that the College Council was anxious that she should apply for the position. The Civil Service Commission appeared to be in no hurry to act whereas Whitelands College intended advertising in early January. Clearly time was the critical factor. In the circumstances she told Cox that she had no choice 'I MUST put in for Whitelands …. I can't let the opportunity slip can I?' Sir Charles Jeffries, the Deputy Under-Secretary, agreed with her. She was clearly torn between her natural ambition and her love for the work she was doing: 'If only there were a chance that a woman could be considered for a Deputy Advisorship sometime — it would be so encouraging … yet the thought of any break with the real thing — people — plans — progress and so on is more than I can bear'. She was thankful that Cox would be back in London before any irrevocable decisions needed to be made. 'Forgive me for disturbing you with it all', she wrote, 'but I couldn't let it be in the air even, without telling you and as I say NOTHING will happen till you are back.'

Two days later she wrote again to Cox after receiving a letter from him which boosted her flagging morale.[27]

> Thank you a thousand times. I feel exhilarated again after days of doubt and gloom — you make me feel again the urgency and the importance of people and personal relations and the need to keep these close and friendly links with people grimly yet cheerfully doing unenviable jobs under conditions incomprehensible to bureaucrats here — But you know its only frequent and regular injections of going to the jungle or bush or island or kampong or reserve that keeps me believing in the value of an assistant adviser.

She then told Cox what she really yearned for:

> Let me boldly (but with shame!) state what I wish *could* happen — It presupposes a value of myself which I *don't* claim but wish I could — I *wish* it were possible to have a Woman Deputy Adviser … one who was really a full member of the team to the office at large instead of just to you and to the many nice people in the colonial territories who pay me that complement. The 4/5ths of the Deputy Adviser's salary would remove the need to consider Whitelands on financial grounds …. I'm risking an awful lot in revealing to you so uncompromisingly, the horrid depths of my nature — but I could do no less in these circumstances.

In the same letter she told Cox that she had just been advised that the Treasury had agreed to a revised *ad hoc* salary scale of £1050–1200 for the permanent post 'so I could start at the bottom!' Frank Ward and Harold Robison, two of her Whitehall colleagues, advised her to take the Whitelands job if it was offered.

> They know I'm not a file-loving, docile, disciplined, proper-channels, humble and obedient (civil) servant — Should I ever be? …. *Am I breaking faith (a) with the CO. and (b) MOST IMPORTANT, with the people in the field,* if I do consider the relative claims of both instead of turning resolutely my back on Whitelands and taking the risks of the C.O. So while I curse myself for telling you all this, I also, with immense relief ask your help and advice as I have done so often since January 1946.

Freda's strong sense of injustice prompted her to compile a memorandum — 'A Woman in the Education Advisory Team' — a copy of which, she sent to Cox.[28] He subsequently drew on it extensively in pressing for an establishment post at a higher salary than that originally decided upon. In the memorandum Freda highlighted the fact that educational salaries were raised in the United Kingdom in December 1950. As a result, she thought it highly unlikely that the Colonial Office would succeed in attracting either a staff inspector at the Ministry of Education, a principal of a Teachers' Training College, a university lecturer, or the headmistress of a large school to fill a permanent advisory position unless the salary scale was raised.

In mid January she wrote again to Cox, this time to express her dislike of the impersonal way the Colonial Office viewed her situation.

> We are cogs in a vast impersonal machine as far as our terms of employment, responsibility and salary are concerned — In Whitehall no one cares a jot or tittle if I come or go — but this four years can't just be washed away and leave no trace — can it? I wish I *could* face going on being a philanthropist and apply for a job at a salary that is less than I ought to be trying for — but I can't and the Civil Service knows it and has the whip hand — Take it or leave it! So there we are — *BUT* nothing is irrevocable YET and in spite of your nightmares that I'm covered with shame and confusion …. I shan't have sent my *application* in to Whitelands till long after you return.

She concluded by saying if only she had a private income she could follow her heart and not her head. Whatever happened, however, she vowed not to waste away the fruits of four exciting and absorbing years — 'and THANK YOU — more than I can say for all you have done to make them so happy'.[29]

Soon afterwards, Cox returned to London and immediately drafted a strongly-worded memorandum in support of a revised salary scale.[30] He spoke highly of Freda's work over the past four years:

> It was a new post which had to establish its value. That, I submit, the first holder has done once and for all in a way that cannot be contested. In the field her influence … has become such that her advice is widely sought and is now having far reaching consequences not only in respect of the specific problems of the education of women and girls but on the professional side of education generally, particularly in teacher training; two striking examples, the impending revolution in attitudes towards, and organisation of, teacher-training in the always sensitive Malayan territories where I should judge her influence has been the

decisive factor in convincing the Director of Education and the designate Director of Education Malaya that in this key field their systems were several decades behind the times, and secondly, the support given by the West African governments for her project for modernising the local conception of teacher-training by sending 40 practitioners to this country to join English practitioners in a conference specially designed by the Ministry of Education ....

He was also convinced that the large sums invested in her touring since 1947 were paying off. 'It would be a great pity', he concluded, 'if her work was to end because the terms of the post of Woman's Assistant Educational Adviser could not attract a successor of similar calibre'. His advice was heeded and the position was eventually advertised in the salary range £1050–£1350.

There were five applicants for the position; two school inspectors, the vice-principal of a teachers' college, the headmistress of a girls' grammar school, and Freda, who at 43 years of age was the youngest of the applicants.[31] Mrs Mee, who had originally suggested her for the position created in 1947, and Cox acted as her referees. Mrs Mee spoke highly of Freda's personal qualities and her capacity to win ready cooperation and respect for the schemes she proposed. She suggested that it would be difficult to imagine anyone more suited to the post. Cox wrote that she had performed her duties with 'outstanding ability' and shown

that the post is of greater importance and influence than I myself had realised it could be. She has in fact made the post what it is. She has won the complete confidence not only of her colleagues at home but of those working in the field, from Governors downwards, with far-reaching consequences, and she has most effectively become, over a wide professional field, the principal personal link between Colonial education and educational practitioners, organisers and thinkers in this country. Both her professional knowledge and her personality are exactly right for the job.

Such glowing testimony ensured that she eventually joined the permanent staff. In the meantime, however, she had applied for and been offered the principalship at Whitelands Teachers' College. Moreover, Cox had acted as her referee.[32] The College Council gave her additional time to make her decision because she was still awaiting the outcome of her application to the Colonial Office. She finally received word of her appointment to the permanent staff on 1 September while she was touring in Nyasaland. She wrote back to Cox saying what a great relief it was. Now she could plan and look ahead with long term conviction and feel she really belonged to the great work she was engaged in.[33]

Throughout her many years of travelling she was a constant and invaluable source of inside knowledge to Cox. Her letters from abroad were always highly informative and frank, and suggest a very close working relationship with him. Her comments about A. L. Binns (Chief Education Officer, Lancashire), his wife, and Professor B. A. Fletcher, when she accompanied them on their tour of East and Central Africa as the Binns Commission in 1951, were typical of the feedback that Cox received. Writing in bed on a Sunday morning in Zomba in August 1951,[34] she wrote of Mrs Binns as an uninhibited and down-to-earth sort of person who said exactly what she thought about all, including her husband 'Arthur'. Freda described him as a good story-teller who goes down well. In an earlier letter she had described how they got on first name terms. Binns had approached her early in the tour by saying; 'Here is a leading question for you. If we are going to be together for six months or more, I can't go on calling you Miss Gwilliam. Can I call you Freda?' She said that she would be delighted; to which he replied, 'Good then. Now here is the second question. Do you think that you could bring yourself to call me Arthur?' Freda said she was sure she could. 'So I do!' Fletcher was described as 'charming'. Evidently his 'physical attributes' were immediately appreciated by women. He was also 'awfully good educationally and we argue on so many things and I sit metaphysically at his feet'. Later in the tour she wrote that 'the shell of Olympian calm round Fletcher (who will remain Prof Fletcher till the bitter end, we are sure!) has been cracked a bit, and occasionally a delightful boyishness comes through. It's such a relief! He is *excellent* professionally and invaluable to us. He and I see eye to eye on so much. So all in all, I think you can rest in peace'.[35] In another letter she included a humorous account of Binns and Fletcher receiving a Roman Catholic delegation: 'Everyone was so polite. We all parted firm friends each knowing the other knew he knew …'.[36] Of some local officials she was less complementary; — 'has improved a lot (plenty of room for it!) … is an efficient and kindly yes-man — no leader; is a keen but spoilt adolescent — charming if everything goes his way — tiresome and fractious if crossed'.

She also provided Cox with valuable comments about directors of education and their departments. In February 1950, she visited Malaya, then a political trouble-spot, and a territory with a very conservative-minded educational administration. She wrote Cox a very detailed analysis of the educational situation to prepare him for his follow-up visit after her departure. 'my *goodness*, you are needed here. I'm re-Christening myself

Johanne la Baptiste and going before you …. There are many personalities
involved [in education] — nice people with antique ideas and not-so-nice
people with modern ideas'. She then commented on several of the senior
educational staff who would soon be heading for London during the
'leave season'. One was rumoured to be next in line for the director's job:
'all very hush hush — Oh THAT IT COULD BE HUSHED RIGHT
UP!'[37] A few days later she changed her tune:

> To my surprise, delight and confusion, the once serene and
> confident and what-have-you-come-for attitude of the Education
> Department seems to have dissipated and they are all so friendly
> and ready to discuss and open their hearts to an outsider and
> their minds to suggestions that I'm quite abashed and feel quite
> sure I'm talking too much …. Do you know, I believe, in their
> heart of hearts they are anxious to be right inside our company
> of people educating the empire — Cox's Own! and are just
> realizing how much of that comradeship they are missing.[38]

In the same letter she asked Cox if he would mind if she did not visit
Mauritius: 'I'm rather like a fat squelchy, soaked sponge — just about
holding it all now, but bound to leak if anything more is poured in'. Her
love of travel was matched only by her wish, after many months away,
to return 'HOME'!

In December 1951, she was called upon to comment on the DE in
Uganda, at a time when 'education [had] hit rock bottom'.[39] Unfortunately
the Director was frequently over-ruled by the Financial Secretary — 'the
dictator and power behind the scenes'.[40] There was also a general feeling
of *laissez-faire* and no confidence in the Education Department because
'Entebbe can always queer the pitch'. Freda spoke at length to the
Director and concluded that he was 'PATHETIC — no drive,
no confidence or vision'. Two weeks later she was equally outspoken:

> I think we shall all burst soon! The rich material here in Africans
> and the grim reality of delay, procrastination, negation, lack of
> drive, lack of plan, lack of initiative and general futility, has worn
> our courtesy so thin and our discretion so holey, that it's just
> as well we are leaving Uganda soon …. A clean sweep appears to
> us to be what the country needs. There is no confidence either in
> the [Education] Department or in … I am completely exhausted
> with the frustration and unhappiness of it all ….[41]

Soon afterwards, the DE was replaced on the order of the new governor
Sir Andrew Cohen.

A further example of Freda's outspokenness occurred during her visit to Kenya in 1957. She commented to Cox that the Kenya Education Department was 'the weakest anywhere'. Good work was being done in the field but the Headquarters staff and some of the Provincial Education Officers were 'just *not* the calibre to match the need — is well gone and there are several others whose replacement would be a godsend'.[42] After a break for lunch she resumed; 'I've just reread — how *pompous* I sound. I've done too much public speaking lately — I must get back to normal! *Very sorry*'.

Freda freely admitted to being an unashamed imperialist. In July 1952, while attending an annual conference of the International Bureau of Education in Geneva, she wrote: 'It is a most interesting new experience — most educative for so confirmed and Blimpish an Imperialist as I am — It's also very satisfying to find how well our Commonwealth countries shape'.[43]

Several months earlier she had been in Kenya when King George VI died. She commented on the genuine expression of grief in Kenya and then remarked; 'Now for an Elizabethan age and the best and finest Empire yet — we *must* link our developing Women's work in the Colonial territories with the reign of our Queen — I have ideas brewing!'[44] At the same time she was no sentimental paternalist. While in East Africa in late 1951, she was moved to anger in her correspondence:

> Confound the Swahili [language] that gives the old hands such a lovely warm comfortable feeling of "understanding the African" and denies to the African his right to understand and enter into the heritage of the English-speaking world: that lulls the delightful but heavily paternal administrators into such bliss as "No politically-minded Africans here, thank goodness!" "Excellent race relations here as long as we are left to determine the pace of our own progress." Who is "we"? Ask the Africans who <u>can</u> speak English and you get another story — But let their ostrichism shelter them a little longer from the rude awakening for they are doing a fine job in the old manner — Bwanas for ever![45]

When not away on tour, Freda spent much of her time recruiting and interviewing prospective female staff for service abroad. As her obituary stated 'she ensured the establishment of girls' schools and colleges throughout the colonies; she recruited scores of remarkable British women to teach in them or to administer them and she kept in personal touch with them all'. She also 'enabled hundreds of indigenous women

teachers from those [colonial] countries to study in the United Kingdom
and knew most of them by name'.[46]

Freda made no claim to academic scholarship — writing reports
reduced her to pulp[47] — but she was a popular and frequent lecturer
to students in the Colonial Department at the Institute of Education in
London in the 1950s. When in London, she also regularly attended the
monthly meetings of the Advisory Committee on Education in the
Colonies and served on numerous of its sub-commitees She was also
deeply involved in the staging of the Cambridge conference on African
education in 1952 and the first Commonwealth education conference
at Oxford in 1959.

Her dislike of 'office routine' was well known. Cox mentioned
it when supporting her application for a permanent position in 1951 but
dismissed it as of no consequence because of her long tours overseas and
the nature of her duties when domiciled in the United Kingdom.
Nevertheless, at least one of her advisory colleagues was greatly irritated
by her frequent failure to read files.[48] She also made what some of her
colleagues thought to be rather hasty judgments about some people; her
'pets' was how one official described some of those she championed.[49]
She, in turn, told Cox that the same official could 'petrify' her when he
was in a bad mood.[50]

For Cox she had an undying admiration which remained
undiminished to the end of her life. When he was away on tour she
frequently wrote to say how much she missed his presence in the office:
'I miss you badly. Its awfully dull and unlively [sic] when you are not
here'.[51] She was likewise ecstatic when she received letters from him:
'Your letters are wonderful. You must hardly sleep'.[52] But there was never
any hint to suggest that their relationship was anything other than that of
close professional colleagues. Freda readily acknowledged that she
belonged to that generation of women who paid the price for the carnage
of the First World War. 'In the 1920s and early 1930s eligible young
women far outnumbered their male counterparts', she once remarked
to the author.

Her career in Whitehall, which she once described as the most
satisfying, exciting, often infuriating, but wholly absorbing 23 years that
anyone could have had,[53] spanned both the demise of the Empire and the
transition to the present Commonwealth of Nations. From 1947 until
1961 she worked in the Colonial Office. Then the education advisory staff
were transferred to the newly formed Department of Technical
Cooperation. Three years later, she and her colleagues moved again to
become part of the new Ministry for Overseas Development from which
she retired in 1970. Her services to colonial education were formally
acknowledged by the awards of the OBE and the CBE and an honorary

DLitt from the New University of Ulster, Coleraine, however, at least one of Britain's foremost educators in the 1960s, thought she should have received more. Near the end of her professional life, Sir John Newsom asked Cox why she had not been knighted in recognition of her 'tremendous achievements' and why she was not listed in 'Who's Who'?[54] Cox mentioned 'major bureaucratic problems':

> Even in the affluent old days, when "recognition" was a facile occupational hazard of the Civil Service, Ralph Furse, who was a freak in his position of influence and achievements, was the only civil servant ever to get a K[nighthood] as a mere head of Department (Assistant Secretary). Freda, alas, is only an Adviser and not a Principal or Deputy, *and* it is 88 times harder nowadays for any civil servant to get any? [high-ranking award].[55]

He promised to look into the matter before she retired but nothing transpired. By the late 1960s Freda was ready to retire. She had led a very active professional life but she increasingly felt that her time was past and that new blood and new ideas were needed in Whitehall. In May 1968, she informed Cox that she would like to retire in the following year. She claimed there were many reasons for her decision: 'I *am* getting older and feel tired-er as I keep up the pace and feel more and more out of touch with the shape of things to come'. She was also conscious of living increasingly on her past experiences and relationships. What ODM wanted, she claimed, was someone who could look squarely and freely to the future.

> I should go — a young, enterprising, professionally competent and experienced woman in teacher education should have the chance of going ahead with the ODM in a changing role she would help to shape. I couldn't do this — I'm the Great Aunt figure — the batterer at doors that are opening ajar — unable to move with the young (why should I — with my life behind me).

She contrasted herself with Cox: '... you are ageless in years and in flexibility and soaring in mind. Your established world position — your unique place in the national and international university world, makes any comparison as laughable as unrealistic'. She also mentioned that she had just come of age in the Civil Service [i.e. 21 years of service from 1 May 1947 to 1 May 1968] and concluded: 'My life — thanks to that 1946 day when I met you — has been exciting, rewarding and unique. THANK you!'[56]

Her last major assignment was to lead the British delegation to the conference on Education in Rural Areas held at the University of Ghana in March 1970. On the eve of her 63rd birthday and her impending retirement, she wrote once more to Cox:

> I suppose everyone as they wind up their professional lives, looks back nostalgically to those good days — I certainly can and do — competence, busy-ness, planning, policies, all continue effectively — but the *panache* has gone! the figures larger than life — the makers of a history through which we have lived — but so much to look back on and dream about and delight in — What a part you played! Thank you a thousand times.[57]

The next day she wrote of the new advisory team; 'The best of luck to them — *but*, poor things, — they have not the memories of the great days — the venture — the fun — the people — that we have!'[58] Several weeks after they had both retired she wrote once more to Cox:

> I must say — financial stringency apart, which is going to be a bind, I find retirement busy, interesting and full of enjoyment. *If* and *when* I give an old colleague in ODA a thought — or meet them as I occasionally do — *They* say its all so dull since we left! What nicer epitaph could they give us![59]

Freda lived out her well-earned retirement in a picturesque cottage in the village of Frant, in Sussex. To the end of her life she remained active in community affairs. Her last major public engagement occurred in 1972 when she served as the only woman member of the Commission of Enquiry led by Lord Pearce, which visited Rhodesia to determine whether the people supported proposals for a settlement of the constitutional crisis. She died unexpectedly on 14 August 1987, aged eighty.

It is fitting that this portrait of Freda, who was truly one of the most memorable characters of the twilight years of British colonial rule, should conclude with an extract from her obituary in *The Times,* including the last two sentences which were omitted from the printed version:

> She belonged to that nearly extinct breed of tough and tireless ladies who fostered the education of girls across the globe. When she entered the colonial service, the education of girls was rare indeed; by the time she retired it was the accepted thing. No 'feminist', she helped many thousands of females in the developing countries. No 'do-gooder', she did untold good.[60]

NOTES ON CHAPTER

1. This essay first appeared as 'Miss Freda Gwilliam (1907–1987): A portrait of the "Great Aunt" of British Colonial Education in the *Journal of Educational Administration and History* 24/2 (1992), pp 145–163.
2. A full record of the Committee's Minutes 1924–1961 is to be found in the Sir Christopher Cox Papers (CP) at the Public Record Office in Kew, Ref. CO 1045/1, 2, 3, 4, 5, 6, 7, 8, 9, 10, 11.
3. Advisory Committee on Education in the Colonies (ACEC), *Report of a sub-committee on the Education and Welfare of Women and Girls in Africa,* CO Colonial 1169, HMSO 1943
4. 'Sub-Committee report on the recruitment and training of women for the Colonial Education Service', ACEC 5/43, in Conference of British Missionary Societies' archives, A/G 3, File on Education and Welfare of Women and Girls 1940–1946, SOAS Library, University of London.
5. CP CO 1045/344
6. CP Cox to Sir Martin Roseveare, 9 Mar 1946 CO 1045/363
7. CP Cox to Dr Margaret Read, 1 Jan 1946 CO 1045/363
8. CP Cox to Philip Morris, 11 Feb 1946 CO 1045/363
9. CP Gwilliam to Cox, 26 Feb 1946 CO 1045/344
10. CP Cox to Gwilliam, 7 Mar 1946 CO 1045/344
11. CP Gwilliam to Cox, 14 Mar 1946 CO 1045/344
12. CP 18 Mar 1946 CO 1045/344
13. CP Cox to Gwilliam, 22 Mar 1946 CO 1045/344
14. CP Gwilliam to Cox, 24 Jul 1946 CO 1045/344
15. CP 26 Sep 1946 CO 1045/344
16. CP 11 Apr 1946 CO 1045/344
17. CP Minute 13 Jun 1946 CO 1045/344
18. CP Minute 24 Jun 1946 CO 1045/344
19. Details of Freda's father were kindly provided by her niece Ms Philippa Gwilliam. Details of Freda's early career were obtained from her application for the position of Woman Assistant Educational Adviser, CP CO 1045/344 and from her obituary in *The Times*, 18 Aug 1987.
20. Address by Ms Gillie Warr at the funeral of Freda Gwilliam, Frant, Aug 1987. A copy of the address was kindly made available to the author by Ms Philippa Gwilliam.
21. Obituary, *The Times*
22. Margaret Read was the head of the Colonial Department at the University of London Institute of Education.
23. Report on the education of women and girls in Northern Rhodesia and Nyasaland, ACEC 6/48 CO 987/13
24. Study of Educational Policy and Practice East and Central Africa, ACEC 21/52. An abbreviated version of the report appeared in *African Education*, The Nuffield Foundation and the Colonial Office, 1953.
25. Interview with Gordon Rodger, former DE in Fiji, Suva 1973
26. CP Gwilliam to Cox, 19 Dec 1950 CO 1045/344
27. CP 21 Dec 1950 CO 1045/344
28. A copy of her memorandum is included in CO 1045/344
29. CP Gwilliam to Cox, 16 Jan 1951 CO 1045/344
30. The memorandum is dated 21 Feb 1951 CO 1045/344

31. Details of Freda's application and referees' statements are included in CO 1045/344
32. A rough pencilled draft of his statement on her behalf has survived although it is difficult to read. As one might expect it was very supportive. He thought her great strength lay in personal relationships. CO 1045/344
33. CP Gwilliam to Cox, 1 Sep 1951 CO 1045/1479
34. CP 26 Aug 1951 CO 1045/1479
35. CP 1 Sep 1951 CO 1045/1479
36. CP 23 Sep 1951 CO 1045/1479
37. CP 19 Feb 1950 CO 1045/1478
38. CP 23 Feb 1950 CO 1045/1491
39. CP 26 Jan 1951 CO 1045/344
40. CP 3 Dec 1951 CO 1045/1479
41. CP 18 Dec 1951 CO 1045/584
42. CP 12 Feb 1957 CO 1045/1482
43. CP 10 Jul 1952 CO 1045/1479
44. CP 17 Feb 1952 CO 1045/344
45. CP 21 Oct 1951 CO 1045/1479
46. I am indebted to Mr W. A. Dodd for an original copy of the text of the obituary which appeared in *The Times*, 18 Aug 1987.
47. CP Gwilliam to Cox 26 Jan 1952 CO 1045/344
48. CP L. McD. Robison to Cox 13 Jan 1955 CO 1045/667
49. *Ibid.*
50. CP Gwilliam to Cox 22 Jan 1953 CO 1045/661
51. *Ibid.*
52. CP 1 Dec 1954 CO 1045/672
53. Gillian Warr
54. CP Newsom to Cox 15 Oct 1968 CO 1045/1498
55. CP Rough notes of Cox's reply CO 1045/1498
56. CP Gwilliam to Cox 2 May 1968 CO 1045/1497
57. CP Gwilliam to Cox 28 Jul 1970 Cox Archive New College, Oxford
58. *Ibid.*, 29 Jul 1970
59. CP Gwilliam to Cox 17 Dec 1970 CO 1045/1484
60. Original version as written by W. A. Dodd

14. William A. Dodd

Colonial and Post-Colonial Educator

The process of decolonization and localization, which gathered pace in the 1950s, meant that many people who joined the CES after 1945 were subsequently caught in mid career with the prospect of 'staying on' as public servants of newly independent governments or returning to Britain in the hope of resuming their careers in a local setting. William 'Bill' Dodd was one such person. Much of the first half of his educational career was spent administering education in Tanganyika. After independence he returned to Britain to a university post but later went on to become Chief Education Adviser and Under Secretary in the Overseas Development Administration. No one better epitomises the transition from the CES of the pre-independence era to that of the post-independence years with their new emphasis on financial aid and technical assistance to developing countries.[1]

Dodd was born on 5 February 1923 in the town of Winsford, located some 30 miles due east of Chester. At the time his father was the administrative secretary at Garner's salt works but he later lost his job when the firm was taken over by the Salt Union.

In 1930, Dodd's father got work in Chester as an accounts clerk in the Surveyor's Department of the Cheshire County Council and the family moved to the rural setting of Newton, on what was then the outskirts of Chester. In Winsford, Dodd attended the Gladstone Street elementary school (1927–30), and in Chester the nearest local authority elementary school for Hoole and Newton (1930–35). He recalls wearing a school uniform and sitting in rows in classes of some 40 pupils controlled by a very strict disciplinary code. In retrospect, he claims that the elementary education offered in that period was efficient and served well a middle class child who had ability.

At the age of 11 he unsuccessfully sat the entrance examination to the City and County Secondary School (later called the Chester City Grammar School). The following year he sat again and was successful. He attended the grammar school for six years (1935–41). It was a boys only establishment run on semi-public school lines. Each year four or five boys gained university places which was highly commendable at a time when the majority of the school population never even attended a secondary school. Dodd was never sure what he wanted to do for a career when at secondary school but readily recalls the constant backdrop of impending war which overshadowed his youth. He sat the school certificate examination in the summer of 1938 — the same year as Chamberlain sold out at Munich! — and performed creditably. Two years later he sat the higher school certificate examination and gained 'distinctions' in history and English. The following year he again sat the higher school certificate examination, this time at the 'scholarship' level, and obtained an 'excellent' in scholarship history. He attributes his life-long love of history to a 'very tough but interesting' teacher at the grammar school. The common theme of high academic achievement in either classical or modern history amongst the men and women examined in this study is clearly evident and reflects the high status that both subjects enjoyed in the late nineteenth and for much of the twentieth century.

In the 1940–41 academic year Dodd also sat two entrance examinations for admission to Oxford colleges and one for a group of Cambridge colleges but to no avail, although he got through to the interview stage on three occasions. Persistence was finally rewarded, however, when he won a Chester City scholarship and a 'Sizarship' to Christ's College, Cambridge. At school Dodd displayed all the leadership qualities that the CES sought in its recruits. He was successively a house captain, prefect, and in his last year [1941] Captain of School. He also played soccer and cricket, and was a member of the debating club, the music society and the air cadet force.

His experience of Cambridge was interrupted by war service. He went up to Cambridge in October 1941 and lived in college on the same staircase as C. P. Snow. Life at Cambridge was greatly affected by the war. Undergraduate numbers were much reduced and Christ's College was partly occupied by American military forces and by the 'rump' of SOAS, the University of London's School of Oriental and African Studies. Socially speaking, Dodd found life as an undergraduate rather dull both during and after the war when he returned from military service. In his first year at Cambridge he joined the officer training corps [OTC], This automatically made him a member of the Home Guard. On 20 February 1942 he was conscripted into the army but allowed to complete the academic year although he was still obliged to attend parades on week nights and at weekends. Despite these distractions he did well academically gaining a 'First' in Part 1 of the History Tripos. He also won the College 'History Prize' and became an 'Exhibitioner' i.e. he got an allowance of £30 per year from the College towards his expenses.

In October 1942 he was directed to present himself for training with the Pre-OCTU [Officer Cadet Training Unit] at Wrotham in Kent. One Sunday morning while reporting at Wrotham he volunteered for the Indian army. He claims that his decision was based partly on the fact that he had been thinking of joining the prestigious Indian Civil Service after the war. He left England in January 1943, and after a nine-week sea voyage via South Africa, finally arrived in Bombay, from whence he moved to Bangalore in southern India. He arrived in the sub-continent at the height of the 'Quit India' campaign being conducted by Mahatma Gandhi and the Congress Party. One of his first tasks was to get acquainted with the Urdu language. He was commissioned in September 1943 in the 8th Gurkha Rifles and posted to the Arakan in Burma. On 9 January 1944 he received shrapnel wounds in his back while resisting a Japanese attack but recovered and returned to his regiment in early March. He was then promoted to the rank of Captain with special responsibility for recruit training and stationed at Quetta. He recalls that for a 21 year old his new role was a major responsibility. In July 1945 he was posted to a jungle camp south of Dehra Dun in preparation for the invasion of Malaya but the war ended abruptly when the Japanese surrendered a month later. Soon after, at the request of Christ's College, he was given a 'Class B release' and left India on 10 October. By mid November he was demobbed and back at Cambridge.

The immediate post-war years at Cambridge were dominated by older undergraduates who were also war veterans and often married. Dodd recalls the absence of political interest amongst many of them. They had survived and most were simply glad to be back studying once more. The war had a profound effect on many young men: 'You grew up very quickly and gained confidence in your ability to do things'. He continued his studies in history but found it harder than when he first went up to Cambridge and finally settled for a class II (1) Hons. degree. While at Cambridge the second time round he edited the Christ's College magazine (1946), was an active member of the debating society and, in 1947, was secretary of the junior combination room committee i.e. leader of the students' union. He vividly recalls the long bitter winter of 1947, the spring floods which followed, and food rationing! Nevertheless, he still managed to enjoy watching cricket at Fenners. As he approached the end of his degree studies he considered teaching as a possible career — Independence had ended any plans he might have had for an administrative career in India. It was, therefore, somewhat fortuitous when he was invited by an undergraduate colleague to consider a post as senior history master at Ipswich School. He duly visited the school in May 1947, was offered the post, and accepted it even though, at the time, he had no professional teaching qualification. The following year he took steps to rectify this deficiency by enrolling in a part-time correspondence course run by the Wolsey Hall Tutorial College. In 1949 he was awarded a Certificate of Education with a grade of '1st Class' for the written examination and 'Excellent' for the practical teaching component. He taught at Ipswich for the next five years (1947–52), but had no intention of staying long term. He had seen India and sought wider horizens.

Ipswich School was akin to a modest public school. It was a town grammar school founded about 1400, with strong links to Oxbridge. It had a preparatory school, a boarding establishment, and played rugby rather than soccer, and cricket. While at Ipswich Dodd also gave Workers' Educational Association lectures in the evenings in Ipswich and neighbouring Dedham. In 1949 he got married. He had known his wife Marjorie when they were at secondary school — she went to Chester Girls' High School. Her father, an early graduate of the London Day Training College, was Dodd's French teacher at the grammar school! The relationship only blossomed, however, years later after she had graduated from the University of Liverpool and become a medical social worker at the Royal Infirmary in Liverpool.

By the early 1950s Dodd was ready for a career move. He applied for a lectureship in history at Dartmouth College and was interviewed for a similar position at Makerere College in Uganda but was unsuccessful in both instances. At this point John Hennings, a Principal at the Colonial Office, who had come to Ipswich to talk to the current affairs class, suggested that he apply for a post in the CES. He did and he was successful! He was interviewed in London by T. [Tommy] H. Baldwin, one of Christopher Cox's assistant educational advisers, who read ancient Greek for relaxation,[2] and who had formerly been deputy DE in Nigeria. Dodd remembers little of what was said except that Baldwin advised him to take a comfortable camp bed and a crate of gin with him to Africa! In late 1952 he went out to a posting in Tanganyika where he was to work for the next 13 years. His first job was at the government teachers' training college in Mwanza. It was here that he first met John Cameron, then principal of the college. The meeting was to prove the start of a lifelong friendship not only in Tanganyika but later also on the staff of the London Institute of Education. Dodd was to spend much of his time in Tanganyika as a district education officer in various parts of the Territory. In the lead-up to independence he worked in the headquarters of the Department of Education and after independence the Ministry of Education in Dar-es-Salaam. At the independence celebrations in December 1961, he organised the youth rally which was attended by the various visiting heads of state. He also held the position of senior education officer for three years before his return to Britain in 1965.

Initially, he was paid less in Tanganyika than at Ipswich and had to learn Swahili in order to be confirmed in his appointment; he has since claimed that his acquaintance with Urdu, while in India during the war, helped him learn Swahili because there are similarities between the two languages. One of his first recollections upon arrival in Tanganyika was of Cameron greeting him and in the same first sentence telling him he was on a three week Swahili course on the following Monday. It was actually a course for missionaries but he was allowed to sit in. He went out some three months ahead of his wife to get domestic matters like the purchase of a car, accommodation, servants etc arranged before she arrived. As must have been the case with many such overseas postings, her family was not happy at the prospect of their only daughter going out to live in Africa but she soon adjusted to her new surroundings, partly because there were many other European staff and their families located at nearby Mwanza. Dodd still recalls Cameron's insistence that 'everyone' attended the 'Mwanza Club' on Friday nights. As a result culture shock was minimised.

Dodd's recollections of education in Tanganyika in the 1950s are dominated by the so-called 'Holy War' waged between the various rival missions and between them and local government authorities. As a district education officer, Dodd was responsible for advising on the payment of government grants-in-aid. This required him to visit schools on a regular basis to check their enrolments and ensure that they were conforming with grant regulations. Inevitably this placed him at the centre of local conflicts — to use his phrase he was an umpire in the 'Holy War' — and he was twice condemned from the pulpit by the Bishop of the White Fathers, Bishop Langtot, who was eventually called to order by the Provincial Commissioner. Rivalry between the missions was long-standing but it was intensified in the 1950s because of the rapid expansion of schooling and the new emphasis placed on developing government and local authority schools. The missions frequently surrounded each other's schools with inferior bush schools in order to draw off potential pupils. Unlike many government education officials in late nineteenth century India, Dodd and his colleagues had no inherent dislike of the missions.[3] He found the Roman Catholics were invariably hospitable — one was frequently offered a whisky — but they kept a close watch on his daily movements to ensure that he did not arrive at a school without prior warning, The Protestants were equally friendly but they tended to be more puritanical and whisky was certainly not on offer!. The scope for conflict with the missions in Tanganyika was increased by their diversity and the high proportion of their staff who were not native English speakers.

In the early 1950s Dodd saw the CES as a career which would last until he turned 50. At that time he recalls no sense of living on borrowed time. Even the granting of independence to India had not changed his view. It was only in the late 1950s that he became aware that decolonisation was gathering pace and would effect his long term career prospects. Julius Nyerere, the nationalist leader in Tanganyika, had planned to achieve independence by 1970 or thereabouts but the process was speeded up. It was in his second tour of duty [1956–60] that Dodd became aware that Nyerere and his TANU party were more important than he had previously thought. Years later Dodd was somewhat critical of Nyerere's education policy as enunciated in *Education for Self-Reliance*.[4] The attempt to create an idyllic 'Arcadia' was, he argued, impracticable and really little more than a restatement of the 'adaptation' theory of the inter-war years. Nevertheless, the statement sounded so logical that for a time it beguiled Tanzanians and foreign academics alike.

In 1954, Dodd rejected the offer of a post at Makerere College and also a transfer from education to administration i.e. to district commissioner. During the last three years of his stay in Tanganyika he worked in the Department and later Ministry of Education at a senior level. During that period he created a primary school inspectorate and a district education administration staffed by Africans. He also created a unified teaching service and drafted regulations in amplification of the 1961 Education Act which founded a united education system to replace the former racially based schools. Despite this heavy workload he still found time to be secretary of the Tanzanian Cricket Association for two years. The decision to leave Tanzania, [the name adopted by Tanganyika in 1964 after the union with Zanzibar] was dictated by both the imminent Africanization of his post and also by the education of his two daughters born in 1954 and 1957 respectively.

In Dodd's view, African education in Tanganyika in the early 1950s was economically efficient in what it did but it was severely limited in scope and there was little time for field officers like himself to engage in theoretical speculation. He still recalls an early experience, again with Cameron, which brought home to him the realities of colonial education at that time. In response to a question about his views on African education, Cameron ordered Dodd to organise a squad of a dozen or so Africans to go and dig a series of field latrines, insisting that they had to be 12 feet deep! Once that task was completed Dodd was ordered to organize another squad of men to break up some large slabs of disused concrete. Cameron subsequently commented that his views on African education could wait! Clearly, immediate practicalities left little time for field officers to indulge in theory. The apparent inability of many Whitehall officials to appreciate the practical problems of those who worked 'in the field' was a criticism frequently voiced by a wide range of colonial officials from governors like Sir Philip Mitchell downwards. The emphasis on community development as part of colonial education policy after 1945 was a classic case in which there appeared to be a vast difference in perception between what colonial officials in London thought it was possible to achieve and their counterparts in the territories who were saddled with both the responsibility for implementing policies and overcoming practical problems.[5]

Dodd returned to Britain in 1965, to a temporary lectureship in the Department of Education in Developing Countries at the London Institute of Education. He owed his new post to Professor John Lewis who visited Tanganyika as leader of a Unesco mission in 1962. The Unesco mission interviewed him several times in his capacity as a member of the inspectorate in Tanganyika. At the end of the visit John Cameron organized a farewell party and everyone was obliged to perform a party act. Dodd and his wife sang the song 'Green grow the rushes O' with ever faster accompanying actions. After the climatic end to the song Dodd sat down next to Lewis and was immediately asked if he would like a job at the Institute in London. The lectureship was made permanent in 1966, the same year in which he turned down a permanent position at Reading University. During the next five years he made various overseas trips. In 1967–68 he was a visiting lecturer at Teachers' College, Columbia, and in 1969–70 at Soche Hill College, University of Malawi. He also made various trips to Africa under the AAA [Afro-Anglo-American] Programme funded by the Carnegie Corporation. This programme was designed to encourage the establishment of institutes of education in Anglophone Africa. Dodd supported the entry of the Americans into the educational field but he was critical of their lack of any long-term commitment — 'They were here today but gone tomorrow'. He also claims that they were keen to get involved in Africa because of the Cold War but were destined to learn the realities of African education the hard way! At first they thought themselves very superior to the Europeans serving in Africa and they were also very critical of British imperialism but those who stayed on soon changed their views as they confronted the stark realities of life in Africa. Dodd also had mixed thoughts about Unesco's educational work in Africa: 'There were some bright spots and many problems but with experience Unesco learnt where it could be most effective — in science, adult education, the training of educational planners, and in the provision of books and other teaching materials'.

In 1970, Dodd and John Cameron combined to produce *Society, schools and progress in Tanzania*, a highly successful book in a series on the same theme in various countries. A year earlier Dodd had published his critique of education for self-reliance in Tanzania. In the late 1960s and early 1970s he also wrote several other studies including *The Teacher at Work*,[6] *Teacher education in the developing countries of the Commonwealth: a survey of recent trends*,[7] and *Primary school inspection in new countries*.[8]

In 1970, at the instigation of Professor John Lewis, Dodd was seconded as an education adviser to the ODM, the Ministry of Overseas Development, later renamed the ODA or the Overseas Development Administration. Again he travelled extensively, especially in eastern Africa. From 1975 to 1977 he was Deputy Chief Education Adviser and then Chief Education Adviser (1978–83) and Under Secretary (1981–1983). During his time in ODA he attended two Commonwealth education conferences (1974 and 1980) as a member of the British delegation, as well as the Commonwealth Specialist Education Conference in 1979, and various Unesco conferences in 1976, 1977, 1979 and 1981 respectively. When he retired in 1983 few people could match his wide-ranging experience of education in Africa both before and after independence. In the same year he was awarded the CMG for his services to education.

His role as an education adviser in Whitehall was, as he put it, 'largely what you made of it' but he identified seven major functions. The first was to advise the Minister and senior officials in ODM/ODA on educational issues, for example, to draft speeches and answers to parliamentary questions; to accompany Ministers on overseas visits or represent them on official bodies or at conferences. Interviewing teachers seeking overseas appointments and advising on the placement of overseas students in the United Kingdom were two further activities which took up much of his time as an adviser. Likewise, it was necessary to keep in close touch with British universities and colleges which took overseas students and provided expert staff for overseas consultancies. Liaising with the British Council, which was an operational arm of the ODM/ODA, and comparable bodies like VSO, the Commonwealth Secretariat, the BBC, Unesco, Unicef, the World Bank and the European Community was also an aspect of the adviser's task. Finally, as much as two to three months in each year was taken up with overseas travel to discuss and negotiate with governments over educational components of aid programmes and attendance at Unesco and Commonwealth conferences concerned with education in developing countries.

In 1970 Sir Christopher Cox finally retired after 30 years as Education Adviser to the Colonial Office, the Department of Technical Co-operation and ODM respectively. He was replaced by Jack Thornton[9] and a small team of advisers who each had a designated geographical area to deal with. Dodd was given responsibility for an area of eastern Africa stretching from Egypt to Swaziland, including the Seychelles, Mauritius, Madagascar, Gibraltar, Malta, Cyprus and the Middle East. From 1978 to 1983 his focus changed to Asia where he assumed responsibility for Burma, Thailand, Malaysia and Singapore. In the 1970s economic advisers were uppermost in the ODA and educational aid had to be justified on the basis of its contribution to manpower planning and economic growth. In later years the economists went out of fashion and were replaced by sociologists with their stress on more education for women and girls, a renewed emphasis on primary education, and the need for a primary school curriculum more relevant to children living in rural areas. Overall, Dodd claims that education was not accorded a very high priority in aid programmes eminating from London but it was highly valued by the recipients. In the 1970s the British government sought to reduce the flow of 'aided' expatriate teachers but this was resisted by recipient countries.

In the late 1970s and early 1980s Dodd was deeply involved in the overseas student fees issue and appeared before a Select Committee of the House of Commons in both 1980 and 1981. In 1979, the Thatcher government had decided to charge overseas students the full cost of their courses instead of a nominal fee. The decision generated widespread protests both at home and abroad, especially from those institutions in Britain that specialised in training overseas teachers. These included the London Institute of Education, Moray House College of Education in Edinburgh, and the universities of Reading, Bristol, Exeter, Manchester, Leeds, Newcastle, Birmingham, and Cambridge. The government remained stead-fast in its resolve and eventually quelled the storm of protest both in Britain and overseas by increasing the number of scholarships and awards granted to overseas students.[10]

As Chief Education Adviser, Dodd served on the Unesco Executive Board, the Board of the British Council, the Boards of Governors of Imperial College and the London School of Oriental and African Studies respectively, the Commonwealth Scholarships Commission, and the Council of Voluntary Service Overseas. Visits abroad to learn more about the education systems of other states, to judge the impact of aid policies, to advise on further aid, to conduct detailed negotiations with local officials, and the compilation of appropriate reports, often meant long working days — 8.30 am to 7.30 pm — and additional work done at home.

During Dodd's time as Chief Education Adviser, British membership of Unesco caused major misgivings in Whitehall and he became deeply involved in the issue. The British link with Unesco was originally the responsibility of the Ministry of Education but by the 1970s the ODM had taken over and maintained a permanent office in Paris. Dodd attended two general conferences — in 1978 and 1980 — when 'education' as well as science and culture was debated. The Unesco Executive Board comprised some 50 members. Dodd was an alternative Executive Board Member in 1982–3 and a full Board Member during the years 1983–5. Membership of the Board involved living in Paris for five to six weeks each year.

The British contribution to Unesco was widely respected but by the early 1980s there were growing doubts in Whitehall about the value of continued membership. There were claims that it was too bureaucratic, that it was exploited by Eastern Bloc states and some developing countries for their own political ends, that it dabbled in matters beyond its remit, for example, disarmament and world peace, that it spread its programmes and activities too thinly, and that it was impractical. The issue facing the Thatcher government was whether the UK should remain a member and try to reform Unesco from within or withdraw completely. The UK National Commission for Unesco voted overwhelmingly — 78 to 2 — to stay in. The All Party Select Committee on Foreign Affairs similarly supported staying in as did the Commonwealth countries, Britain's European partners and the British Minister Timothy Raison. Despite this weight of opinion, Thatcher still chose to withdraw because she claimed that the organisation was overly political, financially extravagant and insufficiently practical. Dodd suggests that Britain withdrew because of an agreement between President Reagan and Thatcher that both countries would withdraw. The USA did so in 1984 and the UK and Singapore followed a year later. In Dodd's opinion, both Reagan and Thatcher wanted to fire a warning shot across the bows of the United Nations system and chose Unesco as the means to make their point. In the lead up to Britain's withdrawal Dodd was uniquely and critically mentioned by name in a *Times* editorial on the matter.

Dodd retired from the ODA in 1983 when he turned 60. At that point he was invited to return to the London Institute of Education as a consultant on overseas initiatives, a position he occupied until his eventual retirement in 1991. Initially, the contract was for five years but he stayed for eight and was asked to stay longer. He described his job as something akin to 'Foreign Secretary' of the Institute. He advised on the enrolment and care of foreign students, especially those from developing countries, and on overseas consultancies by the staff of the Institute. The success of the venture depended on Dodd's many contacts with ODA, the British Council, the Foreign Office, embassies and Unesco etc. As a member of the steering committee of the Child-to-Child Trust he also made several visits to eastern Africa (Somalia 1986, Zimbabwe 1988, Tanzania 1988,

Lesotho 1990, Zanzibar 1989, 1991) during his second spell at the Institute.

The introduction of full fees led to a serious drop in the number of overseas students in the early 1980s but by mid decade the number had been restored to over 400 per year, in some part due to Dodd's efforts. During this period he spent much of his time on student welfare, regular liaison with the British Council, and on the loan of Institute staff for overseas projects. Unfortunately, during the 1980s the Institute's long-standing overseas links declined despite various public pronouncements to the contrary. As Dodd puts it, 'No later Director [of the Institute] felt as Lionel Elvin did in the 1970s'. Also, by the 1980s, the Department of Education in Developing Countries, later called the Department of International and Comparative Education, was disintegrating and losing its status abroad. At the same time some of the other departments also evinced little interest in the overseas role of the Institute. Finally, education departments in other universities were becoming far more positive in promoting their role internationally and increasingly attracted more British Council and overseas government support. By the time Dodd retired he felt he was swimming against the tide as the Institute, understandably, became increasingly preoccupied with its place and role within the United Kingdom.[11]

Dodd belongs to that generation which grew up in the depression ridden years of the 1930s but was old enough to be actively involved in the Second World War. It was also his personal misfortune to have his studies at Cambridge interrupted by war service although he would be the first to claim that his experiences with the British army in India taught him to be confident in his own ability and gave him a taste for foreign parts which subsequently played a major part in his decision to join the CES. He joined the Service several years after Major Sir Ralph Furse, whose name will forever be linked with recruitment to the Colonial Service, had retired,[12] but Furse would surely have heartily approved of such a promising recruit. A product of trustworthy middle class origins; a sound grammar school and Oxbridge education, including a 'good honours degree'; a love of sport, especially cricket; several years of successful teaching experience; and, as an added bonus, several years of active war service, all made Dodd the epitome of the type of recruit that Furse sought so assiduously to attract throughout his long association with recruitment to the Colonial Service. Soundness of character, intellectual ability, athletic prowess, and a deep commitment to serve the Empire, were all present in the young education officer who went out to Tanganyika to serve Queen and country in 1952.

Furse would equally have felt vindicated in his criteria for selection by Dodd's subsequent record of service. In a memorandum that he prepared early in 1943, on post-war training for the Colonial Service,[13] Furse stressed how the war was hastening major changes to the balance of power in the world and generating new aspirations for freedom and progress. Colonial officials, he argued, would have to come to terms with a vastly changing world once the war was over. At the time even Furse could not have foreseen how rapidly the British Empire would be dismantled and replaced by independent soverign states. Dodd's professional career was played out against the backdrop of the profound social, economic and political changes that Furse had predicted. By his own admission, in Tanganyika he was an 'actor' who helped shape and implement education policy. After independence and his return to London he became a 'prompter', someone who offered advice and assistance but only if and when asked for it. The role of adviser was no less important — most former colonies were still in desperate need of aid and advice — but the change of roll was profound and a new experience for those who had formerly exercised both executive and administrative responsibility. By any standards Dodd succeeded in bridging the colonial and post-colonial worlds with distinction. Not only was he a highly regarded educational administrator in Tanganyika both before and after independence, but later he also became the most senior adviser to the British government on educational aid to developing countries

A full and critical account of the role which Britain has played as a major donor of educational aid to developing countries since the 1960s has yet to be written but Dodd has highlighted the primary distinction between bi-lateral and multi-lateral aid as a key issue for consideration. In the first flush of independence much of Britain's educational aid was of the bi-lateral type, i.e. country to country, but by the 1980s multi-lateral aid via international agencies was fast gaining the ascendency. Dodd preferred bi-lateral arrangements because of their more intimate nature. In the 1960s and 1970s most senior officers in the ODA also had colonial experience to call upon, and this facilitated a degree of empathy between the leaders in the new states and ODA officials. By the early 1980s, however, most of the former colonial staff had retired and the ranks of the ODA were being filled from a new generation of university graduates whose on-the-spot experience of conditions in developing countries was mainly confined to ODA projects.

In conversation with former colonial officers like Dodd, one inevitably asks why they chose to serve abroad. In his case he claims that it was mainly because of his wartime experience in India and images of India that he recalled from childhood. The talk on the Colonial Service given by a Colonial Office official when Dodd was a schoolmaster in Ipswich was also highly significant. He also readily admits that at the time when he decided to go abroad he had no insurmountable family ties. He was married but had no children and his wife was supportive of the idea. He refutes any suggestion, whatsoever, that the men and women who served abroad were any better or worse than those who chose to stay at home, but he does believe that most of those who served overseas had a dab of missionary zeal about them. The colonial experience also gave most of them the chance to exercise responsibility at a much earlier age than if they had stayed at home and this later helped many of them to readjust successfully when they returned to Britain, often in mid-career, after independence.

In retirement Dodd has maintained many former contacts and acted in a variety of capacities including chairman of the Sir Christopher Cox Memorial Fund, a trustee for the International Extension College, Deputy Chairman of the Friends of Unesco, adviser to the Marsh Arabs (AMAR) Appeal, and Chairman of the Probus Club in his home town of Sevenoaks. Always an ardent cricket enthusiast, he continues to be a member of the MCC and Sevenoaks Vine cricket clubs. By his own admission he played cricket on a regular basis in Tanganyika and was a wicket-keeper of about 'club' level. In 1965 he took up walking together with 'watching' cricket. Since 1979 he has completed many major walks with his long-time friend and academic colleague John Cameron. He has also dabbled in oil painting and has long enjoyed classical music, opera and the theatre. As if time might ever hang heavily on his hands, he also maintains his membership of the Cambridge Society, the Institute of Education Society, the Ramblers' Association, the Royal Society for the Protection of Birds, and the National Trust.

In the preface to this volume it was suggested that to brand the likes of Frank Ward or Arthur Mayhew as imperialists in any pejorative sense was to stretch credibility to breaking point. The same comment applies to 'Bill' Dodd. A sound historical training at Cambridge followed by a lifetime spent in promoting education in developing countries has generated in him a deep commitment to the welfare of Britain's former colonies but that does not preclude him from making critical judgments of the educational policies of both British and overseas governments. Whatever we may think, British colonialism is a fact of history. Its origins were diverse and its legacy is complex. If we are to achieve a clearer understanding of Britain's imperial past it is as equally important to listen to men like Dodd who served abroad, while there is still time, as it is to assess the academic validity of armchair theories of colonialism.[14]

NOTES ON CHAPTER

1. Much of the information used in compiling this account of the life and work of W. A. Dodd was obtained from a private unpublished autobiography and two interviews conducted at the London Institute of Education in Apr 1998 and Nov 2001 respectively.
2. Information supplied by the late W. E. F. Ward.
3. Hostility towards mission educators in late nineteenth century India by some government officials was generated by the government's policy of strict religious neutrality. Christian missionaries were frequently viewed as potential troublemakers because of their desire to convert the Indians.
4. See Dodd's book *Education for self-reliance in Tanzania; a study of its vocational aspects*, New York, Teachers' College Press, Columbia University, 1969
5. For elaboration on this theme see the author's article *'When the Bush Takes Fire': A Study of the Origins and Purpose of Non-Formal Education in British Colonial Policy*, pp 191–202 in James Lynch, Celia Modgil and Sohan Modgil

(eds), *Education and Development: Tradition and Innovation*, Vol. 4 *Non-formal and Non-governmental Approaches*, London, Cassell, 1997.

6. *The Teacher at Work*, London, OUP, 1970
7. *Teacher education in the developing countries of the Commonwealth: a survey of recent trends*, London, Commonwealth Secretariat, 1971
8. *Primary school inspection in new countries*, London, OUP, 1968
9. For details of Jack Thornton's life [1915–1996] and work see *Who's Who 1996*, and his obituary in *The Times*, 30 Apr 1996.
10. A comprehensive analysis of the student fees issue is contained in Peter Williams, *A Policy for Overseas Students Analysis Options Proposals*, London, Overseas Students Trust, 1982.
11. This period in the Institute's history is covered in the recently published centennial history. See Richard Aldrich, *The Institute of Education 1902–2002 A Centenary History,* Institute of Education, University of London, 2002.
12. For more details of Furse see his autobiography *Aucuparious Recollections of a Recruiting Officer*, London, OUP, 1962
13. 'Memorandum on Post-War Training for the Colonial Service', included in Colonial Office, *Post-War Training for the Colonial Office Report of a Committee appointed by the Secretary of State for the Colonies*, London, HMSO 1946, Colonial No. 198, pp 20–46

Bibliographical Note

The sources used for biographical work are often exceedingly varied as in this study. The annotated notes at the end of each chapter provide full details of all sources consulted and for that reason they are not repeated here. It should be emphasised that this study has relied extensively on archival sources together with the more familiar biographical publications.

Information on members of the Indian Education Service was derived mainly from the *Proceedings of the Indian Government* (Education series), annual editions of the *India Office List*, British parliamentary papers, obituaries and tributes in *The Times*, and the standard biographical sources such as *Alumni Oxoniensis, Alumni Cantabrigienses, Who Was Who, Who's Who, the Dictionary of National Biography,* and C. E. Buckland's *Dictionary of Indian Biography*. By far the richest source of information, especially on the lesser known personnel, was the Government of India records (formerly the India Office library), now housed in the British Library in Euston Road, London.

Material on members of the Colonial Education Service was also derived principally from archival sources, together with personal reminiscences. Three archives were especially important. The first was the Sir Christopher Cox Papers, a vast array of official, semi-official, and personal papers that Cox collected during the 30 years that he spent as a public servant in Whitehall. These are now housed in the Colonial Office series (CO 1045) at the Public Record Office in Kew. Another much smaller collection of papers relating to Cox's life before he joined the Colonial Office is housed in New College library, Oxford. A large collection of material gathered as a result of the Oxford Development Records Project, housed at the Rhodes House Library in Oxford, was also a rich source of biographical information. So too, were the voluminous Colonial Office territorial and subject records in the P.R.O. at Kew. The London Institute of Education also has a valuable library collection and archive for biographical purposes. There were also two extensive mission archives which yielded important information. The first was that of the Conference of British Missionary Societies (CBMS). The original papers are housed in the library at the London School of Oriental and African Studies but they are also available on microfiche. The second was the extensive archive of the International Missionary Council/ Council of British Missionary Societies (IMC/CBMS), also housed at SOAS and now available on microfiche. Family archives were also important in compiling this work, especially in relation to the chapters on Vischer, Hussey, Gwilliam and Dodd. Likewise, personal communication was a rich source of information, especially in relation to Ward and Dodd. Amongst printed sources, the annual *Colonial Office List, The Dictionary of National Biography, Who Was Who,* and *Who's Who,* were regularly consulted.

Index